Intelligent Systems for IoE Based Smart Cities

Edited by

Arun Solanki
Department of Computer Science and Engineering
School of ICT, Gautam Buddha University
Greater Noida, India

&

Anuj Kumar Singh
Department of Computer Science and Engineering
Adani University
Ahmedabad, India

Intelligent Systems for IoE Based Smart Cities

Editors: Arun Solanki & Anuj Kumar Singh

ISBN (Online): 978-981-5124-96-5

ISBN (Print): 978-981-5124-97-2

ISBN (Paperback): 978-981-5124-98-9

First published in 2023.

need for a court order if at any point you breach any terms of this License Agreement. In no event will any delay or failure by Bentham Science Publishers in enforcing your compliance with this License Agreement constitute a waiver of any of its rights.

3. You acknowledge that you have read this License Agreement, and agree to be bound by its terms and conditions. To the extent that any other terms and conditions presented on any website of Bentham Science Publishers conflict with, or are inconsistent with, the terms and conditions set out in this License Agreement, you acknowledge that the terms and conditions set out in this License Agreement shall prevail.

Bentham Science Publishers Pte. Ltd.
80 Robinson Road #02-00
Singapore 068898
Singapore
Email: subscriptions@benthamscience.net

BENTHAM SCIENCE

CONTENTS

FOREWORD

The continuing dispersal of Internet of Things (IoT) technologies is opening new opportunities, and the foremost amazing application is the smart city concept, which is endlessly progressing in many dimensions. Generally, a smart city can be defined as integrating IoT and other Information Communication Technologies (ICT) into city management, controlling, or monitoring to address the exponential rise in urbanization and population, therefore significantly improving people's living standards. The smart city model is also strictly associated with the aspects of sustainability. But with the evolution of the Internet of Everything (IoE), which provides connectivity not only among things, but also among people, data, and processes, smart cities will become smarter. The IoE enhances connectivity and intelligence to about every entity in the system, including things, data, processes, and people, giving it special functions. This integration will have a vivid impact on every aspect, from city management to planning, controlling, and health.

Intelligent Systems for IoE-based Smart cities are emerging as a primary need for Cyber-Physical Systems (CPS) across the world. Advances in Artificial Intelligence (AI) and Machine Learning (ML) algorithms have played an important role in the progress and automation of city operations and in supporting the development of CPS in cities. Extensive use of intelligent decision-making and data-driven modelling under uncertainty are establishing the basis for advancements in public services, safety, connectivity, transportation, and health services. The examples include improved public transportation systems, advanced traffic solutions, energy modelling, smart emergency response and autonomous driving, being some of the applications that have benefited from the methodologies of principled decision-making.

This book focuses on the characteristics, requirements, issues, challenges, and development of intelligent systems for smart cities based on IoE. The allied topics, including data science and open-source data sets for IoE-based smart cities, decision-making for IoE-based smart cities, design of intelligent systems for IoE smart cities, and challenges in deployment, equity and fairness in IoE smart cities, and security and privacy in AI for smart cities are being addressed in this book. Since the smart infrastructure paradigm is now shifting from IoT to IoE, this book will certainly be appealing to readers. The fusion of three main technologies, including intelligent systems, smart cities, and IoE, has been presented in this book, which is a relatively unique approach.

Anand Paul
The School of CSE
Kyungpook National University
Daegu, South Korea

PREFACE

There are many challenges affecting decision-making for Cyber-Physical Systems in smart cities. With the initiation of IoT, sensor data is being produced at high speed and in large volume that is hard to process and make conclusions from it. Requirements of the smart cities dictate that a large amount of processing occurs on edge, making it imperative in a way that fast and tractable methods of decision-making are designed. Concurrently, there is an increasing requirement for automated applications to be secure, fair, and resilient. Moreover, with the advent of the Internet of Everything (IoE), which tends to integrate things, people, data, and processes, it is essential to develop smart and intelligent systems that facilitate smart cities in the IoE environment. The book aims at covering all the necessary aspects of the development of intelligent systems for IoE-based smart cities.

This book has been organized into three sections where **Section 1** consists of four chapters highlighting the technological aspects related to smart cities, **Section 2** presents intelligent systems in IoE/IoT-based smart cities and includes four chapters, and **Section 3** comprises three chapters that focus on utilizing cloud and blockchain in IoE/IoT based smart cities.

Chapter 1 of the book first introduces smart cities, and then it elaborates on the technical aspects of the physical layer in a smart city environment, enabling the utilization of the Internet for the operation of various devices. **Chapter 2** focuses on identifying the most prominent enabling technologies in making smart computing environments intelligent. The ten foremost intelligence-enabling technologies – predictive analysis, deep learning, artificial neural network, big data analytics, intelligent edge, human-computer interaction, computer vision, explainable artificial intelligence, natural language processing, and robotics in context to a smart computing environment, have been discussed in this chapter. **Chapter 3** analyses the role and importance of Smart sensors and actuators along with their applications, challenges, and opportunities, followed by various future trends in the domain of the smart city. **Chapter 4** explores numerous IoE applications which are also concerned with smart cities. This chapter discusses existing technologies that have a great contribution to the development of various prominent areas of smart cities. The chapter also identifies and categorizes several challenges that are being faced by the stakeholders and officials in the construction of smart cities.

Chapter 5 focuses on a definite area of AI called Natural Language Processing, which helps and enhances human lives living in smart cities. These use cases and various applications, scopes, techniques, advantages, disadvantages, and future scopes of NLP in the context of smart cities have been discussed in this chapter. The goal of **Chapter 6** is two-fold. First, it intends to analyze the security issue in VANET by reviewing the most important vulnerabilities and proposed countermeasures. In a second part, it introduces a comprehensive Machine Learning framework to design VANET IDs. It has used the framework to evaluate the performances of several Machine Learning techniques to detect position attacks using the VeReMi security dataset. In **Chapter 7**, through the use of trilateration, an application has been devised that takes the help of Wi-Fi signals and does position fixing in an indoor environment. The trilateration method is implemented to calculate the unknown position of a device under the environment. It collects all the Wi-Fi signals and finds the exact matches with the database to calculate the user's actual position on the map. **Chapter 8** of the book emphasizes the deep-seated relationship between IoT and sensors from the perspective of state-of-the-art research. It offers discussions on the usage of various types of sensing devices, associated data, and their contribution towards solving specific research problems in the respective IoT-based applications. This includes the Video Camera, Inertial Measurement

Unit (IMU) Sensors, Ultrasonic Sensors, Electrocardiogram (ECG) Sensor, Passive Infra-Red (PIR) Sensor, Electromyogram (EMG) Sensor, and some commonly used sensing devices for Environmental and Agricultural Smart system development. A pertinent case study is also included in this chapter to demonstrate the role of sensors in the development of IoT-based systems.

Chapter 9 focuses on the Internet of Things, cloud computing, and data mining, and tries to find the connection between them in terms of users, services, and applications. The goal is to identify how data analytics can be applied to real-life IoT and cloud-based applications.

Along with explaining the security requirements in smart cities, **Chapter 10** proposes a security framework focused on providing secure access control and authentication services delivered over the cloud-based system used in smart cities. This chapter also covers the concepts on convergence of IoE and cloud computing in smart cities and challenges faced by future generation cities employing IoE.

Chapter 11 here provides an insight into how blockchain technology works for smart contracts, which deliver numerous services in Smart cities ecosystems in more reliable, data secured, and beneficial for the population in Smart cities. The chapter has contributed to the planning of Smart cities planners, developers, architects, and thinkers for the usage of smart contracts for delivering various services in the smart city's governance.

Arun Solanki
Department of Computer Science and Engineering
School of ICT, Gautam Buddha University
Greater Noida, India

&

Anuj Kumar Singh
Department of Computer Science and Engineering
Adani University
Ahmedabad, India

List of Contributors

Aditya Gupta	Amity University, Noida, Uttar Pradesh, India
Aman Verma	Amity University, Noida, Uttar Pradesh, India
Amit Wadhwa	GL Bajaj Institute of Technology and Management, Greater Noida, Uttar Pradesh, India
Amartya Chakraborty	University of Engineering and Management, Kolkata, India
Anuj Kumar Singh	Department of Computer Science and Engineering, Adani University, Ahmedabad, India
Ankit Garg	Apex Institute of Technology, Computer Science and Engineering, University Center for Research and Development, Chandigarh University, Mohali, Punjab, India
Anand Paul	The School of CSE, Kyungpook National University, Daegu, South Korea
Arun Solanki	Department of Computer Science and Engineering, School of ICT, Gautam Buddha University, Greater Noida, India
Chitra Krishnan	Symbiosis Center for Management Studies, Symbiosis International Deemed University, Noida, India
Hanaa Hachimi	University Sultan Moulay Slimane, Beni Mellal, Morocco
Hanen Idoudi	National School of Computer Science, University of Manouba, Manouba, Tunisia
Jafar A. Alzubi	Faculty of Engineering, Al-Balqa Applied University, Salt-19117, Jordan
Jayanta Kumar Ray	Sikkim Manipal Institute of Technology, Sikkim Manipal University, Gangtok, Sikkim, India
Mohamed Mosbah	LaBRI(UMR5800) CNRS, University of Bordeaux, Talence, France
Neelesh Thallam	Amity University, Noida, Uttar Pradesh, India
Neerja Arora	Ajay Kumar Garg Engineering College, Ghaziabad, Uttar Pradesh, India
Olfa Masmoudi	National School of Computer Science, University of Manouba, Manouba, Tunisia
Parth Malkani	Amity University, Noida, Uttar Pradesh, India
Quazi Mohmmad Alfred	Aliah University, Kolkata, India
Rabindranath Bera	Sikkim Manipal Institute of Technology, Sikkim Manipal University, Gangtok, Sikkim, India
Sanjib Sil	The A.K. Choudhury School of Information Technology, University of Calcutta, Kolkata, West Bengal, India
Sanjay Kumar Sharma	Department of Computer Science and Engineering, School of ICT, Gautam Buddha University, Greater Noida, India
Sandeep Kumar	Gautam Buddha University, Greater Noida, Uttar Pradesh, India
Saptarshi Paul	Department of Computer Science, Assam University, Silchar, India
Sartaj Ahmad	KIET Group of Institutions Delhi-NCR, Affiliated to AKTU, Lucknow, UP, India

Tarana Singh   Department of Computer Science and Engineering, School of ICT, Gautam Buddha University, Greater Noida, India

CHAPTER 1

On Physical Layer Design for Smart Cities

Jayanta Kumar Ray[1,*], Rabindranath Bera[1], Sanjib Sil[2] and Quazi Mohmmad Alfred[3]

[1] *Sikkim Manipal Institute of Technology, Sikkim Manipal University, Gangtok, Sikkim, India*

[2] *The A.K. Choudhury School of Information Technology, University of Calcutta, Kolkata, West Bengal, India*

[3] *Aliah University, Kolkata, India*

Abstract: In the future, the real world will convert to a smart world around 2025. One could predict that there will be a changeover from 4G LTE to 5G NR. In pandemic conditions, 4G LTE has been found to provide good online support, such as accessing the Internet for education, administration, banking, official works, *etc.*, anywhere in the real world. But there are some limitations, such as operating machines in industries, and driving vehicles on the road with the help of the Internet. These facilities will be provided by 5G NR as there is a large difference between 4G LTE and 5G NR. In 4G LTE, only Mobile Broad Band (MBB) is present, but in 5G NR, there are three terms, *i.e.*, Enhanced Mobile BroadBand (eMBB), Ultra-Reliable and Low Latency Communication (URLLC) and massive Machine Type Communication (mMTC). As a result, the city will convert into a smart city. It is possible by applying intelligence in various technologies. Applying intelligence will lead to the improvement of smartness in the environment, mobility, building, home, administration, health, education, *etc.* The smartness of the item includes the utilization of the Internet in various devices, which means the Internet of Things (IoT). In previous times, humans communicate with humans, but in IoT, a human will communicate with the device. In the future, it will be realized using NXP Semiconductors. NXP semiconductors manufactured various chips, which should be beneficial for the formation of smart cities. In the near future, facilities will be increased in a more massive manner than the present time. By 2030, the goal will have been fully attained, and IoT will have evolved into the Internet of Everything (IoE), meaning that everything will be made possible by the Internet. Device-to-device communication will be a possibility in IoE side-by-side. This outlines how 5G to 6G will change.

Keywords: 3GPP (Third Generation Partnership Project), 4G LTE (Long Term Evolution), 5G NR (New Radio), EMBB (Extended Mobile Broad Band), IoT (Internet of Things), MMTC (Massive MachineType Communication), NXP (Next eXPerience) Semiconductors, URLLC (Ultra Reliable Low Latency Communication).

---

[*] **Corresponding author Jayanta Kumar Ray:** Sikkim Manipal Institute of Technology, Sikkim Manipal University, Gangtok, Sikkim, India; E-mail: jayantakumar.ray@gmail.com

INTRODUCTION

Telia Sonera had previously introduced 4G technology in Finland by the year 2010. Third Generation Project Partnership (3GPP) standardised LTE-Advanced [1]. High data speeds, decreased latency, seamless connections, improved Quality of Service (QoS), distribution across heterogeneous networks, capacity in high network infrastructure, and simple infrastructure are some of the characteristics of LTE [2]. Between 4G and 5G, there is a connection made through LTE-Advanced [2]. High data speeds, decreased latency, seamless connections, improved Quality of Service (QoS), distribution across heterogeneous networks, capacity in high network infrastructure, and simple infrastructure are some of the characteristics of LTE [2].The advancements made possible by Radio Access Networks (RAN) in 5G technologies are basically made possible by LTE-Advanced. Microwave frequency (sub-6GHz) is used for LTE-Advanced. Nevertheless, 5G uses both microwave and millimeter wavelengths, therefore, the range of frequencies is 6 GHz to 100 GHz. By 2020, 5G will be commercially accessible and will essentially be an end-to-end support system. In this place, a society is created where connections and mobility are made possible. Massive MIMO, which is an upgrade of the MIMO seen in 4G LTE-Advanced, is used in 5G technology.

Radio Access Networks (RAN) advancements in 5G technologies are made possible by LTE-Advanced. Microwave (sub-6GHz) frequency is used for LTE-Advanced. In contrast, millimeter and microwave frequencies are used in 5G, resulting in a frequency range of 6 to 100 GHz. A complete support system will be provided by 5G technology, which will be ready in 2020. A civilization that allows for connections and mobility is created in this instance. Massive MIMO, which replaces the MIMO used in 4G LTE-Advanced, is a 5G technical innovation.

There are significant differences between 5G and 4G in terms of several important needs [3]. Whereas 5G's peak data rate is 20 Gbit/sec, 4G LTE's peak data rate is 1 Gbit/sec. In 4G, the user-experienced data rate is 10 Mbit/sec, while in 5G, it is 100 Mbit/sec. Mobility for 4G is 350 km/h, whereas it is 500 km/h for 5G. The required latency for 4G is 10 ms, whereas for 5G, it is less than 1 ms. In comparison to 5G, which has a connection density of 106 devices per square km, 4G has 105 devices per square km (Fig. **1**).

The Microwave Horn antenna (Fig. **2a**) can be used for 4G LTE's microwave frequency (sub-6 GHz), whilst the Millimeter-wave Dish Antenna (Fig. **2b**) can be used for 5G NR's millimeter-wave frequency (28 GHz). The two antennas were compared in SMIT. It has been noted that there is a significant disparity between their received signal strength indicators, which are given in dBm and are, respectively, -97.2 dBm for microwave and -43.8 dBm for millimeter-wave [4]. In comparison, there is also a significant difference in the Signal Noise Ratio (SNR), which is 31 dB for microwaves and 49 dB for millimeter waves [4].

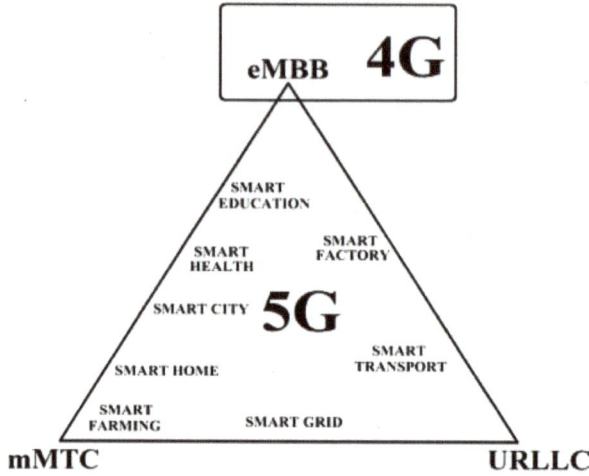

Fig. (1). 4G *vs.* 5G.

Fig. (2a). Microwave horn antenna.

Fig. (2b). Millimeter-wave dish antenna.

The real world will evolve into a smart world in the future. The equipment in the "smart world" can operate through automation. The center piece of the smart world is the smart city. A "smart city" [5] is essentially a city where technology, government, society, *etc.*, will evolve along with an increase in intelligence for things like the economy, mobility, environment, people, home, administration, *etc.* Smart data are gathered through a variety of installed devices and sensors on streets, cars, people, *etc.*, in a smart city.

The growth of smart cities is accelerating. Using a smart communication system, which may use wired or wireless media, smart data is transmitted [6]. In this case, the software is being used to execute information [7]. There will be a need for advanced instrumentation, connectivity, and intelligence in the smart city. The built environment, economic development, energy, health, payments, safety and security, telecommunication, transit, waste management, and other areas are all made easier by the smart city [8].

There will be enhanced effects on sustainability, economic development, and quality of life (QoL) as a result of the development of smart cities [9]. Every citizen's quality of life will be raised. According to population, location, and economic development, it varies for different cities. It covers a range of topics such as civic responsibilities, culture, economy, ecology, housing, socialism, technology, *etc.* The primary network is the Internet. The Internet of Things (IoT) [10] will be introduced once the 4G network has been upgraded to 5G. In contrast to 5G, which combines human-to-human and human-to-machine communication, 4G is a human-to-human network. The term "smart city" can mean many different things, including digital cities, electronic communities, flexi cities, information cities, intelligent cities, knowledge cities, mesh cities, teli cities, wireless cities, *etc.*

Information and communication technologies (ICT) are used to create smart city globally [5]. A smart city still involves a variety of things, including politics, city administration, business, institutions, buildings, special interest groups, *etc.* Intelligent data from different industries are gathered, analyzed, and decisions are made. A system of interconnected infrastructure is present in a smart city. The exchange and fusion of smart data is the key component of the smart city. Instrumentation, the availability of real-time data from various sources, data visualization, automation, a network of collaboration spaces, and other traits define smart cities. Better service will be provided by smart cities, and citizens will benefit from it [11]. ICT enhances the smart city to provide services, decision-making, and public engagement. Smart cities have several indicators, such as knowledge workforce, broadband connectivity, digitalization, innovation and marketing [12].

The smart city will offer a variety of services, such as those related to governance, solid waste management, solid waste management, energy, finance, and fire and emergency response. A smart city will have a smart environment, such as the ones shown in Fig. **(3)** [13], which includes the political and social environment, economic environment, socio-cultural environment, and natural environment. The term "smart city" refers to a place where people, technology, and information are all integrated and where services are reliable and the infrastructure is sustainable and resilient. In a smart institution, the current classroom will be transformed into a smart classroom where different pupils will receive helpful information. Teachers are able to automatically impart knowledge to kids by gathering information from them. On the other hand, the students can attend the class taken by the teacher and become knowledgeable through the automation process.

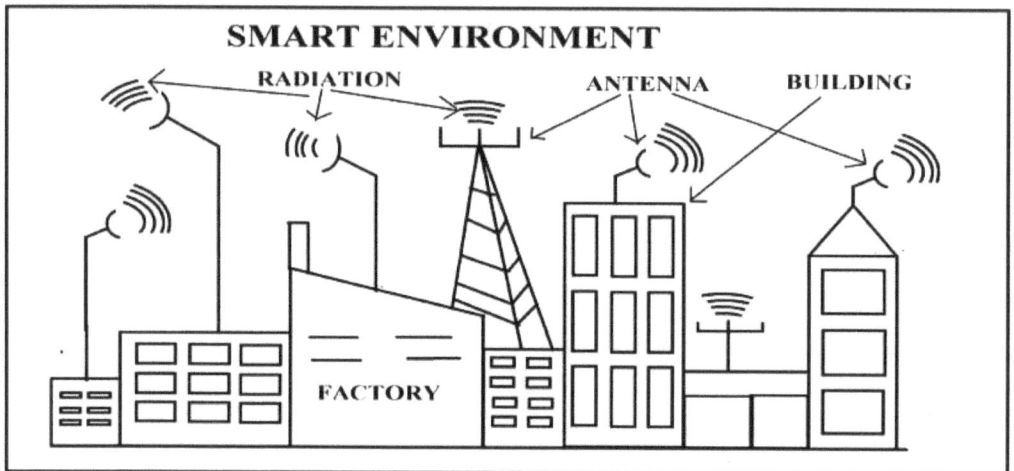

Fig. (3). Smart city.

As a result, the concept of smart class is specified in the smart institution. In smart institutions and offices, the attendance of the students and office staff can be taken by the process of automation. Smart security is applied to protect the area from unauthorized users during the period of restriction. The smart fire alarm system delivers the message of the incident to the police station and the fire departments about the location of the incident. The building manager manages the smart building.

It carries out the obligation for routine tasks. It is essential for communication that a smart bridge has a variety of sensors to monitor the structure. Smart cities were created as a result of the powering, enabling, and integration done by digital technologies. One of the greatest developments of the twenty-first century is the smart city. As a result, the expectation of the citizens will be fulfilled, and various opportunities will expand. The urban population will increase rapidly. The aim of a smart city is the transformation of lives, comfortability and safety of the citizens [14]. The critical technological and financial developments for the smart city include public-private partnerships, development of emerging technologies, expansion of ICT infrastructure, focus on cyber security, edge computing, big data analytics, *etc.* The real world is transformed into a smart environment in smart cities. Smart cities are made possible by a number of innovations, including cloud computing, the Internet of Things (IoT) [15, 16], the semantic web, open data, internet technologies, *etc.* The development, financing, and delivery of the digital infrastructure for smart cities will be carried out using a three-tier development [12]. The aim of Tier 1 is to fulfill the needs for service capability and infrastructure of the smart city. Here, the public group utilizes the private sector to apply the specific technologies or services in which the needs of the city planners will be the main goal. Examples are traffic management, LED street lighting, Wi-Fi connection, and water management. The main characteristics of this tier are that the economic arrangement provided by public organizations gives good support to the private sector so that the services, solutions and technology will be managed. In Tier 2, there will be some additional opportunities required for additional services. There are two functions, i.e., improvement of services to citizens, and verification of expanded digital services. Here the public organization makes an understanding with the private sector, which is called public-private partnership. Examples are the usage of financial items such as payment mechanisms. The private sector has much customer's support base. In Tier 3, there is the involvement of the new development in smart city projects. The main characteristics of this tower are the development of a digital ecosystem in the digital infrastructure. As a result, various opportunities will be available in the smart system. These opportunities are new services, products, businesses, revenues *etc.* One such example is smart streetlight, which includes sensors, WiFi, digital display, *etc.* When these technologies are deployed, a digital platform will be created in which new services are being developed. By following these three-tier development model, six developments take place for smart city development, which are a public partnership, development in emerging technologies, expansion of ICT infrastructure, increased focus on cyber security, edge computing, big data analysis, *etc.* [12]

The distribution of components occurs at random in a smart city. Smart data presents a number of issues, including those related to analysis, assessment, integration, validation, and visualization. The Internet of Things (IoT) elements create the framework for the smart city [16]. The smart city becomes synchronous when a synchronization procedure is present. The creation of a smart city involves a number of tasks. These various tasks are activation of mobility as a service, utilization of non-motorized transport, involvement of citizens to make decision, diversity in political management, adaptation due to climatic change, reduction of pollution, *etc.* Smart city needs software-based technology and can be applied with the help of devices such as sensors, analysis tools, and output from machine learning and artificial intelligence [17]. The advantages of a smart city are sustainability, prevention of disaster, business, safety and enhancement of the quality of standard of life. The smart city has six key domains: energy and environment, economy, safety and security, health and living, mobility, education and administration. The term "smart city" primarily refers to the intelligence of numerous components, including the environment, life, water, people, governance, health, waste, *etc.* Advanced and innovative technologies are used to create smart cities. The initiatives for smart cities will be launched in a number of nations throughout the world, including Kenya and South Africa in Africa, China, Dubai, Hong Kong, and Japan in Asia, Barcelona, Romania, Sweden, the United Kingdom, and the United States of America in Europe. A smart city is said to be an Intelligent city because Intelligent technologies are being applied. IoT is basically the current communication technologies, which have been launched. In IoT [18], essential things for everyday life, such as home appliances, cameras, sensors, actuators, displays, vehicles, *etc.*, will be embedded with microcontrollers, transceivers for digital communication, suitable protocol stacks which have the ability for communication between each other and help the user to make it easy to access and become an integral part of the Internet. As a result, in a smart city [19], new applications are available which facilitate the residents, organization, *etc.* These new applications include automation in the home, workplace, medical field, energy and traffic management, as well as smart grids. Urban IoT must be installed for the smart city. Public services, including transportation and parking, lighting, security, preservation, heritage, trash collection, schools, hospitals, and other areas, all benefit from an urban IoT in various ways. Urban IoT gathers an enormous amount of smart data that can be used to improve the signal's dependability [20]. On the other hand, the application of IoT in a smart city makes people attractive. Smart city project is said to be the deployment of the Proof of Concept (PoC). For the realization of the urban scale platform, urban IoT [21] is the main element behind the development. Smart city is created by increasing the smartness, interconnection among various devices, sustainability, availability and gathering of information. In a smart city, there is a combination of various technologies, such as edge computing, blockchain, and artificial intelligence. In urban IoT, there is a processing of massive data. Smart data are not homogeneous, but they are heterogeneous because data are available in heterogeneous elements such as energy, vehicle, home, water, *etc.*

This chapter is organized as follows:

Technology Evolution towards Smart Cities: Future smart cities will be built with the aid of 5G technologies. As a result, a smart environment is created. The real world will change into a smart world as daily intelligence increases.

Importance of Internet of Thing (IoT) in Smart Cities: The Internet is a crucial component that offers complete facilities and utilities for running various gadgets in smart cities. IoT refers to the operation of things with the assistance of the Internet. IoT will eventually evolve into the Internet of Everything (IoE).

Physical Layer Aspects in Smart Cities: The hardware of the system for smart cities is referred to as the Physical layer. The hardware of the system should be constructed such that it may operate numerous gadgets in the surroundings by using the Internet.

Realization of Smart Cities: Several chips made by NXP Semiconductors will be used in the creation of smart cities.

TECHNOLOGY EVOLUTION TOWARDS SMART CITIES

The new secret to fixing many problems is the smart city. These issues include urban ageing, pollution, heavy traffic, a lack of vitality, criminal activity, *etc.* In essence, a smart city is a massive information system. Large-scale facilities and opportunities are provided by smart cities to the public sector for the development of quality [22]. A smart city integrates several services, as seen in Fig. (**4**), including health, education, transportation, and power. Smart city basically means smartness in the metropolitan area. The data rate for a smart city is from 10 Gbps to 1 Tbps. Side by side, the spectrum efficiency is from 30 bps/Hz to 100 bps/Hz. The frequency bands are Microwave (Sub-6 GHz), Millimeter-wave and Sub Millimeter-wave.

The broadest possible frequency range is between 90 GHz and 10 THz. Smart data from any domain is used to process the operations in a smart city. Each autonomous device has a central connection to data management platforms that store large amounts of data. Smart cities involve the intelligence of many different things, including economics, governance, mobility, environment, people, and way of life.

Smart Mobility

Smart mobility is applicable to movable devices, *i.e.*, autonomous vehicles. Here, the infrastructure determines the sustainability, innovation and safety of the transport, and the information can be accessed. Smart mobility is one of the important features which have a reduction in pollution, faster activation, cheap transport, green environment. The components of smart cities include sensors, dynamic street lights, global positioning systems, vehicle identifiers, navigation facilities, communication systems, data integration, *etc.* [23]. The latency should be 1 ms, and the reliability should be 99.99999%. As a result, road safety, traffic management, pollution reduction, user reception, accessibility, *etc.*, can be improved. Smart mobility provides smarter decisions in which the usage of the transport network is possible by delivering the essential message to the user. The mobility support should be 500 km/hr to 1000 km/hr.

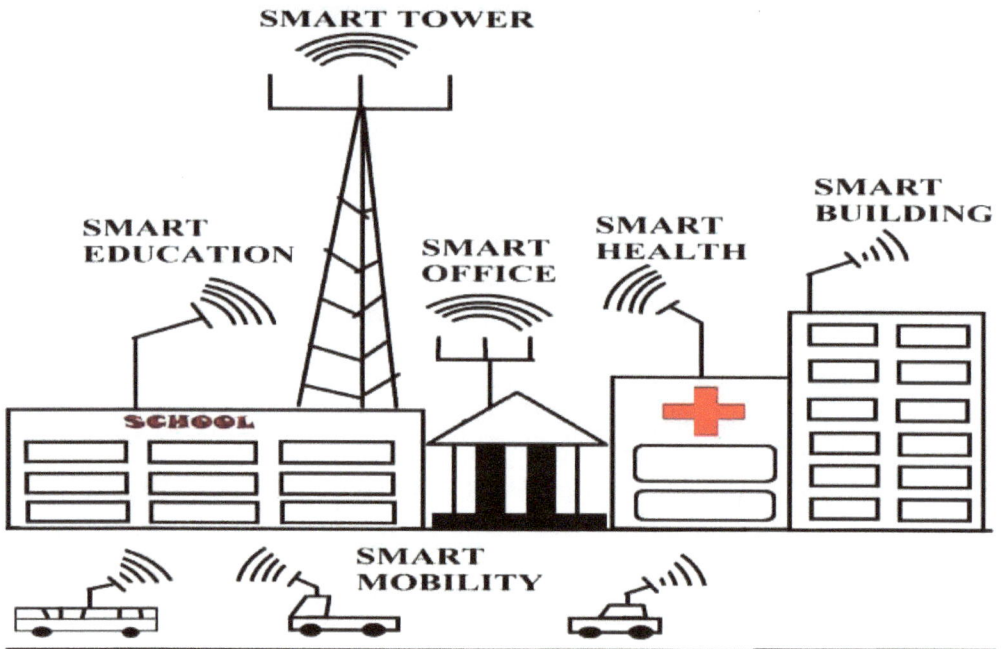

Fig. (4). Smart city with its constituents.

Smart vehicles basically mean vehicles interconnected with computing, sensing, processing device, *etc.* These are used to improve protection, reliability, Quality of Service (QoS). In the Intra Vehicular Sensor Network (IVSN), the wireless mode reduces the vehicle's weight. An IVSN can able to fulfill its targets such as transmission rate, low delay, stationary sensors and robustness. Smart transport is designed to activate traffic management, mode in advanced transport, driving and services in the car. In the smart transport system, Road Side Unit (RSU) is the main term. When the smart transportation system [24] is applied by the vehicle, the vehicle can able to change its communication from one RSU to another RSU given in Fig. (**5**). In smart transportation, 5G enables a software-defined vehicular network. It is an architecture that has 3 planes, *i.e.*, data plane, social plane and control plane. The smart bus facilitates passengers by delivering high-quality service by applying several transit features and making it possible by using information and communication technology, which integrate and send the service to the user.

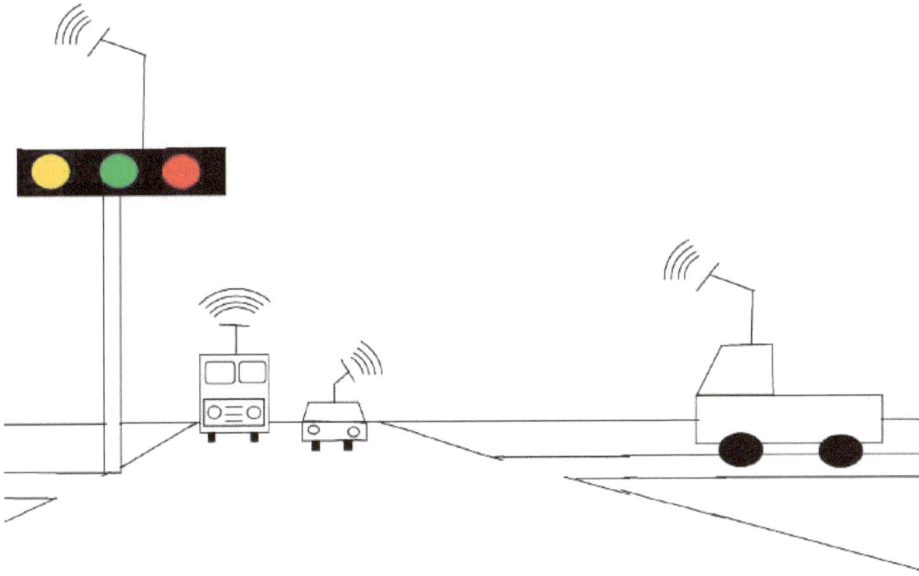

Fig. (5). Smart transportation.

Smart Environment

The smart environment determines the conservation of the natural environment, steps for environmental protection, pollution control, resource management, *etc.* [25]. Here the environmental changes can be verified, and the information about the pollution can be delivered. In the smart environment, the system is equipped with the power required for processing, actuator, sensor, displays, *etc.* These parts ought to be incorporated into the devices along with other commonplace items. For achieving smart environments, the main requirements are autonomy, adaptability and user interaction [23]. Smart environment communication includes WSNs, RFID tags and mobile networks. The device types are smartphones, sensors, drones, smart implants, DLT devices, CRAS, *etc.* The service level should be virtual reality, augmented reality and Tactile Internet.

Smart Building and Smart Home

The applications of IoT [26] in homes and buildings are essentially what smart homes and smart buildings refer to. It will encourage homes to use power and water sparingly. The ideal delay is 10 ms. By producing smart data, sensors will manage and keep an eye on the smart home. The key components of smart cities are smart houses and smart buildings. Smart homes have the capacity to provide users with opportunities. The user can design their own level of comfort. There are often two tiers employed in smart buildings.

Physical Level

The efficiency of the wired and wireless network and its integration with a power supply, transportation systems, switching devices, *etc.,* are all included in the physical structure of the building.

Virtual Level

The virtual level refers to the facilities available in virtual mode. It includes the delivery of information, collaboration, intercommunication among people, and its application. The data are rectified by RFID CRC check and collision detection mechanism.

In the smart home, energy management is the main function. With the help of energy management, several devices can be switched on/off according to user needs and the electricity bill can be reduced. Several sensors and actuators control humidity, temperature, light, *etc.* When these parameters are controlled, the comfortability of life will be achieved. Activation of the alarm is done by the smoke detector when harmful gas is detected.

The smart home leads to smart living. When IoT [27] will be applied in smart homes and buildings, energy consumption, energy analytics, fire safety and environment management will be monitored given in Fig. (**6**). As a result, a new environment will be created in which the cost will be reduced for any services such heating or cooling and positive return will be obtained.

Smart Administration

Smart administration refers to city management, socialism, mass communication, development strategy, *etc.* Here urban IoT [28, 29] is the main item that provides various services to achieve perfect administration. The energy consumption should be verified. On the other hand, the detailed report of the energy consumption by different services such as street lights, transportation, traffic lights, camera, buildings, *etc.* As a result, energy efficiency can be improved. In smart administration, action transparency is mandatory. Using advanced technologies, information can be transferred to citizens by applying efficient, connected systems. Smart infrastructure, where data are generated, is necessary for smart administration [30]. The city authority alters these data in order to produce fresh insights. The goal is to create a viable value chain for these data as well as a business model for the data at various stages. Enabling of big data and analysis can be done through the reduction of tax evasion. Smart administration [31] includes watching of the activities and behavior for the proper administration of the city. The technology includes the LTE Advanced, New Radio, and New Radio Access Technologies. A few elements, such as TeraHertz Communication, Artificial Intelligence, smart cars, haptic communication, satellite integration, *etc.*, ought to be totally applicable. The administrator's primary responsibility is to keep an eye on government services [32]. Electric supply, irrigation, *etc.*, should be controlled for the improvement of efficiency, quality, and equity for the residents. Smart administration generally means smart governance in which political activities, residential facilities, and administrative functions are included. The functions of smart administrations are security, health, education, environment and urban planning, business, water and energy, transportation, *etc.*, as given in Fig. (**7**). For providing facilities to residents in a region, there is a requirement of computers, devices, internet, *etc.* This system is called electronic government [33]. On the other hand, in case of natural disaster conditions, there is a need for emergency response. In the case of hospitality, there is a need for emergency response. Its architectures are massive MIMO and Intelligent surfaces. In smart administration [34], one important term is used, which is called public safety. For public safety, residents and organizations need protection against various threats.

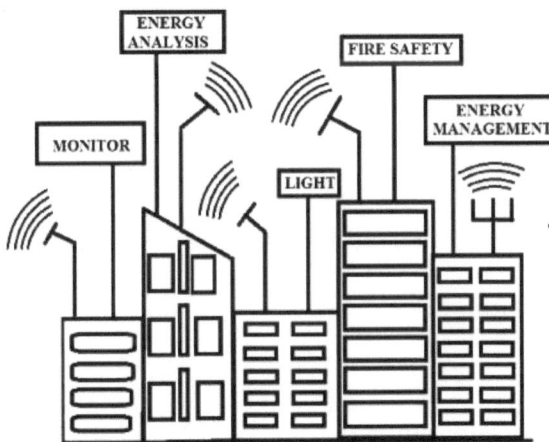

Fig. (6). Smart building.

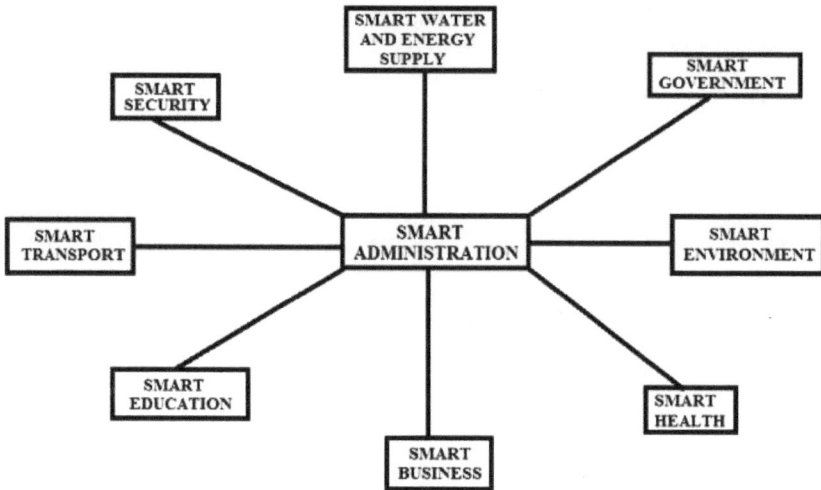

Fig. (7). Smart administration.

Smart Education

Teachers will get great assistance from data and analytics so that the teacher will feel easier for proper guidance to students. Smart education facilitates both teachers and students in a proper manner by providing high-quality teaching. On the other hand, students can able to take high-quality education. As a result, the Quality of Learning (QoL) will be improved [35]. Due to the development of smart education, student performance can be monitored, and development of teaching methods for the improvement of learning outcomes. Smart education is initiated by educated persons. Smart education leads to smart classroom buildings. In smart classroom buildings, the participants are students, teachers, visitors, cleaners, food suppliers, maintenance staff, *etc.* [36], and the services are IT services, academic services, technology services, *etc.* In smart classroom buildings, information and communication technologies are applied, which can make connectivity to different systems present in the building and essential information will be sent to different users; as a result, there will be an improvement in the techniques of learning, teaching and service experience. The smart education includes a smart board, video conference, learning, smart control, smart table, *etc.*, given in Fig. (**8**).

Smart Health

Smart health mainly refers to electronic health and telecare services, and it will provide opportunities for some people like the elderly, the disabled, and disease patients. The use of robotic technology is here. The use of intelligent robots that adhere to patents and provide appropriate direction and information will be undertaken. Big data and artificial intelligence technology are used in smart robots [37]. The creation of smart health care is currently a pressing need. By utilizing sensors and actuators, smart health [38] can raise people's quality of life. Analytics are combined with data. Smart healthcare can be activated when there is a facility to use technology such as big data, which are used for the development of prediction and identification of hotspots. Here, the data refers to health-related data with the help of which digital health records, residential health services, treatment, patient verification systems, *etc.* The health condition of citizens is monitored by the health care unit using smart and network technologies. The transmission of medical data is from the sensing plane to the data plane. The applications of smart health given in Fig. (**9**) expand in various behaviors, and social and medical fields. In smart hospitals, three layered architecture will be used: device layer, edge layer and cloud layer. In the device layer, sensors capture the biomedical signals from the human body. These signals are being sent to the gateways through the wireless mode. In the edge layer, smart electronic health gateways are present, which are capable of supporting protocols and device-to-device communication in wireless communication. In the cloud layer, data analytics is performed by cloud computing.

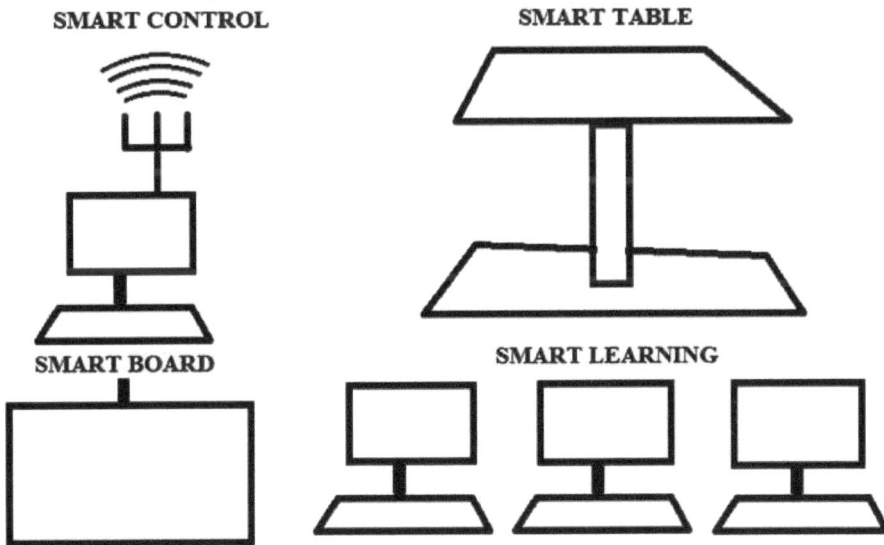

Fig. (8). Smart education.

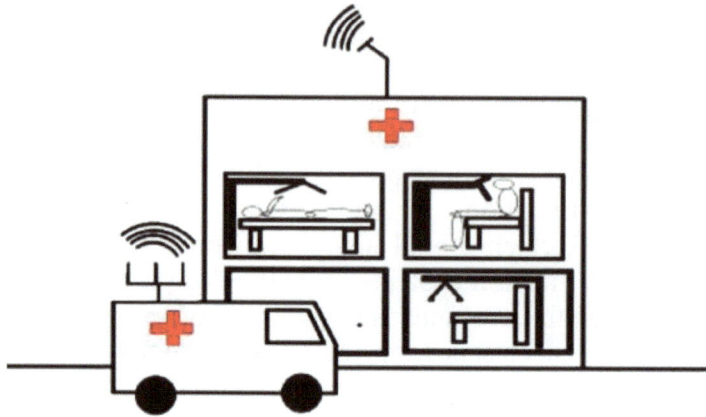

Fig. (9). Smart health.

IMPORTANCE OF INTERNET OF THINGS (IOT) IN SMART CITIES

In order to connect IoT with other devices and perform a variety of operations and services, IoT has the ability to integrate heterogeneous technologies with the communication infrastructure. The Internet of Things (IoT) will expand quickly, converge with other technologies, and large data will be used effectively. IoT is a new item faced by the real world in the future in which usable things are connected to a network. The usage of IoT will be such that specific tasks should be achieved where high intelligence is required. For high intelligence, IoT devices are connected with sensors, actuators, processors and transceivers. IoT is basically the combination of various technologies that can be executed with the help of the Internet. IoT is the main network in which the interconnection and communication between physical devices such as buildings, vehicles, hospitals and other devices will be fulfilled. IoT's primary purpose is to gather data, which residents and government agencies will have simple access to. IoT is essentially a method in which objects are linked together using sensors, actuator processors, and communication lines in order to achieve a goal. IoT forges a connection between the real world and the digital one [39].

The possibility of a relationship between the physical and digital worlds is due to the application of sensors and actuators. Sensors collect data that will be used for storage and processing in an intelligent manner in order to get useful information from it. IoT [40] is the network in which the interconnection and communication between physical devices such as building, vehicles, hospitals and other devices will be fulfilled. IoT [41] is a new platform having the combination of massive devices joined with the Internet and the identification takes place with the help of IP addresses and protocols. The embedding of devices takes place with sensors and actuators, shaving the connectivity to the network in wireless mode. The facilities are provided to the persons with the help of the pattern of connection and communication between sensors and the application of incoming information. Radio Frequency Identification (RFID) is basically the required item for IoT so that all devices can be identified with the help of radio units. There are varieties of IoT peripheral nodes depending upon many characteristics: powering capacity, network importance, sensor, actuator technologies and link layer technologies [42]. In the future, IoT will be updated to the Internet of Everything (IoE). It is the design, updating and extension for the replacement of IoT. As a result, life comfortability in cities will increase. The facilities present in IoE are much more than that of IoT. IoE can provide massive connectivity to every object with intelligent technologies.

As a result, various advantageous functionalities will be achieved. IoT executes on the massive number of interconnected devices given in Fig. (10). The ability of IoE is to carry the collected and created information by these things and allows communicating with massive things. When there is, an interconnection of intelligent objects and everybody from anywhere can able to access it., then the IoE forms a new and innovative era. In IoE, Internet infrastructure and interconnection of networks are applied. As a result, the incoming information from the devices will be managed. On the other hand, an application will be developed which can fulfill user satisfaction both in the public and private sectors and reduce the complexity of the network by the utilization of API (Application Program Interface).

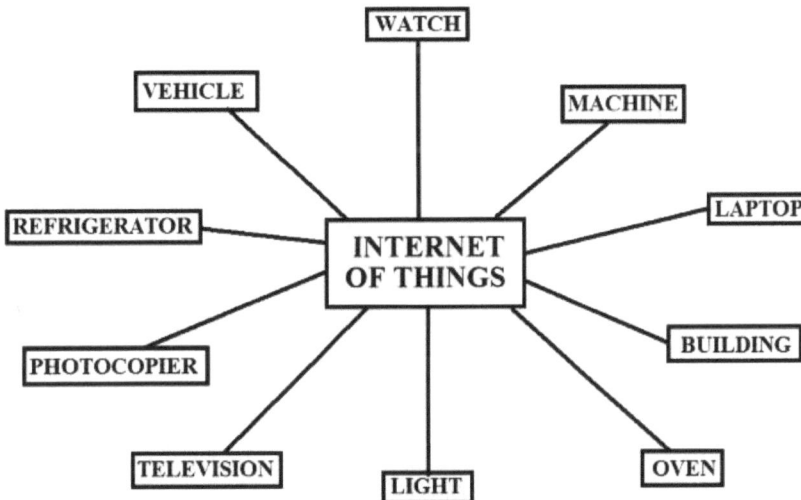

Fig. (10). Internet of things.

PHYSICAL LAYER ASPECTS IN SMART CITIES

In order to design the physical layer for 5G IoT [43], several features like energy efficiency, reasonable cost, spectral efficiency, Quality of Service (QoS) should be fulfilled. The probability of these features will be successful if there will be the possibility of the removal of interference. The removal of interference is possible with the help of intelligent interference management techniques. In wireless IoT, there are several application areas such as WBAN(Wireless Body Area Network), WSN (Wireless Sensor Network), D2D (Device to Device), M2M (Machine to Machine), Satellite Communications and 5G network. For these applications, we have to undergo the characteristics of the physical layer. In wireless IoT, the different enabling physical layer techniques are cognitive techniques, dynamic carrier allocation, adaptive power allocation, distributed beam forming, adaptive waveforms, Millimeter wave technology, orthogonal/non-orthogonal multiple access, energy harvesting and efficient techniques, low complexity cooperative techniques, compressive and spectrum sensing, interference/fade mitigation techniques and different protocols. The physical layer is the perception layer in which the sensors are used for sensing, collecting and processing information about the environment. Some physical parameters are sensed with the help of a physical layer, and hence the smart objects are identified. IEEE 802.15.4 (ZigBee) supports low-energy communication at the physical layer.Another physical layer protocol relevant to IoT is IEEE 802.15.6. Bluetooth Low Energy, LTE A, NFC, *etc.* The sensor is one of the important components in the physical layer of IoT applications because the collection of data is possible with the help of sensors. Side by side, the sensor determines the smartness of the objects. The important feature of the Internet of Things is context awareness which is done by sensor technology. Basically, the sensors are small in size, cheaper, power saving capacity. Context awareness is the procedure of affecting a change in the physical world. It is dependent upon the conditions at that time.

Wireless Body Area Network (WBAN)

For proper diagnosis and analysis of the body, the WBAN [43] is an important item. Its usage is for monitoring the patient. The nodes present in WBAN are inside the body and on the body. Wireless Medical Telemetry Services (WMTS) in licensed mode, Ultra Wide Band (UWB), Medical Implant Communication Service (MICS) in a licensed mode which ranges from 402 to 405 MHz, ISM in unlicensed mode, which is operated at 24 GHz. In WBAN, there are three different tiers of communication. In tier 1, Intra WBAN communication is present in which there is an interaction of nodes and ranging of transmission within 2 metres in and around the body. Tier 2 represents Inter WBAN communication which includes the interconnection of a WBAN with different networks. The networks can be Internet and cellular. In tier 3, the Beyond WBAN communication is represented in which the connection between the Internet and the medical server is specified by using a gateway device. In WBAN, the communication aspects in the physical layer include antenna design, transmission and receiving of radio frequencies, coupling of electromagnetic waves and signal propagation. In the physical layer, the Physical Layer Service Data Unit (PSDU) is transformed into Physical Layer Protocol Data Unit (PPDU). Here, for WBAN, IEEE 802.15.6 is used where human body communication, UWB, the narrow band is specified.

Wireless Sensor Network (WSN)

The design of WSN [43] is required for gains in high diversity, maximization of efficiency in energy, and reduction of computational burden. Categorization of research aspects includes various techniques such as energy efficiency with the design of a transceiver having high reliability and rules for data fusion having less complexity. For energy efficiency with the design of the transceiver, there is an involvement of the techniques in spatial diversity, *i.e.*, Space Time Block Code (STBC) and the beam formation having single or multiple antennas present at each sensor node and energy efficient modulation with the techniques of detection. Every sensor has the capability of sensing in which a certain quality of information is provided, depending upon the employed application. In the sensing technique, the detection ranges from simple to complex eigenvalue. The WSN is composed of heterogeneous nodes. Hence there is a requirement of the investigation by the cooperative sensing techniques for addressing the problem in the hidden node. The critical issues for IoT sensors are selection and searching, and there needs the investigation for the new approaches as there is a problem in accuracy for the traditional text-based searching while capturing the important characteristics of the sensor.

Machine Type Communication (MTC)

Machine Type Communication [43] includes a large number of connected devices, which is 100 times more compared to the current wireless network. MTCs include Machine to Machine (M2M), Device to Device (D2D), and Vehicle to Vehicle (V2V). Here there is a development of direct communication between the nodes without the usage of base stations in the cellular systems. As a result, there is an improvement in performance in the spectrum and efficiency of energy. For monitoring the radio resources present at the cross-layer, the latency is required to be examined along with the throughput of the physical layer. Majorly, the machine type Communication depends upon IEEE 802.11p, in which the carrier sense multiple access having collision avoidance can be facilitated.

Such an event is dependent upon the sensing procedure at the transmitter. The performance is decreased than the previous stage due to the problems held in the hidden terminals. Various techniques, such as conventional orthogonal, Non-Orthogonal Multiple Access (NOMA), are utlised for the detection of the problem. With the help of these techniques, realization can be done easily but cannot fulfill the requirement for MTC. Hence the cognitive radio having algorithms of spectrum sensing is used for the detection of the invisible problem.

Satellite Communication

Due to the presence of satellite communication [43], broadband services are spread over a vast area and applicable to various sectors such as avionics, transport, defence, disaster, shipping, mobile phones, safety, relief, *etc*. The sensors cum actuators are utilized in a large area, but in remote areas, there is no facility of accession. Satellite Communication will able to fulfill this facility of accession, and hence a new term arises called the Internet of Remote Things (IoRT). Satellite Communication is done by Low Earth Orbit (LEO) Satellite. It helps in the distribution and automation control in a smart grid having the need for latency.

LTE-Advanced/5G Networks

For the improvement of QoS for the IoT applications in 5G systems, several parameters such as the reduction of latency, massive connectivity, and increase of efficiency in spectrum and energy are mandatory. To fulfill these parameters, an air interface is required, which should be scalable and flexible. By following the technical procedures, the physical layer and Medium Access Layer (MAC) can be configured in a flexible pattern. The enabling of IoT is possible through the usage of Millimeter waves. In comparison to Microwaves, Millimeter-wave has high significant bandwidth. Along with the Millimeter wave, there will be the usage of massive antenna array elements will be utilized in which massive MIMO should be present for the improvement of performance. The performance includes beamforming and multiple access availability. Nowadays, hybrid digital and analog beamforming is used for the improvement of performance.

REALIZATION OF SMART CITIES

The position of smart cities is currently established. Smartness in different areas, including security, health, the house, automobiles, *etc*., is a feature of smart cities. Authors and industries should be responsible for bringing smart cities to life.

Realization by Industries

One of the international semiconductor companies, NXP Semiconductor [44], has developed several technologies for building secure links with the infrastructure of the future intelligent world. The target market's research and development are ongoing at NXP. NXP launched "Secure Connections for a Smarter World" with the goal of transforming the physical environment into a more intelligent one. NXP Semiconductor seeks to develop civilization in a number of areas, including automation, business, mobility, communication infrastructure, and home and city smartness. Total quality, flexibility, capability, and talent are key elements of NXP Global operations [44]. Total quality refers to new technologies in the coming future, which basically include perfection, on-time delivery, quality standardization of the product, and their process of automation. The flexibility includes the capacity of cost, competitive, and security through the process of flexible industrialization. The capability and talent mean the performance of the organization and user capability. In the "Secure Connections for a smarter world", various solutions for new features are included, such as connected cars, the Internet of Things, portability & wearability, and cyber security. In the future, new applications are Automotive (In-vehicle networking, vehicular access and entertainment, lighting, telematics, speed & angular sensors), identification (identity, transactions, tagging and authentication), Consumer (TV, satellite, cable, set-top box, outdoor units of satellite), Computer (Tablet PCs, notebooks, netbooks, desktop, power supplies, monitors, peripherals), wireless infrastructure (wireless base stations, point to point), cable TV infrastructure, broadcasting), lightning (drivers, networks, backlighting), industrial (smart grid, white goods, automation, power supplies), mobile (devices, portability of power supplies, health check up, chargers).

Access

It is safe, contactless and convenient used for different type of attractions and services in a smart city. For improvement of the security and safety, legacy technologies will be more helpful [45]. The examples of legacy technologies are barcodes or magnetic stripe cards.

Various organizations and multinational companies are dependent on secure technologies in contactless form produced by NXP semiconductors for an access control system. For providing access to smart cities, Access control and smart lock systems are used. In Access Control, the access control means physical and logical access control and its provision for solutions in a few corporate sectors, campuses, *etc.* The access control includes access management and building security. In Access management, access should be managed to buildings and information is different for different sectors. NXPs physical and logical access [46] is scalable and can be tailored by the combination of MIFARE products, Bluetooth, NFC, UWB technologies. As a result, the integration form factors such as smart cards, mobile phones *etc.* The Logical Access includes the utilization of a smart card and reader given in Fig. (**11**).

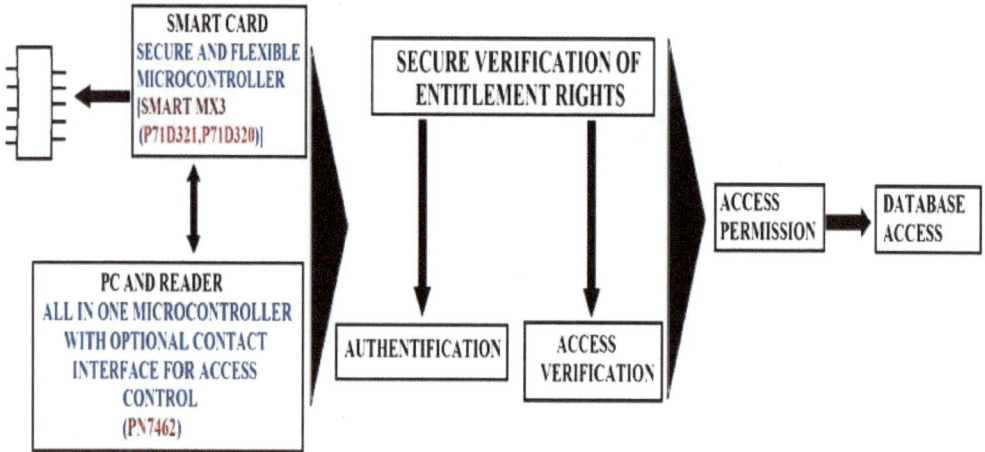

Fig. (11). Logical access.

Building Security

In building security [47], there are various options for solutions. MCUs (Microcontroller Unit) are the accurate devices which provide the required solutions. MX RT MCUs give a perfect solution for video processing, and data management used for wireless IP video cameras and its utilization areas are motion and occupancy sensors (Fig. **13**), and surveillance cameras. Fig. (**12**) shows the Microcontroller Unit solution for face recognition.

Fig. (12). Microcontroller Unit (courtesy [47]).

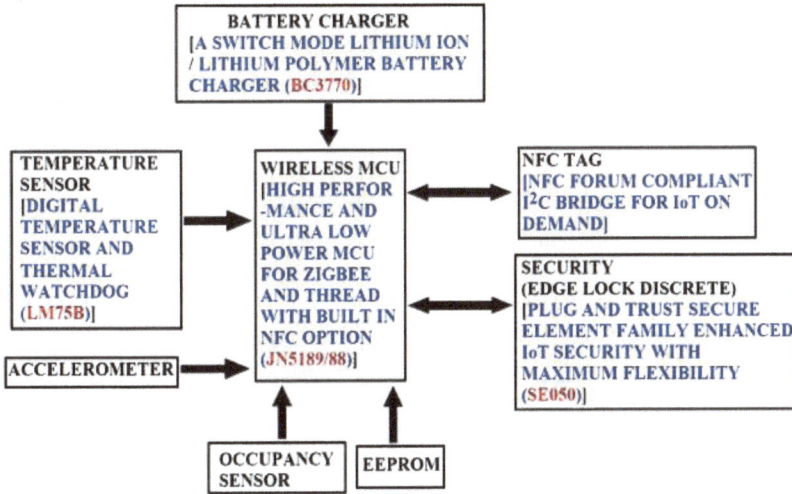

Fig. (13). Wireless occupancy sensor.

Smart Lock System

In the Smart Lock system [48], low-energy solutions are included, which are required to open gates to have security and convenience. The accession of smart locks is possible using NFC contact or contactless technology and Ultra Wide Band (UWB) (Fig. **15**). On the other hand, the function of the smart lock is to communicate with the user's Smartphone in Fig. (**14**).

Identification

NXP Semiconductor is a reliable organization that provides various services such as identification, security, authentication, and electronic government services [49]. As a result, various electronic items are introduced, for example, electronic identity cards, electronic passports, electronic health, electronic driving licenses, *etc.*

National ID

It is an electronic ID document. In National ID [50], the national specification includes security options given in Fig. (**15**). Here, the execution will be easier and more secure. It will be accessible to public, private, online or offline, where identification will be required. Several countries utilize NXP's electronic ID to give every citizen a new opportunity where government administration, authorities and organizations provide benefits or services.

Fig. (14a). Electronic Demo Guide with the Microcontroller Unit courtesy [48].

Fig. (14b). Smart lock.

Electronic Passport

It is a travel document having high security, which helps to protect sensitive data designed by a chip [51]. It is an RFID-based biometric passport which creates a new travel experience. It makes no delay in waiting in line and proving the identity in an efficient way. It is a smart card IC product with high security that can take various steps against various attacks and keep the data having high safety and security in a chip given in Fig. (**16**).

ONLINE IDENTIFICATION

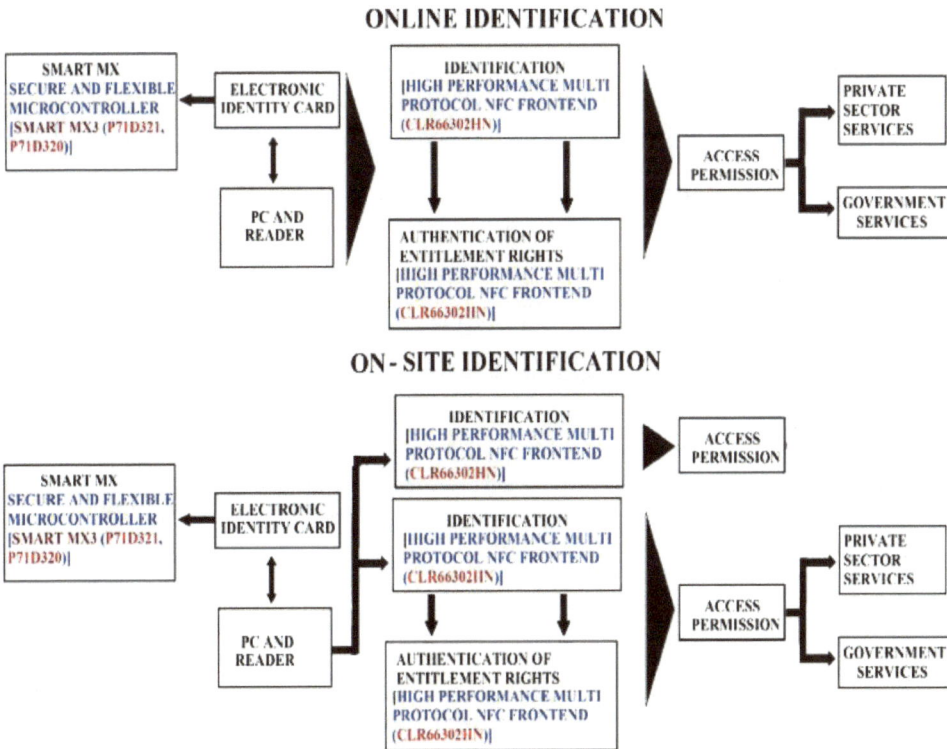

ON-SITE IDENTIFICATION

Fig. (15). National identification.

Electronic Health ID

It is one of the highly secured products developed by NXP semiconductors (Fig. **17**), making the healthcare systems efficient in protecting personal and critical data [52]. It stores health records and emergency data. As a result, health projects around the world are deployed in an easy manner. Many countries are using NXP semiconductor chips for the prescription process and online services, which makes it advantageous to doctors, patients and health insurance.

Electronic Vehicle License (eVL)

It is an electronic document with opportunistic proof for the vehicular driver [53]. It is a secured identification element used when smart governance executes inspections. As a result, road safety will be improved by reducing fraud and assisting administrative official in their responsibilities. It is a smart card that contains registration documents, fine collections and the storage of traffic violations. This chip is developed by NXP Semiconductor, which keeps the sensitive data in protected mode (Fig. **18**). As a result, the reliable infrastructure for online service is created.

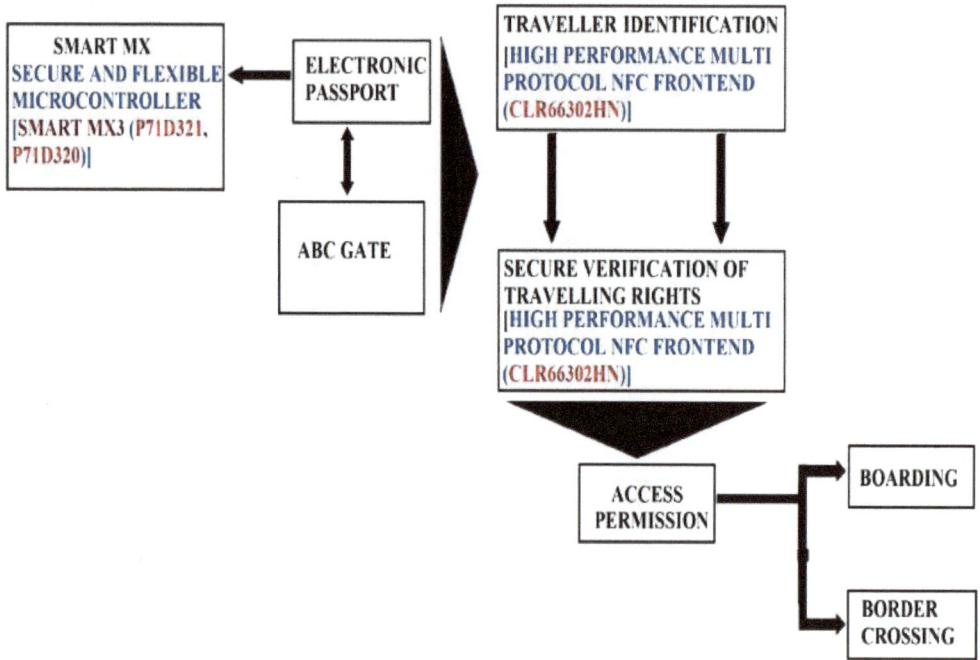

Fig. (16). Electronic passport.

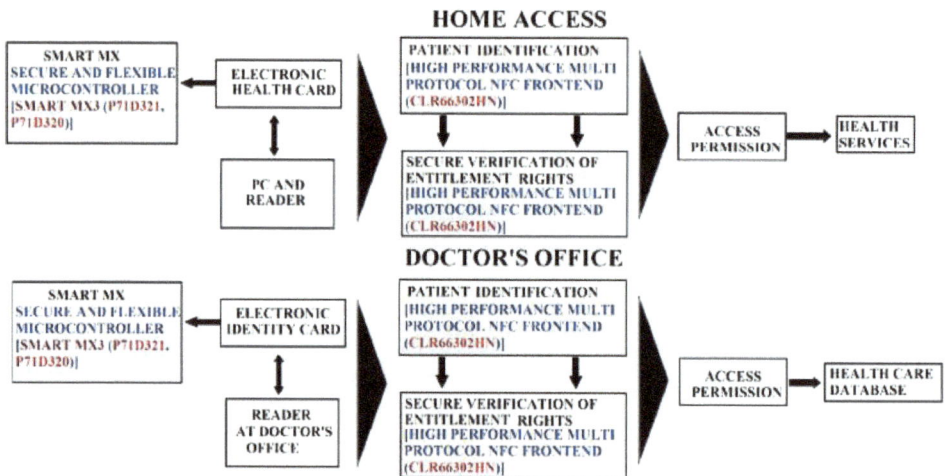

Fig. (17). Electronic health identification.

Fleet Management

It entails a variety of tasks, including route optimization, driver, speed, and fuel management, cargo tracking, tracking and diagnostics, and more (Fig. **20**) [54]. Future decision-makers such as drivers, logistic managers, technicians, and others will be able to do so with ease thanks to artificial intelligence (AI) and machine learning (ML). (Fig. **19**) depicts the Time Sensitive Networking solution for Industrial IoT. The NXP processor includes a variety of components, including sensors, real-time networking, RFID tracking applications, high-security components, and electronic intelligence to provide the necessary ecosystem. As a result, a highly effective fleet management system will be developed.

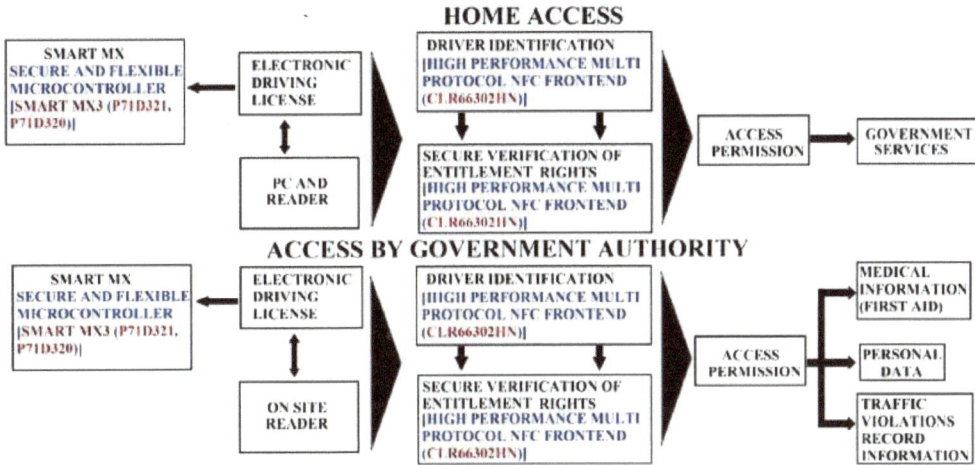

Fig. (18). Electronic vehicle license.

Transportation

Transportation includes safety, security and efficiency in mobility in the city. For Intelligent transportation systems, NXP Semiconductor develops reliable, secret identification and authentication solutions [55]. This technology assists the user in choosing the best, safe and secured ways for roaming themselves, cargoes and big data.

Fig. (19). Time Sensitive Networking [54].

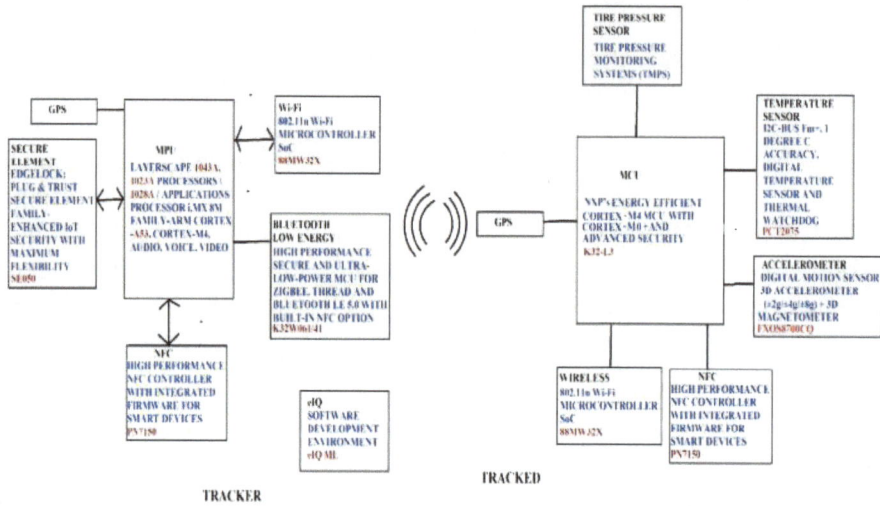

Fig. (20). Fleet management.

V2X Communications

In V2X technology [56] (Fig. **22**), both LOS and NLOS communication, safe and efficient driving are enabled by the vehicles. As a result, invisible objects will become visible, and traffic injuries and fatalities will be reduced. For the improvement of safety, the traffic flow should be optimized, and traffic congestion must be reduced. For safety and intelligent transport system, Vehicle to Vehicle (V2V) and Vehicle to Infrastructure (V2I) communications are provided. (Fig. **21**) shows the automotive telematics box solutions. It is a reference design board utilized for telematics with automation phenomenon.

Fig. (21). Automotive telematics box [56].

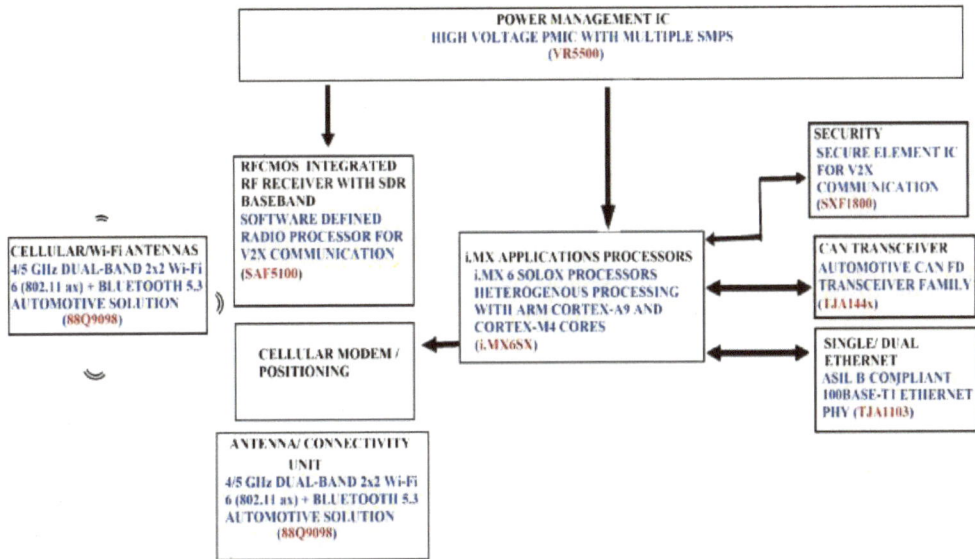

Fig. (22). V2X communications.

Car and Bike Sharing

It is basically the vehicle sharing system and its solutions can fulfill the requirement for flexible and cost-efficient transport [57]. By keeping the cost low, using smart cards, and mobile phones, creating seamless end-user experiences, and providing car and bike sharing solutions are developed by NXP Semiconductor. Its application is car and bike sharing (Fig. **23**).

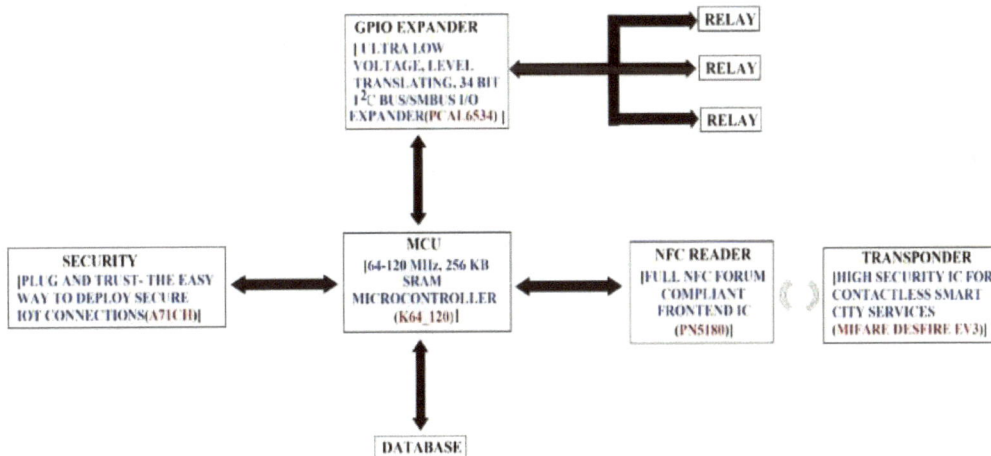

Fig. (23). Car and bike sharing.

Automatic Vehicle Identification

Its utilization is the identification of vehicles in traffic situations having critical conditions with security, reliability and cost efficiency. As a result, AVI is used [58] (Fig. **24**) in access control, speed control and electronic toll collection. An RFID tag should be present on the license plate, and it should execute as a government-issued document, and it can protect the document from fake and duplication. RFID tags read and find out which vehicles have stolen license plates. Its application areas are access control, electronic toll collection, road tolling, and speed control.

Inventory and Supply Management

It has the ability to enable tracking of assets in quick and accurate manner. There is a provision of high visibility, catching theft, increasing productivity and reducing the cost, and high control of the supplied chain process. In NXP Semiconductor, different RFID families such as UCODE, ICODE and NTAG [59] are available. The connectivity and processing provide suitability to supply chain optimization efforts. Its application areas are cold storage monitoring (Fig. **25**), food safety, healthcare safety, industrial safety, inventory management, logistics (Fig. **26**), self-service library, self-service library and warehousing.

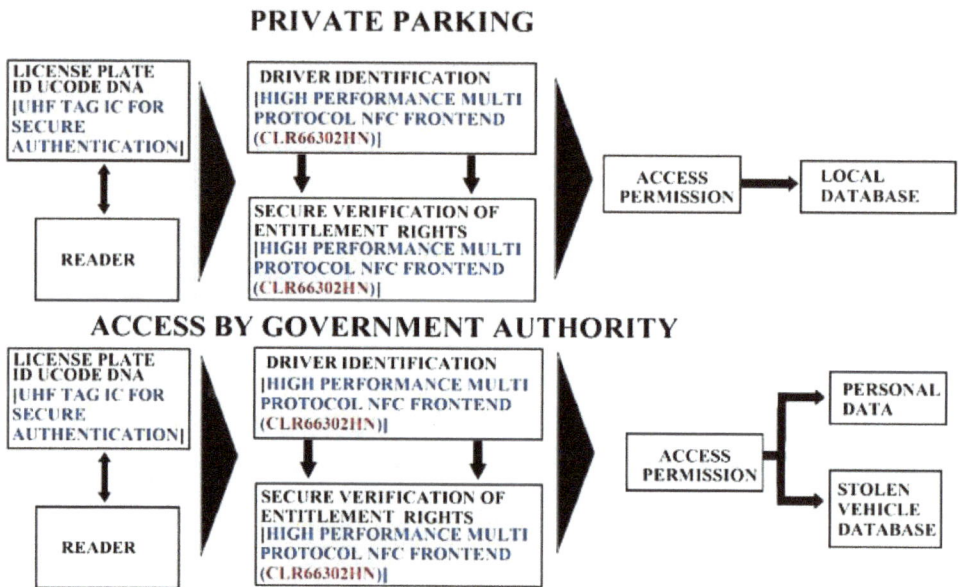

Fig. (24). Automobile Vehicle Identification.

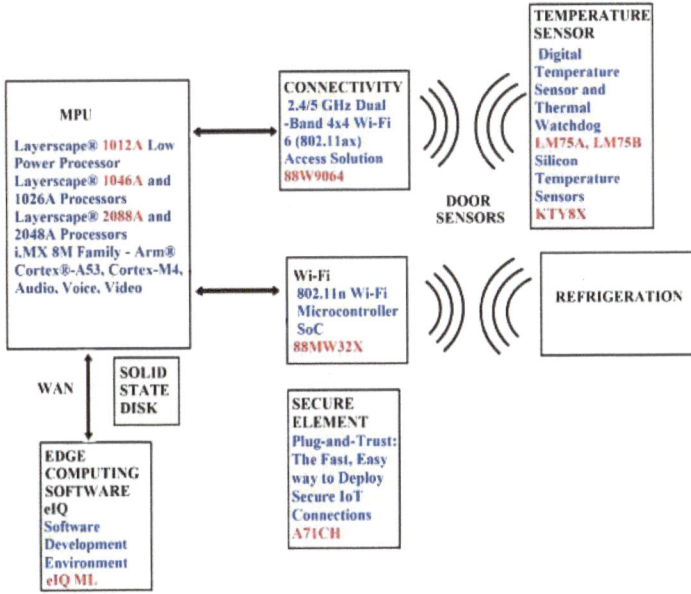

Fig. (25). Cold storage monitoring.

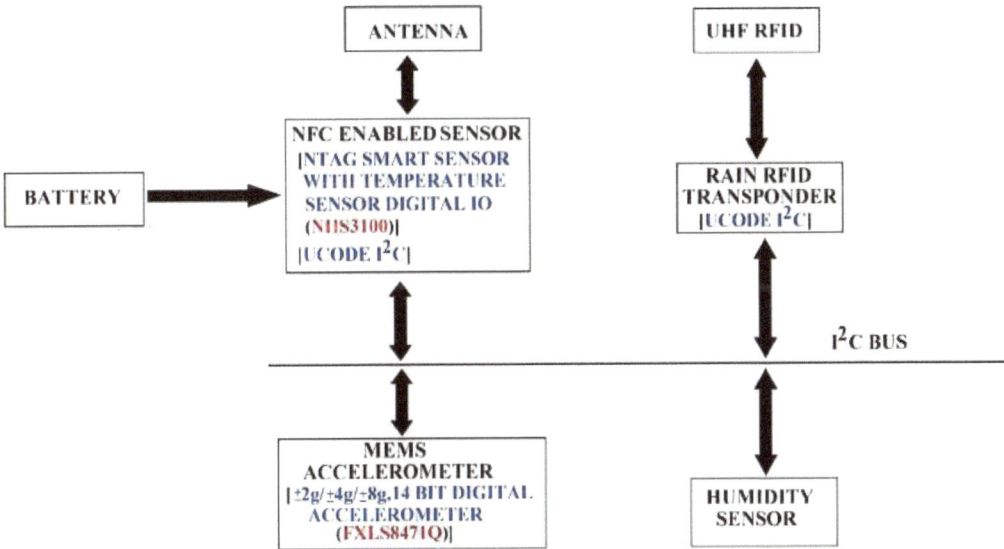

Fig. (26). Smart logistics.

Broadband Modem and Residential Gateway

Data, voice and video signals having broadband frequencies are delivered to home or user areas by broadband gateway [60]. As a result, the performances of internet services facilitate the home. Hence it is called Smart Home Gateway (Fig. **28**). Broadband data service will be utilized by both TV and video, and then it will be utilized by other voice-controlled services. A Residential Gateway LS1043A (Fig. **27**) is a comprehensive with respect to home-based router platform. Here the design cycles are decreased, and the time will be reduced for marketing. The modem residential gateways having gigabit-class network processors used for hardware packet processing, QoS, WiFi, IoT radios, *etc.*, are solved by NXP Semiconductors.

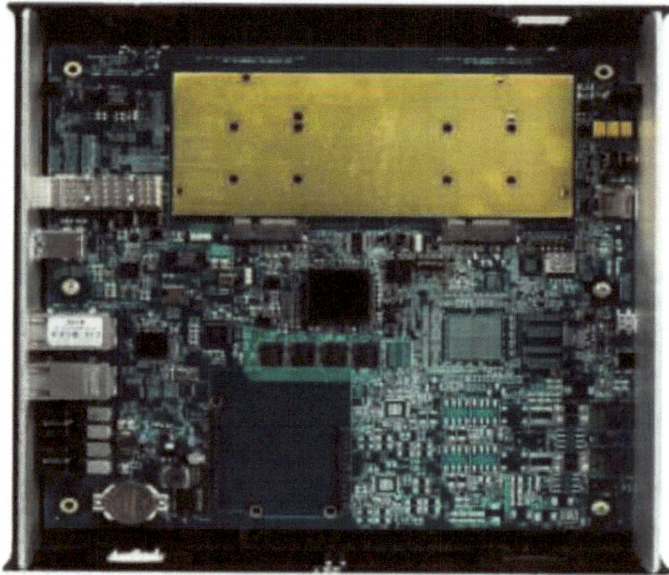

Fig. (27). LS1043A Residential Gateway [60].

Realization by Authors

Prof. Bera, with his family members, is driving his Electric Smart Car to enjoy the tour to The Floating Market (Fig. **29**) of a Smart City, Kolkata. Prof. Bera is assisted by the following facilities out of his Smart Car:

Facility 1- SMART CAR with RADAR Sensor with ACC Mode:

He invoked the ACC (Automatic Cruise Control) RADAR mode of his Smart Electric Car to assist the driver (him) in automatic driving while he was on EM Bypass Road, Kolkata. In this ACC radar mode, his car is driven by the front car and has velocity synchronised by the front vehicle. In this way, he enjoys high speed from his vehicle and ensures ' No Accident' .

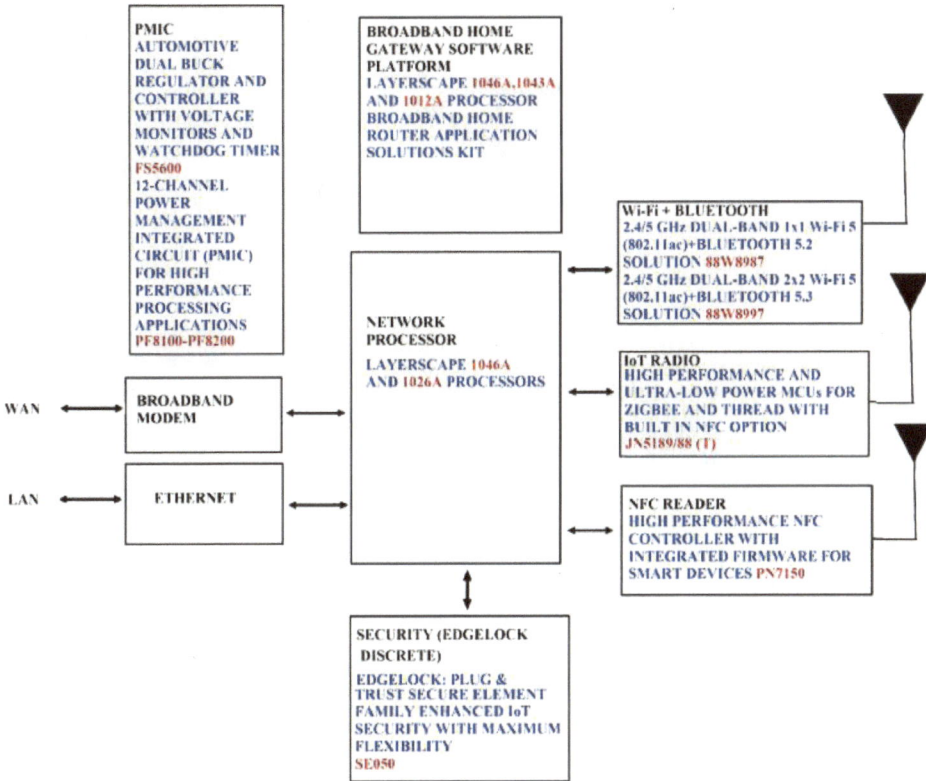

Fig. (28). Smart home gateway.

Facility 2- SMART CAR with 5G_URLLC Communication System:

Near the market entry, at the road crossing, he was warned on the Car Dashboard about some vehicles at the nearby crossing, which is totally invisible to his eye as it is the crossing. His vehicle is always '5G CONNECTED CAR' mode 5G_URLLC system embedded in the car. Here also, the 5G_URLLC Communication system assisted him, thus ensuring further safe travelling.

Facility 3- SMART CAR Radar Sensor with Parking Assistance mode:

Thus, Prof. Bera has reached the destination, 'The Parking area of the Floating Market' with the safest journey. He also invoked the Parking Radar mode of his vehicle and successfully parked his vehicle.

Fig. (29). Floating market.

Facility 4- Smart Car with 5G_eMBB communication system:

During the journey, the family members enjoyed a lot of the Communication systems like Live TV, Live Music, Video calling, Live gaming, and other Internet Facility.

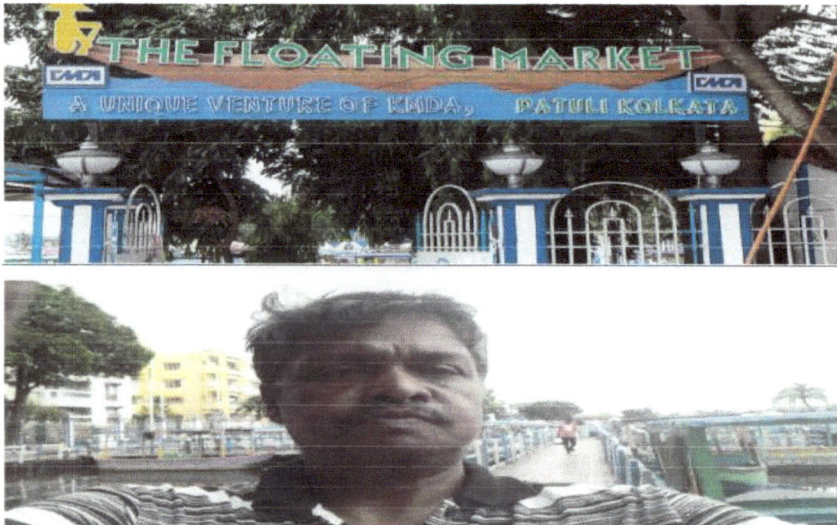

Fig. (30). Prof. Bera in Floating Market.

The above Venture of 'THE FLOATING MARKET' by KMDA (Kolkata Metropolitan Development Authority) (Fig. **30**) is really enjoyable and praised by the citizens of Kolkata.

- Recent Up-gradation to MBB (Mobile Broad Brand) Service by Jio, Mobile Service Provider
- AirSynergy 2000

With Air Synergy, an innovative Pico base station from Airspan that uses Software Defined Radio (SDR) technology, you can have wireless backhaul and data access from the same device.

- Jio has installed the above Picco Base Station near the Floating market.
- Mobile users are enjoying data rates of more than 60 Mbps on their 4G cellphones while watching HD LIVE TV, listening to LIVE music, making video calls, and using other High-Speed Internet Access.

THE FUTURE TOUR WITH MORE ELECTRONIC SERVICES

The IoT-enabled Smart Grid Upgradation with efficient use of the street lamps control on the tour site can be made smart towards IoT enabled.

TOUR DESIGN AND DEVELOPED BY ECE DEPT., SMIT

The tour extends towards:

i) MBB upgradation to 5G_eMBB with data rate always more than 100 Mbps.

ii) Introducing New 5G_IoT service through 'IoT enabled Smart Lamps'.

iii) Introducing New 5G_IoV/ 5G_URLLC service through 'IoV enabled smart Vehicles'.

All the above Up-gradation can be designed and developed by ECE, SMIT under the Centre of Excellent project running @ ECE, SMIT and supported by the Endowment Fund of SMU (Sikkim Manipal University).

TOUR IMPLEMENTATION

Presently, the above concept has been validated by ECE, SMIT as POC (Proof of Concept), and the 5G_IoT Group of ECE, SMIT is working towards the implementation of the same Smart Floating Market.

CONCLUSION

The 5G technology was already made available in the actual world by 2020. The advancement of internet technology has made the transition from 4G to 5G possible. In addition, the 4G facilities already provide good support during a pandemic crisis. The city will eventually become a smart city thanks to this development, which will include smart homes, smart cars, and smart health systems. NXP semiconductors have previously released a few Integrated Chips for the creation of smart cities (IC). Some of the applications used for the creation of smart cities will be satisfied by these chips.

NOTES

[**] eMBB = Enhanced Mobile Broad Band; URLLC = Ultra Reliable Low Latency Communication

REFERENCES

[1]   E. Ezhilarasan, and M. Dinakaran, "A Review on Mobile Technologies: 3G, 4G and 5G", *International Conference on Recent Trends and Challenges in Computational Models (ICRTCCM)*, pp. 369-373, 2017.
[http://dx.doi.org/10.1109/ICRTCCM.2017.90]

[2]   K. Gopal, "A comparative study on 4G and 5G technology for wireless applications", *IOSR J. Electr. Commun. Eng. (IOSR-JECE)*, vol. 10, no. 6, pp. 67-72, 2015.

[3]   G. Barb, and M. Otesteanu, "4G/5G: A comparative study and overview on what to expect from 5G", *43rd International Conference on Telecommunications and Signal Processing (TSP)*, pp. 37-40, 2020.
[http://dx.doi.org/10.1109/TSP49548.2020.9163402]

[4]   J.K. Ray, S. Sil, R. Bera, P. Biswas, A.S. Biswas, and Q.M. Alfred, Millimeter Wave Based Reliable V2X Communication.J.K. Mandal, and D. De, *Advanced Techniques for IoT Applications. EAIT 2021. Lecture Notes in Networks and Systems* vol. 292. Springer: Singapore, 2021.
[http://dx.doi.org/10.1007/978-981-16-4435-1_59]

[5]   J. Winkowska, D. Szpilko, and S. Pejić, "Smart city concept in the light of the literature review", *Eng. Manag. Prod. Serv.,* vol. 11, no. 2, pp. 70-86, 2019.
[http://dx.doi.org/10.2478/emj-2019-0012]

[6]   L.U. Khan, I. Yaqoob, N.H. Tran, S.M.A. Kazmi, T.N. Dang, and C.S. Hong, "Edge-computin-
-enabled smart cities: A comprehensive survey", *IEEE Internet Things J.,* vol. 7, no. 10, pp. 10200-10232, 2020.
[http://dx.doi.org/10.1109/JIOT.2020.2987070]

[7]   G. Betis, C.G. Cassandras, and C.A. Nucci, "Smart Cities Scanning the Issue", *Proc. IEEE,* vol. 106, no. 4, pp. 513-517, 2018.
[http://dx.doi.org/10.1109/JPROC.2018.2812998]

[8]   R. Nelson Pacheco, D. Ana, S. Gonçalo, R. Mário, Q. Alexandra, and R. Carlos, "Smart cities and public health: A systematic review", *Procedia Comp. Sci.,* vol. 164, pp. 516-523, 2019.
[http://dx.doi.org/10.1016/j.procs.2019.12.214]

[9]   R. Sánchez-Corcuera, A. Nuñez-Marcos, J. Sesma-Solance, A. Bilbao-Jayo, R. Mulero, U. Zulaika, G. Azkune, and A. Almeida, "Smart cities survey: Technologies, application domains and challenges for the cities of the future", *Int. J. Distrib. Sens. Netw.,* vol. 15, no. 6, 2019.
[http://dx.doi.org/10.1177/1550147719853984]

[10] F. Cirillo, D. Gómez, L. Diez, I. Elicegui Maestro, T.B.J. Gilbert, and R. Akhavan, "Smart City IoT services creation through large-scale collaboration", *IEEE Internet Things J.,* vol. 7, no. 6, pp. 5267-5275, 2020.
[http://dx.doi.org/10.1109/JIOT.2020.2978770]

[11] C.S. Lai, Y. Jia, Z. Dong, D. Wang, Y. Tao, Q.H. Lai, R.T.K. Wong, A.F. Zobaa, R. Wu, and L.L. Lai, "A review of technical standards for smart cities", *Cleanroom Technol.,* vol. 2, no. 3, pp. 290-310, 2020.
[http://dx.doi.org/10.3390/cleantechnol2030019]

[12] PWC. Creating the smart cities of the future. A three-tier development model for digital transformation of citizen services. Available from: https://www.pwc.com/gx/en/sustainability/ assets/creating-th--smart-cities-of-the-future.pdf

[13] J.H. Jo, P.K. Sharma, J.C.S. Sicato, and J.H. Park, "Emerging technologies for sustainable smart city network security: Issues, challenges, and countermeasures", *J. Inform. Proce.Sys.,* vol. 15, no. 4, pp. 765-784, 2019.

[14] N. Zakaria, and J. A, "Smart city architecture: Vision and challenges", *Int. J. Adv. Comput. Sci. Appl.,* vol. 6, no. 11, 2015.
[http://dx.doi.org/10.14569/IJACSA.2015.061132]

[15] A. Zanella, N. Bui, A. Castellani, L. Vangelista, and M. Zorzi, "Internet of things for smart cities", *IEEE Internet Things J.,* vol. 1, no. 1, pp. 22-32, 2014.
[http://dx.doi.org/10.1109/JIOT.2014.2306328]

[16] H. Rajab, and T. Cinkelr, "IoT based smart cities", *International Symposium on Networks, Computers and Communications (ISNCC),* pp. 1-4, 2018.
[http://dx.doi.org/10.1109/ISNCC.2018.8530997]

[17] K. H. Law, and J. P. Lynch, "Smart City: Technologies and challenges", *IT Professional,* vol. 21, no. 6, pp. 46-51, 2019.
[http://dx.doi.org/10.1109/MITP.2019.2935405]

[18] R.R. Harmon, E.G. Castro-Leon, and S. Bhide, "Smart cities and the internet of things", *2015 Portland International Conference on Management of Engineering and Technology (PICMET),* pp. 485-494, 2015.
[http://dx.doi.org/10.1109/PICMET.2015.7273174]

[19] C. Kyriazopoulou, "Smart city technologies and architectures: A literature review", *2015 International Conference on Smart Cities and Green ICT Systems (SMARTGREENS),* pp. 1-12, 2015.
[http://dx.doi.org/10.5220/0005407000050016]

[20] H. Wang, L. Xu, W. Lin, P. Xiao, and R. Wen, "Physical layer security performance of wireless mobile sensor networks in smart city", *IEEE Access,* vol. 7, pp. 15436-15443, 2019.
[http://dx.doi.org/10.1109/ACCESS.2019.2895338]

[21] S. Pallavi, and R. Smruti, "Internet of things: Architectures, protocols, and applications", *J. Electr. Comp. Eng.,* vol. 2017, 9324035, p. 25, 2017.
[http://dx.doi.org/10.1155/2017/9324035]

[22] L.G. Anthopoulos, and A. Vakali, "Urban Planning and Smart Cities: Interrelations and Reciprocities", In: *The Future Internet. FIA 2012.,* F. Álvarez, Ed., vol. 7281. Springer: Berlin, Heidelberg, 2012.
[http://dx.doi.org/10.1007/978-3-642-30241-1_16]

[23] Kaptan Hadi, and Kantarci Soyata, "Smart city system design: A comprehensive study of the application and data planes", *ACM Comp. Surv.,* vol. 52, no. 2, pp. 1-38, 2019.
[http://dx.doi.org/10.1145/3309545]

[24] R.K. Radovan Novotny, "Smart city concept, applications and services", *J. Telecommun. Sys. Manag.,* vol. 3, no. 2, 2014.
[http://dx.doi.org/10.4172/2167-0919.1000117]

[25] D.P. Abreu, K. Velasquez, M. Curado, and E. Monteiro, "A resilient internet of things architecture for smart cities", *Ann. Telecommun.*, vol. 72, no. 1-2, pp. 19-30, 2017.
[http://dx.doi.org/10.1007/s12243-016-0530-y]

[26] J. Zhang, S. Rajendran, Z. Sun, R. Woods, and L. Hanzo, "Physical layer security for the internet of things: Authentication and key generation", *IEEE Wirel. Commun.*, vol. 26, no. 5, pp. 92-98, 2019.
[http://dx.doi.org/10.1109/MWC.2019.1800455]

[27] L. Chettri, and R. Bera, "A comprehensive survey on internet of things (IoT) toward 5G wireless systems", *IEEE Internet Things J.*, vol. 7, no. 1, pp. 16-32, 2020.
[http://dx.doi.org/10.1109/JIOT.2019.2948888]

[28] J. Lin, W. Yu, N. Zhang, X. Yang, H. Zhang, and W. Zhao, "A survey on internet of things: Architecture, enabling technologies, security and privacy, and applications", *IEEE Internet Things J.*, vol. 4, no. 5, pp. 1125-1142, 2017.
[http://dx.doi.org/10.1109/JIOT.2017.2683200]

[29] H.N. Saha, "IoT solutions for smart cities", In: *8th Annual Industrial Automation and Electromechanical Engineering Conference (IEMECON)*, Bangkok, Thailand, 2017, pp. 74-80.
[http://dx.doi.org/10.1109/IEMECON.2017.8079565]

[30] J. Sahoo, and M. Rath, "Study and analysis of smart applications in smart city context", *2017 International Conference on Information Technology (ICIT)*, pp. 225-228, 2017.
[http://dx.doi.org/10.1109/ICIT.2017.38]

[31] A.M. Gonsalves, and D.K. Sreekantha, "Applications of IoT in smart city: A study", *Int J Engg Res Tech (IJERT)*, vol. 8, no. 5, 2019.

[32] K. Su, J. Li, and H. Fu, "Smart city and the applications", *Interntional Conference on Electronics, Communications and Control (ICECC)*, pp. 1028-1031, 2011.
[http://dx.doi.org/10.1109/ICECC.2011.6066743]

[33] A. Monzon, "Smart cities concept and challenges: Bases for the assessment of smart city projects", *2015 International Conference on Smart Cities and Green ICT Systems (SMARTGREENS)*, pp. 1-11, 2015.
[http://dx.doi.org/10.1007/978-3-319-27753-0_2]

[34] P.J. Navarathna, and V.P. Malagi, "Artificial intelligence in smart city analysis", *2018 International Conference on Smart Systems and Inventive Technology (ICSSIT)*, pp. 44-47, 2018.
[http://dx.doi.org/10.1109/ICSSIT.2018.8748476]

[35] G. Sarin, "Developing smart cities using internet of things: An empirical study", *2016 3rd International Conference on Computing for Sustainable Global Development (INDIACom)*, pp. 315-320, 2016.
[http://dx.doi.org/10.2139/ssrn.2780756]

[36] N. Dlodlo, O. Gcaba, and A. Smith, "Internet of things technologies in smart cities", *2016 IST-Africa Week Conference, Durban, South Africa*. IST-Africa Week Conference, Durban, South Africa, pp. 1-7, 2016.
[http://dx.doi.org/10.1109/ISTAFRICA.2016.7530575]

[37] H. Arasteh, "Iot-based smart cities: A survey", *IEEE 16th International Conference on Environment and Electrical Engineering (EEEIC)*, pp. 1-6, 2016.
[http://dx.doi.org/10.1109/EEEIC.2016.7555867]

[38] C.X. Mavromoustakis, G. Mastorakis, J.M. Batalla, Ed., Internet of Things (IoT) in 5G Mobile Technologies.*Modeling and Optimization in Science and Technologies* Springer: Cham, 2016, pp. 1-499.
[http://dx.doi.org/10.1007/978-3-319-30913-2]

[39] H. Rahimi, A. Zibaeenejad, and A.A. Safavi, "A Novel IoT Architecture based on 5G-IoT and next generation technologies", *Electronics and Mobile Communication Conference (IEMCON)*, pp. 81-88, 2018.

[http://dx.doi.org/10.1109/IEMCON.2018.8614777]

[40]   E. Okai, X. Feng, and P. Sant, "Smart cities survey", *IEEE 20th International Conference on High Performance Computing and Communications,* pp. 1726-1730, 2018.
[http://dx.doi.org/10.1109/HPCC/SmartCity/DSS.2018.00282]

[41]   Y.C. Hsiao, M.H. Wu, and S.C. Li, "Elevated performance of the smart city—a case study of the IoT by innovation mode", *IEEE Trans. Eng. Manage.,* vol. 68, no. 5, pp. 1461-1475, 2021.
[http://dx.doi.org/10.1109/TEM.2019.2908962]

[42]   E. Gomes, M.A.R. Dantas, D.D.J. de Macedo, C. De Rolt, M.L. Brocardo, and L. Foschini, "Towards an infrastructure to support big data for a smart city project", *2016 IEEE* 25th International Conference on Enabling Technologies: Infrastructure for Collaborative Enterprises (WETICE) Paris, France, pp. 107-112, 2016,
[http://dx.doi.org/10.1109/WETICE.2016.31]

[43]   S.K. Sharma, T.E. Bogale, S. Chatzinotas, X. Wang, and L.B. Le, "Physical layer aspects of wireless IoT", *2016 International Symposium on Wireless Communication Systems (ISWCS),* pp. 304-308, 2016.
[http://dx.doi.org/10.1109/ISWCS.2016.7600919]

[44]   NXP Semiconductors, "Secure Connections for a smarter world", Corporate Overview. Available at: https://www.nxp.com/docs/en/supporting-information/NXP-CORPORATE-OVERVIEW.pdf

[45]   XP Semiconductors, "Access", Smart city-Access. Available at: https://www.nxp.com/ applications/smart-city/access:ACCESS

[46]   NXP Semiconductors, "Access Management", Smart city/Access Management. Available at: https://www.nxp.com/applications/smart-city/access/access-management:ACCE-S-MANAGEMENT-ASP

[47]   NXP Semiconductors," Building Security", Smart city/Access/building security. Available at: https://www.nxp.com/applications/smart-city/access/

[48]   NXP Semiconductors," Smart Lock", Smart city/Access/smart lock. Available at: www.nxp.com/applications/smart-city/access/smart-lock

[49]   NXP Semiconductors, "Identification", Smart city/Identification. Available at: www.nxp.com/applications/smart-city/identification

[50]   NXP Semiconductors, "National ID (eID)", Smart city/Identification/ National ID. Available at: https://www.nxp.com/applications/smart-city/identification/national-ideid:NATIONAL-ID

[51]   NXP Semiconductors, "Electronic Passport(ePP)", Smart city/Identification/electronic passport. Available at: https://www.nxp.com/applications/smart-city/identification/electronic-passportepp :ELECTRONIC-PASSPORT

[52]   NXP Semiconductors, "Electronic Health ID (eHID)", Smart city/Identification/ electronic Health card. Available at: https://www.nxp.com/applications/smart-city/identification/electronic-health-id-ehid:ELECTRONIC- HEALTH-CARD

[53]   NXP Semiconductors, "Electronic Vehicle License (eVL)", Smart city/Identification/ electronic vehicle license. Available at: www.nxp.com/applications/smart-city/identification /electronic-vehicl--license-evl:DRIVING-LICENSE

[54]   NXP Semiconductors, "Fleet Management", Smart city/retail/ fleet management. Available at: www.nxp.com/applications/smart-city/retail/fleet-management:FLEET-MANAGEMENT

[55]   NXP Semiconductors, "Transportation", Smart city/transportation :mobility. Available at:www.nxp.com/applications/smart-city/transportation

[56]   NXP Semiconductors, "V2X Communications", Smart city/automotive/connectivity/V2X Communications. Available at: www.nxp.com/applications/automotive/connectivity/v2x-comm

[57]   NXP Semiconductors, "Car and Bike Sharing", Smart city/transportation/Car and bike sharing. Available at: www.nxp.com/ applications/smart-city/transportation/car-and-bike-sharing

[58]   NXP Semiconductors, "Automatic Vehicle Identification", Smart city/transportation/automatic vehicle identification, Available at: www.nxp. com/applications/smart-city/transportation/automatic-vehic-e-identification

[59]   NXP Semiconductors, "Inventory and Supply Chain Management", Smart city/retail/inventory and supply chain management, Available at: www.nxp.com/applications/smart-city/ retail/inventory-an--supply-chain-management:SUPPLY-CHAIN-MGMT

[60]   XP Semiconductors, "Broadband Modem and Residential Gateway, Available at: www.nxp.com/applications/smart-city/transportation/broadband-modem-and-residential-gateway:BRO ADBAND-GATEWAY

CHAPTER 2

Enabling Technologies for Intelligent Systems in Smart Computing Environment

Anuj Kumar Singh[1,*] and **Ankit Garg**[2]

[1] *Department of Computer Science and Engineering, Adani University, Ahmedabad, India*

[2] *Apex Institute of Technology, Computer Science and Engineering, University Center for Research and Development, Chandigarh University, Mohali, Punjab, India*

Abstract: Smart computing environments have evolved with the dawn of the Internet of Things, incorporating pervasive or ubiquitous computing. Besides using sensors and smart devices, the main objective has been to make these environments intelligent by utilizing different kinds of artificial intelligent methods and algorithms. Making a system intelligent requires inclusion and implementation of various tools and technologies to facilitate artificial intelligence. This chapter focuses on identifying the most prominent enabling technologies in making smart computing environments intelligent. The ten foremost intelligence-enabling technologies – predictive analysis, deep learning, artificial neural network, big data analytics, intelligent edge, human-computer interaction, computer vision, explainable artificial intelligence, natural language processing and robotics have been discussed in this chapter.

Keywords: Artificial intelligence, Computer vision, Deep learning, Edge intelligence, Enabling technologies, Explainable artificial intelligence, Human-computer nteraction, Intelligent systems, Smart Computing.

INTRODUCTION

The human age is in the process of transition from "Society 4.0, also labelled as Information Society" to "Society 5.0 declared as Super Smart Society ought to be people-centric largely". Society 4.0 refers to the economic and social processes influenced by the apparent "4th Industrial Revolution," which concentrated on the massification of technological advancement around the globe. The advent of Big Data and the processing of massive volumes of data about people at the compassion of enterprises are two important characteristics of Society 4.0, as is the establishment of an Economy of Orders that fostered different forms of labour using various kinds of digital platforms. Industry 4.0, also known as Intelligent

---

* **Corresponding author Anuj Kumar Singh:** Department of Computer Science, Adani University, Ahmedabad, India; E-mail: anuj.singh@adaniuni.ac.in

Industry, is a real-world concept that involves the digitalization and transformation of industrial operations, either through sensors or information systems, to make them more efficient [1]. Cross-discipline exchange of information and knowledge was not there in Society 4.0, and collaboration was challenging. While in Society 5.0, virtual cyberspace and tangible physical space have a high level of convergence. Persons have been able to access and use the storage services offered by the cloud in virtual cyberspace via the Internet in Society 4.0, and thus will access, obtain and analyze vital information.

In Society 5.0, in the physical environment, a large volume of information from the devices and sensors is collected in virtual cyberspace. Intelligent systems and Artificial Intelligence techniques analyze this large volume of data in virtual cyberspace, and the outcomes are communicated to humans in tangible physical space in numerous ways. Thus, Society 5.0 is going to be an ecosystem that will ensure long-term viability in all dimensions, including social, economic, political, and environmental, with an emphasis on people and value generation. Owing to the rapid transition in the present society and integration of it with the latest AI-based technologies, it is significant to understand the role of new-age intelligent systems in building people-centric super smart Society 5.0.

Intelligent and Smart Environment

We use the term "environment" to refer to any location in our immediate surroundings. Although some individuals contemplate virtual environments, we mainly denote tangible physical spaces in each of their forms, like a house, a building, a street, a field, a sea or space region, and so on. When we use the term "intelligent" in reference to environments, we typically mean Artificial Intelligence achieved by using various tools and techniques. An Intelligent Environment would be one where self-programming and pre-emptive mechanisms (*e.g.*, artificially intelligent agents) help facilitate the actions of multiple interconnected control systems (controlling different aspects of an eco-system) to create dynamic comprehensive and integrated features and functions that improve occupant experiences [2].

Basic Principles of Intelligent Environment

Further, to describe what we mean by Intelligent Environment, a list of key principles that we feel any Intelligent Environment should strive for, are listed below [2]:

• To be intelligent enough to identify and recognize a condition where it can provide help.

- To be able to discern when it is appropriate to assist.
- To provide support based on the requirements and preferences of individuals being assisted.
- To meet its objectives deprived of requiring the technical expertise of the user in order to get an advantage from its assistance.
- To consider the safety of the user first at all times.
- To safeguard the user's privacy.
- To follow those principles that perhaps the users are holding the charge and the system follows, not the other way around.
- To be able to act independently.
- To be able to work without enforcing modifications on the environment's feel and look, and also the occupants' normal routines.

From these principles, it can be analyzed that a proactive attitude is needed in an intelligent environment, which is constantly figuring out how to assist the users. The field of Intelligent Environments is determined by the comparative ripeness and the success level attained in a variety of distinguished computer science domains shown in Fig. (**1**). The potential applications of intelligent and smart environments include healthcare, education, transportation, smart offices, intelligent supermarkets, energy conservation, smart cities, smart industries, *etc.*

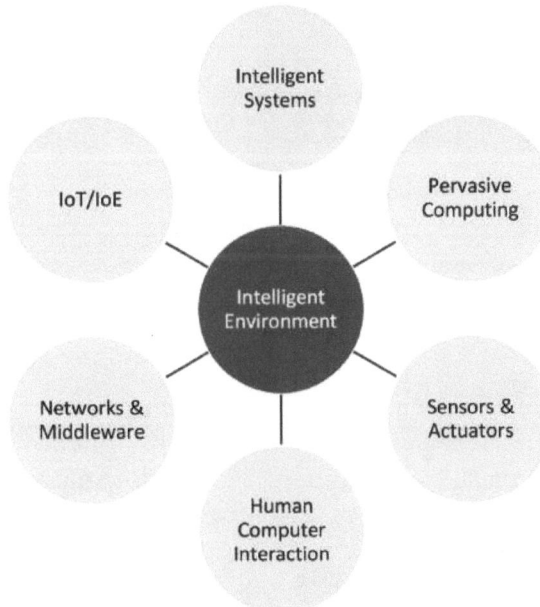

Fig. (1). Association of intelligent & smart environment with other disciplines.

Intelligent Systems for Smart Environment

An intelligent system can be defined as a machine/device with an integrated, Internet-enabled computer that can collect data and analyze the information as well as communicate it to the other machines/devices. Additional characteristics of intelligent systems include the learning ability from former experiences, security, privacy, connectivity, adaptability with respect to the changing conditions/data, and the capacity to monitor and function them from remote locations. Intelligent systems are also apprehensive about how these techniques and tools communicate with humans in mutable and real-time physical and social conditions. Intelligent systems are capable of reasoning, learning, solving a problem, and making perceptions. They can be characterized as a tool (1) that functions in a complicated world with limited resources, (2) exhibits primary cognitive capabilities such as action control, perception, reasoning, or language usage, and (3) demonstrates complex intelligence accompanied by capabilities such as learning adaption, rationality, or the ability to articulate the application of information through introspection [3]. A smart environment requires the implementation and usage of intelligent systems at various levels. Typically, artificial intelligence systems can be categorized as Artificial Narrow Intelligence (ANI) systems, Artificial General Intelligence (AGI) systems, and Artificial Super Intelligence (ASI) systems, as depicted in Fig. (**2**).

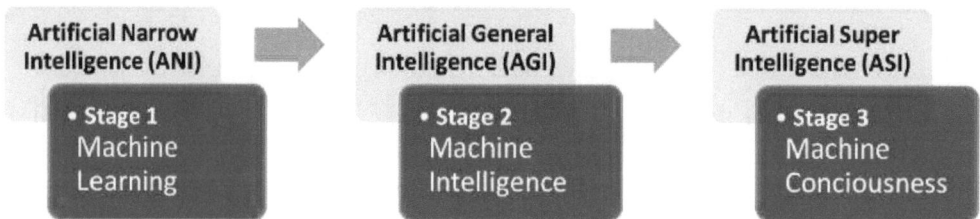

Fig. (2). Types of intelligent systems.

ANI Systems

These AI systems are envisioned to address an explicit problem and are skillful in the accomplishment of the specific assignment extraordinarily effectively. They possess few competencies by definition, like endorsing a product/service to something like an e-commerce buyer or forecasting the environment. They have the ability to emulate, and in certain cases even outstrip, the performance of humans in very particular circumstances, but in tightly controlled settings with a specific variety of parameters.

AGI Systems

It is characterized as AI with a cognitive ability comparable to humans in a varied assortment of disciplines, comprising computational reasoning, image processing, language processing, and many more. To emulate human logic, an AGI system would have to be composed of thousands of ANI computing systems functioning in unison and communicating with each other.

ASI Systems

ASI system will certainly outstrip humans in each possible way. This will comprise effects, such as making improved art and developing emotive associations, as well as sensible decision-building.

When AGI is realized, AI systems can rapidly develop their own skills and magnify into situations that one cannot think of. In a smart environment, different types of intelligent systems can be deployed depending on the requirements and application. Therefore, it is significant to understand the hierarchical taxonomy of intelligent systems for a smart environment that has been presented in Fig. (**3**). This taxonomy is not meant to be comprehensive or exact; rather, it is meant to present existing systems while showing their primary differences. This hierarchical taxonomy can be considered to be approximate because it incorporates various interpretations to represent the different categories in a tree structure.

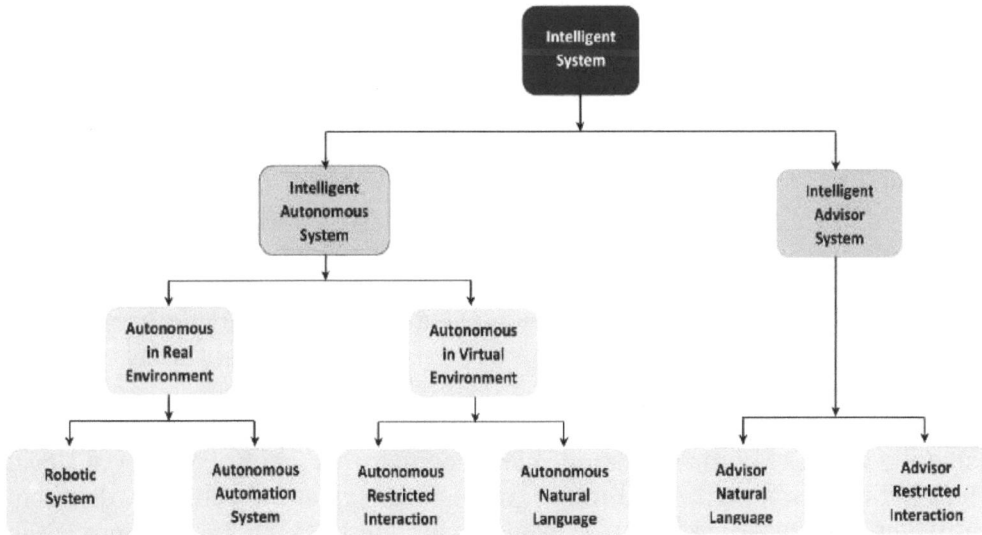

Fig. (3). Taxonomy of intelligent systems for smart environment.

Autonomy is a desirable attribute that an intelligent system can have when networking with other agents. An autonomous system, in general, decides on its own to act in the environment to perform a task that has been allocated to it by another agent. In the real world, an autonomous system operates to support the user. This means the user delegates a task to the system, the system determines and executes appropriate actions in the environment that enables the task to be completed autonomously. In contrast, an intelligent advisor system supports user actions in the real world. In this situation, the user is the entity that decides what actions to perform, and the system's duty is to provide guidance by supplying helpful information to aid decision-making. This data can be gathered using predictive or descriptive analysis techniques (like diagnostic approaches, pattern recognition, or temporal projection). Furthermore, the system can advise what actions should be done employing prescriptive methods (*e.g.*, scheduling, resource assignment, or planning).

Security and privacy have been prevalent concerns for computing systems, and for smart systems in IoE/IoT settings, it becomes a big challenge since the number and types of devices are huge. The security requirements, the challenges and the potential security solutions for the low computing power devices employed in IoE/IoT settings have been surveyed in [4]. The authors in [5] have presented a security framework for resource-constrained devices like sensors, smart cards, and radio frequency identification tags. In the development of intelligent smart computing applications, the issues of security and privacy must also be taken into account in a way that when these applications are deployed, they are secured from potential threats and attacks.

ENABLING TECHNOLOGIES FOR AN INTELLIGENT SMART ENVIRONMENT

Smart environments are proving to be an extended form of ubiquitous or pervasive computing. Three different classes of smart environments can be seen in the form of: (1) virtual computing environments, which allow smart devices or components to use appropriate services at any time and from any place, (2) physical environments, which may contain a range of smart devices, such as sensors, tags, and controllers, (3) human environments, consisting of human beings using smart devices in various forms like smartphones, wearable smart devices, *etc.* [6]. For building the smart environment, various technologies, including wireless communication, cloud computing, IoT/IoE, sensors design, information theory, signal and image processing, semantic web, crowdsourcing, multilayered software architecture, middleware, networking, parallel processing, and many others are utilized. In addition to these, to make the smart environment intelligent too, big data analytics, predictive analytics, edge intelligence, deep learning, natural language processing, computer vision, explainable artificial intelligence, robotics and automation, artificial neural network, and human-computer interaction are the key technologies. The evolution and existence of a smart environment (smart cities, smart healthcare, smart transportation system, smart workplaces, and smart government) has become possible due to the empowerment of these technologies. The ten prominent technologies enabling the intelligence in a smart environment have been highlighted in Fig. (**4**). This section intends to explain these ten technologies in context of the smart environment. Out of these technologies, edge intelligence and explainable artificial intelligence are the two recent technologies that are going to revolutionize the smart intelligent environment.

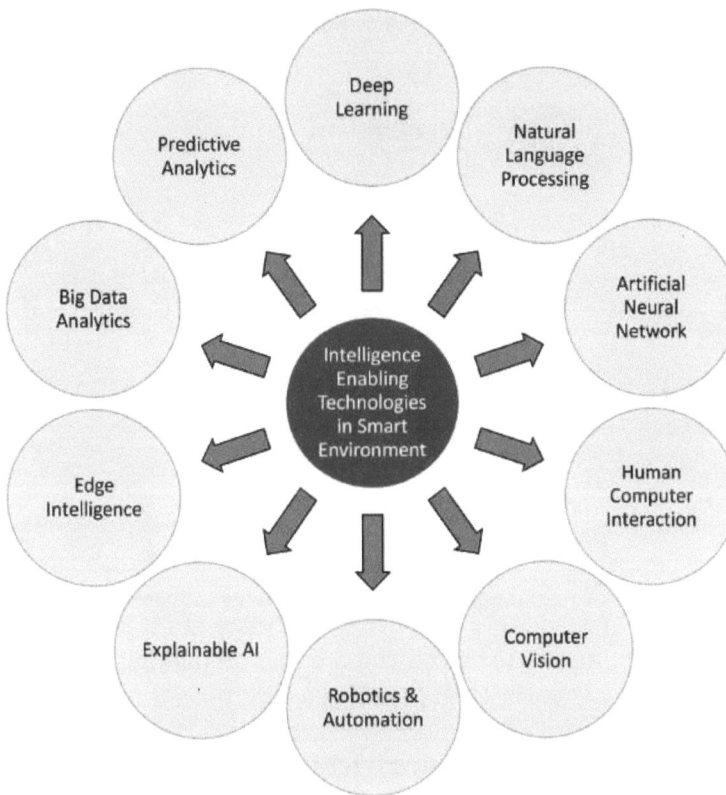

Fig. (4). Prominent technologies enabling intelligence in smart environment.

Big Data Analytics

The key goals of a smart and intelligent environment are to progress the welfare of the people and boost financial growth while ensuring sustainability. Smart and intelligent environments are built on an information and communication technology (ICT) framework that includes IoT as a technology that facilitates the generation of huge volume of heterogeneous data generally identified as Big Data [7]. If critical information or data can be gathered and analyzed from huge volume of heterogeneous of data, big data analytics can be very valuable to smart environments. To extract value from massive amounts of data, however, it should be accessed and processed at the appropriate time. This is possible with the appropriate amalgamation of people, processes, and technology. Smart city environments can be benefited significantly from big data analytics, which is focused with analyzing trends and detecting patterns in data. In addition to these, big data analytics can contribute in the enhancement of critical processes, activities, and roles. By transforming data into intelligence, big data analytics can progress business performance. The three significant big data analysis techniques (Fig. **5**) that can be employed in smart environment are edge analytics, semantic analytics, and security analytics.

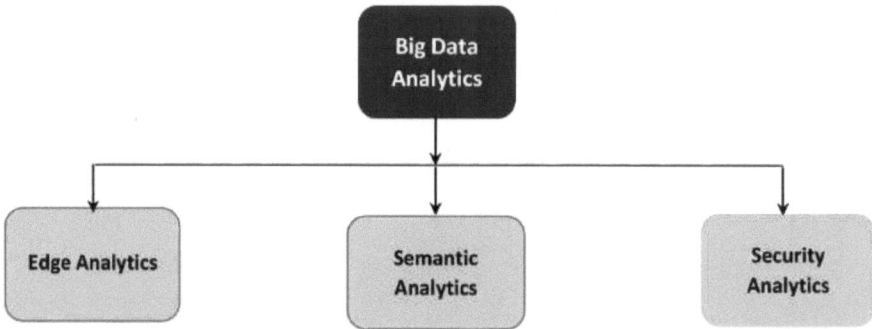

Fig. (5). Big data analysis techniques for smart environment.

Edge Analytics

Edge analytics is a method of collecting the data and analyzing it though automatic analytical computation performed over the data generated by a sensor or other device in the network. Edge analytics advances things to another level, capturing more data and performing complex analytics before enchanting speedy action. On connected machines and devices, analyzing data as soon as it is generated can help in reducing the latency in decision-making. Scalability is another major advantage of edge analytics in a smart environment. Monitoring edge device is one of the most prominent use case for edge analytics. This has been found especially true for IoE devices active in a smart environment. A platform for data analytics might be utilized to observe a huge number of heterogeneous devices for ensuring that they are all functioning suitably. If difficulty ascends, an edge analytics platform could be able to automatically rectify the situation and take corrective action.

Semantic Analytics

The capability of technology to comprehend the meaning of words and the relationship of context between a set of words is known as semantic analytics [7]. Textual data analysis and Semantic Web technologies are combined in this topic of study. Semantic analytics evaluates the interconnectivity of various ontological principles. Businesses can use semantic analysis-driven solutions to retrieve relevant and meaningful information from unstructured data like support issues, emails and comments received from customers. Systems might be trained to achieve precise predictions on the basis of former experiences by loading semantically improved machine-learning procedures along with textual samples. A method based on semantics for machine learning entails a set of sub-tasks, including relationship extraction and word sense disambiguation [8].

Security Analytics

Security analytics is a set of software, algorithms, and analytic procedures that are used to identify potential vulnerabilities to computer systems. Due to the rapid enhancements in malware, spyware, and other cyber-attacks, the demand for security analytics tools is intensifying. Conventional security methods and technologies like intrusion detection and prevention systems, and firewalls will necessitate automation and real-time analysis to identify and mitigate intrusions in order to stay on top of professional criminal groups. This will necessitate the use of security analytics [9]. To identify and diagnose vulnerabilities, security analytics explanations use both historical data as well as present information. Security analytics collects information from a multitude of sources and explores patterns and anomalies. Various data analysis methods may be employed by a security analytics solution. Conventional rule-based methods, statistical analysis and machine learning are among them. Other components can also be integrated to automate and coordinate events.

Predictive Analytics

Predictive analytics extracts data from current data sets, which is then utilized to identify usage trends and estimate possible future consequences. Predictive analytics, on the other hand, cannot guarantee precise outcomes exactly. Rather, it leverages "what-if" models, and risk assessment approaches to forecast the degree to which a specific event or activity might happen in the future based on the data accessible. Predictive analytics can be applied to smart environments, including smart business solutions, banking and retail, and smart telecommunication. Predictive analytics methods like logical regression, time series analysis, and decision trees can be applied to make near-accurate predictions in a smart environment. The four major aspects of predictive analytics are descriptive –

concerned with what happened, diagnostic – identifying why it happened, predictive – forecasting what will happen in future, and perspective – deals with how to make it happen. The working of predictive analytics in a smart environment has been shown in Fig. (6). Predictive analytics provides precise and dependable information, enabling businesses to solve problems and discover new opportunities. Predictive analytics can be used to detect frauds, reduce risks, optimize marketing, make accurate decisions and enhance the efficiency of operations in a smart environment.

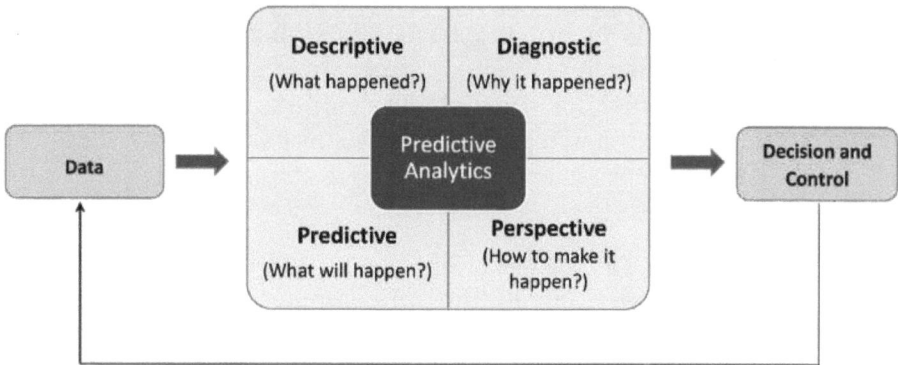

Fig. (6). Predictive analytics in smart environment.

Deep Learning

Deep learning is a sub-domain of machine learning in which a computer program or algorithm learns to execute categorization tasks directly on complicated data such as text, image, or voice. Deep learning approaches like long short-term memory (LSTM), convolutional neural network (CNN), and recurrent neural network (RNN), can be applied with time series analysis and image recognition in the smart environment connected to an IoT network. Deep learning, on the other hand, is effective in the majority of circumstances, such as the well-known instance of automatically sorting fish based on their innate characteristics. The application of deep learning prototypes for analyzing data in smart computing has become increasingly popular in recent times [10]. This is due to the fact that deep learning models are well suited for interpreting the extremely complex data generated by smart devices. In a smart computing environment, deep learning methods can be used for network anomaly detection, human activity recognition, intrusion detection, traffic prediction, and forecasting resources. The employment of deep learning in a smart environment has been demonstrated in Fig. (7), where deep learning techniques are applied at all the levels of computing – edge level, middleware, and at cloud level to facilitate intelligent computing for smart city, smart transportation, smart retail, smart banking, smart healthcare, *etc*.

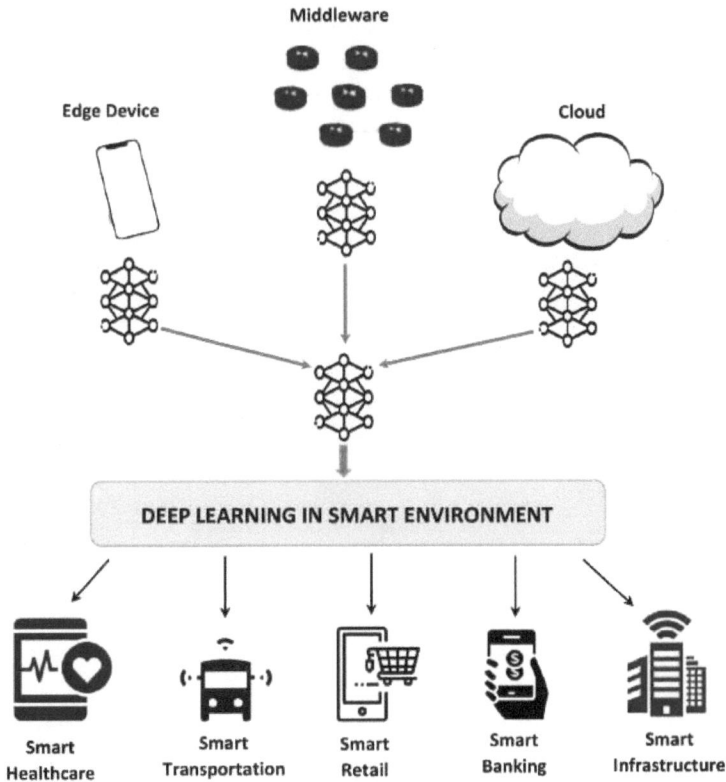

Fig. (7). Deep learning in smart environment.

Deep learning provides training from data models using supervised, semi-supervised, and unsupervised learning techniques. Deep learning's functioning is based on the following points:

- It replicates the functioning of a human brain for data management and pattern formation, enabling decision-making.
- The nature of the trained dataset can be diverse, interrelated, and complex.
- Larger the data set will, more effective the training will, and it will have a direct impact on decision-making.

Natural Language Processing

Natural Language Processing (NLP) is a relatively different sub-area of artificial intelligence that deals with empowering computer systems to interpret text and vocal language in style comparable to that of humans. NLP integrates rule-based modeling of natural languages and computational linguistics with deep learning models, statistical models, and machine learning. NLP enables computers and smart devices to converse with human beings in their native language while accomplishing language-related activities. NLP is proving to be a vital component of computing as it helps resolve phonological vagueness and contributes helpful statistical meaning to data for many application areas, like voice recognition and text analytics. The computing with NLP has been demonstrated in Fig. (**8**).

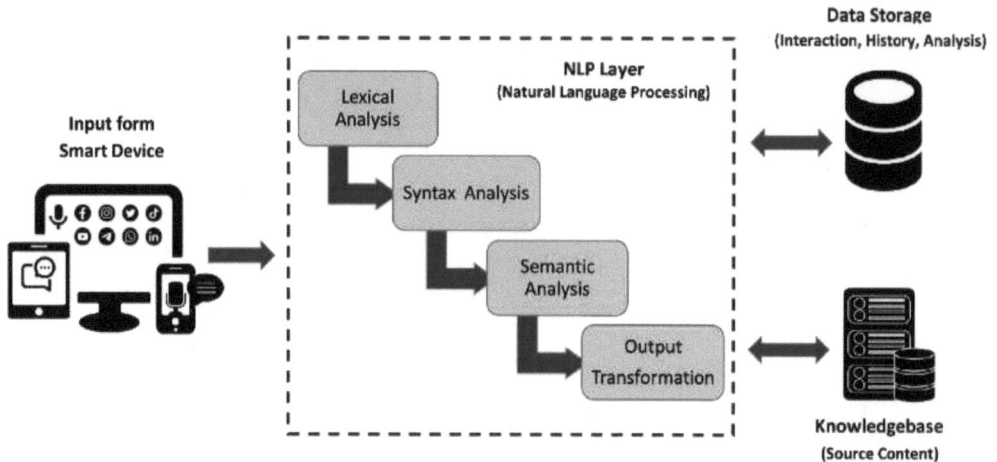

Fig. (8). Computing with natural language processing.

As shown in Fig. (**8**), the natural language is captured by the smart device, which is fed into the NLP layer for processing. The NLP layer performs four operations – lexical analysis, syntax analysis, semantic analysis, and output transformation. A knowledge base is used in producing significant output from the whole process, which is then stored in the database for further interaction and analysis. The use of NLP in smart environment applications can support differently-abled and old persons in controlling gadgets and performing everyday tasks by inputting their voices into the system [11]. This can aid in security as well as human multitasking. Many researchers are now addressing the solutions in a smart computing environment using NLP; like in [12], the authors have applied NLP in controlling operations in a smart home, realizing voice recognition, while in [13], NLP is utilized in smart healthcare. In fact, NLP is a technique that can now be utilized in any smart application connected to IoE or IoT environment.

Artificial Neural Network

Artificial Neural Networks (ANN) are connectionist models that offer means to deal with multifaceted pattern-oriented tasks, including both time series and classification. ANN is the technology that involves the functioning of the brain and nervous system. ANN models tends to mimic the electrical activity of the nervous system and the brain. Neurons that are the processing elements in ANN, are typically organized in the form of different layers that are interconnected to many other elements of the processing chain [14]. Industrial smart IoE devices frequently transmit data to the cloud for intelligent processing. However, reliable network connections are not always available everywhere, which limits the ability to meet real-time necessities. The execution of processing information using ANN employed directly on IoT devices could be a valid solution to this challenge. The stability of Internet access would have no effect in this scenario. Therefore, ANN for smart IoE devices and edge computing is grasping an increased attraction and demand. Fig. (**9**) illustrates the deployment of ANN in a smart computing environment [15]. The data produced by the sensors and actuators are captured by the IoT/IoE device, which is forwarded to the server. The server with the ANN module performs the necessary computations by retrieving/storing the required information from/to the cloud *via* the gateway.

Human-Computer Interaction

Human-computer interaction (HCI) is a topic of transdisciplinary research that emphasizes computer technology design for interaction between humans and computer systems. HCI originated with computer systems, and it has now evolved to encompass practically all aspects of information technology design. HCI is an amalgamation of computer science, cognitive science, and engineering factors related to human beings, and the same has been depicted in Fig. (**10**).

Smart computing systems generally utilize sensor-enabled cameras for capturing the pictures and video of the human user making interacting with the system. The capability to recognize and track motion patterns of humans and postures in the visual field of the sensing device is one of the most important features of camera-based HCI systems [16]. Although most of the public's gadgets remain simple instruction setups utilizing less complicated physical hardware, the focus of research has been on the development of intelligent and adaptable interfaces. Intelligent HCI schemes are user interfaces that integrate intelligence within the perception or responsiveness to users. Another aspect of intelligent interfaces to explore is that most HCI designs that are not intelligent tend to be passive in nature, implying that they would only react only when the user invokes them, whereas ideal intelligent and adapting designs are active interfaces [17]. From a smart computing perspective, HCI is now being used in many smart computing applications and is being proven an effective technology in the IoE/IoT environment.

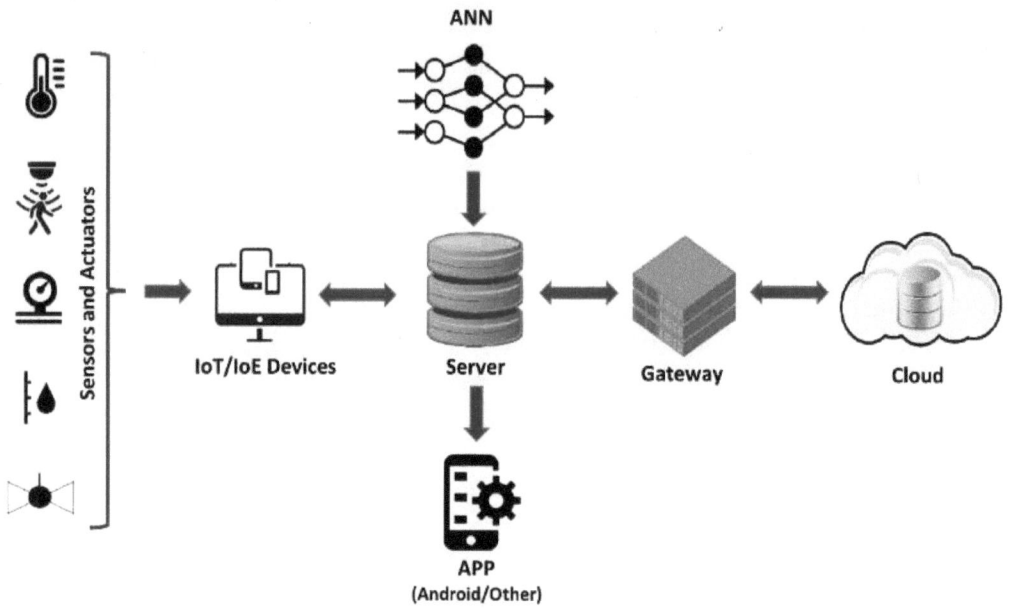

Fig. (9). ANN for smart computing.

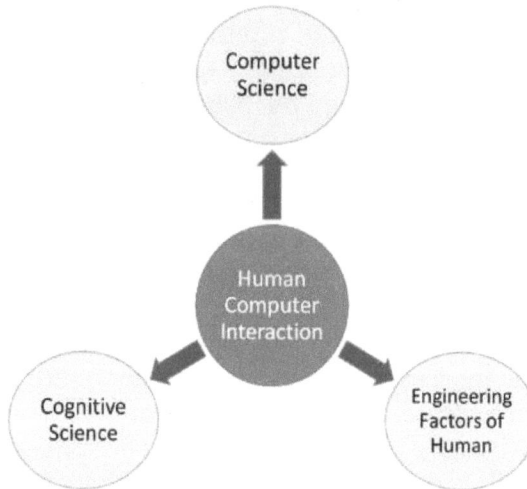

Fig. (10). Associated fields of human-computer interaction.

Computer Vision

Computer vision is a domain of artificial intelligence that is related to developing digital systems having the capability to interpret, process, and comprehend visual input (pictures or videos) similar to humans. Computer vision is predicated on training computing systems for interpreting and understanding images at the pixel level. Pattern recognition is the backbone of today's computer vision algorithms. Computers are trained to analyze huge amounts of visual information, including photos and videos, process these, label items on them, and find patterns within these object items. Computer vision involves different areas of computing science, including artificial intelligence, image processing, cognitive science, machine learning, computer graphics, machine learning, and computer algorithms [18]. An illustration of using computer/machine vision in a smart ubiquitous environment [19] has been provided in Fig. (**11**).

The edge servers can be utilized in cooperative network learning as well as to interact with the radio access network that facilitates end-to-end-resource orchestration. Cloud orchestration means the organization and synchronization of automated tasks that result in a fused process or workflow. Cloud orchestration is a technique for optimizing the automated benefits of agility while reducing expenses. Adaptive machine/computer vision tools and methods are then applied to the captured data sent by smart cameras and devices.

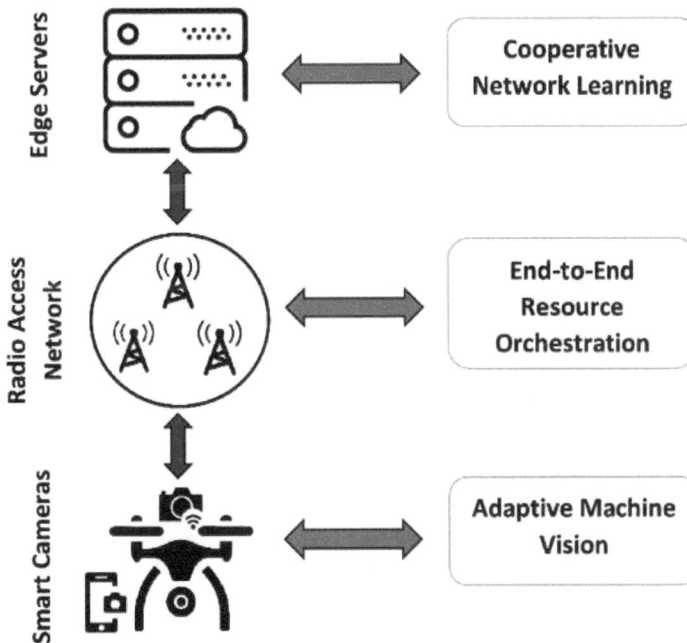

Fig. (11). Computer/machine vision in smart computing.

Robotics and Automation

Robotics is a domain of engineering that is concerned with the design, development, and deployment of robots, as well as the use of computing to control and operate them. Robotics and automation control mechanisms and information technologies are being used in engineering to minimize the requirement for manual effort in producing goods and services. Robotics is the science of the design, development, and implementation of robots to perform tasks, while automation is concerned with self-operating physical machinery, software, and other techniques to carry out the tasks that would normally be performed by humans. Applying the domain of robotics and automation in a smart computing environment has given rise to the evolution of the Internet of Robotic Things (IoRT) [20]. Smart manufacturing industries can use IoRT systems to perform complex operations like packaging, welding, assembling, quality control management, and so on independently and remotely. IoRT systems are also gaining attraction outside of the manufacturing industry, including sports, museums, and entertainment. IoRT is at the core of robotics-integrated IoT-based systems, where cloud computing and connectivity can be used to execute difficult operations, enabling robots to exchange, network, and acquire different types of information from both human users and machines. In Fig. (**12**), it can be seen how IoT/IoE, robotics, and cloud computing are all intertwined.

Edge Intelligence

Edge intelligence is a way forward from edge analytics, in which one can take actions depending on the outcomes of the analysis at the edge, employing Artificial Intelligence. This differs from cloud intelligence and cloud analytics, wherein we transmit all of this information across the internet to a centralized database and perform analysis to make decisions. An intelligent edge node will have a flow enabling storage of meta-data as an alternative. Edge Intelligence is built around the idea of transferring the processing of data from the cloud to the edge, or to the smart computing environment, where sensors and equipment are placed. Employing edge intelligence in smart computing results in intelligence at low latency, information storage at low bandwidth, linear scalability, decreased operational costs, and enhanced privacy. Edge intelligence architecture is composed of the following four primary components, according to recent studies - edge training, edge inference, edge caching, and edge offloading [21]. The interaction among these four components of edge intelligence has been demonstrated in Fig. (**13**).

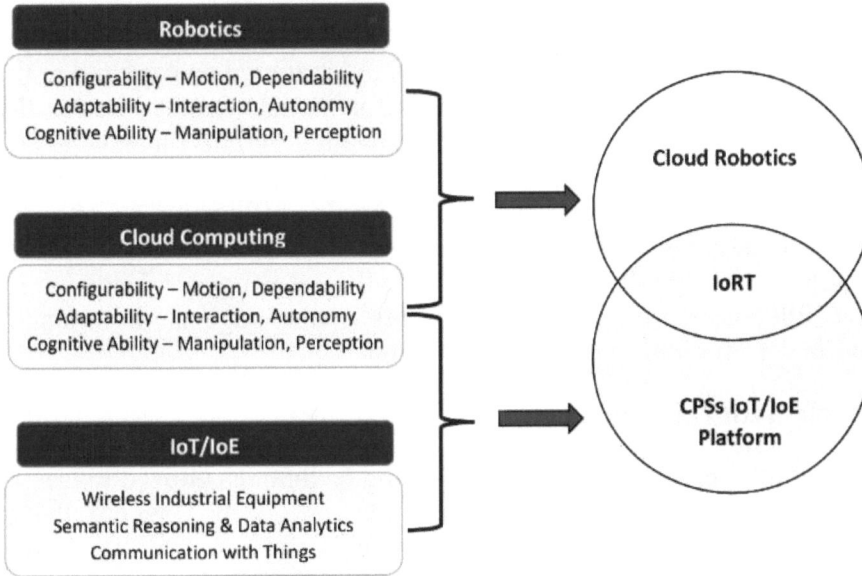

Fig. (12). Integration of IoT/IoE, cloud computing, and robotics for IoRT.

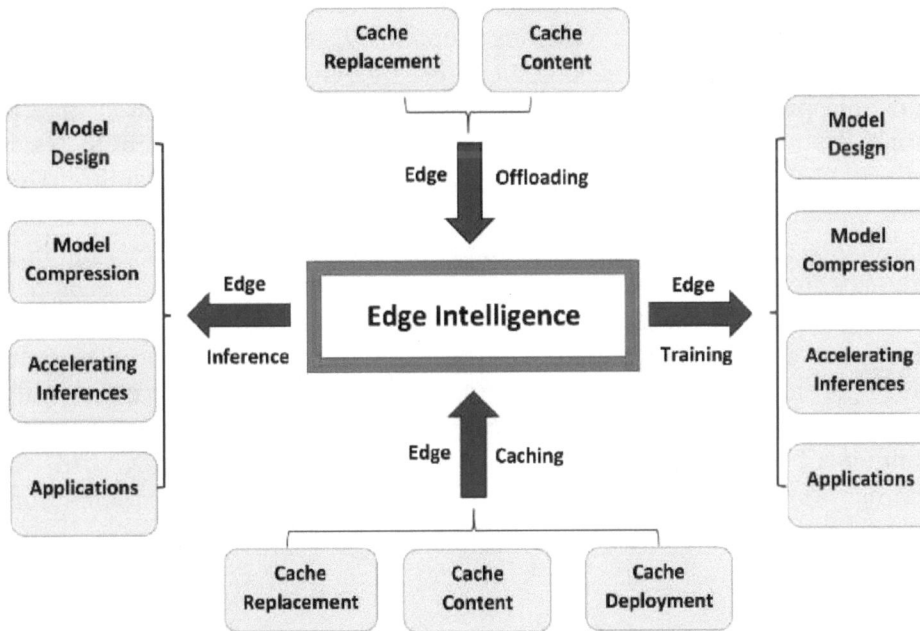

Fig. (13). Major components of edge intelligence architecture.

Edge caching principally deals with the incoming data from end-users and the surrounding environment settings directed at your edge devices. Edge caching incorporates both this data and the data produced by edge devices. Edge training is the procedure of revealing hidden features in learning data captured at the edge or establishing optimal weights and biases for models deployed on data. Edge inference refers to the process method of calculating outputs on an edge device in order to evaluate the performance of the model or algorithm trained on a dataset. Another key component of edge intelligence is edge offloading, which permits an edge device to assign part of its tasks, such as edge caching, edge training, or edge inference, to other edge devices connected to the network [22]. Edge intelligence will have full access to available resources in the edge environment if it is deployed in an efficient and structured manner.

Explainable Artificial Intelligence

The artificial intelligence and machine learning techniques utilized to examine the big data generated use the fundamental of a black box where the system designers, as well as the end-users, cannot identify and elucidate why an AI system has reached at a specific inference or decision. Explainable Artificial Intelligence (XAI) contrasts to the conventional artificial intelligent systems since the results, inferences, decisions, and conclusions can are comprehensible by the people. XAI-based methods are based on three significant principles: transparency, interpretability, and explainability, which are also a primary requirement of people-centric smart computing environment. XAI is a set of methods and processes that permits human end-users to comprehend, interpret, and trust the conclusions, results, and output produced by machine learning algorithms [23]. XAI derives notions from different fields, including cognitive sciences, philosophy, and psychology, to yield a range of procedural methodologies that can produce explainable results for the end-users, not having enough background in Artificial Intelligence. The main emphasis has been placed on the progression of XAI that encompasses the human end-user in the cycle and therefore, become human-centric. XAI-based intelligent systems will facilitate enhanced prediction accuracy with a comprehensible decision and traceability of actions performed, and have a significant impact in the smart computing environment. The four significant dimensions of explainability in XAI for smart computing - explainability to control, explainability to discover, explainability to justify, and explainability to improve, have been shown in Fig. (**14**).

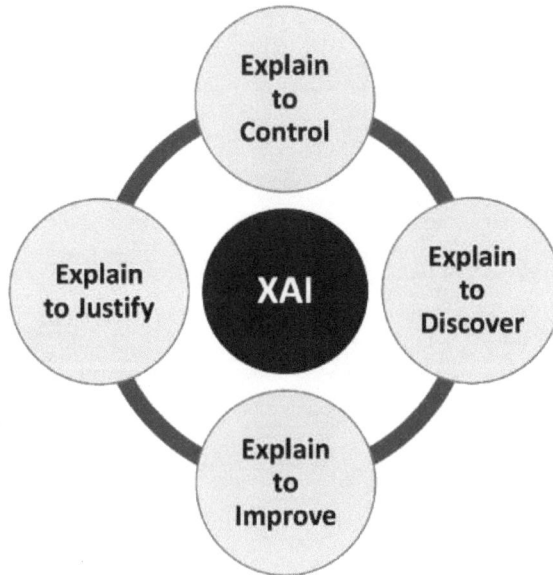

Fig. (14). Dimensions of Explainability in XAI.

XAI focuses on creating a set of machine learning and deep learning models that:

- Build further explainable methods, while retaining the highest point of learning outcome (*i.e.*, prediction accuracy),
- Empower human users to comprehend, properly trust, and successfully handle the emergent production of artificially intelligent allies.

CONCLUSION

Smart computing environments are now evolving everywhere in human life, facilitating the daily tasks and computing needs to save time and effort. These can be made more effective by adding intelligence to the computing systems employed in smart environments. This chapter has first introduced the need for intelligent systems in human-centric super-smart society and has also highlighted the taxonomy of intelligent systems that can be utilized in a smart computing environment. The ten major intelligence-enabling technologies for smart computing, namely predictive analysis, deep learning, artificial neural network, big data analytics, intelligent edge, human-computer interaction, explainable artificial intelligence, computer vision, natural language processing, and robotics, have been briefly explained in this chapter. The application of these varieties of techniques in a smart computing environment, including smart cities, smart banking, smart retail, *etc.*, is still an open problem area for the research community. The ten major technologies presented in this chapter can be utilized in designing and developing smart and intelligent applications for facilitating the computing requirements of the end users in the internet of everything environment.

REFERENCES

[1] M.V. Mairano, "Emotions and digital delivery platforms: An approach to the configuration of sensibilities during the isolation caused by the COVID-19 Pandemic", In: *Socio-Economic Effects and Recovery Efforts for the Rental Industry: Post-COVID-19 Strategies.* IGI Global, 2021, pp. 178-193. [http://dx.doi.org/10.4018/978-1-7998-7287-0.ch010]

[2] J.C. Augusto, V. Callaghan, D. Cook, A. Kameas, and I. Satoh, "Intelligent environments: A manifesto", *Human-centric. Comp.Inform. Sci.,* vol. 3.1, pp. 1-18, 2013.

[3] M. Molina, "What is an intelligent system?", *arXiv,* vol. 2009, p. 09083, 2020.

[4] A.K. Singh, and B.D.K. Patro, "Security of low computing power devices: A survey of requirements, challenges & possible solutions", *Cybern. Inf. Technol.,* vol. 19, no. 1, pp. 133-164, 2019. [http://dx.doi.org/10.2478/cait-2019-0008]

[5] A.K. Singh, and B.D.K. Patro, "Signcryption-based security framework for low computing power devices", *Rec. Adv. Comp. Sci. Commun.,* vol. 13, no. 5, pp. 845-857, 2020. [http://dx.doi.org/10.2174/2213275912666190617161732]

[6] S. Poslad, "Ubiquitous computing smart devices, smart environments and smart interaction", *Ubiquitous Computing Smart Devices.,* Smart Environments and Smart Interaction, pp. 115-133, 2009. [http://dx.doi.org/10.1002/9780470779446.ch4]

[7] V. Bassoo, "Big data analytics for smart cities. Internet of things and big data analytics toward next-generation intelligence", In: Springer: Cham, 2018, pp. 359-379. [http://dx.doi.org/10.1007/978-3-319-60435-0_15]

[8] R. Wolff, "Semantic Analysis", Available from: https://monkeylearn.com/blog/semantic-analysis/ (Accessed 15 Feb, 2022)

[9] I. Birzniece, *Security Analytics: Dispelling the Fog.* BIR Workshops, 2018.

[10] T.J. Saleem, and M.A. Chishti, "Deep learning for internet of things data analytics", *Procedia Comput. Sci.,* vol. 163, pp. 381-390, 2019. [http://dx.doi.org/10.1016/j.procs.2019.12.120]

[11] S. Kumar, S. Benedict, and S. Ajith, "Application of natural language processing and iotcloud in smart homes", *2nd International Conference on Intelligent Communication and Computational Techniques (ICCT) IEEE,* 2019. [http://dx.doi.org/10.1109/ICCT46177.2019.8969066]

[12] G. Alexakis, S. Panagiotakis, A. Fragkakis, E. Markakis, and K. Vassilakis, "Control of smart home operations using natural language processing, voice recognition and IoT technologies in a multi-tier architecture", *Designs,* vol. 3, no. 3, p. 32, 2019. [http://dx.doi.org/10.3390/designs3030032]

[13] B. Zhou, G. Yang, Z. Shi, and S. Ma, "Natural language processing for smart healthcare", *EEE Reviews in Biomedical Engineering,* 2021.

[14] S. Walczak, and N. Cerpa, "Artificial Neural Networks", In: M. Robert A., *Encyclopedia of Physical Science and Technology* 3rd. Academic Press, 2003, pp. 631-645.

[15] K. Hameed, "An intelligent IoT based healthcare system using fuzzy neural networks", *Scientific Programming,* 2020.

[16]   O.D. Alao, J.V. Joshua, and J.E.T. Akinsola, "Human Computer Interaction (HCI) and Smart Home Applications", *IUP Journal of Information Technology,* vol. 15, no. 3, pp. 7-21, 2019.

[17]   F. Karray, M. Alemzadeh, J.A. Saleh, and M.N. Arab, "Human-computer interaction: Overview on state of the art", *Int. J. Smart Sensing Intell. Syst.,* vol. 1, no. 1, pp. 137-159, 2008.
[http://dx.doi.org/10.21307/ijssis-2017-283]

[18]   A.K. Singh, and A. Garg, "Applications of signal processing", In: *Machine Learning in Signal Processing.* Chapman and Hall/CRC, 2021, pp. 73-95.
[http://dx.doi.org/10.1201/9781003107026-4]

[19]   Available from: https://ece.charlotte.edu/spotlights/ubiquitous-machine-vision

[20]   G.H. Phan, C. Hansen, P. Tommasino, A. Budhota, D.M. Mohan, A. Hussain, E. Burdet, and D. Campolo, "Estimating human wrist stiffness during a tooling task", *Sensors,* vol. 20, no. 11, p. 3260, 2020.
[http://dx.doi.org/10.3390/s20113260] [PMID: 32521678]

[21]   Available from: https://www.einfochips.com/blog/edge-intelligence-enabling-intelligence-beyond-cloud/

[22]   A. Garg, and A.K. Singh, "Applications of internet of things (IoT)", In: *Intelligence of Things: AI-IoT Based Critical-Applications and Innovations.,* G. Computing, Ed., Springer: Cham, 2021, pp. 1-34.
[http://dx.doi.org/10.1007/978-3-030-82800-4_1]

[23]   A. Barredo Arrieta, N. Díaz-Rodríguez, J. Del Ser, A. Bennetot, S. Tabik, A. Barbado, S. García, S. Gil-López, D. Molina, R. Benjamins, R. Chatila, and F. Herrera, "Explainable artificial intelligence (XAI): Concepts, taxonomies, opportunities and challenges toward responsible AI", *Inf. Fusion,* vol. 58, pp. 82-115, 2020.
[http://dx.doi.org/10.1016/j.inffus.2019.12.012]

CHAPTER 3

Smart Sensors and Actuators for Internet of Everything Based Smart Cities: Application, Challenges, Opportunities, and Future Trends

Tarana Singh[1,*], Arun Solanki[1], Sanjay Kumar Sharma[1] and Hanaa Hachimi[2]

[1] Department of Computer Science and Engineering, School of ICT, Gautam Buddha University, Greater Noida, India

[2] University Sultan Moulay Slimane, Beni Mellal, Morocco

Abstract: Cities across the globe are installing sensors, actuators and other devices, to become safer, greener, sustainable, and efficient with the hope of improving the urban interests of people. Sensing and collection of records are at the heart of any smart infrastructure, which can display itself and act on its own intelligently. Using sensors to screen public infrastructures, including bridges, roads, and homes, presents cognizance that enables more efficient use of resources based on the facts amassed by those sensors. As smart sensors, actuators, *etc.*, play a critical role in the smart infrastructure, this chapter explores the smart sensors and actuators in IoT-enabled smart cities. As the domain of smart cities is emerging in the present days with a huge number of research opportunities for the researchers, also data collection and sensing play their role at the heart of the infrastructure. This chapter will critically explore the role and importance of Smart sensors and actuators and their applications, challenges, and opportunities, followed by various future trends in the domain of the smart city.

Keywords: Actuators, Artificial intelligence, Big data, Internet of everything, Internet of things, Machine learning, Sensors, Smart city, Sensing.

INTRODUCTION

With the rapid growth in population density in city environments, infrastructure and facilities are needed to meet the desires of inhabitants. As a result, devices, which include sensors, actuators, smartphones, and smart devices, have grown significantly, attaining the huge enterprise goals of the Internet of Things (IoT) through being joined and setting up all devices. Over the Internet, it has been difficult to combine these digital devices in the past. Similarly, collecting that

---

*[*] **Corresponding author Tarana Singh:** Department of Computer Science and Engineering, School of ICT, Gautam Buddha University, Greater Noida, India; E-mail: taranasingh14@gmail.com

Arun Solanki and Anuj Kumar Singh (Eds.)

information for daily action organization and enduring growth planning in urban areas is essential. For example, specific information about the public real-time location and usage, parking space occupancy, transportation such as traffic congestion, and other information such as weather conditions, road conditions, air and noise pollution, water pollution, and energy consumption. It needs to be collected continuously [1]. In the past, various technologies have been applied according to the characteristics of each application. The required technology covers a wide range of ranges from the bodily layer to the information and alertness layers. The continuous development of generations has created new possibilities. It simplifies normal existence and provides extra green services and manufacturing tactics. With digitalization, "smart" is the center of continuous technology development. In reality, the advanced Internet of Things era is seen as one of the primary columns of the 4th Industrial Revolution. Huge innovation capacity and useful blessings to the populace, on the alternative hand, each development assignment makes use of restricted resources and leaves behind a one-of-a-kind environmental footprint, especially one-of-a-kind types of pollution. Future traits in diverse regions, together with engineering, agriculture, and medicine, depend on the Internet of Things (IoT) expertise, and some ability programs of Internet of Things generation in different unexplored areas are, however, unknown [2]. Or it is unclear how to deal with them, which clearly shows that this will carry out more research activities in difficult areas to bring new great benefits to society. Therefore, the relevance and significance of future Internet of Things technology may be very clear and anticipated to play an important role [3]. A smart city is a very broad domain, so there are plenty of research opportunities in this domain. Smart cities have several components represented in Fig. (1). These components work together to achieve the objective of the smart city implementation.

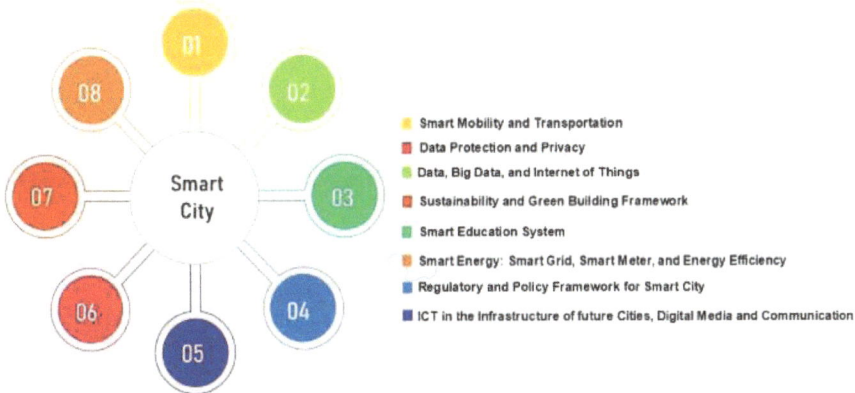

Smart City

01 Smart Mobility and Transportation
02 Data Protection and Privacy
03 Data, Big Data, and Internet of Things
04 Sustainability and Green Building Framework
05 Smart Education System
06 Smart Energy: Smart Grid, Smart Meter, and Energy Efficiency
07 Regulatory and Policy Framework for Smart City
08 ICT in the Infrastructure of future Cities, Digital Media and Communication

Fig. (1). Smart city with its components.

It should be emphasized that there is no doubt about what the Internet of Things technology brings, such as bringing various beneficial advantages to the community and refining the complete value of life expectancy. Internet of Things technologies can change our lives and habits, so each technology has certain problems and shortcomings that need to be scrutinized and investigated [4, 5]. In order that let everyone recognize the enduring implications of the speedy development of the Internet of Things, some vital facts need to be emphasized while discussing the IoT generation.

- The IoT technology has increased the utilization of partial possessions and unprocessed resources, some of which are deficient (such as certain precious metals used in electronic products).
- Electronics prices have become more acceptable, production has increased, and ultimately more resources have been used. In this sense, the reflective effect is possible.
- The long-term impact of IoT technology on the environment is unknown. It takes a lot of energy to the establishment of construct and process of IoT policies.
- E-waste is expected to increase because of the large variety of IoT-based total gadgets anticipated to exist in the near destiny.
- In some sectors, Internet of Things technology can impact society due to reduced human demand and limited direct social contact. This is an essential and important aspect for everyone.

The focus of the above points is not to suggest and create a negative attitude towards the Internet of Things technology, but for a careful analysis of the global aspects and to be a valuable opportunity for humankind to be intelligent of the Internet of Things technology which ensures the sustainable development [6]. The application of the internet of things in the domain of smart cities is represented in Fig. (**2**).

The world is changing rapidly. In other words, development in the technical sense is growing rapidly. In the current world, according to the economic prospect, all technological developments are costly. This can be achieved with the extensive use of limited fossil resources and produces a variety of environmental impacts. The population is steadily increasing at an annual rate of about 1.1%, and the current population exceeds 7.7109 [7]. As mentioned above, the population is concentrated in cities. By 2050, the United Nations predicts that about 68% of the population will live in cities (UN, 2018). As urbanization accelerates, urban infrastructure is expected to face significant pressure. Therefore, new technology solutions are essential for a city to function properly in a given complex and demanding environment [8].

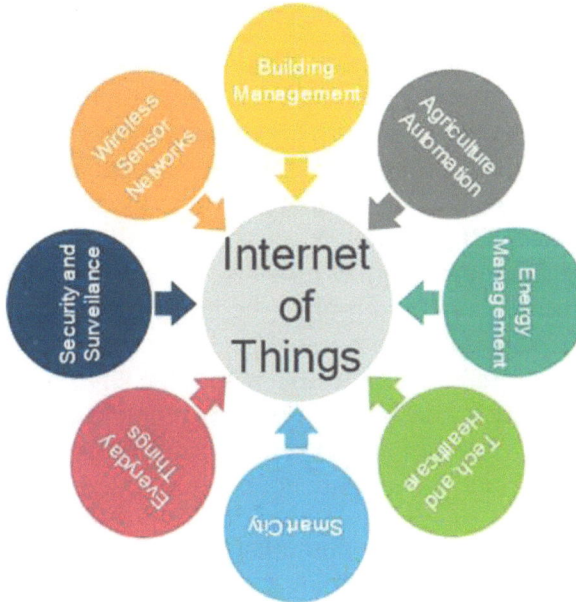

Fig. (2). IoT in smart city.

In the traditional sense, the Internet of Things and conventional programs of smart generation performs a key function in helping clear up some of the city's principal infrastructure issues. The needs of the Internet of Things technology are closely related to technological advances and continuous digitization, and specific digital products need to be connected in a convenient manner. Generally speaking, it requires more green offerings and flexible techniques [9]. This can be performed by efficaciously enforcing the IoT era. Internet of Things generation permits an expansion of green services and smart grids, packages, or gadgets to offer beneficial interactions and generate earnings. The maximum significant advantage of the IoT era is its connectivity, which has awesome ability [10].

Smart cities use statistics and ICT to recover working performance, and percentage statistics through the general community and enhance authorities' service best and civil well-being. The fundamental area of smart cities is to use smart technology and information analysis to optimize city capabilities, promote monetary increase, and improve the great existence of its residents. The value lies not only in the number of technologies available but also in how they are used [11]. Urban intelligence includes technology-based infrastructure, environmental protection measures, efficient and powerful public transportation, confident and progressive city planning, and the ability of people to live and use their resources in the city. Depending on the characteristics of smart cities normally provide related solutions using an expansion of software, consumer interfaces, conversation networks, and the IoT. The IoT is a community of linked devices used to communicate and trade records [12]. This consists of the whole lot, from cars to appliances and street sensors. The information accumulated from those devices is saved in the cloud or on servers, growing the efficiency of the private and non-private sectors, presenting monetary advantages, and enhancing the lives of residents. The number of IoT devices utilize superior computer science to make certain, *i.e.*, individually, the maximum appropriate and significant information is sent to conclude the communication network [13]. The protection structure is executed to guard, screen, and manipulate the broadcast of statistics on the smart metropolis network, stopping unauthorized get entry to the IoT community of the urban records platform. In addition to IoT solutions, smart towns also use APIs, AI, cloud computing, dashes, system knowledge, gadget-to-device communication, mesh networks, smart sensors, and actuators [14]. The types of sensors used in the smart city development are represented in Fig. (**3**).

The combination of automation, machine learning and the IoT allows smart city technology to be applied to a very wide range of requests. For instance, smart parking can support drivers and finds parking spaces and even enable electronic payments [15]. Another case is smart parking organization. It is used to manage circulation with the flow and optimize traffic lights to mitigate congestion. Carpooling facilities can likewise be achieved of the SC structure. Smart town capabilities additionally encompass strength savings and environmental performance, together with dimming road lighting while the street is empty [16]. This smart grid technology can improve the whole lot from operations to protection, making plans, and power. Smart city plans can also address climate exchange and air pollutants and collect waste *via* the Internet, trash cans, and waste management structures for waste control and sanitation. In addition to services, smart cities can also provide security measures such as monitoring high-crime areas and using sensors to alert early to events such as floods, landslides, hurricanes, and droughts [17]. Smart homes can also provide real-time space control or physical well-being monitoring and remarks to decide when maintenance is needed. People also can get the right of entry to the device to inform the government of problems consisting of potholes. Sensors also can monitor infrastructure issues along with water pipe leaks. In addition, the smart town era can improve the performance of production, city agriculture, energy consumption, and further [18]. SC can join a variety of offerings to deliver residents a time-honored solution.

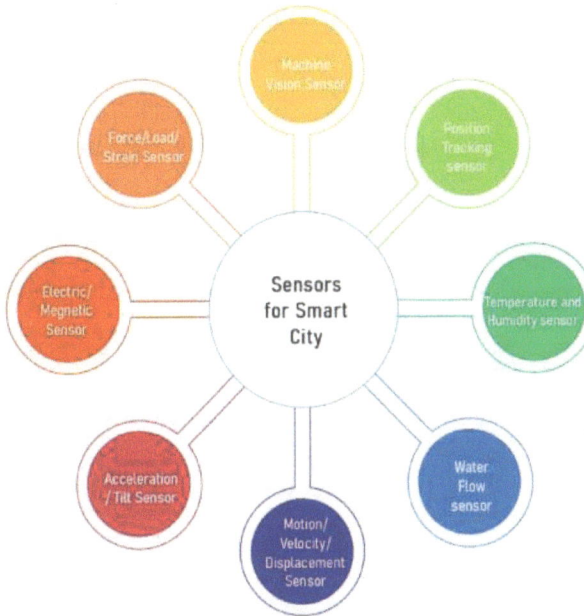

Fig. (3). Smart Sensors in the IoT/IoE-enabled smart cities.

Over a previous couple of centuries, the description of "Smart Cities" has advanced to cruel plenty to many. However, there may be one factor this is identical. Part of "smartness" is using ICT and the web to satisfy city-demanding situations. The number of city inhabitants is increasing by way of approximately 60 million per year. Moreover, by 2050, further than 60% of the sector's populace will stay in cities. Therefore, people who occupy the most effective 2% of the area of terrestrial consume about three-quarters of their capital. In addition, greater than a hundred cities with a population of one million may be constructed over the subsequent 10 years [19]. Cities these days face a selection of demanding situations, inclusive of task advent, financial increase, environmental sustainability, and social resilience. In light of these traits, knowledge in which is in the development of the web is essential for the upcoming metropolis planning manner. From a level or technology perspective, Cisco believes that many companies are actually familiar with the IoT, the network construction of physical gadgets [20].

As functions such as environmental awareness, processing power, and energy independence improve and the information is connected to more people, the "Internet of Things" builds billions and even billions of networks. It is becoming the Internet of Things. Unprecedented opportunities and novel jeopardies. In fact, we are witnessing the development of a new mission for the general public and industry leaders [21]. "Digital city planning" is rapidly flattering dominant support of city organizers, designers, planners, transportation providers, and the provision of public services. From the perspective of public sector leaders, metropolises can be seen as typical of the organized systems that make up all of the Internet. In fact, metropolises are "fertile lands" to realize the value of the Internet [22]. However, to achieve this, city leaders understand the components of IoE: people, processes, data, and things, and show a precise role and effort collectively (Fig. **4**) to help future cities. And the community needs to be empowered.

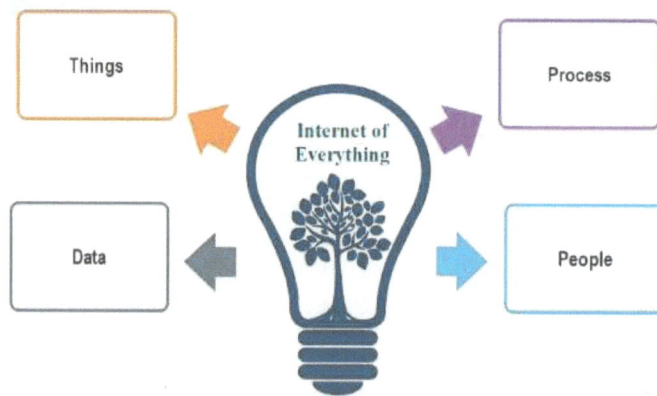

Fig. (4). Representation of the Internet of Everything.

- **People:** The Internet of Everything allows people to link to the net in countless ways. Today, utmost individuals join the Internet using devices (PCs, tablets, TVs, smartphones, *etc.*) and public links (Facebook, Twitter, LinkedIn, Pinterest, *etc.*). As Cyberspace grows towards all Internet, it allows connecting with each other in a more appropriate and appreciated way. For instance, in the future, people will be able to swallow pills, check gastrointestinal health *via* a secure internet connection, and report it to their doctor. In addition, sensors placed on the skin and sewn on clothing provide information about a person's vital signs. According to Gartner, people themselves become nodes on the

  Internet, with both static information and a system that constantly broadcasts activity.
- **Data:** In the Internet of Things, devices typically collect data, and deliver it over the Internet to a central source, where it is analyzed and processed. As networked objects continue to improve, they become smarter by combining data with more useful information. Connected objects not only report raw data, but

also soon send higher levels of information to machines, computers, and people for more detailed evaluation and decision-making. Converting data into information with IoE is very important. This allows for faster and more informed decisions and more effective control over the environment.

- **Thing:** This group consists of physical elements such as sensors, consumer devices, company assets, *etc.*, both of which are connected to the Internet and interconnected. At IoE, these factors detect more data, become context-sensitive, and provide more empirical information to help people and machines make better and more valuable decisions. Examples of IoE "things" include smart sensors embedded in structures such as bridges and disposable sensors placed in daily necessities such as milk cartons.
- **Process:** This process plays an important role in how each of these entities (people, data, objects) work together to create value in all interconnected worlds. Through the right process, connections are relevant and add value because the right information is delivered to the right people at the right time and in the right way.

According to the current analysis, Cisco has 21 major "use cases" by 2022 that apply to five business parts: asset utilization, employee productivity, supply chain, and logistics, customer experience, and innovation. It can be calculated that there is a possibility of realizing the Internet. The value (net profit) of private enterprises in the world will reach 14.4 trillion [23]. This "endangered value" is based on the ability to achieve low cost and high revenue through the strategy and applications of the Internet of Everything. Use illustrations to cover regions that include smart grids, smart homes, connected healthcare, and patient tracking, smart factories, linked personal training, connected land (business) vehicles, marketing, and related marketing, connected games, and freedom.

The main motivation behind this chapter is to provide quick guidance to new researchers and developers to get started with their research work. In this chapter, the primary objective is to identify and discussion of the roles of smart sensors and actuators for Internet of Everything-based smart. This chapter will also discuss various applications, challenges, opportunities, and future trends in a smart city. Basically, this chapter will provide great help for the new researchers and students who are exploring the domain and are very new to the domain. The chapter also aims to provide a quick guide to address the applications, challenges, and future research opportunities in the domain of the smart city.

The whole chapter is divided into a few subsections, and each subsection is dedicated to a particular aspect of the concept. Section I provides a general introduction to IoT, IoE, Smart City, and Sensors used in the smart city. Section II contains a brief discussion of different types of sensors and actuators used in the smart city. Section III discusses the applications of sensing devices in IoE-enabled Smart Cities. Section IV contains the challenges in the implementation of IoT-enabled Smart Cities. Section V contains a brief discussion of the opportunities and future trends in the domain of the smart city. The final section of the chapter contains the conclusion of the whole chapter, followed by the references.

ROLE OF SENSORS AND ACTUATORS IN SMART CITIES

By 2020, a further 50 billion gadgets can be associated with the web, and this new associativity goal has previously begun. The number of things linked to the web has extended exponentially, revolutionizing our global. The listing is divided into 12 distinctive disciplines, showing that the IoT is the following scientific revolution. This comprises the maximum popular eventualities inclusive of smart cities. In this scenario, the sensor can provide offerings, including smart parking (finding free parking space on the street) and managing the intensity of streetlights to keep electricity. Weather variation, ecological protection, water quality, or CO_2 emissions also are talked about by sensor systems. These are a few examples of the smart water and smart surroundings phase of the document. Industrial manipulation, logistics, retail, and more [24]. Sections cover greater targeted system efficiency programs inclusive of supplying facts for shelving, re-shelving and product placement for marketing purposes. The list includes smart meters, safety, and emergency smart. Agriculture, animal rearing, home automation, home automation e-health applications. Now you can collect data from the environment, infrastructure, business, and even your own location. This vast amount of information is stored, analyzed, and it is creating a new business opportunity ecology for accessibility. Systems. Basically, smart cities need to extend their smart capabilities with four sensor technologies, as shown in Fig. (**5**).

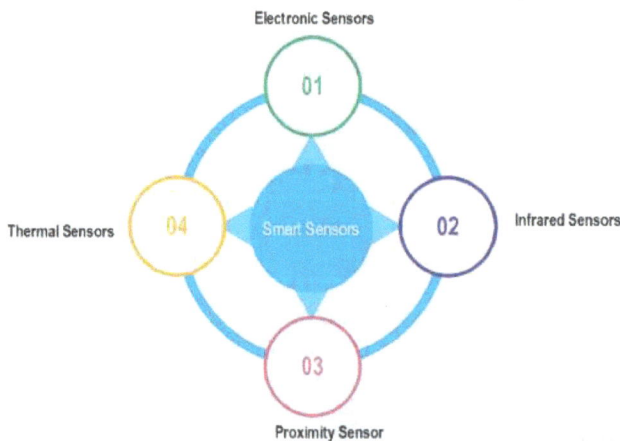

Fig. (5). Type of sensing device which work for smart city.

- **Electronic Sensors:** They are established in environmental monitoring sensors and speedometer sensors. These sensors are usually used in smart towns to perform various responsibilities, along with electricity and modern-day stage tracking for fault detection. The main characteristic of digital sensors is to hit upon numerous styles of electricity, the usage of voltage detectors, magnetic anomalies, and voltage detectors. Instances of digital sensors consist of environmental monitoring sensors, parking sensors, and speedometer sensors. The wireless competencies of the sensor cause restrictions along with maximum strength utilization, low flexibility, and maximum difficulty. Monitor power and present-day tiers to make sure that screw-ups are detected in time. This guarantees the performance of digital sign transmission. In addition, infrared sensors are utilized in technological advances and are designed to generate unbiased information crucial for rapid decision-making procedures in adverse environments. Radar sensors, in contrast, use complicated computer statistics to perform capabilities. Smart sensors can examine and interpret films from many sensors, together with avenue protection cameras and mobile phones. The precision in generating and transmitting records from gesture moves and other actions can provide wise facilities in human-computer interaction [10, 12]. SC uses sensors related to neural networks to expand and examine records from speech popularity, video, photos, and NLP. They analyzed statistics that might be used to make important choices to make sure the protection of citizens and to monitor the surroundings.
- **Radar sensors:** Radar sensors in comparison, use complicated systems information to perform features. Smart sensors can study and interpret films from many sensors, together with avenue protection cameras and cell telephones. The precision in producing and transmitting data from gesture actions and different moves can offer intelligent offerings in human-computer interaction [10, 12]. Smart cities use sensors related to neural networks to increase and analyze information since speech popularity, video, photographs, and NLP. The analyzed information might be used to make crucial decisions to make certain the protection of citizens and to monitor the surroundings.
- **Infrared Sensors:** It helps generate impartial statistics on inactive and volatile situations to help smart city decisions. Radar sensors can be used to analyze important information about archaeological sites using complex computer data. Thermal sensors accurately track electricity distribution, at the same time as other smart sensors help energy control at the call for the side. Therefore, smart grid sensors assist in enhancing power performance. Proximity and lidar sensors assist in increasing automated car systems, which are essential to making a city completely wise.
- **Smart Grid Sensors:** Smart grid era is divided into five key elements, relying on its role, sensors, advanced components, communications, selection guide

structures, and different distinctly progressed components [16]. A style of sensors is used in smart grids to make certain green strength era, transmission, and power distribution from energy resources to quit-users. The use of thermal sensors related to climate situations plays a vital role in accurately tracking power switches and distribution [13]. In this regard, smart personal sensors ensure electricity efficiency thru power management at the call-for aspect. In addition, wireless sensor networks provide immediate records about transmission strains as a way to enhance strength performance [14]. Smart meters are additional sensors used to screen power transmission on the smart grid. The analysis of monitored electricity indicators is primarily based on the IEEE 1459-2010 well-known and is useful for actual-time choice-making methods [22]. These choices are supposed to cast off conditions characterized by using poor first-class and interruptions in the end consumer's power delivery.

- **Biosensors:** The leading-edge feature of biosensors is to detect anolyte in biomedicine. Current biosensors encompass sensors for ionization and standard particle sensors, which include neutron and MEMS sensors and lots of other biosensor devices. The drawback of biosensors is that they can best feature inside the discipline of biomedicine. Biosensor's paintings are simplest *via* signal transduction. For example, scent-binding proteins are utilized in biosensors to offer sensitive information that indicators are detected by way of electronic systems [25, 26]. Factors such as high accuracy and timely results make the use of optical technology in biosensors advantageous. These benefits describe the generation, transmission, and distribution of biosensors. Electrochemical biosensors, on the other hand, apply basic knowledge of electrical and chemical sensors to the anomaly detection process. Electrochemical sensors use the electric and chemical properties of numerous ions to show the concentration of anolyte. Therefore, non-polar molecules can be effectively measured [28].

- **Chemical Sensors:** Chemical sensors currently encompass carbon dioxide sensors, oxygen sensors, digital noses, and catalytic ball sensors. If chemical substances are involved, they're enough to discoverability issues with the chemicals. That is, it may be used to stumble on chemical reactions and physical residences of the system or environment. Chemical sensors have been used to generate and transmit crucial information approximately the feasibility of digital nasal within the diagnosis of patient allergies [30]. The important alternative to chemical sensors is environmental tracking sensors, whose use isn't always restricted. Sensors can correctly hit upon oxygen or carbon monoxide in the surroundings or substances.

APPLICATIONS OF SENSING DEVICES IN IOE ENABLED SMART CITY

Behind the grand emergence of smart cities, the key factor that performs a very vital role is the sensors. Almost in every field, without the sensors, it is impossible to achieve any tasks, whether it is a smart city, smart agriculture, smart environment, smart education, or smart healthcare. Basically, sensors are the backbone of smart cities. Here in the coming sections, some of the applications of sensing devices in IoE-enabled smart cities are given and also represented in Fig. (**6**).

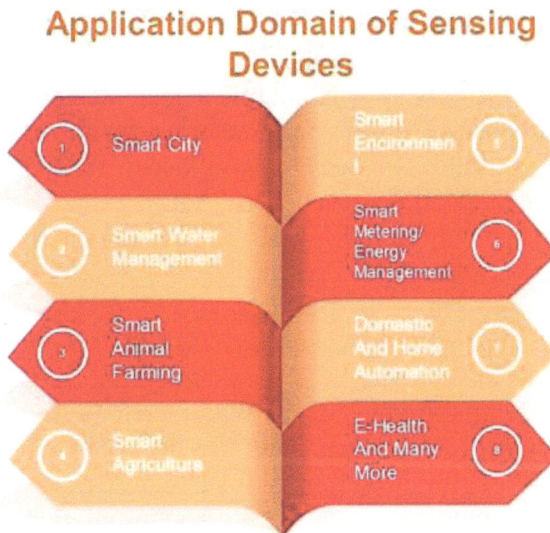

Fig. (6). Application domains of sensing devices.

- **Smart Cities:** In smart cities, smart parking can monitor the availability of parking spaces in the city. It is not permitted to monitor the structural health and material condition of vibrations of buildings, bridges, and historic buildings. Noisy city maps do not provide real-time sound monitoring in bars or central areas. Smartphone detection can detect not only iPhone and Android devices, but all devices that normally operate with a WiFi or bluetooth interface. Field levels are used to measure the energy radiated from cellular stations and WiFi routers. Congestion enables screening the level of cars and pedestrians to optimize driving and walking routes. Smart lighting provides street lights with smart, weather-adaptive lighting [26, 27]. Waste management can detect waste levels in containers and optimize waste collection routes. Smart Roads are smart highways that issue warning messages and deviations based on weather conditions and unexpected events (such as accidents and traffic jams).

- **Smart Environment:** Wildfire detection allows to reveal of smoke and preventive hearth situations and defines caution areas. Air pollution allows for managing carbon dioxide emissions from factories, pollution from motors, and toxic gases from farms. By tracking the extent of snow, you may degree the level of snow to recognize the fine of the slopes in actual time, and safety forces can prevent avalanches. Landslide and avalanche prevention helps screen soil moisture, vibration, and soil density to come across risky patterns of soil situations [27]. Early detection of earthquakes permits the allotted manipulation of earthquakes at unique locations.

- **Smart Water:** Drinking water monitoring video display units the high-quality faucet water inside the city. River chemical leak detection detects leaks and waste from river factories. Remote pool metering for far-off monitoring of pool status. The marine pollutants stage displays ocean leaks and wastes in actual time. Water leak detects the presence of liquid outside the tank and strain modifications along the pipeline [28]. River Floods permit monitoring changes in water stages in rivers, dams, and reservoirs.

- **Smart Metering:** The smart grid allows you to reveal and manipulate your strength intake. Reservoir stages are used to display the stages of water, oil, and gas in garage tanks and reservoirs. PV systems can display and optimize the overall performance of PV vegetation. Water drift is a measure of the water stress in a water transport gadget. The silo stock calculation allows you to measure the empty level and weight of your cargo [28].

- **Security and Emergencies:** Peripheral access manipulation can provide entry to manage confined areas and detection of unauthorized persons. Liquid detection in data facilities, warehouses, and touchy construction websites saves from malfunctions and corrosion. Radiation ranges allow disbursed measurements of radiation stages near nuclear energy flora to generate leak warnings. Explosive and hazardous gases are used to stumble on gas ranges and leak inside the industrial surroundings, around chemical flowers, and in mines [29].

- **Smart Retail:** Supply chain management can monitor the storage status of the entire supply chain and track products for traceability. NFC payments support payment processing based on the location or duration of activities such as public transport, gyms, and theme parks. The smart shopping app provides POS recommendations based on customer habits, preferences, the presence of allergens, or expiration dates [30]. Intelligent product management helps automate the replenishment process by controlling product rotation on shelves and warehouses.

- **Logistics:** The quality of the shipping conditions allows you to monitor vibration, impact, container openings, or cold chain maintenance for insurance purposes [31]. Item locations allow you to search for a single item in a large area (such as a warehouse or harbor). Detecting storage incompatibilities can alert containers that store combustibles near other containers that contain explosives. Fleet tracking can control the route of sensitive items such as drugs, jewelry, and dangerous goods.

- **Industrial Control:** The M2M application supports machine self-diagnosis and asset management. Indoor air quality helps to ensure the safety of workers and property by monitoring the toxic gas and oxygen content of chemical plants. Temperature monitoring is used to control the temperature inside industrial and medical refrigerators, including sensitive items. The presence of ozone helps to monitor ozone levels during the drying of meat in food factories. Use active (ZigBee) and passive (RFID / NFC) tags to track the indoor location of an asset. Vehicle self-diagnosis can collect information and send real-time alerts in emergencies and provide recommendations to drivers [32].

- **Smart Agriculture:** To improve the quality of the wine, and can monitor the soil moisture and trunk diameter of the vineyard to control the sugar content of grapes and the health of grapes. Greenhouses can control microclimate conditions to maximize fruit and vegetable yields and quality. Golf courses allow selective irrigation in dry areas, reducing the water resources required for the green. A network of meteorological stations helps to investigate the weather conditions at the site to predict changes in icing, rain, drought, snow, or wind. Compost helps control humidity and temperature levels in alfalfa, hay, straw, *etc.* To avoid fungal and other microbial contamination [33, 34].

- **Smart Animal Farming:** Hydroponics allows you to control the exact condition of plants that grow in the water to obtain the most efficient crops. Descendant care controls the growth conditions of the offspring on the farm to ensure the survival and health of the offspring. Animal tracking Identify the location of animals grazing in open pastures and large stables. Poisonous gas levels are used to study farm ventilation and air quality and detect harmful gases in feces.

- **Demotic and Home Automation:** Energy and Water use energy consumption and water tracking to get advice on how to save costs and resources. Remote control devices can be opened and closed remotely to prevent accidents and save energy. Intrusion detection systems detect door and window openings and crack to prevent intruders. Preservation of art helps to monitor the condition of galleries and art granaries.

- **E-Health:** Fall detection supports the aged and people with disabilities who stay independently. Medical fridges are used to govern the situation of fridges that store vaccines, drugs, and organic dependents. Sportsmen Care lets you screen critical signs in excessive-performance facilities and regions. Patient tracking is used to display the condition of patients in hospitals and nursing houses. Ultraviolet rays are a measure of the sun's ultraviolet rays to warn human beings no longer to be exposed to the solar at unique instances.

CHALLENGES IN THE IMPLEMENTATION OF IOE ENABLED SMART CITIES

The community and financial influences of virtual passage are undeniable. It is essential to discover a number of the primary tasks inside the software of community sensors as essential mechanisms of SC. Due to the gap restriction, it is discovered that the following challenges are the major.

- **Security and Safety Organization:** Alternative facilities have enhanced significantly, but delays in reporting and response times continue to kill the city. Therefore, it is important to focus not only on crime and risk prevention but also on mitigation strategies. Police and fire brigades may not know about accidents or crimes until then. This delay can be eliminated by installing gunshot, accident, and noise sensors in the city. In addition, connecting smoke sensors to a central repository based on an artificial intelligence system facilitates rapid response by police, ambulances, and firefighters. The main challenge that security management may encounter is the availability of voice communication equipment supported by the Internet of Things [35]. The telecommunications model is essential to understanding the role of noise sensors. In addition, the confidentiality and security of data transmitted over the Internet of Things network are essential to the development of smart cities. Therefore, using an integrated RFID sensor completely solves the security issues of cellular IoT systems. Using cellular networks for IoT devices can solve the risks of scalability and reliability.
- **Service Delivery and Optimization:** Municipalities face challenges in providing light and sanitation facilities to large inhabitants. Some cities rely on physical and basic operating structures. These systems are error-prone and interfere with optimal management. By deploying more sensor nodes than the urban people to facilitate the integration of smart city systems, it may be possible to simplify facility distribution [32]. Integrating information on or after these sensors provide feedback on the day-to-day processes and management of SC. Though, tasks together with scalability and strength boundaries restrict the effective use of wi-fi community sensors in facility distribution. The function of wi-fi nodes promoted by the MAC protocol is the primary cause of electricity boundaries. In this regard, the creation of different styles of MAC protocols, relying on the nature of the network structure, can extend the existence of wireless sensor networks [33]. As an end result, the performance of diverse sensors, which includes conservation sensors and waste sensors, is enhanced.

- **Traffic Management and Parking:** The city has lost millions of dollars due to traffic jams. The pause wasted high-quality time and fuel on the road. In addition, these traffic jams reduce the quality of life in the city. It is also clear that the purpose of congestion is the difficulty of securing parking areas. Moreover, in the age of electrical automobiles, site visitor control is paramount, so smart metering equipment can correctly cope with demanding situations [34]. These facilities shop the value of all parties concerned in the transportation industry. In addition, smart towns can take advantage of the likelihood of the GPS to through site visitors. In cities, it could be essential to equip automobiles in the relevant region with smart place sensors. First, the sensor can process primary records approximately the parking space (and who desires to be booked) and use this information to remedy a specific avenue. Therefore, smart grid sensors can be used to clear up parking troubles and decrease visitor congestion.
- **Smart Building:** In the conventional machine, building control turned outsourced to every real estate supervisor. Not just the costs of appointment and preserving actual estate administrators excessive, but operational performance also can be inconsistent. For instance, it could take numerous days to file and reply to a tenant's protection necessities. In addition, traditional systems require security guards to constantly monitor the access and exit of homes to enhance safety. With the help of smart buildings, the challenges could take away, which were posed by conventional systems. Smart towns can take benefit from automation, which is the center of smart buildings. Smart constructing automation can include included structures that are accessed through disbursed structures [35]. Through this gadget, you could screen lighting, heating, security, and carrier structures. Here, the provider machine refers to repeated rubbish series operations and cleansing obligations. In addition, the security monitoring subsystem can be incorporated with the town safety machine. The fundamental hassle in integrating wise building systems into urban systems is the distinction in the IT infrastructure used in the construction. Due to different tastes, this trouble arose in the early stages of construction. In this regard, it is vital to set up standards for every metropolis in an effort to manipulate the varieties of IoT infrastructure that are followed.
- **Public Transport:** Most public delivery stops at the bus prevent in preference to preventing. However, ordinary stops may be a waste of time, as there may be no commuters. There is likewise the hassle of losing time because the bus runs the targeted course outdoors, and there may be no opportunity for commuters. Therefore, it's miles feasible to escape those variations by growing a structure that connects the terminal to the bus station and bus dashboard. This machine enables car drivers to collect records that they can use to ensure efficiency. Implementation of this solution requires the improvement of a data gadget related to a far-flung terminal in a smart town. GPS is vital for tracking bus

actions. Both terminals are connected to the input device, which is the source of the fact for the general public delivery organization structure. It is a control structure that capabilities as a verdict care structure and proposes whether to prevent at each bus forestall. However, the principal task you can stumble upon is the generalization of control systems. This project limits the feasibility of the answer however may be resolved by means of strictly adhering to the coverage concerning the relationship between a particular bus terminal and the vicinity of the bus.

- **Environment:** Smart sensors can exacerbate the deterioration of the environment. However, thru improved and efficient electricity manufacturing and intake, it's miles viable to satisfy the climate exchange-demanding situations going through smart cities. The principal task is to grasp the widely deployed sensors and acquire reliable facts.

OPPORTUNITIES AND FUTURE TRENDS IN THE DOMAIN OF IOT

Based on the above discussion, some opportunities and future trends can be concluded. The role of smart sensors in the development of smart cities is very important. At the same time, this field offers many research opportunities in the future. The next part of this chapter describes some search possibilities. First, we need to improve security and security by eliminating delays in reporting and responding to incidents. In addition, connecting smoking and sound sensors using the Internet of Things solves safety and security issues. Second, sensors can be used to improve service delivery and integrate information from unused and preservation sensors. Third, sensors can be utilized to guide traffic, remove congestion, and accomplish car parking lots. Fourth, smart grids can be used to develop smart structures. These are constructions with automatic structures for managing public and general services. Fifth, we will inspect the effect of smart towns on the environment and public transportation. Sixth, we plan to investigate worldwide ethical problems surrounding smart sensors, consisting of privacy and regulatory frameworks. Recommendations for these problems keep emerging and guide the implementation technique. Finally, we will achieve our goal of implementing the strategy by emphasizing the use of network sensors to solve smart city problems.

CONCLUSION

The Internet of Everything (IoE) replaces the Internet of Things. Today, the security of IoE networks is paramount. These security and privacy issues are the main challenges of the Internet of Everything. Different IoE security requirements apply to different industries, such as home automation, smart cities, and smart agriculture and automation system. This article described the role of smart sensors in smart cities that support IoE. This chapter emphasizes the advantages of smart sensors for towns and considers the pressures modeled by using these advances. These parts are advantageous to each community and personal resident. In houses and groups, smart sensors help manage sources and trade statistics. In addition, smart sensors are significant in the community area because they can improve the manner services are introduced. Municipalities and cities can benefit from smart technologies, including optimized facilities such as parking, social site monitoring, lighting, maintenance, and monitoring. In specific, sensor knowledge can be used to detect shootings and trigger a quick response from law enforcement agencies. It is being described that the sensing devices, IoT, IoE, and Big Data go hand in hand and effectively accomplish the dedicated tasks and provide technologically smart surroundings.

REFERENCES

[1]   S. Phuyal, D. Bista, and R. Bista, "Challenges, opportunities and future directions of smart manufacturing: A state of art review", *Sustainable Futures,* vol. 2, no. March, p. 100023, 2020.
[http://dx.doi.org/10.1016/j.sftr.2020.100023]

[2]   J. P. Talari, "A review of smart cities based on the internet of things concept", *Energies,* vol. 10, no. 4, p. 421, 2017.
[http://dx.doi.org/10.3390/en10040421]

[3]   H. Mahdi, "A review on Internet of Things (IoT), Internet of Everything (IoE) and Internet of Nano Things (IoNT)", *2015 Internet Technologies and Applications (ITA),* pp. 219-224, 2015.

[4]   S. Nižetić, and P. Šolić, "Sustain ability energy cities", *J. Clean. Prod.,* p. 122877, 2020.
[http://dx.doi.org/10.1016/j.jclepro.2020.122877]

[5]   A.H. Alavi, P. Jiao, W.G. Buttlar, and N. Lajnef, "Internet of things-enabled smart cities: State-of-the-art and future trends", *Measurement,* vol. 129, pp. 589-606, 2018.
[http://dx.doi.org/10.1016/j.measurement.2018.07.067]

[6]   T. Singh, A. Nayyar, and A. Solanki, "Multilingual Opinion Mining Movie Recommendation System Using RNN", Springer Singapore, 2020.
[http://dx.doi.org/10.1007/978-981-15-3369-3_44]

[7]   V. Stepaniuk, J. Pillai, B. Bak-Jensen, and S. Padmanaban, "Estimation of energy activity and flexibility range in smart active residential building", *Smart. Cities.,* vol. 2, no. 4, pp. 471-495, 2019.
[http://dx.doi.org/10.3390/smartcities2040029]

[9]   S.P. Singh, A. Solanki, T. Singh, and A. Tayal, "Internet of intelligent things: Injection of intelligence into iot devices", In: *Artificial Intelligence to Solve Pervasive Internet of Things Issues.* Academic Press, 2021, pp. 85-102.
[http://dx.doi.org/10.1016/B978-0-12-818576-6.00005-8]

[10]   T. Singh, A. Solanki, and S. K. Sharma, "Role of smart buildings in smart city—components, technology, indicators, challenges, future research opportunities", In: *Digital Cities Roadmap: IoT-Based Architecture and Sustainable Buildings* Wiley Online Library, 2021, pp. 449-476.

[11]   S.P. Mohanty, U. Choppali, and E. Kougianos, "Everything you wanted to know about smart cities: The internet of things is the backbone", *IEEE Consum. Electron. Mag.,* vol. 5, no. 3, pp. 60-70, 2016.
[http://dx.doi.org/10.1109/MCE.2016.2556879]

[12]   R. Khatoun, and S. Zeadally, "Smart cities", *Commun. ACM,* vol. 59, no. 8, pp. 46-57, 2016.

[http://dx.doi.org/10.1145/2858789]

[13] E. Bellini, P. Bellini, D. Cenni, P. Nesi, G. Pantaleo, I. Paoli, and M. Paolucci, "An IoE and big multimedia data approach for urban transport system resilience management in smart cities", *Sensors,* vol. 21, no. 2, p. 435, 2021.
[http://dx.doi.org/10.3390/s21020435] [PMID: 33435451]

[14] P. Singh, A. Nayyar, A. Kaur, and U. Ghosh, "Blockchain and fog based architecture for internet of everything in smart cities", *Future Internet,* vol. 12, no. 4, p. 61, 2020.
[http://dx.doi.org/10.3390/fi12040061]

[15] S. Talari, M. Shafie-khah, P. Siano, V. Loia, A. Tommasetti, and J. Catalão, "A review of smart cities based on the internet of things concept", *Energies,* vol. 10, no. 4, p. 421, 2017.
[http://dx.doi.org/10.3390/en10040421]

[16] S. Anand, and M.V. Ramesh, "Multi-layer architecture and routing for internet of everything (IoE) in smart cities", *2021 Sixth International Conference on Wireless Communications, Signal Processing and Networking (WiSPNET),* pp. 411-416, 2021.
[http://dx.doi.org/10.1109/WiSPNET51692.2021.9419428]

[17] M. Lata, and V. Kumar, "Internet of energy IOE applications for smart cities", In: *Internet of Energy for Smart Cities*. CRC Press, pp. 127-144, 2021.
[http://dx.doi.org/10.1201/9781003047315-5]

[18] S. Tripathi, and S. De, "Pathway and Future of IoE in Smart Cities: Challenges of Big Data and Energy Sustainability", In: *In Internet of Energy for Smart Cities* CRC Press, 2021, pp. 277-302.

[19] H.B. Sta, "Quality and the efficiency of data in "Smart-Cities"", *Future Gener. Comput. Syst.,* vol. 74, pp. 409-416, 2017.
[http://dx.doi.org/10.1016/j.future.2016.12.021]

[20] G.S. Aujla, N. Kumar, and A. Jindal, *Internet of Energy for Smart Cities: Machine Learning Models and Techniques.* CRC Press, 2021.

[21] M.H. Miraz, M. Ali, P.S. Excell, and R. Picking, "A review on Internet of Things (IoT), Internet of Everything (IoE) and Internet of Nano Things (IoNT)", *2015 Internet Technologies and Applications (ITA),* IEEE, pp. 219-224, 2015.

[22] T. Snyder, and G. Byrd, "The internet of everything", *Computer,* vol. 50, no. 6, pp. 8-9, 2017.
[http://dx.doi.org/10.1109/MC.2017.179]

[23] L. DeNardis, *The Internet in Everything.* Yale University Press, 2020.

[24] X. Fan, X. Liu, W. Hu, C. Zhong, and J. Lu, "Advances in the development of power supplies for the internet of everything", *InfoMat,* vol. 1, no. 2, pp. 130-139, 2019.
[http://dx.doi.org/10.1002/inf2.12016]

[25] A. Jara, L. Ladid, and A.F. Gómez-Skarmeta, "The internet of everything through IPv6: An analysis of challenges, solutions and opportunities", *J. Wirel. Mob. Networks Ubiquitous Comput. Dependable Appl.,* vol. 4, no. 3, pp. 97-118, 2013.

[26] B. Di Martino, K.C. Li, L.T. Yang, and A. Esposito, *Internet of everything: Algorithms, methodologies, technologies and perspectives.* Springer: Singapore, 2018.
[http://dx.doi.org/10.1007/978-981-10-5861-5]

[27] Y. Liu, H.N. Dai, Q. Wang, M.K. Shukla, and M. Imran, "Unmanned aerial vehicle for internet of everything: Opportunities and challenges", *Comput. Commun.,* vol. 155, pp. 66-83, 2020.
[http://dx.doi.org/10.1016/j.comcom.2020.03.017]

[28] B. Kang, D. Kim, and H. Choo, "Internet of everything: A large-scale autonomic IoT gateway", *IEEE Trans. Multi-Scale Comput. Syst.,* vol. 3, no. 3, pp. 206-214, 2017.
[http://dx.doi.org/10.1109/TMSCS.2017.2705683]

[29] M.K. Karthiban, and J.S. Raj, "Big data analytics for developing secure internet of everything", *J.*

ISMAC, vol. 1, no. 02, pp. 129-136, 2019.

[30]   M. Civas, O. Cetinkaya, M. Kuscu, and O.B Akan, "Universal transceivers: Opportunities and future directions for the internet of everything (IoE)", *arXiv,* vol. 2107, p. 01028, 2021.

[31]   J.N. Pelton, and I.B. Singh, "Challenges and opportunities in the evolution of the internet of everything", In: *Smart Cities of Today and Tomorrow* Copernicus, Cham, 2019, pp. 159-169.
[http://dx.doi.org/10.1007/978-3-319-95822-4_10]

[32]   P. Padhi, and F. Charrua-Santos, "6G enabled industrial internet of everything: Towards a theoretical framework", *Applied System Innovation,* vol. 4, no. 1, p. 11, 2021.
[http://dx.doi.org/10.3390/asi4010011]

[33]   M. Ayaz, M. Ammad-Uddin, Z. Sharif, A. Mansour, and E.H.M. Aggoune, "Internet-of-things (IoT)-based smart agriculture: Toward making the fields talk", *IEEE Access,* vol. 7, pp. 129551-129583, 2019.
[http://dx.doi.org/10.1109/ACCESS.2019.2932609]

[34]   K. Saravanan, E.G. Julie, and Y.H. Robinson, "Smart cities & IoT: Evolution of applications, architectures & technologies, present scenarios & future dream", *Intelligent Systems Reference Library,* vol. 154, pp. 135-151, 2019.
[http://dx.doi.org/10.1007/978-3-030-04203-5_7]

[35]   N. Havard, S. McGrath, C. Flanagan, and C. MacNamee, "Smart building based on internet of things technology", *2018 12ʰ International Conference on Sensing Technology (ICST)*, pp. 278-281, 2018.
[http://dx.doi.org/10.1109/ICSensT.2018.8603575]

CHAPTER 4

IoE in Smart Cities: Applications, Enabling Technologies, Challenges, and Future Trends

Ankit Garg[1,*], Amit Wadha[2] and Jafar A. Alzubi[3]

[1] *Apex Institute of Technology, Computer Science and Engineering, University Center for Research and Development, Chandigarh University, Mohali, Punjab, India*

[2] *GL Bajaj Institute of Technology and Management, Greater Noida, Uttar Pradesh, India*

[3] *Faculty of Engineering, Al-Balqa Applied University, Salt-19117, Jordan*

Abstract: The innovative concept of smart cities drives economic growth and provides a standard of life through better services to the citizens. The incorporation of advanced technologies in smart cities projects smart outcomes that can be provided to the citizens. In the growth of smart cities, various public sectors, such as education, health care, and communication are adopting recent technologies such as IoE, Cloud/Fog computing, and Big data. These existing technologies integrate various IoE-based networks to manage various activities of smart cities. Many smart city projects are being implemented in different countries. Although various challenges are being faced, still, recent technologies are extensively being deployed in various projects of smart cities. To provide solutions to smart cities many standards have been implemented globally. These standards provide various solutions and concrete guidelines for the proper functioning of smart cities. The concept of smart cities is also facing some challenges in their planning, design, and implementation. Security and privacy of the IoE systems is one of the major challenges faced in the projects of smart cities. The main objectives of smart cities are to provide smart solutions to humans for their daily life problems and to create a sustainable environment. Researchers are developing various models of smart cities that can be implemented in real life to support the sustainable development of smart cities. This chapter explores numerous IoE applications which are also concerned with smart cities. The chapter discusses existing technologies that have a great contribution to the development of various prominent areas of smart cities. The chapter identifies and categorizes several challenges that are being faced by the stakeholders and officials in the construction of smart cities. At the end of the chapter, some research directions have also been discussed that can be helpful in the implementation of IoE-based applications and their deployment in smart cities.

Keywords: Big data, Cloud computing, Internet of everything (IoE), Information Communication and Technology (ICT), Machine learning, Smart cities.

---

* **Corresponding author Ankit Garg:** Apex Institute of Technology, Computer Science and Engineering, University Center for Research and Development, Chandigarh University, Mohali, Punjab, India; E-mail: ankitgitm@gmail.com

Arun Solanki and Anuj Kumar Singh (Eds.)

INTRODUCTION

With the advancement of smart cities and to improve their operational efficiency some solutions are required. These solutions are essential to increase the productivity of smart cities and minimize their maintenance cost [1]. Various IoE-enable devices are being equipped in smart cities, such as TV, mobile phones, smart door locks, and other electronic appliances. IoE plays a major role in Industry 4.0 revolution. From the intensive analysis of the current scenario of smart IoE networks, it has been predicted that by end of the year 2021, approximately 20.8 billion IoE-enabled devices will be interconnected across the world [2]. In the ongoing projects of smart cities, software platforms play a major role in designing, implementing, deploying, and managing applications for smart cities [3]. These IoE-based applications have three main components such as (1) generation of useful data, (2) management of data, (3) effective handling of the application [2]. The waste management applications implemented based on smart city requirements can provide real benefits to citizens. Through these applications, they can know about the actual condition of the dustbins or waste containers in their society or nearby areas [4]. These applications provide data about the condition of waste containers to the teams of garbage collectors so that they can schedule and optimize their routes in pickup services [4]. Integration of intelligence to the IoE sensors and actuators in the development of smart cities regularly keeps tracking the environmental conditions.

The intensive work on standards-based information technology infrastructure can satisfy the requirements of smart cities. In such types of infrastructures, recent technologies such as machine learning, artificial intelligence, and analytics tools can be used to provide better solutions to problems [1]. Widely known organizations such as international standards organizations ISO [2], the International Electrotechnical Commission (IEC) [3] and the International Telecommunication Union (ITU) [4] develop different standards to set a benchmark and to measure the performance of smart cities. Citizens in smart cities can improve their standard of living through proper management of transportation [5], traffic control [6], air pollution [7], waste management [8], health care [9], public safety [10], water [11], energy [12], and emergency management [13]. Fig. (**1**) shows the model of the smart city. Initially, smart cities implement a data-sharing platform with the public. Information shared with the public can be related to the new policies of the government and other private sector companies, fire detection, crime prevention, floods, and climate prediction [14]. To connect the cities with the citizens, pervasive wireless connectivity through a unified framework is highly desirable [15]. Low power wide area networks in smart cities are integrated with IoE-enabled devices, which are cost-effective and consume less power in their operation. Integration of recent technologies such as LTE Cat M, NB-IoE, LoRa, and Bluetooth contribute their major role in the connection of smart cities [16]. A heavy investment related to IoE-enabled hardware and software is required to build smart cities and to generate high revenue from them. Through proper implementation of privacy and security in smart cities, the government can generate high costs from service revenues. Attackers can capture control and hamper the functioning of integrated IoE devices in smart cities, such as CCTV cameras, locking systems, traffic lights, *etc*. To get rid of such type of privacy concerns, third parties in private or government sectors must explore the trade-offs between shortcomings and effectiveness in security.

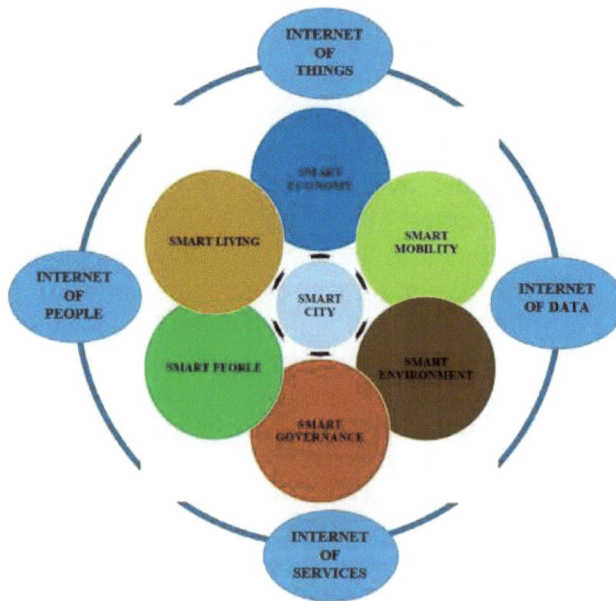

Fig. (1). A smart city model.

Smart cities of any country can generate various types of requirements that can be fulfilled through the implementation and integration of cloud-based applications. These applications can be accessed by equipped IoE devices in smart cities. Mainly two types of services are being provided to smart cities to fulfill their requirements. The first type of service is mainly provided to the end-users and various IoE devices which are equipped in smart cities. The second type of service is concerned with the administration of smart cities by their existing municipal system [17]. According to [18], it is estimated that by the end of 2025, the market size of smart cities will be USD 2.57 trillion. The ultimate objective of smart cities is to provide better services and a decent lifestyle with minimum cost [19]. Different services that are being provided by smart cities should be easy to use and can be capable to create a sustainable environment around them.

To improve the aging infrastructures of the cities, various smart city projects are popping up across the world. It has been estimated that by 2023, various ongoing projects of smart cities would spend more than $189 billion [20]. The goal of smart city projects is to optimize the process of public transport and traffic system. Many high-priority-funded projects related to public safety, the construction of a smart grid, and video surveillance in sensitive areas of cities have been initiated by the government of different countries. According to data obtained from the Ministry of Housing and Urban Affairs, it is estimated that out of 5,151 ongoing smart city projects, only a total of 1,638 projects have been completed [21].

In numerous completed projects, the Indian government has invested a total of INR 2, 05,018 crores. In this amount, a total of INR 26,700 crore has been spent on the resources that are required for the development of smart cities. For a positive impact, the government should formulate new strategies, explore advanced sustainable models, and increase investments in the various identified locations of smart cities. The standards defined for the development of smart cities contribute to their role in the regularization of various activities so that their social advancement can be recognized globally. Various factors have been identified to check the smartness of smart cities, which are mentioned in the report of the Vienna University of Technology [22, 23]. In this report, a total of six major areas of smart cities are identified to determine their performance or level of smartness, such as economy, social and human capital, smart governance, mobility, and smart living. These major areas are further characterized into 33 main factors. Fig. (2) shows the categorization of major areas of smart cities to measure their level of smartness.

The concept of the smart city is evolved to provide solutions to the challenges that are modeled in the process of urbanization. To build smart cities, the concept of information and communication technologies (ICTs) is being incorporated by the private and government sectors. Through the inclusion of ICT in the IoE, novel features are being introduced to smart cities. In the present scenario, smart cities are improving their economy, living standards, and governance through the implementation of IoE in their services. The integration of IoE in smart cities can generate a massive amount of data that can be further used to fulfill the requirement of advanced IoE-based hardware and software systems.

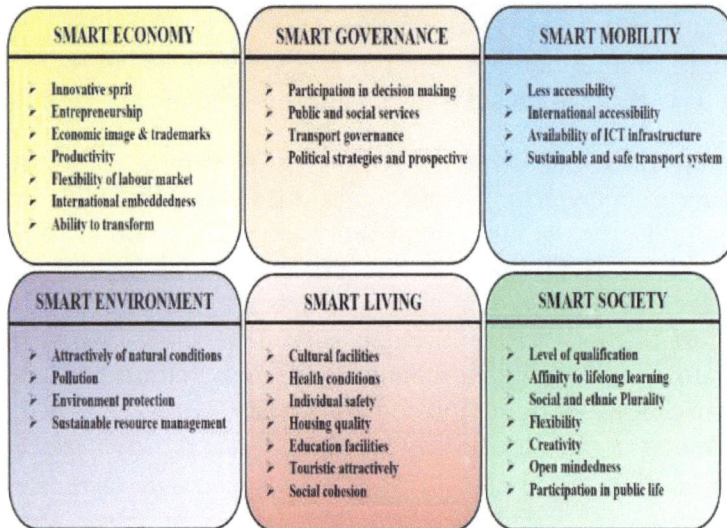

Fig. (2). Categorization of main factors to measure the smartness of smart cities.

The data generated from IoE devices can be used to explore new tools and technologies. The explored advanced technologies can be used to build advanced features for future smart cities. Nowadays, many cities of the world have transformed into smart cities. Many companies in the private sector are financing the development of smart cities as well [24]. In 2010, IBM initiated a smarter city challenge in which a total of 130 cities worldwide participated. IBM positioned a total of 700 specialists for assistance in providing various solutions to these cities [25]. Other private companies such as Siemens and Intel are trying to develop some innovative technologies based on IoE so that some improved services can be provided to the citizens without their interaction with private and government agencies. explore the probable advancements of the Internet of Everything (IoE) in the sustainable growth of smart cities.

In this chapter, Section 2 presents a literature review that identifies some prominent areas of IoE and smart cities to explore the advancement in the technologies, smart cities security, and smart cities projects. This section also discusses the investments by the government and private agencies in the deployment of smart cities. Section 3 explores a total of eight different applications of IoE in smart cities. Section 4 explains the advancements of existing technologies and their worth in the sustainable growth of smart cities and their surrounding areas. Section 5 provides a detailed discussion of the IoE challenges that are being faced in various aspects of smart cities. Finally, based on some observations in the field of IoE and smart cities, Section 6 presents the conclusion and future scope. In this section, some significant areas of research have been explored.

The major contributions of the chapter are summarized as follows:

- The chapter intends to clarify the significance of IoE in the design, management, and deployment of smart cities.
- The chapter explores the importance of smart cities for the economic growth of the country.
- The chapter contributes to explore major areas that are needed to be primarily focused on to provide a deep sense of decent life to the citizens, which is the ultimate goal of smart cities.
- The contribution of this chapter is to present the importance of recent technologies and their advancements in smart cities.
- This chapter contributes to suggest solutions to various challenges in the deployment of IoE systems in smart cities.
- Further, it contributes to explore some significant areas of research and future directions concerned with the smart development of smart cities.

LITERATURE REVIEW

In the development of smart cities, many organizations are facing various challenges in planning, designing, and investing due to complex political and technical guidelines. This literature review summarizes the literature relevant to some key areas such as security [26, 27], privacy [27 - 29], emerging technologies [14], projects and funding [30, 31], and risk management [32], IoE standards in smart cities, challenges and issues within smart cities. This literature review delivers a valuable fusion of some recent and past literature. To organize this literature review, published papers are selected based on some specific keywords such as smart cities, IoE in smart cities, applications of IoE in smart cities, enabling technologies in smart cities, smart city projects, IoE standards in smart cities, and challenges and issues for smart cities. The main sources of literature are renowned journals, conference proceedings, reports, and published magazines. All the published materials are selected with a high level of scholarly recognition based on the number of citations. In the end, the literature review discusses future research directions that are needed to be followed by the researchers and practitioners to provide some innovative research frameworks.

It is fascinating to incorporate various IoE applications in the development of smart cities. In smart cities, IoE-enabled networks equipped with IoE devices improve the daily lifestyle of human beings. Many companies in the private and government sectors realize the concept of smart cities and are trying to find out the optimal ways to effectively adopt Internet and Information Technology (ICT) solutions in various services [14]. In IoE based network, various IoE devices are integrated, such as sensors, actuators, and other physical things. These IoE-enabled devices are being used in smart cities to get useful data from IoE-based consumer goods [33], industrial equipment [34], smart cities infrastructure [35], logistics connectivity [36], and so on. Various technologies have emerged to support the development of relevant applications based on cloud computing [37, 38], data science [39], machine learning (ML), and Artificial Intelligent (AI) [40]. In smart cities, traffic management data is helpful to provide a solution to the challenges that citizens are facing during their routine work [14]. Through the implementation of smart parking systems in smart cities, the arrival and departure of vehicles can be tracked to avoid the rush in these areas [41]. The information about empty parking slots can be sent to the citizen in advance for the proper management of traffic through some visualization techniques [14]. To exchange data in smart cities, companies are establishing Wi-Fi networks that are being implemented through 4G and 5G technologies. The utilization of these adequate techniques provides insights to the decision-makers to manage uncontrollable situations in communication systems [42]. Wadhwa *et al.* [43 - 45] performed a comparative analysis of various security models and their related issues and proposed frameworks to provide better solutions.

Nowadays, smart cities are being equipped with RFID technology [46, 47] to identify the vehicle number automatically and to collect the parking fee from the citizens. To facilitate automation in this area, widely known car manufacturing companies are deploying IoE-enabled devices on the onboard units of the cars. The advanced IoE technologies reduce the power consumption within smart buildings, such as the consumption of power and water supply [48]. IoE sensors regularly monitor and control the data received from the various areas of the smart city and utilize the data to provide services. To control the energy-efficient operation of smart grids latest hardware and software applications are being used. The intelligent IoE sensors [28], actuators [27], software with artificial intelligence [40], and various communication protocols [49] improve the communication system between smart grids and their end-users. Integration of the Internet of Everything (IoE) automates the distribution of power supply, minimizes power consumption, increases power generation, and improves service delivery using an advanced energy delivery network [14].

The surveillance system in smart cities can monitor the condition of weather, pollution, and supply of water. For a healthy environment, the information related to these major concerns should be transmitted to the citizen [50]. Despite these concerns, another most important factor is the security and privacy of the citizens in smart cities [27, 28]. In various security automated systems that are being used in smart cities such as noise monitoring systems [51], video surveillance [52], drones [53], and cybersecurity systems, advanced techniques like Machine learning (ML), and Deep Reinforcement Learning (DRL) are widely used [40]. In smart cities, waste management is a very challenging task in developing countries due to the drastic change in human life, exponential growth of population, high urbanization, and growth of Gross Domestic Product (GDP) [54]. In a report reviewed by World Bank, it is stated that by 2050, global waste is anticipated to grow up to 3.40 billion tons.

In Fig. (**3**), the projected global waste generation is shown for three decades. The growth of waste also depends upon the income level of the country. According to this report, daily per capita waste generation in the developed country is estimated to increase by 19% by the year 2050, and in developing countries, it is expected to grow up to approximately more than 40%. The high-income countries are responsible to generate 34% waste or approx. 683 million tons and 5% waste, or 93 million tons, is generated by low-income countries [54]. The region-wise analysis of waste generation is shown in Fig. (**4**). In smart cities, ICT is widely used to automate the entire health care system and improves its quality of service [52]. In this regard, many companies, hospitals, and other associated bodies in the healthcare sector ensure that their telemedicine services should be accessible to as many people as possible [50]. Doctors in the healthcare sector are using many artificial intelligence and machine learning-based applications to diagnose patients [56]. These applications maintain and record real-time health data of the patient that can be used to predict abnormal health conditions.

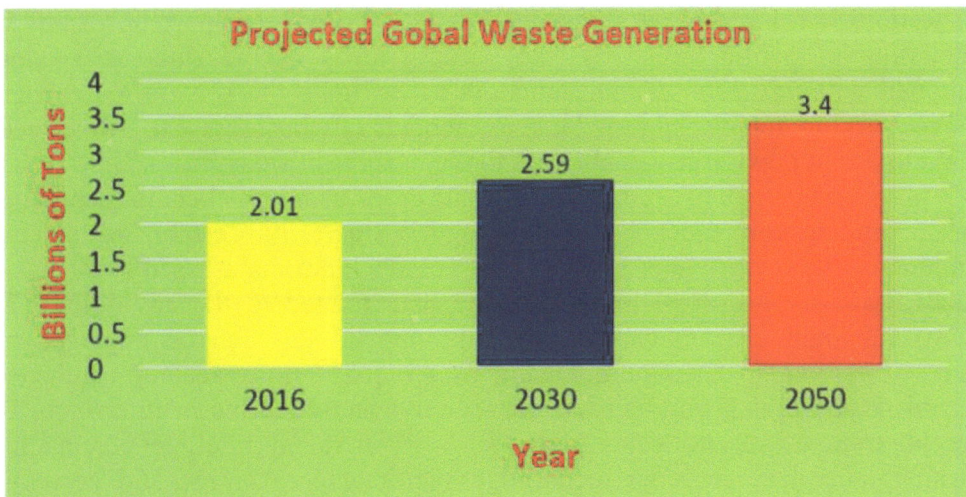

Fig. (3). The estimated global waste generation.

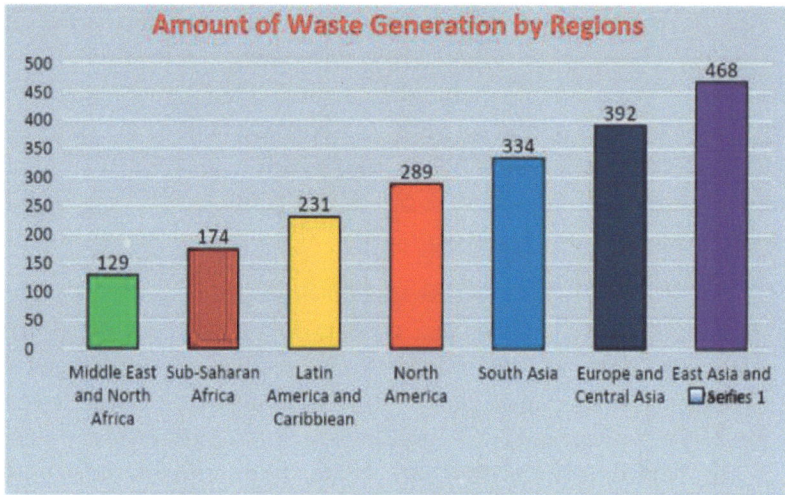

Fig. (4). Estimation of waste generation based on geographical location.

In a smart healthcare system, a massive amount of data, such as medical images and reports, is generated. To minimize the memory requirement, various image retargeting techniques are being used to reduce the size of images [57 - 59].

IoE and Cloud computing services make smart cities capable to exchange health data [17], devise new policies and guidelines, and reduce the cost of healthcare facilities. Recent Information and Communication Technologies (ICT) have resolved various challenges of transportation systems, such as high traffic congestion on roads and parking areas, pollution, high transportation cost, and scheduling of public transport. The parking areas of the smart cities have equipped with IoE sensors and actuators to facilitate the drivers to reach the nearest parking areas. The new business model, *i.e.*, business 4.0 utilize recent technologies to provide sustainable life to the citizens of smart cities. Biswas *et al.* [60] suggested a framework to secure smart cities using blockchain technology. The incorporation of blockchain technology in smart cities establishes a secure communication system. Ibba *et al.* [61] proposed a blockchain-based system using the SCRUM methodology to capture the data related to the environment. A massive amount of data captured by IoE applications can be managed and analyzed by Hadoop, Cassandra, Quantcast, *etc.* [62, 63]. To accomplish the data analysis task, big data can be used in predictive analytics and maintenance. The incorporation of recent technologies such as artificial intelligence, machine learning, and deep learning technology facilitates preventive and corrective decision-making processes [64, 65].

The concept of 5-G enables smart cities to have better communication systems so that citizens can get experience with the advanced framework and sustainable development of new entities [67].

Many projects have been initiated for the development of top smart cities, such as London, San Francisco, Barcelona, Santander, Padova, and Singapore, *etc* [14]. The Malmo Green Digital City project [68] was initiated with two main objectives. The first objective was to develop a carbon-free city by 2020. In the second objective, the project focuses to execute various activities using renewable energy by 2030. The project Scoop@F was initiated in 2016 by the Ministry of Transport, France, to establish an infrastructure for smart vehicles *via* WiFi, 4G, and 5G technologies [69]. A total of 3000 vehicles were connected at different places of the city. The budget estimated in this project was 20 million € to support various requirements of state, organizations, communities, and EU Member States (Spain, Portugal, and Austria) [14]. The Yokohama Smart City project was initiated in japan and the funding for this project was provided by the Ministry of Economy and Trade and Industry. The estimated duration of the project was from the year 2010 to 2015. The goal of this project was to develop a smart city with low-carbon substances in the environment and to provide a decent living to the citizens [70]. For the establishment of smart cities, Saudi Arabia announced a mega smart city project and invested 70 billion dollars in the King Abdullah Economic City [71]. The projected timeline of the project was from the year 2005 to 2020 in alliance with a network-native digital services company. In 2015, South Africa announced a smart city project and planned to invest $7.4 billion to develop a carbon-neutralized public transport environment by 2025. The Indian government has announced the development of 100 smart cities and the estimated cost for the development $1.27 billion. In the literature [72], it is mentioned that the annual revenue for the global smart city technology market to raise from $97.4 billion in 2019 to $263 billion by 2028. Many countries are implementing smart city standards at national and international levels to provide a range of benefits, guidelines, and solutions to the industries that are supporting them. The defined guidelines of the standards specify the process for the attainment of better services in smart cities. The ensure the firm foundation of smart city three standards have been defined based on the strategic level, process level, and technical level [73].

Discussion and inference: This literature review provides a theoretical study about the infrastructure of smart cities and discusses various challenges that are being faced by the investors to implement security and privacy mechanism. With the recent advancement of technology, many IoE platforms are being used to monitor the infrastructure of smart cities. The integrated IoE technology in smart cities improves public transport systems, quality of water, soil, and air. In developing countries, E-waste management is a very critical task that needs to be focused on by initiating some awareness programs in smart cities. IoE-enabled devices are generating a massive amount of information that is being used to develop long-term policies and standards. To create a sustainable environment within smart cities, many organizations in the government and public sectors are investing in smart city projects soon. The incorporation of recent technologies such as Artificial Intelligence (AI), Machine learning, Data science through the Internet of Everything (IoE) exposes various opportunities and enables smart city officials to interact with both communities and city infrastructures. To get the benefits from the smart cities initiatives, it is required to focus on various types of challenges related to technology, operation, and sustainability. Researchers need to focus on the implementation of blockchain technology to improve the infrastructure of smart cities. The government needs to devise new policies and guidelines to resolve various disputes among investors and private companies. Future research can also extend to explore some advanced communication protocols and IoE-enabled devices that can be used to collect data related to pollution, the healthcare sector to improve the prediction capability of new environment models.

APPLICATIONS OF IOE IN SMART CITIES

To develop smart cities, various components are used. Various applications of smart cities have four aspects such as data collection, data transmission, storage management, and data analysis. Various IoE-based applications are used to collect the data from the IoE sensors and transmit it to the clouds for analysis. To accomplish the tasks of smart cities, various technologies, such as Wi-Fi networks, 4G and 5G technologies are being used. Various storage management techniques [65, 66] are being used to manage the massive amount of data in the cloud. To make decisions based on the stored data, various data analysis techniques [40] are being used. To analyze the heterogeneous and complex real-time data, various statistical methods and algorithms based on the concept of machine and deep learning are also being used. Fig. (**5**) shows the various applications of IoE in the development of smart cities.

Smart Transportation

The public transportation system is a major branch of smart cities. Nowadays, many cities are facing lots of traffic problems such as traffic congestion, pollution, scheduling of public transport, *etc*. With the advancement of ICT, vehicles are being connected using three main approaches to communication: (i) Vehicle to Vehicle (V2V), (ii) Vehicle to Infrastructure (V2I), (iii) Vehicle to Pedestrian (V2P) [55]. The incorporation of these approaches in smart transportation systems enables vehicles to communicate useful information about the environment around them. The information related to the number of vehicles, and nearby infrastructures enables the safe mobility of vehicles and chances of accidents even in the high congestion on the roads. The inbuilt Global Positioning System (GPS) devices are used to track the location of the drivers, behaviors, and their pattern of traffic. In smart cities, various applications such as Google Maps and Waze are used to manage public transport using real-time data. These applications enable the driver in mapping the routes, scheduling the trips in advance, and payment. The IoE sensor equipped in the parking areas can send information to the drivers about the free parking slots and the conditions of other nearby parking areas. The government of developed countries should consider urban mobility as a challenging problem in the smart cities mission. For efficient mobility of the citizens, three main areas of improvement such as smart parking, AI-based traffic management system, and Integrated Multi-Modal Transport. Intelligent signboards can be placed at different locations to obtain information related to temperature, weather conditions, and congestion. The equipped sensors in the signboard can sense the data from the cloud using IoE [74]. To improve smart transportation systems, many smart cities such as Malaga, Paris, Amsterdam, and Barcelona are providing services through electric vehicles. Many charging stations have now been installed at different places to provide charging facilities to the drivers or owners of the vehicle. The utilization of such resources in a smart city can reduce the emission of CO_2 and pollution [24].

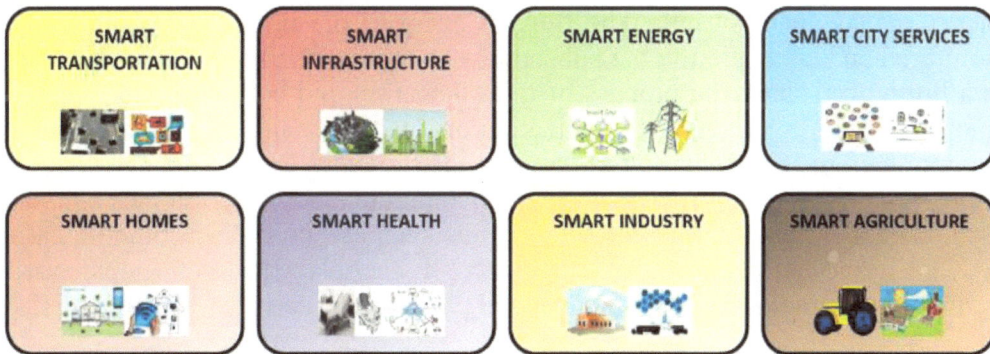

Fig. (5). Internet of Everything (IoE) applications in the growth of the smart city.

Smart Infrastructure

In a smart infrastructure system, the decisions are taken based on the data collected from the IoE sensors related to a specific matter. The collected massive amount of data can be further utilized in monitoring, analyzing, predicting, and measuring the effectiveness of smart infrastructure [24]. Nowadays, various digital technologies are being used for the continuous development of smart cities.

These technologies are used in planning and building energy-efficient sustainable infrastructures. To minimize the emission of CO_2, government and private sector companies are investing in electronic cars and other two-wheeled vehicles. The roadside smart lights reduce power consumption by giving their light when someone walks near them into a defined radius. These IoE-enabled devices can intelligently adjust the level of brightness according to the condition of the weather. The infrastructure of smart cities plays a vital role to provide a standard of living to the citizens. Many companies have initiated smart city projects for the development of new bridges, smart buildings and also maintaining them on a regular basis for their uninterrupted usage. For the normal operation of smart cities, the gathered data from the IoE sensors can be used in predictive maintenance. The whole development process of smart infrastructure should be citizen-centric which expectations of citizens are taken into account. To prevent the infrastructure from various internal and external contingencies, resiliency and sustainability should be maintained in the guidelines and policies. Moreover, smart infrastructure mitigates the risk and ensures the security of citizens from illegal accessing resources [27].

Smart Energy

In smart cities, the living standard of citizens can be improved using the optimal use of available resources. The presence of various complexities and challenges involved in energy management forces smart city developers to an efficient energy management system. The flow of energy from the power plants can be monitored and controlled in the substations using a continuous feedback system. In a big power plant, the process of fault detection and correction takes a huge amount of time. Nowadays, the utilization of smart grids has increased due to the incorporation of ICT technologies that provide flexibility in network topology and improve reliability and efficiency. Several communication technologies are being used to improve the services of smart grids, such as power line communication (PLC), ZigBee, WiMAX, fourth-generation (4G) cellular networks, global system for mobile communication (GSM), general packet radio service (GPRS), *etc.* [24].

The newly installed smart grids in smart cities can intelligently heal themselves. Real-time data about the consumption of energy can be collected at different points on the smart grid for better management of power generation. In a smart grid, every device is capable to provide information about its power consumption and production. The incorporated IoE sensors enable the smart grid to control its services by load balancing and load scheduling [14]. The smart grids also educate their consumers about the proper usage of energy, and cost reduction to take decisions on the efficient utilization of energy and other energy generation resources. Smart metering systems in smart grids can provide real-time data to their consumer about power consumption, new pricing policies, and other routine information.

Smart City Services

Smart cities provide various services to the citizens, such as water quality management, monitoring of water supply, waste management, and control of a sustainable environment. Various IoE sensors are being used to provide information to living entities and municipalities about the change in price, quality of water, and leakage of water tanks and pipes [55]. The intensive investigations in technology and awareness programs initiated by the government can provide solutions to recycle E-waste materials safely and economically. Due to the presence of toxic chemical substances, proper management of E-waste has become an irresistible challenge. The health of humans is also at high risk with the exponential growth of electronic waste elements on earth globally, due to which they face various health issues. Different legislations concerning E-waste have been enacted by the government to resolve its various problems. In the current scenario of E-waste management [35], it has become critical to make some concrete decisions and devise some strategies to address its various issues. In smart cities, the bins are equipped with IoE sensors to store information about their real-time conditions. The relevant authorities can obtain the information from the cloud to schedule their regular tasks. Through AI-based applications, the services can be provided in less time and cost by determining the best routes [24]. IoE sensors can be used to monitor pollution and other environmental conditions.

Smart Home

Smart homes enable IoE devices to communicate with each other. Automation in a smart home can be achieved through IoE-enabled electric appliances, IoE integrated alarm systems, efficient data management, and processing, and AI-based data analyzing capabilities of devices. There are certain challenges for the developer of the smart home are found such as (i) requirement of inbuilt communication technology in the IoE-based devices, (ii) high cost to manufacture IoE-enabled devices, (iii) establishing the connection of each device through IoE sensors, (iv) privacy and security in the smart home [64]. The owner sitting anywhere in the world can monitor/control his/her home appliances remotely. Old people with disabilities can be benefited from smart homes with alarm systems, coincidence anticipation, safety systems, and automatic timers and alarms. The incorporation of such a mechanism in the smart home raises the confidence and sense of independence among them.

Moreover, their relatives can take care of them 24 hours being in contact with the automated systems through their mobile phones. The data generated from smart homes can be used by different industries, such as the energy industry, hardware industry, and health industry. The information related to the consumption of energy in the smart home can be used to cut down the electricity bills and devise new guidelines on energy consumption. The digital health monitoring system can send the health-related data of cities to the nearest doctor in case of emergency. Through real-time data, the hospitals can keep tracking of the visit of the patient and can arrange many facilities in advance for them. The adoption of IoE technologies in the smart home can save millions of lives. After considering all the requirements in the smart home, the ratio of the healthy population can be considerably increased, which is the first step towards the attainment of the goals of smart home industries [75].

Smart Healthcare

In smart healthcare systems, the security and privacy of data and information are crucial. The researchers have identified various challenges to build a secure information architecture and provide solutions through the adoption of IoE-enabled sensors in various smart health care applications. To advance the eminence of services in smart healthcare sectors, ICT is being used [28]. In smart health care systems, numerous mobile health software has been developed in mobile operating systems. Examples of such applications are First Aid, Instant Heart Rate, Fooducate, Glucose Buddy—Diabetes Log, *etc*. [24]. The current healthcare systems have become overburdened due to the exponential growth of the population, which is the main reason for the rising cost of various services. Smart health care sectors are utilizing recent technologies such as AI, machine learning, and deep learning in their telemedicine services to improve their diagnosis assistance through the analysis of real-time data [14]. Through IoE sensors, real-time data related to ECG, body temperature, and oxygen level can be captured. The health tracker applications can record patient's daily activity and also can detect their abnormal movements. To make a better decision, smart healthcare systems should be leveraged with cloud computing and edge computing capabilities to reduce the overall cost of services and resources [37]. The proper management and utilization of these capabilities cab minimize the burden on healthcare facilities.

Smart Industry

The industry 4.0 paradigm emphasis the integration of various functions of the industries to improve productivity with low utilization of available resources [68]. The integration of IoE in the industry enables the intermediate departments to work in tandem. Various IoE-enabled devices are equipped within machines to optimize the production process, quality of products, safety of the workers, and improve sales. Due to the use of heterogeneous IoE devices in industries, many challenges are being faced. To overcome these challenges, cyber-physical systems (CPS) should provide flexibility to conFig. the IoE devices in real-time and quick implementation of IoE-based applications. To improve the services of industries, the industry 4.0 paradigm incorporates Artificial Intelligence technology in the deployment of IoE. To automate the production, marketing, sales, and other departments of industries, AI-based sensors are being embedded in the machines. The data collected by these sensors can be used to monitor the health of machines, faults, and facilitate the maintenance department to initiate various preventive measures in advance. The other aspects of Industry 4.0 such as the Internet of Services (IoS) and Internet of Energy (IoE). The Internet of services (IoS) refers to smart mobility and smart logistics in smart cities [36]. Internet of Energy (IoE) ensures the proper utilization of natural resources in an efficient way. The smart interconnection of the Internet of everything (IoE), Internet of Services (IoS), Internet of People (IoP), and Internet of Energy (IoE) can optimize the production of goods, services, and provide sustainable development of society [76].

Smart Agriculture

With the exponential growth of the world population, lands are being utilized in the development of house, companies, and markets, leading to many challenges in food production through agriculture. The recent technologies enable farmers to monitor field conditions through IoE-based applications installed in their smartphones. The inbuilt IoE sensors in the tractors can predict soil moisture and uncertainty in weather conditions. To make smart farming precise and cost-effective various data management techniques are being used to collect data about humidity and temperature [8]. Recent technologies, such as cloud computing [37], artificial intelligence [40] and deep learning [39], are expected in smart agriculture to improve the entire process of farming. With the utilization of Big Data [37] in agriculture, a massive amount of data related to various framing operations can be captured and analyzed for effective decision-making. The real-time operational decisions enable farmers to cope with the enhanced business models of agriculture industries. In a smart agriculture system, RFID [43] is widely used to track the intrusion of animals and protect the crop from them. With the incorporation of intelligent irrigation technologies, the supply of water and electricity can manage to accomplish various farming activities. The precise seeding and spraying of fertilizers can be achieved using recent technologies and advanced wireless sensor networks. The IoE-based sensors are being deployed to gather data that can be used to understand the growth of plants and to promote research in the agriculture field carried out in various institutions around the world.

EXISTING TECHNOLOGIES IN SMART CITIES

To improve the standard of living, humans are continuously adopting advanced technologies in their routine life. The incorporation of recent technologies in daily activities achieves some level of automation and improves decision-making capabilities. The world is now moving towards business 4.0 and Industry 4.0, and to cope with the changing environment, the utilization of technologies is essential for a sustainable lifestyle. For the development of smart cities, it is required to integrate modern technologies to set up connections among the network of devices and various objects of a smart city.

The main goal of any smart city project is to provide smart interconnectivity among the participating objects. The incorporated technologies, such as cloud/edge computing, support the dynamic change in the configuration of the network according to the changing requirements of the citizens. To deal with the massive amount of data produced by the IoE devices, various data management and processing applications are being used. The traditional security mechanism is not capable to provide the security of heterogeneous interconnected devices on the network. To improve security and privacy novel, security mechanisms are required that can provide a highly secured network of participating objects in the smart city ecosystem. Fig. (**6**) shows recent technologies that are being used to govern major routine operations and to develop plans for the future.

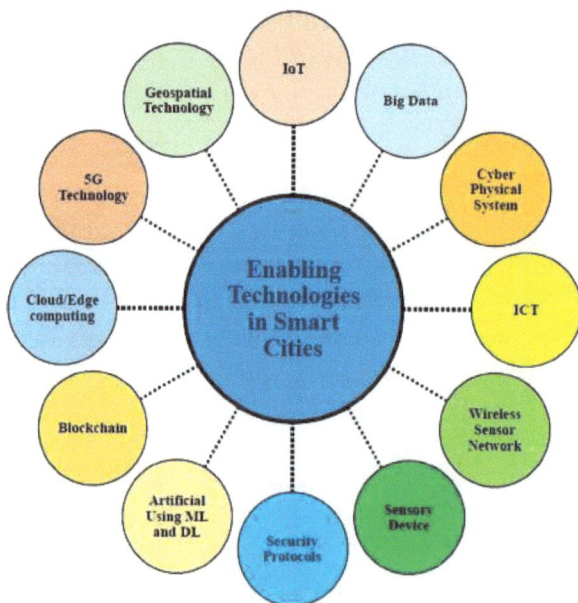

Fig. (6). Advanced technologies incorporated in the smart cities.

Internet of Everything (IoE)

The concept of IoE is widely used to integrate uniquely identified objects over the network. To develop smart cities, three major components of IoE, such as hardware, middleware, and presentation layer, are used [77]. The massive amount of data collected from the IoE sensors is used to adopt IoE technologies in various smart city platforms. The collected data from IoE hardware can be transmitted to interconnected networks to provide better services to citizens. Researchers have suggested the potential usage of IoE in health monitoring systems, transportation systems, waste management, green computing [78], and monitoring infrastructure. The integration of IoE networks and recent technologies such as wireless communications and wireless sensor networks (WSN) enable the object's intelligence. The objects like food products, electronic appliances, vehicles, healthcare devices, *etc.*, are equipped with Internet-addressable artificial intelligence up to some extent. These IoE-enabled objects share the information with other integrated objects to produce the data for further analysis and decision-making [64].

Big Data

Big Data is a set of technologies through which a massive amount of data can be stored and processed using various tools. Big data provides various mechanisms to handle the huge amount of data that are not available in the conventional relational database and its related data handling tools. IoE-enabled devices and recent technologies produce a massive amount of data, *i.e.*, Big Data. The gathered data obtained from various sensors and wireless networks should be managed properly on the cloud are need to be analysed to extract the patterns. The extracted patterns are further used for the development of applications, maintaining services to citizens, and effectively integrating various ICT approaches. The improvements are required in many key areas such as public information systems, energy management, public transportation system, security and emergency services, and waste and waste management to provide better services to the residence. In all these services, three major operations are performed such as (i) data acquisition, (ii) data processing, (iii) data analysis [55]. To storage and process the data, local servers and various cloud processing techniques are being used. The processed data on cloud networks are analyzed for the implementation of advanced services such as smart economy, smart governance, smart sustainable environment, and smart mobility [64]. The amount of data obtained from the big data tools is transmitted to other interconnected sensor networks to analyze the condition of various prominent areas of the city. The type of information that is needed to be shared can be temperature, quality of air, pollution, weather conditions, *etc.* Public transport such as buses and taxies send information to their customers about price and position on their smartphone. There are various Big Data tools such as NoSQL databases, Hadoop, and Apache Storm [77].

Cyber-Physical System

A Cyber-Physical System is a collection of physical and virtual devices over the network and has the capabilities of processing, management, and computation, communication, and storage. The real word applications gain profit with the existence of CPS, such as healthcare systems, smart grids, public transportation systems, and robotics, which are specific to a particular domain [75]. Conventional ICT does not support applications that can deal with the changing behavior of the networks. To overcome this limitation, CPS introduces some applications that can manage the activities over heterogeneous networks and their dynamically changed requirements. The applications in CPS are aware of in advance about the change in the physical context. These applications can change their execution and processing capability accordingly. An example of such CPS WreckWatch [77] which is widely used in smart cities to detect traffic accidents. In CPS various mobile applications enabling the Global Positioning System (GPS) to track the location of the driver, speed, distance, and driving patterns. The prediction models implemented in the WreckWatch can generate data that can be analyzed on the centralized server. The analyzed data is further transformed as an alert to indicate the occurrence of an accident in the traffic.

Information Communication and Technology (ICT)

ICT is used to improve the living standard of citizens, services, and infrastructure, and also strengthens the relation between citizens and city stakeholders. The services and applications that are being executed in smart cities due to the existence of ICT infrastructure can be used to provide real-time data and responses for the standard of living [79, 80]. In the development of smart cities, the stakeholders and citizens can be benefited from the intelligent ICT infrastructure design. To design such a structure, different networks within the smart cities should be unified and managed as a single entity. The simplified management of networks minimizes complexity and increases efficiency. The below-mentioned areas need to be focused on for the development of smart city infrastructure.

- Effectively adoption and transformation of new strategies in smart cities.
- Solution of various issues and challenges in the existing smart city infrastructure.
- Implementation and integration of Information Communication Technologies

(ICT) in smart cities.

- Risk management involved in the handling of the massive amount of smart cities data.
- Automation of various business processes and routine activities of stakeholders and citizens to provide a standard of living.

The smartness of smart cities can be measured based on the four pillars of ICT such as economy, governance, environment, and society [81]. All three pillars play a major role in the development of a sustainable environment, smart services, and a decent lifestyle. The improvement of all the attributes of these pillars reflects how the citizens of smart cities are secure, and prosperous in terms of wealth, health, and education. The three pillars of ICT have various applications such as information sharing, forecasting, disaster management [13], and integration of resources. In smart cities mainly, three types of infrastructures such as physical, digital, and service, are generally found in smart cities. The service infrastructure of a smart city provides services to the various attributes of physical and digital infrastructure, such as education, healthcare, building, public transport, information technology, communication technologies, *etc*. The digital infrastructure of a smart city enables various operations to be performed optimally.

Network Technologies

The IoE in smart cities depends upon the data gathered by different IoE sensors placed at various locations. The collected data is used to make decisions and perform various complex actions to provide services to the citizens from the service providers. The devices on the IoE networks can be connected through various network topologies such as point-to-point, star, tree, and mesh [55]. In smart cities, mainly three types of network architectures are generally used, such as Home Area Networks (HANs), Wide Area Networks (WANs), and Field/Neighborhood Area Networks (FANs/NANs). The rage of Home Area Networks is very low and the central node generally performs the exchange of information.

The wireless sensor networks (WSNs) are the essential component in the development of the smart city framework. The network is widely used to transmit information that is used for effective decision-making in various major areas, such as public transport systems, traffic congestion management, and temperature control in a smart city. In this type of network, various communication protocols such as Zigbee [28], Bluetooth, and WiFi are being used to transmit the information. To communicate over long distances, Field Area Networks are widely used, which provide the connection between the user and service providers. Moreover, Wide Area Networks are also used for long-distance communication and use in many IoE applications such as smart grids and public transport. These network architectures are not much dense as compared to the HANs and FANs [55]. These networks are equipped with the latest technologies, such as cellular services, fiber optics, and some low-power protocols. The type of network architecture and selection of the protocols is depended upon the requirement of the applications. The main goal of any network protocol is to maintain the desired Quality of Services (QoS) for the end-user. To implement wireless networking in smart cities, various communication protocols such as Radio Frequency Identification (RFID), Near Field Communication (NFC), Z-Wave, Li-Fi, Wi-Fi, Zigbee, Wi-SUN, Cellular, LoRaWAN, 6LoWPAN, SigFox, and NB-IoE are being used to exchange the data at a long and short distance [55]. Fig. (7) shows the three types of network architecture and communication protocols used in the development of smart cities.

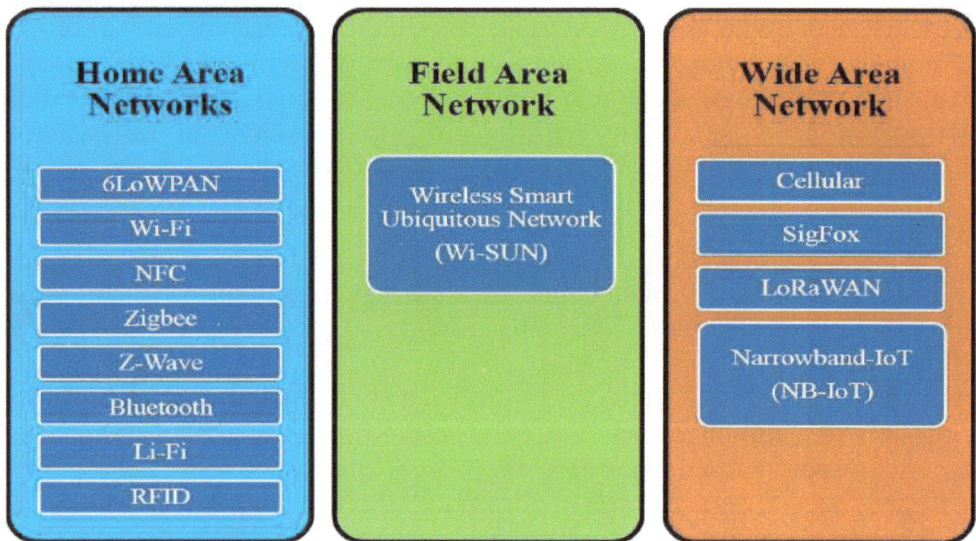

Fig. (7). Types of network and communication protocols.

Sensing Technologies

In a smart city, numerous sensors are connected to collect and exchange data to share knowledge. The shared knowledge through sensors is used in innovation and decision-making. The citizens of smart cities utilize IoE sensors as a key entity for their interaction and to obtain various services. The selection of the sensors depends upon the requirement of applications. For example, various sensors such as ambient, motion, electric, identification, position, chemical, and hydraulic sensors are widely used in the development of smart homes. The developer of smart cities can face various challenges in the handling of data generated by the multiple sensors due to the diversity in their features, requirements, and behavior of operation. The list of various sensory devices used in smart cities and their usage are given below [55].

- Ambient Sensors: Used to measure temperature, humidity, the intensity of light, and pressure.
- Bio Sensors: Used to measure heartbeat, breath, pulse, and blood pressure.
- Chemical Sensors: Used to measure carbon monoxide (CO), carbon dioxide (CO_2), smoke detection, and water quality monitoring.
- Electric sensors: Used to measure power consumption, and voltage.
- Hydraulic Sensors: Liquid measurements, water level, water flow, leak detection.
- Identification Sensors: To initiate payments and exchange of data.
- Motion Sensors: Used to detect motion, activity tracking, and vibration sensing.
- Presence Sensors: Human motion, security in the locking system, measure distance of objects to determine position.
- Other Sensors: Sensing visual information, sound and to measure signal strength, quality of data

Security and Privacy

With the advancement in network structure and the advent of new connecting devices improve the communication process and make network system less secure. In complex IoE network systems, approximately 70% of the data is found heterogeneous. The interconnected IoE devices in smart cities' wireless networks can be attacked by various commonly known security attacks such as Trojan horse, Man-in-the-middle [49], Distributed Denial of Service (DDoS) [28], spoofing and session hijacking, and eavesdropping [29]. In smart cities, the major security requirements comprise privacy, integrity and authenticity, confidentiality, prevention of device tampering, and secure accessibility of data. In the secure communication system, network access control plays a significant role. To prevent the leakage and tempering of information from intruders, an adequate IoE security framework is required to design. The integrated platform SMARTIE [79] is used to maintain the user's privacy even in the decentralized accessing of IoE devices over the network. Other technologies such as blockchain [60], cryptography, biometrics, machine learning and data mining [60], game theory [28], and ontology can be used to maintain the security and privacy of the system. Various networking protocols are being used to connect IoE devices integrated within the IoE network. Wadhwa *et al.* suggested and analyzed different frameworks and techniques to secure critical data over the cloud [82 - 85].

Artificial Intelligence and Machine Learning

The application area of artificial intelligence and machine learning is very wide. These technologies play a significant role in the field of scientific research, industry automation, the development of medical tools, and robotics. IoE-enabled devices are being developed based on artificial intelligence (AI) and Machine learning (ML) to effectively manage citizen's routine life and essential activities [66]. The IoE network based on these technologies is connected with heterogeneous sensors that produce a massive amount of data. The proper management of such an amount of data and predicting a course of action based on data analysis is a very challenging task. Many AI-based applications are being used in smart homes. These applications are capable to customize their execution based on the behavior of the end-users in their routine activities, such as walking in a smart home, cooking, taking medicine, and gardening. In smart cities, the individual smart home is equipped with advanced artificial intelligence (AAI) systems that enable the user to be benefited from various AL/ML-based home services [64]. To improve the efficiency of the security infrastructure in smart cities, machine learning (ML) techniques are being employed in intrusion detection systems. The adoption of these technologies provides security and privacy for data from attackers. Researchers are implementing various techniques to secure Wireless sensor networks (WSNs) within smart cities, which has been assumed as a key component. The recently developed models are being used to extract features and patterns from the sensed data to detect attacks on the WSN and Wi-Fi networks [28]. Various other AL/ML models are developed to secure biometric systems and sensitive information obtained from Data Mining (DM) technologies [40]. From the network, a massive amount of information is collected from IoE sensors and other IoE-enabled devices that are integrated around the citizens of smart cities. To provide better services and maintain data security, information such as location and behavior patterns should not be disclosed to other users. To fulfill such requirements, many companies are adopting some recent privacy-preserving data mining (PPDM) technologies in the development of smart cities [55].

Blockchain Technology

Blockchain technology has especially emerged for cryptocurrencies such as Bitcoin and Litecoin [60]. Nowadays, the concept of Blockchain is widely being used to develop applications related to smart cities. It provides various opportunities to the developers of smart cities because of having various features such as information sharing, transparency, distribution, and security. In this technology, no central body exists to validate the transactions. Despite this, blockchain is considered to be secure and reliable due to the presence of consensus protocol [61]. The consensus algorithm ensures that each new node is first verified by all the existing nodes before adding to the blockchain network. The consensus algorithm helps the peers to come to a common agreement on the trust of unknown peers that is trying to be added to the distributed computing environment. The consensus protocol comprises some other objectives such as collaboration, cooperation, equal rights to every node, and participation of each node in the consensus process. In this technology the usage of data obtained from the public is transparent. The citizen of smart cities are aware of the contribution of each other and also have information about how the government is using the data. The sensitive information is first encrypted before storing in the chain of blocks. In a blockchain system, applications that are being used automatically collect the data from the IoE devices and generate the outputs. In a smart city, various objects are linked with each other, which increases the cost of their operations. Blockchain technology reduces the operating cost of physical devices and also keeps track of the coordination among them. Presently, many IoE systems are implemented based on client-server technology [29]. Various authentication protocols are being used to make the communication system reliable and robust. The client-server-based architectures are facing the problem of data latency. The intrinsic feature of the blockchain provides the decentralization of services to reduce management cost and improve the efficiency of the network. Biswas *et al.* [60] proposed a reliable and efficient blockchain-based framework that ensures security in the exchange of information among various devices in a smart city. The existing clouds are not compatible with the new demands that are needed to be fulfilled to extend the IoE network. The combination of blockchain and other recent technologies, such as fog computing and software-defined networking (SDN) technology, can satisfy the need to develop a novel distributed architecture.

Cloud Computing

The IoE systems are now equipped with cloud computing technologies in which the processed data obtained from various IoE components are stored on clouds. The Cloud computing facilitates the users to access and share data without any kind of interruption in computation, data management, and services. Cloud computing technologies enable IoE systems to dynamically allocate the resource to the network activities without any intervention from the users. A variety of platforms are now available to schedule a pool of activities of IoE objects on the networks [75]. Cloud computing technology is capable of providing hardware and software services to the IoE applications that are being used by the citizens of smart cities. The centralized management platforms control the IoE systems by executing various commands. The execution of commands and their corresponding actions are based on the data retrieved from the IoE-enabled device integrated into the network. Various data mining techniques are being adopted to explore the relevant information from the massive amount of data available on the IoE network. The extracted data can be used in planning and decision-making based on pattern analysis [17]. The cloud computing model of IoE has some disadvantages. First, the network traffic can be congested due to the transmission of the massive amount of data through IoE sensors on the clouds. In cloud computing models, data latency is also another disadvantage. The problem of data latency occurs due to the transmission of information from various sensing devices on the cloud. The reliability of the IoE network is also a challenging issue in the cloud computing model. Researchers have found various challenges to incorporate robust data transmission mechanisms in the IoE network as the size of the network will become bigger.

5G Technology

The 4G systems can only support the speed of data transfer up to 100 Mbits/s. 5G enables effective communication by software-based communication network architecture in which the data rate is up to 10 Gb/s. The high data rate in 5G technology supports the transfer of ultra-high-definition video and images [67]. The high speed of 5G allows downloading of web pages and real-time video in smartphones and is also used in various innovations. 5G supports the execution of real-time applications in which the data latency requirement is less than 1 millisecond. This technology also supports applications that do not require time-critical process control and services. IoE is one of the emerging technology, and its impact can be visible in various smart city's infrastructure due to the adoption of 5G technology [54]. 5G supports various application areas of IoE, such as smart transport systems, smart grids, smart healthcare, and smart industries. To fulfill the requirements of these application areas 5G technology supports massive machine-type communication (MMTC) to send and receive a huge amount of information through IoE sensors and actuators. 5G supports the interconnection of various IoE devices over the network regardless of their position and time to support power grid management and public transportation systems. The incorporation of 5G technology in these areas can save money, time, energy, and resources [64, 86]. Telecom operators are investing in 5G projects for an impact of 5G technologies in the smart city infrastructure. Governments have also initiated awareness programs that support the utilization of 5G infrastructure for the sustainable growth of smart cities.

Geospatial Technology

Geospatial technology is a field of information technology that enables the user to perform various activities on the data, such as data management, analysis, and presentation. Mainly the acquired data provide information about geographic locations, and temporal and spatial relationships of data. In smart cities, geospatial technologies cover various applications such as surveying, photogrammetry, and remote sensing. Systems based on geospatial technologies obtain data from various sensors placed at different locations of smart cities and interpret it to produce useful information such as latitude, longitude, postal codes, *etc.* [80]. The invention of the Global Positioning System (GPS) is a good example of geospatial technology. Geospatial technologies is a multidisciplinary technology that includes remote sensing, Geographic Information System (GIS), Global Positioning System (GPS), and Internet mapping technologies that can be used in smart cities to improve services and minimize costs. Nowadays, geospatial technologies are being integrated with Machine Learning (ML) and Artificial Intelligence (AI). Geospatial AI apps provide real-time data about weather conditions, traffic patterns, trade flow information, *etc.*, to the users. In all geospatial applications, the accuracy of the data is required for better prediction and analysis. Users can demand desired maps using geospatial mapping technology, which is not available online. The customization of the available maps is possible according to the ever-changing behavior of the users. Geospatial imagery and the Mapping as a Service market could reach $8 billion by 2025 [80].

To improve the operations related to agriculture in smart cities, GIS technology can be incorporated. Sensors can collect data about the condition of the land, crop growth, and weather conditions in advance to the farmers for future planning and controlling. Table **1** presents the roles of geospatial technologies in major areas of smart cities.

Table 1. Geospatial Technologies and their applications.

Geospatial Technologies	Applications
Remote Sensing	• Monitoring needs of human beings • Observing ratio of snow melt • Prevention from contingencies • Agriculture • Observing geometry patterns of earth • Defense communities
Geographic Information Systems (GIS)	• To analyses geographic patterns • Environmental analysis • Habitat and archaeological analysis • Natural resource management • Applicable in surveying and operation research

(Table 1) cont.....

Geospatial Technologies	Applications
Global Positioning System (GPS)	• Navigation and control • Monitoring satellite transmission • Construction and mining • Response in emergency • Logistics and services
Internet Mapping Technologies	• Analyzing wind patterns • Traffic patterns on the urban roads • Trade flow prediction • Communication patterns

IOE CHALLENGES FOR SMART CITIES

The concept of IoE enables the digitization of various aspects of citizen's lives and incorporates essential features to the sensing nodes to perform various significant operations. In the successful deployment of IoE networks and integrated IoE-enabled devices, officials of smart cities are facing many challenges. The technological challenges related to the IoE systems and their deployment need to be considered to find optimal solutions. Fig. (**8**) presents various challenges concerned with the security, privacy, data analytics, smart sensors, and networking of IoE-enabled devices.

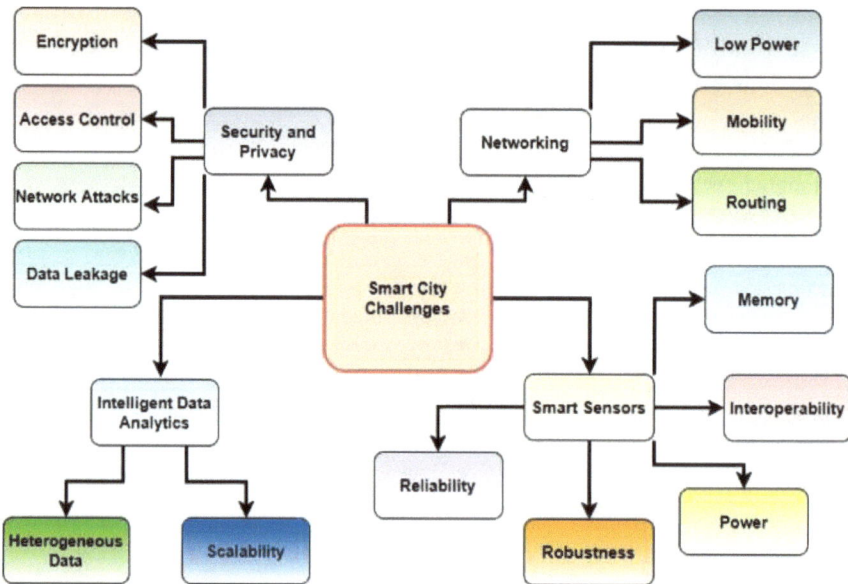

Fig. (8). IoE systems challenges in the sustainable growth of smart cities.

Security and Privacy

Privacy and security are the two main concerns of smart cities. The citizens of smart cities may feel inconvenienced if any defects are found in the operations related to these concerns, and also put the lives of citizens and their properties at high risk. Therefore, security has become the most important aspect of smart cities. In this era, technologies are being advanced day by day, and smart cities are at high risk of being targeted by various attackers over the networks. To protect the user information exchanged through sensors various encryption schemes are being developed and implemented over the networks [46]. To accomplish the smart cities project and their associated tasks, the trust and involvement of the citizens are required. The excess utilization of sensors can also be the main reason for the security breach. The sensitive data related to the various activities of the citizens gathered by the IoE sensors can be exposed to unwanted parties who are not the actual participants/users of the IoE network [19]. Moreover, other third parties can use the sensitive data in targeted advertising. In this context, the secrecy of data and its integrity should be ensured so that effective decisions can be taken on the available data over the network.

Smart Sensors

In an IoE network, the sensors are tangible components that can be used to gather the data of various ongoing activities in smart cities. These devices are manufactured by various vendors that comply with standards and protocols. The data collected by these devices can be used for effective planning, scheduling, and decision-making [14]. In the IoE network, heterogeneous IoE devices are integrated. To bring harmony among these devices and to improve the entire communication system, open protocols and data formats should be utilized to exchange data among IoE devices. The deployment of a standard access point within the IoE systems can also establish compatibility among various IoE-enabled objects to encode and decode the information. The other challenges concerned with smart sensors are dependability and robustness. The sensors are assumed to be reliable and robust so that the entire IoE system can depend on them. In the future, it would be essential to deploy IoE systems in smart cities effectively so that citizens can get a smooth experience of available services. The robust IoE system ensures the availability and quality of services through which the user can get a timely response to their request. IoE systems that are being used to provide critical services such as electricity, water supply, and transport should be decentralized [52]. In present IoE systems, many devices, such as sensors and actuators, require continuous energy to accomplish their assigned operations. The other devices, such as mobile devices and smartwatches consume power from inbuilt batteries to share and access the data from IoE networks. In the future, it is required to develop low-power and low-overhead schemes to exchange data over the IoE network. The development of new schemes of data management can also minimize power consumption and increase the life of inbuilt batteries.

The computation time and requirement of storage can minimize using data compression algorithms in the development of smart cities in the future. To provide solutions concerned with power consumption, it is required to promote energy harvesting mechanisms within the IoE systems. In wireless networks, a limited amount of ambient energy should be utilized to charge integrated wireless devices which are not easily accessible and located at remote locations. The inclusion of energy harvesting mechanisms promotes long-lasting services from the IoE systems [55].

Big Data Analytics

Nowadays, IoE-enabled devices connected to the IoE systems are generating approximately 13.6 Zetta Bytes of data. According to the facts, it is believed that till 2025 this amount of data will increase up to 79.4 Zetta Bytes.

The developers should investigate new data analytics algorithms that can be used for the effective usage of data and to enhance the services and decision-making process. To work on both structured and unstructured data and to develop algorithms based on different parameters of smart cities, some data fusion techniques are essential to be explored [55]. The developers of such algorithms can be leveraged with the inclusion of Data Science and Deep Learning [40] in the area. The newly developed algorithms should be scalable and compatible with the future requirements and ever-changing needs of smart cities. Various techniques, such as predictive analytics and machine learning, are being used in data analytics for the sustainable growth of smart cities. In these techniques, the concept drift is a challenging issue because of variable properties and the nature of data over time which lead to less accurate predictions. To deal with such a problem, Incremental Learning techniques can be utilized. The predicted which is outcome of these techniques should widely acceptable, especially in the case of healthcare systems of smart cities. Rahman *et al.* [87] proposed a deep learning-based healthcare system to improve the healthcare system during the COVID-19 pandemic. The proposed framework is based on Distributed Deep Learning (DDL) paradigm, which generates optimal results. Table **2** shows various challenges of IoE in the sustainable growth of smart cities and some future directions that are needed to be focused on by the researchers.

Table 2. Challenges of IoE systems and some future directions.

Challenges	Solutions/Future Directions
Security and Privacy	• Development of efficient data encryption authentication schemes • New standards to improve services • Inhibit data leakage
Smart Sensors	• Development of open protocols and standards • Incorporation of reliable and robustness IoE sensors • Utilization and implementation of distributed and decentralized services • Incorporation of distributed IoE architectures • Low power consumption • Utilization of energy harvesting mechanism • Development of efficient data management and compression schemes
Networking	• Establishment of low-power networks • Development of network schemes to enable routing
Big data analytics	• Incorporation of recent technologies such as AI, ML, and data science • Development of algorithms to handle different types of data
Socio-Economic	• Planning of awareness programs • Arrangement of funds in advance
Environmental	• Adoption of 5G technology • Initialization of awareness programs • Establishment of new standards

Socio-Economic

The awareness of the citizens plays a very vital role in the cognition of a smart city ecosystem. The dynamic change in technology and its impact on the IoE systems should be acceptable to the citizens of the smart city. Without their agreement on the drastic transformations in various aspects of the smart city, the imagination of their implementation is not possible. Many smart city projects have been initiated by companies in the government and private sectors. There is a chance for the success of the smart city project only when the governments and other private companies arrange proper funds in advance [31]. Due to the non-availability of funds and infrastructure, it is like a dream to complete the projects of smart cities. Educated professionals also have a big hand in the success of the project attached to the smart city. These professionals are well versed with the prevailing technologies nowadays and know very well how to use them in the construction of smart cities. Apart from this, many residents do not have much knowledge of the Internet. They don't know how to mold themselves with the changing technology and development. Such citizens are not well educated and also not aware of the moderation in the guidelines related to smart cities by the government agencies. In this regard, the government should start some awareness programs so that such citizens can get information in time.

Environmental

In the current scenario, stakeholders and officials of smart cities are facing various barriers to the adoption of 5G technology [64, 67]. Natural disasters and preparedness to deal with them are the challenges for the professionals associated with smart city projects. Natural disasters such as floods, earthquakes, and droughts can completely ruin the foundation of the smart city ecosystem. Other challenges, such as problems arising from the adverse effects of greenhouse gases and sudden changes in weather patterns, can also greatly affect the ecosystem of smart cities. The increasing population in smart cities is also responsible for the deterioration of the smart city ecosystem. Pollution and garbage increase with the increasing population. In this context, E-waste management is a very good example. The E-waste management system within the smart cities can be used to schedule various activities of the E-waste management team in advance and also minimize the time and cost of the utilized resources [88]. Many devices are being used in the IoE system of smart cities. The technologies related to these objects have now obsolete. The excessive use of such devices is not environmentally sound. In this context, the government should be taken some concrete steps to establish some standards to minimize their adverse effects on the sustainable growth of smart cities.

CONCLUSION AND FUTURE SCOPE

This paper provides a comprehensive knowledge about the Internet of Everything (IoE) and enabling technologies in the sustainable growth of smart cities. The detailed discussion on different domains of smart cities provides insight into various challenges that are being faced in the deployment of smart cities. The chapter explores various IoE applications and their vital roles in smart city architecture. Although existing technologies are very advanced, the imaginary world of a smart city is like a dream to developing nations. Stakeholders, officials, and the government initiated many steps in this regard to work tighter in this direction. Security and privacy are the primary concerns of the smart city. Efficient and lightweight algorithms and protocols are being deployed to secure the communication process over the IoE networks. The cyber-physical system plays a critical role in the sustainable development of smart cities.

Researchers are trying to develop a novel framework to provide some cost-effective solutions for smart cities. In many smart cities, enabling technologies are being used to provide a holistic environment that is transparent, eco-friendly, secure, and automated. The government has established various standards that need to be focused on to minimize the carbon substances in the environment while deploying smart cities. The international standard implemented by global expert ensure that the technologies and resources that are being used in the deployment of smart cities are safe. The performance and smartness of smart cities can be measured by the adopted standards in the smart cities projects. These standards provide some guidelines to minimize waste disposal in the surrounding areas, energy management in smart grids, and optimal use of services. The advent of nanotechnology influences various application areas, such as smart agriculture, smart healthcare, smart transportation, *etc.* The utilization of nanomaterials in the development of IoE devices reduces space, cost, deployment time, pollution, and energy consumption. In the development of smart cities, the adoption of quantum computing technology can play a crucial role in real-time decision-making and analysis due to its fast response and complex computation capabilities.

Nowadays, the incorporation of recent technologies, such as blockchain, artificial intelligence, and machine learning, re becoming an integral part of smart city architecture. The existence of these technologies in the various aspects of smart cities satisfies various requirements of the citizens and increases a certain level of trust in their minds. The other emerging technology, such as 5G, can be used to devise various strategies to design smart governance and improves B5G communications in smart cities. The technologies discussed in this chapter present their growing role in the development of smart healthcare systems for effective diagnosis, data analysis, and security of IoE-based health monitoring systems. In the existence of recent technologies, researchers in their study trying to discover new medicines, solutions, and effective ways of diagnosis. The concept of industry 4.0 is a building block of the smart city. Industries in smart cities are the essential part that cannot be ignored for their sustainable growth. To develop a fully automated infrastructure of smart cities, it is required to focus on the implementation of efficient information-sharing systems, minimization of resources, smart economy, and accessibility of real-time services. To improve the public transportation systems within the smart cities, some effective transportation service level guidelines should define by the government and other private agencies.

In this chapter, several suggestions related to the utilization of IoE systems in smart cities have been made. After reviewing the literature, it has been found that security and privacy are the major concerned areas in the smart city. Researchers need to focus on the development of more secure encryption schemes, authentication protocols, and more efficient algorithms that can prevent unauthorized access of IoE objects. To deploy smart cities in the nation, recent technologies such as artificial intelligence, machine learning, and blockchain should be adopted for the sustainable growth of smart cities. With the advancement of technologies, attackers are inventing new ways to steal sensitive data from the IoE network. In this case, the most common threat is Phishing.

Stockholders such as research organizations, and government agencies try to find out ways through which blockchain technology can be included in smart city projects. In the development of smart cities, all the hardware and software should be replaced by the smart cities network that is based on obsolete technologies. The utilization of lightweight algorithms and procedures can significantly reduce the power needed for the execution of IoE devices. The network of smart cities should be created by integrating low-power devices to reduce carbon emissions in the environment. The other major area that needs to focus on is the development of some efficient storage mechanisms to store the massive amount of data for better decision and analysis. Researchers need to opt for optimal ways to decentralize the whole system of smart cities to provide real-time services to the citizens. The decentralization of services in smart cities can improve the standard of living of citizens. In the development of smart cities, data fusion technology should be adopted so that useful information can be extracted from the raw data transmitted from heterogeneous sources such as sensors, human feedback, and other IoE-enabled devices over the IoE network. Future research should in focused on the incorporation of nanotechnology and quantum computing to find out the solutions to various challenges and issues of IoE networks within smart cities. Private and government agencies should establish new standards, parameters, guidelines, and evaluation metrics that can be used to quantify the performance of smart cities. Researchers need to discover new sustainability metrics that can incorporate all the parameters and components that can be used to quantify the sustainability of smart cities and their surrounding areas. The government of the nation needs to focus on the legal system and implement new rules and regulations to resolve dispute among stakeholders, officials, and other transacting parties.

REFERENCES

[1]   C.S. Lai, Y. Jia, Z. Dong, D. Wang, Y. Tao, Q.H. Lai, R.T.K. Wong, A.F. Zobaa, R. Wu, and L.L. Lai, "A review of technical standards for smart cities", *Cleanroom Technol.*, vol. 2, no. 3, pp. 290-310, 2020.
[http://dx.doi.org/10.3390/cleantechnol2030019]

[2]   B. Or, and S. Our, "Standards Iso standards are internationally agreed", Available from: https://www.iso.org/standards.html (Accessed 06 March 2022)

[3]   K. Foreman, "Vision and mission", *Strateg. Manag. Sch. Coll.*, 2012. Available from: https://www.iec.ch/what-we-do (Accessed 06 March 2022)

[4]   B.A. Member, and O.F. Itu, "About International Telecommunication Union (ITU)", 2021. Available from: https://www.itu.int/en/about/Pages/default.aspx (Accessed 06 March 2022)

[5]   S. Djahel, R. Doolan, G.M. Muntean, and J. Murphy, "A communications-oriented perspective on traffic management systems for smart cities: Challenges and innovative approaches", *IEEE Commun. Surv. Tutor.*, vol. 17, no. 1, pp. 125-151, 2015.
[http://dx.doi.org/10.1109/COMST.2014.2339817]

[6]   C.T. Barba, M.Á. Mateos, P.R. Soto, A.M. Mezher, and M.A. Igartua, "Smart city for VANETs using

warning messages, traffic statistics and intelligent traffic lights", *IEEE Intell. Veh. Symp. Proc.,* pp. 902-907, 2012.
[http://dx.doi.org/10.1109/IVS.2012.6232229]

[7]   G. Kakarontzas, L. Anthopoulos, D. Chatzakou, and A. Vakali, "A conceptual enterprise architecture framework for smart cities: A survey based approach", *Jt. Conf. E-bus. Telecommun.,* pp. 47-54, 2014.
[http://dx.doi.org/10.5220/0005021400470054]

[8]   G. Zhang, J. Gu, Z. Bao, C. Xu, and S. Zhang, "Joint routing and channel assignment algorithms in cognitive wireless mesh networks", *Trans. Emerg. Telecommun. Technol.,* vol. 25, no. 3, pp. 294-307, 2014.
[http://dx.doi.org/10.1002/ett.2560]

[9]   A. Hussain, R. Wenbi, A.L. da Silva, M. Nadher, and M. Mudhish, "Health and emergency-care platform for the elderly and disabled people in the Smart City", *J. Syst. Softw.,* vol. 110, pp. 253-263, 2015.
[http://dx.doi.org/10.1016/j.jss.2015.08.041]

[10]   J.M. Hernández-Muñoz, J.B. Vercher, L. Muñoz, J.A. Galache, M. Presser, L.A.H. Gómez, and J. Pettersson, "Smart cities at the forefront of the future internet", *The Future Internet,* vol. 6656, pp. 447-462, 2011.
[http://dx.doi.org/10.1007/978-3-642-20898-0_32]

[11]   D. Pérez-González, and R. Díaz-Díaz, "Public services provided with ICT in the smart city environment: The case of Spanish cities", *J. Univers. Comput. Sci.,* vol. 21, no. 2, pp. 248-267, 2015.

[12]   S. Yamamoto, S. Matsumoto, S. Saiki, and M. Nakamura, "Using materialized view as a service of scallop4sc for smart city application services", *Adv. Intel. Sys. Comp.,* vol. 271, pp. 51-60, 2014.
[http://dx.doi.org/10.1007/978-3-319-05527-5_6]

[13]   E. Asimakopoulou, and N. Bessis, "Buildings and crowds: Forming smart cities for more effective disaster management", *Proc. 5th Int. Conf. Innov. Mob. Internet Serv. Ubiquitous Comput. IMIS,* pp. 229-234, 2011.
[http://dx.doi.org/10.1109/IMIS.2011.129]

[14]   B. Hammi, R. Khatoun, S. Zeadally, A. Fayad, and L. Khoukhi, "IoT technologiesfor smart cities", *IET Netw.,* vol. 7, no. 1, pp. 1-13, 2018.
[http://dx.doi.org/10.1049/iet-net.2017.0163]

[15]   E. Ismagilova, L. Hughes, N.P. Rana, and Y.K. Dwivedi, "Security, privacy and risks within smart cities: Literature review and development of a smart city interaction framework", *Inf. Syst. Front.,* pp. 1-22, 2020.

[16]   E. Zanaj, G. Caso, L. De Nardis, A. Mohammadpour, Ö. Alay, and M.G. Di Benedetto, "Energy efficiency in short and wide-area iot technologies : A survey", *Technologies,* vol. 9, no. 1, p. 22, 2021.
[http://dx.doi.org/10.3390/technologies9010022]

[17]   R. Petrolo, V. Loscrì, and N. Mitton, "Towards a smart city based on cloud of things", *Proc. of the 2014 ACM International Workshop on Wireless and Mobile Technology for smart cities,* pp. 61-65, 2014.
[http://dx.doi.org/10.1145/2633661.2633667]

[18]   I. Belle, "The smart city, integrated design and planning and urban tech", *24th International Conference on Urban Development,* pp. 793-798, 2019.

[19]   A. Ali, Z. AlMeraj, and P. Manuel, "Challenges of IoT based smart-government development", *21st Saudi Computer Society National Computer Conference (NCC),* pp. 1-6, 2018.

[20]   Available from: https://www.businesswire.com/portal/site/home/my-business-wire/

[21]   Available   from: https://www.investindia.gov.in/team-india-blogs/smart-city-mission-greatest-opportunity-improve-lives

[22]   R. Giffinger, C. Fertner, H. Kramar, and E. Meijers, "Cities-ranking of European medium-sized cities, January", *Cent. Reg. Sci. Vienna UT,* vol. 9, pp. 1-12, 2007.

[23]   M. Angelidou, *Strategic planning for the development of smart cities* PhD thesis, University of Thessaloniki, IKEE/Aristotle University of Thessaloniki–Library, 2015.

[24]   W. Ejaz, and A. Anpalagan, "Internet of things for Smart Cities: Overview and Key Challenges", In: *In: Internet of Things for Smart Cities. SpringerBriefs in Electrical and Computer Engineering.* Springer, Cham, 2019, pp. 1-15.
[http://dx.doi.org/10.1007/978-3-319-95037-2_1]

[25]   Available from: https://www.smartercitieschallenge.org/

[26]   A.K. Singh, A. Solanki, A. Nayyar, and B. Qureshi, "Elliptic curve signcryption-based mutual authentication protocol for smart cards", *Appl. Sci.,* vol. 10, no. 22, p. 8291, 2020.
[http://dx.doi.org/10.3390/app10228291]

[27]   M. Sookhak, H. Tang, Y. He, and F.R. Yu, "Security and privacy of smart cities: A survey, research issues and challenges", *IEEE Commun. Surv. Tutor.,* vol. 21, no. 2, pp. 1718-1743, 2019.
[http://dx.doi.org/10.1109/COMST.2018.2867288]

[28]   F. Al-turjman, H. Zahmatkesh, and R. Shahroze, "An overview of security and privacy in smart cities' IoT communications", *Trans. Emerg. Telecommun. Technol.,* p. e3677, 2019.

[29]   L. Cui, G. Xie, Y. Qu, L. Gao, and Y. Yang, "Security and privacy in smart cities: Challenges and opportunities", *IEEE Access,* vol. 6, pp. 46134-46145, 2018.
[http://dx.doi.org/10.1109/ACCESS.2018.2853985]

[30]   K. Kavta, and P.K. Yadav, "Indian smart cities and their financing: A first look", In: *From Poverty.* Inequality to Smart City, 2017, pp. 123-141.
[http://dx.doi.org/10.1007/978-981-10-2141-1_9]

[31]   R.S. Galati, "Funding a Smart City: From concept to actuality", In: *Smart Cities.* Springer: Cham, 2018, pp. 17-39.
[http://dx.doi.org/10.1007/978-3-319-59381-4_2]

[32]   M. Vitunskaite, Y. He, T. Brandstetter, and H. Janicke, "Smart cities and cyber security: Are we there yet?A comparative study on the role of standards, third party risk management and security ownership", *Comput. Secur.,* vol. 83, pp. 313-331, 2019.
[http://dx.doi.org/10.1016/j.cose.2019.02.009]

[33]   S. Bayer, H. Gimpel, and D. Rau, "IoT-commerce : Opportunities for customers through an affordance lens", *Electron. Mark.,* vol. 31, no. 1, pp. 27-50, 2021.
[http://dx.doi.org/10.1007/s12525-020-00405-8]

[34]   B-Y. Ooi, and S. Shirmohammadi, "The potential of IoT for instrumentation and measurement", *IEEE Instrum. Meas. Mag.,* vol. 23, no. 3, pp. 21-26, 2020.
[http://dx.doi.org/10.1109/MIM.2020.9082794]

[35]   P. Marques, D. Manfroi, E. Deitos, J. Cegoni, R. Castilhos, J. Rochol, E. Pignaton, and R. Kunst, "An IoT-based smart cities infrastructure architecture applied to a waste management scenario", *Ad Hoc Netw.,* vol. 87, pp. 200-208, 2019.
[http://dx.doi.org/10.1016/j.adhoc.2018.12.009]

[36]   J. Korczak, and K. Kijewska, "Smart logistics in the development of smart cities", *Transp. Res. Procedia,* vol. 39, pp. 201-211, 2019.
[http://dx.doi.org/10.1016/j.trpro.2019.06.022]

[37]   Q. Liu, J. Gu, J. Yang, Y. Li, D. Sha, M. Xu, I. Shams, M. Yu, and C. Yang, "Cloud, edge, and mobile computing for smart cities", *Urban Book Series,* pp. 757-795, 2021.
[http://dx.doi.org/10.1007/978-981-15-8983-6_41]

[38]   O. Iatrellis, T. Panagiotakopoulos, V.C. Gerogiannis, P. Fitsilis, and A. Kameas, "Cloud computing

and semantic web technologies for ubiquitous management of smart cities-related competences", *Educ. Inf. Technol.,* vol. 26, no. 2, pp. 2143-2164, 2021.
[http://dx.doi.org/10.1007/s10639-020-10351-9]

[39]   S. Bhattacharya, S.R.K. Somayaji, T.R. Gadekallu, M. Alazab, and P.K.R. Maddikunta, "A review on deep learning for future smart cities", *Internet Technol. Lett.,* p. e187, 2020.

[40]   Z. Ullah, F. Al-Turjman, L. Mostarda, and R. Gagliardi, "Applications of artificial intelligence and machine learning in smart cities", *Comput. Commun.,* vol. 154, pp. 313-323, 2020.
[http://dx.doi.org/10.1016/j.comcom.2020.02.069]

[41]   N. Neyestani, M. Y. Damavandi, M. Shafie-khah, and J.P. Catalão, "Modeling the PEV traffic pattern in an urban environment with parking lots and charging stations", *2015 IEEE Eindhoven PowerTech,* pp. 1-6, 2015.
[http://dx.doi.org/10.1109/PTC.2015.7232637]

[42]   A. Lavalle, M.A. Teruel, A. Maté, and J. Trujillo, "Improving sustainability of smart cities through visualization techniques for big data from iot devices", *Sustainability,* vol. 12, no. 14, p. 5595, 2020.
[http://dx.doi.org/10.3390/su12145595]

[43]   A. Wadhwa, and V.K. Gupta, "Practical implementation and analysis of MLBAAC model for cloud", *Int. J. Comp. Eng. Tech.,* vol. 9, no. 3, pp. 14-22, 2018.

[44]   A. Wadhwa, "Analysis of multilevel security based service access control and data protection approach for cloud", *Int. J. Adv. Sci. Tech.,* vol. 29, no. 5, pp. 11136-11145, 2020.

[45]   A. Wadhwa, "Security approaches and implementation for data protection over cloud", *J. Emerg. Technol. Innov. Res.,* vol. 6, no. 5, pp. 500-503, 2019.

[46]   A.K. Singh, and B.D.K. Patro, "Security of low computing power devices: A survey of requirements, challenges & possible solutions", *Cybern. Inf. Technol.,* vol. 19, no. 1, pp. 133-164, 2019.
[http://dx.doi.org/10.2478/cait-2019-0008]

[47]   A.K. Singh, and B.D.K. Patro, "Elliptic curve signcryption based security protocol for RFID", *Trans. Internet Inf. Syst.,* vol. 14, no. 1, 2020.

[48]   X. Li, J. Liu, Q.Z. Sheng, S. Zeadally, and W. Zhong, "TMS-RFID: Temporal management of large-scale RFID applications", *Inf. Syst. Front.,* vol. 13, no. 4, pp. 481-500, 2011.
[http://dx.doi.org/10.1007/s10796-009-9211-y]

[49]   I. Jawhar, N. Mohamed, and J. Al-Jaroodi, "Networking architectures and protocols for smart city systems", *J. Internet Serv. Appl.,* vol. 9, no. 1, p. 26, 2018.
[http://dx.doi.org/10.1186/s13174-018-0097-0]

[50]   C. Chakraborty, A. Banerjee, M.H. Kolekar, L. Garg, and B. Chakraborty, *Internet of things for Healthcare Technologies,* Springer, 2020.

[51]   J.P. Bello, C. Mydlarz, and J. Salamon, "Sound analysis in smart cities", In: *Computational Analysis of Sound Scenes and Events,* 2018, pp. 373-397.
[http://dx.doi.org/10.1007/978-3-319-63450-0_13]

[52]   R. Gade, and T.B. Moeslund, "Thermal cameras and applications: A survey", *Mach. Vis. Appl.,* vol. 25, no. 1, pp. 245-262, 2014.
[http://dx.doi.org/10.1007/s00138-013-0570-5]

[53]   E. Vattapparamban, I. Güvenç, A.I. Yurekli, K. Akkaya, and S. Uluağaç, "Drones for smart cities: Issues in cybersecurity, privacy, and public safety", In: *International wireless communications and mobile computing conference.* IWCMC, 2016, pp. 216-221.

[54]   S. Kaza, L. Yao, P. Bhada-Tata, and F. Van Woerden, *What a waste 2.0: A global snapshot of solid waste management to 2050.* World Bank Publications, 2018.
[http://dx.doi.org/10.1596/978-1-4648-1329-0]

[55]   A.S. Syed, D. Sierra-Sosa, A. Kumar, and A. Elmaghraby, "IoT in smart cities: A survey of

technologies, practices and challenges", *Smart Cities,* vol. 4, no. 2, pp. 429-475, 2021.
[http://dx.doi.org/10.3390/smartcities4020024]

[56]   P.A. Keane, and E.J. Topol, "With an eye to AI and autonomous diagnosis", *npj.Digit. Med.,* vol. 1, no. 1, pp. 1-3, 2018.

[57]   A. Garg, and A. Negi, "Structure preservation in content-aware image retargeting using multi-operator", *IET Image Process.,* vol. 14, no. 13, pp. 2965-2975, 2020.
[http://dx.doi.org/10.1049/iet-ipr.2019.1032]

[58]   A. Garg, and A. Negi, "A survey on image resizing methods", *KSII Trans. Int. Inform. Tech.,* vol. 14, no. 7, pp. 2997-3017, 2020.

[59]   A. Garg, A. Negi, and P. Jindal, "Structure preservation of image using an efficient content-aware image retargeting technique", *Sig. Ima.Vid. Proc.,* vol. 15, no. 1, pp. 185-193, 2021.
[http://dx.doi.org/10.1007/s11760-020-01736-x]

[60]   K. Biswas, and V. Muthukkumarasamy, "Securing smart cities using blockchain technology", In: *2016 IEEE 18th International Conference on High Performance Computing and Communications*, 2016, pp. 1392-1393.
[http://dx.doi.org/10.1109/HPCC-SmartCity-DSS.2016.0198]

[61]   S. Ibba, A. Pinna, and M. Seu, "CitySense: Blockchain-oriented smart cities", *Proc. of the XP2017 Scientific Workshops,* pp. 1-5, 2017.

[62]   M.A. Ahad, and R. Biswas, "Request-based, secured and energy-efficient (RBSEE) architecture for handling IoT big data", *J. Inf. Sci.,* vol. 45, no. 2, pp. 227-238, 2019.
[http://dx.doi.org/10.1177/0165551518787699]

[63]   M.A. Ahad, and R. Biswas, "Comparing and analyzing the characteristics of hadoop, cassandra and quantcast file systems for handling big data", *Indian J. Sci. Technol.,* vol. 10, no. 8, pp. 1-6, 2017.
[http://dx.doi.org/10.17485/ijst/2017/v10i8/105400]

[64]   K.E. Skouby, and P. Lynggaard, "Smart home and smart city solutions enabled by 5G, IoT, AAI and CoT services", *2014 International Conference on Contemporary Computing and Informatics (IC3I),* pp. 874-878, 2014.
[http://dx.doi.org/10.1109/IC3I.2014.7019822]

[65]   M. Batty, "Big data, smart cities and city planning", *Dialogues Hum. Geogr.,* vol. 3, no. 3, pp. 274-279, 2013.
[http://dx.doi.org/10.1177/2043820613513390]

[66]   Z. Allam, and Z.A. Dhunny, "On big data, artificial intelligence and smart cities", *Cities,* vol. 89, pp. 80-91, 2019.
[http://dx.doi.org/10.1016/j.cities.2019.01.032]

[67]   Available   from: https://www.techrepublic.com/article/5g-will-bring-smart-cities-to-life-in-un-xpected-ways/

[68]   S.E. Bibri, and J. Krogstie, "Smart eco-city strategies and solutions for sustainability: The cases of Royal Seaport, Stockholm, and Western Harbor, Malmö, Sweden", *Urban Science,* vol. 4, no. 1, p. 11, 2020.
[http://dx.doi.org/10.3390/urbansci4010011]

[69]   Available from: https://team.inria.fr/ease/

[70]   R. Khatoun, and S. Zeadally, "Smart cities", *Commun. ACM,* vol. 59, no. 8, pp. 46-57, 2016.
[http://dx.doi.org/10.1145/2858789]

[71]   R.A. Moussa, "King Abdullah Economic City: The Growth of New Sustainable City in Saudi Arabia", In: *New Cities and Community Extensions in Egypt and the Middle East.* pp. 51-69, 2019.
[http://dx.doi.org/10.1007/978-3-319-77875-4_4]

[72]   K. Saravanan, E.G. Julie, and Y.H. Robinson, "Smart cities & IoT: Evolution of applications,

architectures & technologies, present scenarios & future dream", *Intell. Sys. Ref. Lib.*, vol. 154, pp. 135-151, 2019.
[http://dx.doi.org/10.1007/978-3-030-04203-5_7]

[73] P.S. Saarika, K. Sandhya, and T. Sudha, "Smart transportation system using IoT", *2017 Int. Conf. Smart Technol. Smart. Nat. (SmartTechCon)*, pp. 1104-1107, 2017.
[http://dx.doi.org/10.1109/SmartTechCon.2017.8358540]

[74] M. Lom, O. Pribyl, and M. Svitek, "Industry 4.0 as a part of smart cities", *2016 Smart Cities Symposium Prague (SCSP)*, pp. 1-6, 2016.
[http://dx.doi.org/10.1109/SCSP.2016.7501015]

[75] E.F.Z. Santana, A.P. Chaves, M.A. Gerosa, F. Kon, and D.S. Milojicic, "Software platforms for smart cities", *ACM Comput. Surv.*, vol. 50, no. 6, pp. 1-37, 2018.
[http://dx.doi.org/10.1145/3124391]

[76] M.A. Ahad, S. Paiva, G. Tripathi, and N. Feroz, "Enabling technologies and sustainable smart cities", *Sustain Cities Soc.*, vol. 61, p. 102301, 2020.
[http://dx.doi.org/10.1016/j.scs.2020.102301]

[77] J. White, S. Clarke, C. Groba, B. Dougherty, C. Thompson, and D.C. Schmidt, "R&D challenges and solutions for mobile cyber-physical applications and supporting Internet services", *J. Internet Serv. Appl.*, vol. 1, no. 1, pp. 45-56, 2010.
[http://dx.doi.org/10.1007/s13174-010-0004-9]

[78] A. Garg, and A.K. Singh, "Applications of Internet of Things (IoT) in Green Computing", In: *Intelligence of Things: AI-IoT Based Critical-Applications and Innovations.* pp. 1-34, 2021.
[http://dx.doi.org/10.1007/978-3-030-82800-4_1]

[79] J.M. Bohli, A. Skarmeta, M.V. Moreno, D. García, and P. Langendörfer, "SMARTIE project: Secure IoT data management for smart cities", *2015 International Conference on Recent Advances in Internet of things (RIoT)*, pp. 1-6, 2015.
[http://dx.doi.org/10.1109/RIOT.2015.7104906]

[80] D. Li, J. Shan, Z. Shao, X. Zhou, and Y. Yao, "Geomatics for smart cities-concept, key techniques, and applications", *Geo Spat. Inf. Sci.*, vol. 16, no. 1, pp. 13-24, 2013.
[http://dx.doi.org/10.1080/10095020.2013.772803]

[81] A. Lele, "Internet of things (IoT)", In: *Disruptive Technologies for the Militaries and Security. Smart Innovation, Systems and Technologies* vol. 132. Springer: Singapore, 2019, pp. 187-195.
[http://dx.doi.org/10.1007/978-981-13-3384-2_11]

[82] A. Wadhwa, and V.K. Gupta, "Proposed framework with comparative analysis of access control & authentication based security models employed over cloud", *Int. J. Appl. Eng. Res.*, vol. 12, no. 24, pp. 15715-15722, 2017.

[83] A. Wadhwa, "Comprehensive analysis of security issues and solutions while migrating to cloud environment", *Int. J. New. Innov. Eng.Tech.*, vol. 4, no. 4, pp. 127-130, 2016.

[84] A. Wadhwa, "Proposed technique for securing critical data over cloud", *J. Emerg. Technol. Innov. Res.*, vol. 5, no. 5, pp. 592-595, 2018.

[85] A. Wadhwa, and A. Garg, "Studying and analyzing virtualization while transition from classical to virtualized data center", *Int. J. Comput. Appl.*, vol. 117, no. 14, pp. 10-14, 2015.
[http://dx.doi.org/10.5120/20620-3341]

[86] A.K. Singh, and A. Garg, "Applications of signal processing", In: *Machine Learning in Signal Processing* Springer, 2021, pp. 73-95.
[http://dx.doi.org/10.1201/9781003107026-4]

[87] M.A. Rahman, M.S. Hossain, N.A. Alrajeh, and N. Guizani, "B5G and explainable deep learning assisted healthcare vertical at the edge: COVID-I9 perspective", *IEEE Netw.*, vol. 34, no. 4, pp. 98-105, 2020.

[http://dx.doi.org/10.1109/MNET.011.2000353]

[88]   M. Aazam, M. St-Hilaire, C.H. Lung, and I. Lambadaris, "Cloud-based smart waste management for smart cities", *2016 IEEE 21st International Workshop on Computer Aided Modelling and Design of Communication Links and Networks (CAMAD),* pp. 188-193, 2016. [http://dx.doi.org/10.1109/CAMAD.2016.7790356]

CHAPTER 5

Smart Cities Emergence with Artificial Intelligence- Natural Language Processing

Sandeep Kumar[1,*], **Arun Solanki**[3] and **Anand Paul**[2]

[1] *Gautam Buddha University, Greater Noida, Uttar Pradesh, India*

[2] *The School of CSE, Kyungpook National University, Daegu, South Korea*

[3] *Department of Computer Science and Engineering, School of ICT Gautam Buddha University, Greater Noida, India*

Abstract: In this digital world integrating smart city concepts, a smart city is a technically advanced metropolitan region that collects data using various electronic technologies, voice recognition methods, and sensor devices. It would not be wrong to say that this smart city is based on the Internet of things (IoT) and artificial intelligence (AI). The IoT and AI are closely related. IoT systems generate big data, and data is at the heart of AI and machine learning. Simultaneously, as the number of linked devices and sensors expands, the importance of smart technologies is also growing faster in this domain. These technologies enable contextual understanding and allow smart devices to solve our problems. Today, the applications of computational intelligence in IoT products and smart devices used in smart cities vary. AI can be leveraged to drive efficiency and improve human living quality for the smart cities of tomorrow. NLP gives the powers to AI tools that recognize and respond in natural Language. This chapter focused on a definite area of AI called Natural Language Processing, which helps and enhances human living in smart cities. There are many use cases where this AI technology makes sense for smart cities. Computerized healthcare services assist policymakers in implementing smart cities in becoming brighter, using opinion mining and permission to remodel a house. These use cases are achieved and discuss various applications, scopes, techniques, advantages, disadvantages, and future scope of NLP of AI in Smart Cities.

Keywords: Deep neural network, Internet of things, NLP pipeline, Natural language processing, Smart cities, Text mining, Text summarization.

INTRODUCTION

Nowadays, a Smart city is a trendy concept for any developing nation. The Internet of things helps to achieve the purpose of nation-building and its citizens.

---

* **Corresponding author Sandeep Kumar:** Gautam Buddha University, Greater Noida, Uttar Pradesh, India; E-mail: sk136398@gmail.com

Arun Solanki and Anuj Kumar Singh (Eds.)

With a massive number of homogeneous and heterogeneous systems, it would be possible to communicate transparently and seamlessly, whereas access to data will be selected for designing many digital services. Our life is now being affected by a new word, the Internet of Things. Now the world is becoming borderless. People are linked together by means of technology, goods, electronics, and web-enabled tools, resulting in the development of lucrative and creative new services. The Internet of things (IoT) is a system that connects devices to the Internet. A number of sensors provide access to the physical environment. As of 2011, the number of devices connected to the Internet (12.5 billion) had exceeded the number of humans on the planet (7 billion), which number the number of devices connected to the Internet is expected to be between twenty-six billion to fifty billion worldwide during the year 2020. Various countries, such as the United States, China, North/South Korea and Japan, have preparations to take advantage of IoT services. India is not ready to be left behind in this smart city race. IoT is ready to build faster. The center-sponsored scheme will drive entry into India as a mission. The central government gave a financial proposal of 48,000 crore rupees in support over five years and planned to set up a hundred Smart Cities buildings across the country.

LITERATURE REVIEW

The Internet of Things (IoT) has been established, ultimately resulting from the expansion of traditional networks, which connect billions of connected devices; information and communication technologies have become widely used in regular human activities in recent years and incorporated into urban strategies [1]. This type of technical innovation is regarded to be significant since it is used to bring answers to urban challenges [2]. Furthermore, various elements of people's health issues, transportation, energy usage, education, knowledge transfer, and governance are covered by digital information [3, 4]. With the advent of information and communication technology in urban development actions, the idea of a smart city, which is really the successor to preceding notions (for example, digital city and intelligent city), was proposed [5]. The phrase "smart city" has been around since the late 1990s, but it wasn't until the mid-2010s that it really took off and became widely debated in industry and academic journals [6]. Sustainable cities, smart cities, urban ICT, sustainable urban development, sustainability and environmental challenges, and urbanisation and urban expansion were all used to create this idea [7, 8]. Green building management helps in smart city development and provides the key to a sustainable global solution for smart building [9, 10].

Smart city applications come in a wide variety of shapes and sizes. The strategy for implementation is what they share in common. Municipalities should start a basic smart city platform- whether they want to automate rubbish collection or enhance street lighting. When smart city manager wants to increase the breadth of smart city services in the future, new tools and technologies may be added to the existing architecture without having to rebuild it [11, 12]. To be able to grow, the implementation should begin with the creation of basic architecture, which acts like a springboard for future expansions and agrees with introducing new services without sacrificing functional performance. A basic IoT system for smart cities is made up of four components [13].

The Smart Things Network

Like any other IoT system, a smart city uses smart objects with sensors and actuators. The sensors' primary objective is to gather and transmit data to a central cloud management platform. Actuators enable equipment to do tasks such as changing the lights, limiting water flow to a leaky pipe, and so on.

Gateway

A "tangible" element of IoT devices and network nodes, as well as a cloud part, make up every IoT system. Data cannot easily be transferred from one section to another. Doors - field gates – must exist. Field gateways make data collection and compression easier by pre-processing and filtering data before sending it to the cloud. A smart city solution's cloud gateway guarantees safe data transfer between field gateways and the cloud.

Data Lake

A data lake is a component of IoT. Its main work is to store the original form of data. When the data is needed for relevant insights, it is extracted and delivered to the big data warehouse, where data are stored in a well-structured format.

Warehouse for Big Data

A single data repository is referred to as a vast data warehouse. It includes exclusively structured data, unlike data lakes. Data is extracted, converted, and placed into the big data warehouse once its worth has been determined. It also saves contextual information on related items, such as whether sensors were installed or not and the device commands that control apps send to devices' actuators.

Fig. (1) shows how IoT components collect data from the environment and create big data. A sensor detects some environmental event and translates that into an electrical signal. An actuator is more or less the opposite of an electrical signal, and it causes some event in the environment. The Gateways help to store sensor data in Data Lake. It keeps data in its original form. The data is extracted and sent to the big data warehouse for useful information. In the big data warehouse, data are well structured and well formatted.

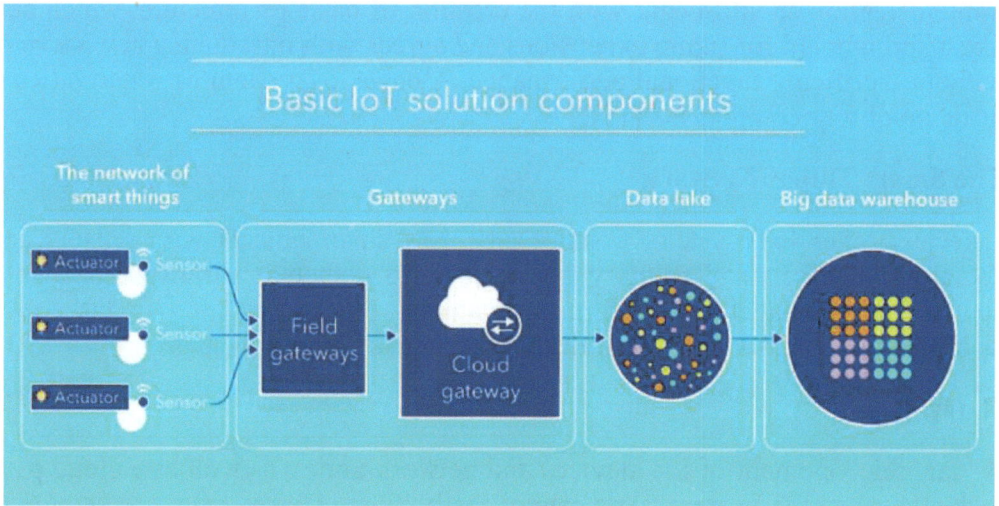

Fig. (1). Basic Smart IoT Device Components [13].

SMART CITY CONCEPTS

Generally, a smart city, on the other hand, is a purpose that uses technology to offer services and resolve issues. Transportation and accessibility, as well as social services, sustainability, and public engagement, are all smart city goals. The term "smart city" is a relatively recent one, but the concept is not-aspects of this concept, such as using technology to make residents' lives easier. Water drainage systems and aqueducts are two examples of how this may be done. The main goals of smart cities are to enhance policy efficiency, reduce waste, improve economic and social quality, and promote social justice. A developed metropolitan area excels in numerous important categories: economy, transportation, environment, people, and government. Strong human capital, social capital, and ICT infrastructure may help you excel in several crucial areas [14].

Smart City Concept

The smart city concepts define how to make a city smarter with multiple perspectives. Fig. (2) shows some perspectives of smart city concepts, such as smart infrastructure, health, energy, traffic, air quality, *etc.*

Fig. (2). Smart city concepts [15].

Smart Infrastructure

For effective structural care, regular monitoring of actual building conditions and identifying regions with the most significant impact by external agents is essential [16]. The Internet of Things may access a distributed database, including structural measures collected by sensors in buildings. Sensors to monitor pollution levels, temperature and humidity sensors, and vibration and deformation sensors to examine building stress are just a few examples. It is possible to include seismic measurements and vibrations to better understand and research the effects of mild earthquakes on municipal structures. The sensors must be installed in buildings and surrounding regions and be connected to a control system.

Smart Health

Patient's vital signs, such as heart rate, temperature, pulse, and breathing, should all be monitored. Warnings and alarms for life-threatening cases are sent in hospitals and at remote patient sites such as ambulances and older people's homes. To assist mentally ill patients, babies, and young children by utilizing pertinent data from various digital sensors inside the IoT network.

Traffic Congestion

The Internet of Things can monitor traffic congestion in a city. Although camera-based traffic monitoring systems are currently in place and used in many metropolitan areas, low-power ubiquitous communication provides a better source of information. GPS tracking is used to keep track of newer automobiles. City officials must control traffic and dispatch cops as required, while residents must plan for a shopping trip or a route to work.

Smart Energy

A service powered by IoT may assist in monitoring the city's energy use, giving authorities and residents a precise picture of how much energy is used for things like public building heating and cooling, traffic lights, public lighting, control cameras, and transit. This will make it easier to isolate the primary sources of energy usage and set priorities accordingly. The power drawing monitoring devices must be connected to the local power grid. Active functions to control local power generation infrastructure can also be added to these services.

Air Quality Management

Due to busy neighborhoods, parks, and other factors, city air is contaminated. The Internet of Things will enable the monitoring of air quality in metropolitan areas. The ICT infrastructure will be connected to the health apps running on the runners' devices. Citizens will have access to their favorite personal training app through the Internet. They are capable of determining the healthiest route for outdoor activities. Air quality and pollution sensors should be put around the city, and sensor data should be made accessible to the public.

The Internet of Things (IoT) as a Smart City Enabler

The authors have recently defined the phrase 'Internet of Things (IoT)' in the literature. "Objects with identities and virtual personalities in smart places employing intelligent interfaces to connect and interact within social, medical, environmental, and user context [17]" is one definition of the IoT. The IoT techniques are predicted to be used in significant networks with tens of thousands of devices and coverage areas of several kilometers. The IoT concept utilizes a wide range of applications and facilities to support Smart City implementations globally. It brings up novel possibilities, like the remote capability to monitor and handle smart devices for information. As a consequence, IoT technologies are revolutionizing cities by improving infrastructure, providing more operative and cost-effective urban services, enhancing transportation services by decreasing traffic congestion, and ensuring human security. Today, IoT items with varied capacities suppose to be related to weather information. Connected objects are used in various industries (healthcare, manufacturing, transportation, and so on).

NLP TASKS USED IN SMART CITY

Natural Language Processing (NLP) is a key technique for extracting data from human speech. Using techniques like tokenization, normalization, stemming, and stop word removal, the textual data is correctly pre-processed to reduce noise. Lexical acquisition, word sense disambiguation, and part-of-speech (POS) tagging are examples of NLP approaches. NLP is the process of converting natural Language into text format, which a computer system may use to gain knowledge and learn about the world [18]. The world's knowledge is occasionally utilized to produce natural language literature representing that knowledge. The most efficient algorithm used for converting natural language into SQL query language can easily store in a relational database [19]. The Latent Dirichlet Allocation (LDA) method and the Word2vec method were used by Qiu *et al.* [20] to harvest information from text. Each text is considered a combination of a small number of latent themes by the LDA algorithm, and each word contributes to one of these topics. LDA can gather the inferred topic distribution of materials given all terms present in each document collection document. Word2vec is a deep learning-based application that Google published in 2013.

In this section, the techniques of NLP are described below that could be used in smart cities for extracting information.

Entity Name Recognition

The most basic popular, and useful technique in NLP is extracting entities in the text. Under this technique, the algorithm highlights the fundamental concept and reference in the text and identifies all the nouns, names, locations, organizations, dates, *etc.* many use cases used daily, such as:

News Categorization

It automatically scans all the news articles and retrieves the short form of the information. That will describe people, companies, places, and celebrity's names from that news article, so using this, devices easily classify articles into different categories.

Customer Supports

Everyday, thousands of feedback are provided by people in different areas; here I am concerning heavy traffic on Twitter. Using NER API, we can quickly pull out all the tags to inform concerned traffic police departments.

Efficient Search Engine

The name entity recognition algorithms are used in different articles, news, and blogs to extract relevant tags and tags stored in a separate database. They are using these tags to make an efficient search engine.

Sentiment Analysis

The most widely used NLP technique is sentiment analysis. Sentiment analysis is instrumental when people express their thoughts and opinions through customer surveys, reviews, and online comments. It measures on three scales: positive, negative, and neutral. In more complicated circumstances, the result might be a numeric score that can be classified into as numerous categories as needed. The supervised and unsupervised algorithms can be used for sentiment analysis. The naive Bayes model is the most often used supervised model for sentiment analysis. It requires a sentiment-labeled training corpus, which is used to train a model and identify the sentiment. Instead of Naive Bayes, ML approaches such as random forest or gradient boosting can also be used. Lexicon-based approaches, also known as unsupervised techniques, require a corpus of texts with associated emotion and polarity [21, 22]. The polarity of the words in the phrase is used to compute the sentence's sentiment score. A library available in python named coreNLP helps in sentiment knowledge discovery [23].

Text Summarization

As the name implies, NLP approaches may be used to summarise vast amounts of text. The text summary is most commonly used in news stories, search engines and academic papers. There are two ways to summarize textual data named extraction and abstraction. The extraction approach extracts elements of the text to construct a summary. The abstraction approach generates new text that expresses the essence of the original text, resulting in a summary. There are several python libraries available that help to summarize the text. LexRank, TextRank, PageRank [24], textSumm, spaCy, Gensim, *etc.*

Topic Modeling

One of the more complex ways of identifying natural subjects in a document is topic modeling. Topic modeling has the benefit of being an unsupervised method. There is no need for model training or a labeled training dataset. Topic modeling is a sort of statistical modeling that is used to find the abstract "themes" that appear in a set of texts. The topic model algorithm is Latent Dirichlet Allocation (LDA), which categorizes text in a document to a particular subject.

Aspects Mining

Aspect mining is a technique for identifying the many features of a text. It pulls comprehensive information from the text when combined with sentiment analysis. Part-of-speech tagging is now one of the simplest ways of aspect mining.

Natural Language Generation (NLG)

NLG is a method of converting raw designed information into plain English (or another language). It is sometimes referred to as data storytelling. This technology, which translates structured data into plain languages for a better comprehension of patterns or comprehensive insights into any business, is highly useful in many businesses where a massive volume of data is handled. Any NLG has a number of phases. Content determination, document clustering, aggregation, lexical choice, referring expression generation, and realization..

Different types of NLP pipelines depend on the task; machine learning and deep learning only understand numeric data. So we need to extract numeric data from text using the NLP pipeline. Some of the NLP pipeline tasks define below.

Tokenization

To begin, understand what tokenization is. The technique of breaking down a text corpus into a series of tokens is known as tokenization. Tokens may be anything, including words, phrases, characters, numbers, punctuation, *etc*. There are two main vital advantages of tokenization: the first is that it significantly reduces search time, and the second is that it efficiently uses storage space. This is an essential aspect of any "Information Retrieval (IR) system since it not only pre-processes text but also creates tokens that are utilized in the indexing and ranking processes" [25]. In the field of Natural Language Processing, several tokenization algorithms are available. "Porter's Algorithm is one of the most well-known tokenization and stemming algorithms" [26].

Stemming and Lemmatization

"Stemming" is the procedure of dropping inflected (or occasionally resultant) words to their root term or base form, which is usually a written rooted version of the word without suffixes. Stemming, *e.g.*, essentially removes all suffixes. For example,

Playing ———————→ Play ⎤
Plays ———————→ Play ⎬— Common root form 'play'
Played ———————→ Play ⎦

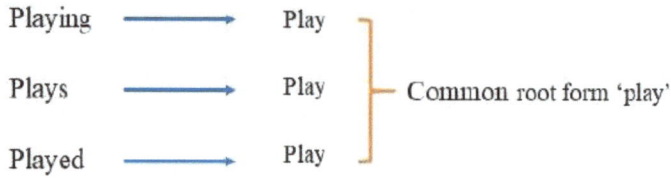

Lemmatization is a term that refers to actions taken through the proper use of vocals and morphological investigation of words to remove only inflectional ends and return the base form of the word or a word in the dictionary, which is also known as the lemma. For example,

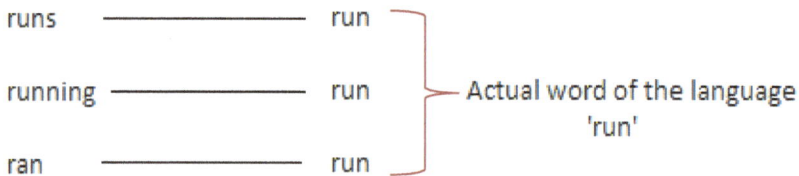

runs ———————— run ⎤
running ———————— run ⎬— Actual word of the language 'run'
ran ———————— run ⎦

"run" is the lemma of all these words since runs, running, and running are all variants of the word run. That means it returns an actual term in the Language and is utilized when valid words are required.

Bag of Word

Bag of Words simply generates a set of vectors containing the number of times each word appears in the page (reviews). It is also a demonstration of any text in a corpus that expounds on or elucidates the occurrence of terms in a text corpus (document). It is also known as "Bag" because its method simply cares about if recognized words are in the document, not where they appear. For example, to understand the bag of word two simple examples that is given below:

"Neha was angry on Sunil, and he was angry on Ramesh".

"Neha loves animals".

As can see two sentences above; we regard each document like a separate entity and produce a list of all the terms included in each document, excluding punctuations.

"Neha", "was", "angry", "on", "Sunil", "and", "he", "Ramesh", "love", "animals"

The 'bag-of-words' method is mostly used to generate features from text data.

Word Embedding

This technique is an improved version of a bag of words and tf-idf. It used cosine similarity in the context of semantics for text.

ADVANCED TECHNIQUES FOR NLP AND SMART CITIES APPLICATIONS

Few advanced deep learning models are used behind it. Deep learning is a subset of machine learning techniques to achieve above mention NLP task efficiently and effectively with good accuracy that is indirectly useful for smart cities. The advanced techniques are given below:

Recurrent Neural Network (RNN)

It is a deep learning algorithm that deals with a sequential type of input data. Sequential data may be in text form, audio or speech signals, financial data, time series data, *etc*. For NLP applications, RNN has become the legally recognized neural network architecture [36]. Concerning NLP problems, recurrent architecture for neural networks has come a long way in the previous several years. RNNs, unlike Artificial Neural Networks (ANNs), deal with sequential data and have their memory cell. A feed-forward neural network is the first and primary ANNs network. The network information flows only in the forward direction through three layers: input layer to output layer via hidden layer; in this network, no backward connections. In a feed-forward neural network, no memory cells for storing previous output data, so it is only based on the current input. These networks solve basic supervised machine-learning problems like regression and classification.

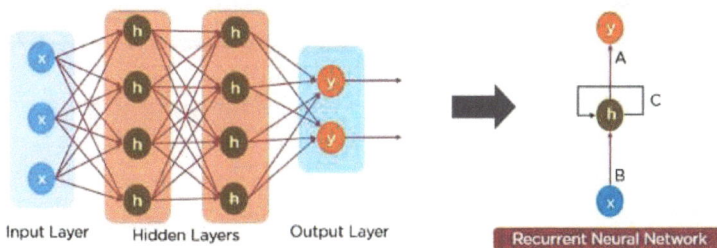

Fig. (3). Feed-Forward Network to Recurrent Neural Network [27].

In Fig. (**3**) all the layer of Feed-Forward Neural Network nodes is compacted to produce a Recurrent Neural network. The network's parameters are A, B, and C.

In below Fig. (**4**), 'x' expresses the input layers nodes, 'h' expresses the nodes of the hidden layer and 'y' expresses the output layers nodes of the network with the period 't'. The network parameters that were employed to improve the model's output. The present inputs are combined with the help of at x(t) input and x(t-1) input. And finally, the output is collected from the network at any given instant in order to enhance it.

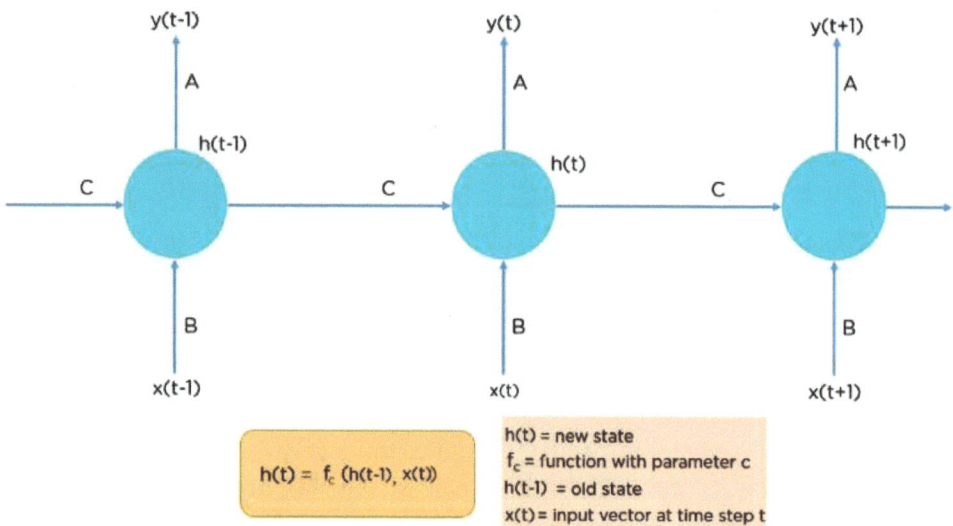

$$h(t) = f_c (h(t-1), x(t))$$

h(t) = new state
f_c = function with parameter c
h(t-1) = old state
x(t) = input vector at time step t

Fig. (4). A fully connect RNN networks [28].

This recurrent neural network was created because of many problems in feed-forward neural networks that could not solve the recent upcoming future tasks. It cannot handle sequential data, considers only the current input, and cannot memorize previous input. There are few applications of RNN where this technique performs well and gives the desired result. Image captioning, time series prediction, text summarization, question answering, machine comprehension, Real Time Analysis of Tweets and many more applications using ML, RNN and Semantic Analysis [23].

Long Short Term Memory (LSTM)

LSTM is a special kind of recurrent neural network capable of handling long-term dependencies. LSTM Network is also called an advanced variant of Recurrent

Neural Network, a sequential network that allows information to persist. It is capable of handling the vanishing gradient problem faced by the Recurrent Neural Network (RNN). The problem of vanishing gradients affects RNNs. Gradients transport information to the RNN and parameter changes become irrelevant when the gradient is too tiny. Long data sequences are difficult to learn because of this. The disappearing gradient problem is also known as information loss over time. The most popular and efficient method for dealing with gradient problems is the LSTM.

There are three basic components of an LSTM network cell name gates. The first component of the LSTM cell is called Forget gate, the second component of the LSTM cell is known as the Input gate, and the third component of the LSTM cell is called the Output gate. It also uses three sigmoid activation functions and one tanh activation function. The LSTM has a hidden state like a simple RNN network where h(t-1) denotes the previous timestamp's hidden state, and h(t) denotes the current timestamp's hidden state. LSTMs contain a cell state too, which is represented by c(t-1) and c(t), respectively, for past and current timestamps. Fig. (**5**) shows the network components process of the LSTM network and its working.

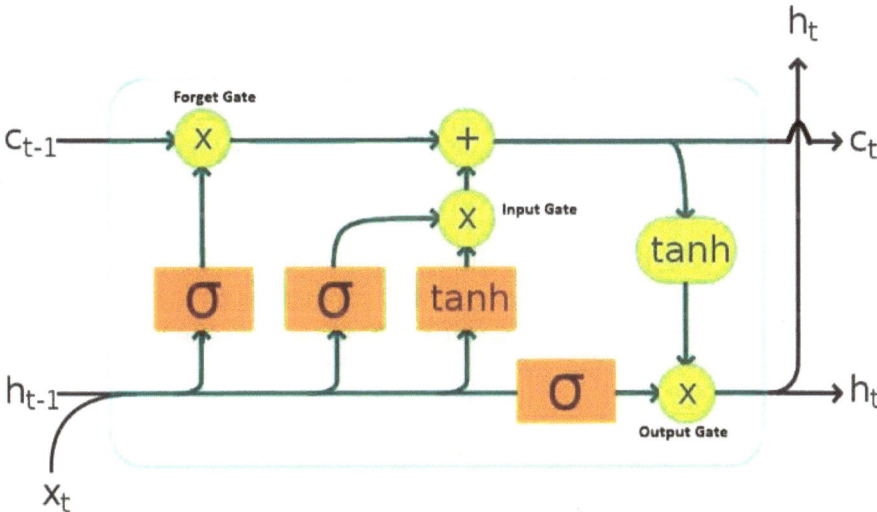

Fig. (5). Long Short-Term Memory [29].

Sigmoid Function

Sigmoid function is an activation function that belongs to networks' non-linear activation functions. The LSTM gate contains this sigmoid activation function. The sigmoid activation function maintains the value between 0 and 1, and updates or forgets the data of the network. Depending on multiplication results, information is considered forgotten when the result is 0 or remembered when the result is 1.

Tanh Function

Tanh function is also a non-linear activation function for LSTM network. In this, the values flow via the network and maintain the values range between -1 and 1. A function whose second derivative may persist for longer is required to avoid information fading.

Forget Gate

It determines whether data needs attention or not. It uses a sigmoid activation function for data value transfer. Sigmoid generates the data value between 0 and 1.

$$F_t = \sigma(Wf.[h_{t-1}, x_t] + b_f) \tag{1}$$

Ft= forget gate at t, Wf= weight matrix between forget gate and input gate, h(t-1)= previous hidden state, xt= input, bf= bias at t timestamp.

Input Gate

The input gate to update the cell state conducts the following processes. The second sigmoid function receives the current state x(t) and the previously concealed state h(t-1). The values are changed from 0 (important) to 1 (unimportant). It uses tanh activation function that will construct a vector c(t). The activation functions provide output values that are appropriate for multiplication on a point-by-point basis. The forget gate and input gate have provided enough information to the network. After that, the information is captured in the cell state from the new state. The f(t) values are multiplied by C(t-1) state values. The final result 0 will indicate the cell state value discarded.

$$i_t = \sigma(W_i.[h_{t-1}, x_t] + b_i) \tag{2}$$

$$C_t = tanh(W_c.[h_{t-1}, x_t] + b_c) \tag{3}$$

i(t)= input gate at t timestamp, C(t)= value generated by tanh, Wc= weight matrix of tanh operator between cell state information and network operator, t= timestamp, bc= bias vector at t concerning Wc.

Cell State

The forget gate and input gate have provided enough information to the network. The information must be stored in this state for future reference.

$$C_t = f_t * C_{t-1} + i_t * C_t \tag{4}$$

Ct=cell state information, Ft=forget gate at t, i(t)=input gate at t, C(t-1)=previous timestamp, C′(t)=value generated by tanh.

Output Gate

This is generated by the value of the hidden states. This state stores data from earlier inputs. The current state and previous concealed state values are sent to the third sigmoid activation function. The tanh activation function is to construct a novel cell state. Both of these outputs are multiplied by a factor of two. The network selects which information the concealed state should convey based on the final value. Prediction is based on this unseen state.

$$o_t = \sigma(W_o[h_{t-1}, x_t] + b_o) \tag{5}$$

$$h_t = o_t * tanh(C_t) \tag{6}$$

O_t= output gate at t, W_o= weight matrix of output gate, b_o=bias vector with respect to Wo, h_t= LSTM output.

The forget gate determines which relevant information from the prior steps is needed. The input gate decides what relevant information can be added from the current step, and the output gates finalize the next hidden state [29].

LSTM network also solves various real-life problems using big data analytics, such as weather forecasting [30].

Sequence to Sequence (Seq2Seq) Modelling

Many systems that we encounter regularly are based on a sequence-to-sequence paradigm. For example, the seq2seq model gives the power to Google Translate, voice-activated gadgets, and digital chatbots. Generally, question-answer, video captioning, and text summarization [31]. These are only a few applications where seq2seq is the best option. This paradigm may be applied to any sequence-based issue, particularly in which the inputs and outputs are of varying sizes and categories. A sequence-to-sequence model aims to convert a fixed-length input to a fixed-length output, even if the input and output lengths are different.

Encoder-Decoder Model

Encode - Decoder Model introduced in the papers "Sequence to Sequence Learning with Neural Networks" [32] and "Learning Phrase Representations using RNN Encoder-Decoder for Statistical Machine Translation" [33] uses Recurrent Neural Network and Long Short Term Memory. It works with together like a Pictionary game. Player1 draws a sketch based on input text, and Player2 guesses the text based on the sketch. The main advantage of this encoder-decoder model is that the input and output lengths may differ. So this opens up the possibility of some highly intriguing applications, like text summarization, question answering, image or video captioning, language translation, *etc*.

There are two processes of this model: one is the encoder, and the other is the decoder. Let's understand the working of each process below and its architectural diagram shown in Fig. (**6**).

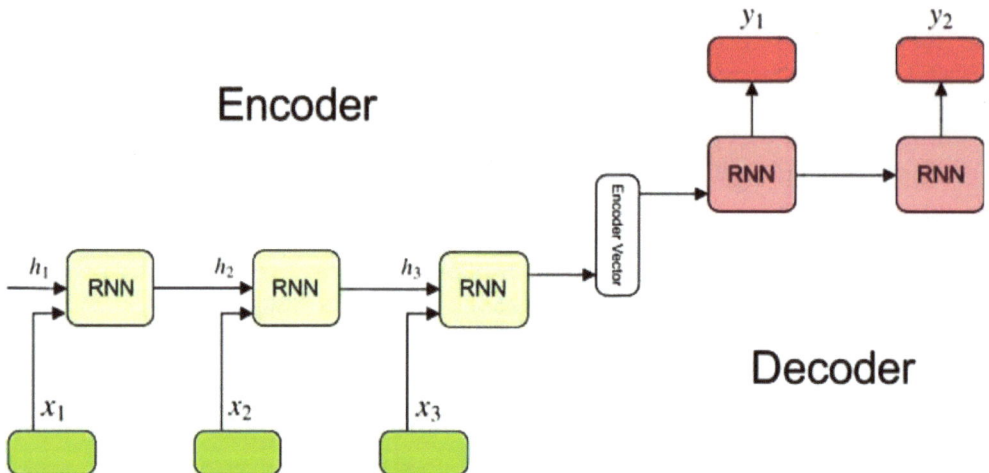

Fig. (6). Encode–decoder recurrent neural network model [23]. c=encoder/context vector, x1, x2…, xt are input sequences for encoder and y1, y2… yt are output sequence to decoder.

Encoder

The encoder is responsible for encrypting the entire sequence of the input time steps into a fixed-size vector called a context vector.

Context Vector

It is the model's final hidden state, generated by the encoder and the formula above to compute it. This vector seeks to incorporate all input element information for correct predictions [26].

Decoder

The term "decoder" refers to converting a coded communication message into understandable language. The second player in the Pictionary game will turn the drawing into a word. The decoder's job in the machine learning model will be to turn the two-dimensional vector into the output sequence.

The formula is used to calculate y(t) as an output using the Softmax function:

$$y_t = softmax\ (W^s * h_t)$$ (7)

The outputs are determined by combining the hidden state ht at present time t with the W^s as a weight. The softmax activation function generates a vector of probabilities that aids in the prediction of the ultimate result.

Attention Mechanism

In Natural Language Processing, the Attention Mechanism is the approach that was created to increase the performance of the Encoder-Decoder Recurrent Neural Network systems and their applications. This approach is later employed in various applications such as computer vision, voice processing, *etc*. Bahdanau *et al*. (2015) [34] proposed a simple yet elegant idea: not only should all input words be considered in the context vector, but the relative value should also be assigned to each of them. As a result, whenever the suggested model constructs a phrase, it looks for a collection of hidden states in the encoder where the most relevant information is available. This concept is known as 'Attention'.

Demonstration of Attention Mechanism

When people try to comprehend a picture, they concentrate on various areas of the image to grasp the whole meaning. Similarly, we may teach an artificial system to focus on specific aspects of an image to obtain the entire "picture." This is how the attention process operates in general. Fig. (7) shows how the attention mechanism focuses on the image and generates the caption for a particular image.

Consider the challenge of picture captioning, in which the system must provide a good caption for an image. In this case, the attention mechanism aids the model in grasping certain aspects of the image that are most significant at that time in order to construct the caption.

To receive input from each time step of the encoder to create the attention mechanism, humans give the timestamps weightage. As illustrated in Fig. (**8**), the weighting is based on the relevance of that time step for the decoder to best create the next word in the sequence:

Fig. (7). Demonstration of attention mechanism [34].

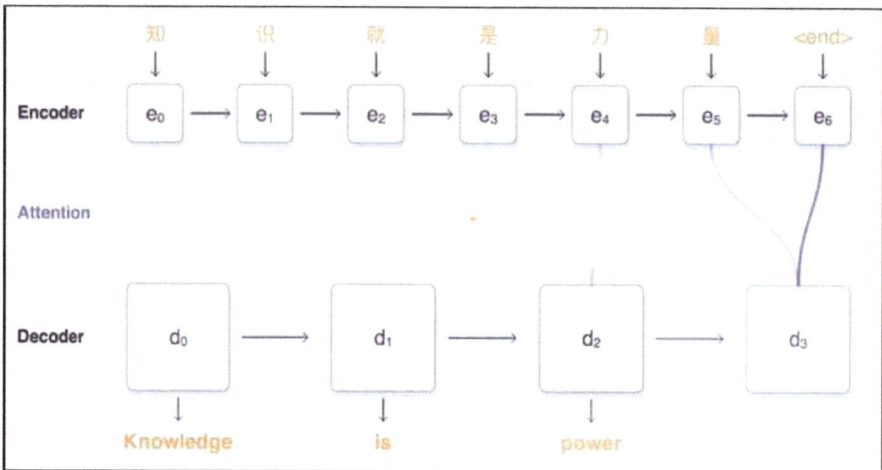

Fig. (8). Attention mechanism demo [35].

This chapter focused on a specific area of AI called Natural Language Processing, which helps and enhances human lives living in smart cities [36]. There are many use cases where this type of AI technology makes sense for smart cities. The four are given below:

Computerized Healthcare Services: We need to make a smart city into a smarter city by using advanced techniques of AI using ML and NLP. Smart healthcare services have become an essential task in smart cities' lives. The basic structure of the NLP application, front end and back end process, and user interaction with the system's front end. Model will take input from the user's data in text or speech. And then apply the pre-processing using a supportive model of the backend process like a Machine learning algorithm, passing the cleaned and extracted data to deep natural language processing techniques like knowledge-based models. Then backend model provides services to the frontend user/customer using speech recognition or machine translation. Fig. (**9**) draws the automatic process of this computerized healthcare service model. Cancer prediction using machine learning is a promising computerized health service [37].

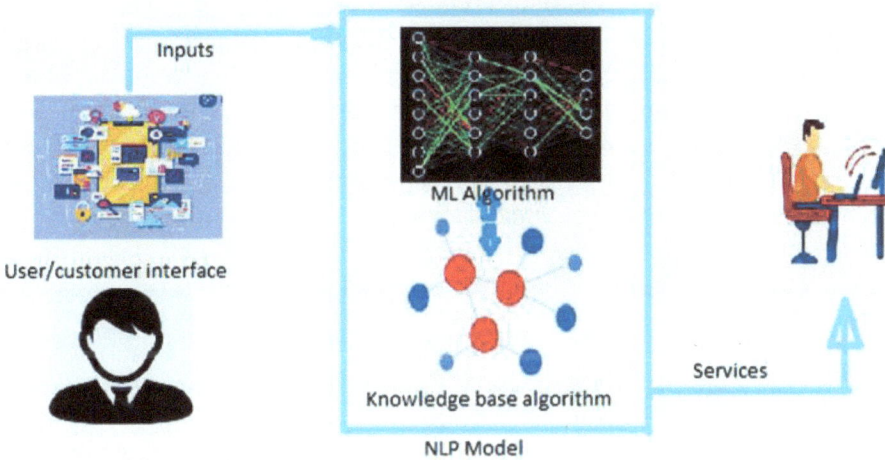

Fig. (9). Computerised health care services.

To Assist Policymakers in Implementing Smart Cities: There are agendas behind policymaking in building a smart city. Whenever the government makes a policy, it thinks that the quality of life of its citizens will be good. In the same context, NLP also provides good quality of life for the people to live in Smart Cities. Whatever problem the citizens have, it should be solved. Policymaking becomes a very difficult task for policymakers. So natural language processing (NLP) will help policymakers to a great extent for this type of task. Let's see how it will work; a collection of policy documents requires gathering documents relevant to smart city policy to clarify the link between "smart city policy" and "local policy" domain. The majority of the materials are gathered from official local websites to guarantee a strong alignment with the policy. After collecting documents for every smart city, it is required to clarify and arrange the content in order to do topic modeling analysis. Once the data file was produced, latent Dirichlet Allocation (LDA) is used for topic modelling [38]. Topic modeling, in general, is a form of a numerical model that uncovers hidden arrangements in textual data. LDA analysis describes every text like a collection of all topics, with every subject represented as a word. Other AI technique also helps to improve the decision-making process, which would help to assist policymaker [39].

To Become Smarter, use Opinion Mining: In today's digital world, where smart city ideas are being integrated, e-governance apps have a huge potential and need. People now look to other people's opinions before purchasing a product, booking a hotel, or eating at a restaurant, and worried consumers post their experiences as a response to the service [40]. However, there is no e-governance mechanism to handle public complaints on COVID-19, new laws, policies, and other government actions. With the growing availability and emergence of opinion-rich data, new possibilities and problems in building large-scale mining technologies may arise. If it is relevant to COVID-19, send out a public notice, get people's opinions, and inform the appropriate agencies and ambulance services. To combat the pandemic, there is a necessity for a natural language processing-based efficient e-governance platform that tracks corona positive patients and gives transparency on the number of confirmed COVID-19 cases, all based on inputs from the relevant health ministry and user feedback. Also, call an ambulance.

Permission to Remodel a House: A building permission, a planning check and inspection reviews are usually necessary for construction projects. For any form of work that will modify or need construction to a current building or land, remodel house permits are necessary for smart cities. Even minor construction projects require many permits, such as updating a bedroom or bathroom. Further issues occur since it is frequently challenging for a permit aspirant to ascertain whether a permit is necessary even after several trips to the city's permit office. The types of permits, rules and regulations differ significantly between cities, making the process of finding building permits complex, opaque, and inefficient, with citizens often having to do a lot of "legwork" [18].

Furthermore, the application procedure is not well-defined. Suppose a building owner wants to get a permit, the procedure entails filling out various forms, giving various relevant paperwork, and typically a lengthy wait for a permission decision. We can propose a modern permit concept using NLP, which any smart city may apply to speed and facilitate the permission request process, to address the abovementioned challenges and deficiencies.

CONCLUSION

Ultimately, the conclusion becomes very important. This chapter described how NLP enables smart city IoT devices to make smarter cities. Firstly, we described smart city concepts such as smart infrastructure, smart health, smart energy, traffic congestion, and air quality management. IoT as a Smart City Enabler. Everyone can see the IoT tools with numerous capabilities (*e.g.*, weather-related information) displayed nowadays. After that, Natural Language Processing (NLP) pipeline techniques are discussed in detail, such as tokenization, stemming, Lemmatization, a bag of words, word embedding, *etc*. These NLP pipelines help achieve important tasks that are helpful for daily human life and make it easy to use and recognize. The task such as Named Entity Recognition, sentiment analysis, text summarization, topic modeling, aspects mining, Natural Language Understanding (NLU) and Natural Language Generation (NLG), *etc.* and also discussed advanced deep learning techniques (Recurrent Neural Networks (RNN), Long Short Term Memory (LSTM), Sequence to Sequence (Seq2Seq), Encoder-Decoder and Attention mechanism models) for NLP. That provides an efficient and effective way with good accuracy. It is indirectly helpful for smart cities. In smart cities, AI-Natural Language Processing helps and enhances human living in these use-cases. Computerised healthcare services to assist policymakers in implementing smart cities, to become more innovative, use opinion mining, and Permission to remodel a house.

REFERENCES

[1]   B.N. Silva, M. Khan, and K. Han, "Towards sustainable smart cities: A review of trends, architectures, components, and open challenges in smart cities", *Sustain Cities Soc.,* vol. 38, pp. 697-713, 2018.
        [http://dx.doi.org/10.1016/j.scs.2018.01.053]

[2]   A. Aldegheishem, "Success factors of smart cities: A systematic review of literature from 2000-2018", *TeMA - J. Land Use Mobil. Environ.,* vol. 12, no. 1, pp. 53-64, 2019.
        [http://dx.doi.org/10.6092/1970-9870/5893]

[3]   Available from: https://www.tandfonline.com/doi/abs/10.1080/10630732.2011.601117 (accessed Mar. 03, 2022)

[4]   J. Desdemoustier, N. Crutzen, and R. Giffinger, "Municipalities' understanding of the smart city concept: An exploratory analysis in Belgium", *Technological Forecasting and Social Change,* vol. 142, pp. 129-141, 2019.

[5]   Available from: https://www.routledge.com/Technology-and-the-City-Systems-applications-and-implications/Yigitcanlar/p/book/9780367871420 (accessed Mar. 03, 2022)

[6]   L.G. Anthopoulos, "Smart Government: A New Adjective to Government Transformation or a Trick?", In: *Understanding Smart Cities: A Tool for Smart Government or an Industrial Trick?,* L.G. Anthopoulos, Ed., Springer International Publishing: Cham, 2017, pp. 263-293.
        [http://dx.doi.org/10.1007/978-3-319-57015-0_6]

[7]   R. Schipper, and A. Silvius, "Characteristics of smart sustainable city development: Implications for project management", *Smart Cities,* vol. 1, no. 1, pp. 75-97, 2018.

[http://dx.doi.org/10.3390/smartcities1010005]

[8]   M. Höjer, and J. Wangel, "Smart Sustainable Cities: Definition and Challenges", In: L. Hilty, and B. Aebischer, *ICT Innovations for Sustainability.* vol. 310. Springer, Cham, 2014, pp. 333-349. [http://dx.doi.org/10.1007/978-3-319-09228-7_20]

[9]   R. Rameshwar, A. Solanki, A. Nayyar, and B. Mahapatra, "Green and smart buildings: A key to sustainable global solutions", In: *Green Building Management and Smart Automation*, 2020. [http://dx.doi.org/10.4018/978-1-5225-9754-4.ch007]

[10]   R. Krishnamurthi, A. Nayyar, and A. Solanki, "Innovation Opportunities through Internet of Things (IoT) for Smart Cities", In: *Green and Smart Technologies for Smart Cities.* CRC Press, 2019. [http://dx.doi.org/10.1201/9780429454837-13]

[11]   H. Kaur, S.P. Singh, S. Bhatnagar, and A. Solanki, "Chapter 10 - intelligent smart home energy efficiency model using artificial intelligence and internet of things", In: *Artificial Intelligence to Solve Pervasive Internet of Things Issues* Academic press, 2021, pp. 183-210. [http://dx.doi.org/10.1016/B978-0-12-818576-6.00010-1]

[12]   S.P. Singh, A. Solanki, T. Singh, and A. Tayal, "Chapter 5 - Internet of Intelligent Things: Injection of intelligence into iot devices", In: *Artificial Intelligence to Solve Pervasive Internet of Things Issues* Academic press, 2021, pp. 85-102. [http://dx.doi.org/10.1016/B978-0-12-818576-6.00005-8]

[13]   Available from: https://www.scnsoft.com/blog/iot-for-smart-city-use-cases-approaches-outcomes (accessed Mar. 03, 2022)

[14]   Available from: https://davra.com/iot-smart-cities-the-big-5-use-cases/ (accessed Mar. 03, 2022)

[15]   V. Snieška, and I. Zykiene, "The role of infrastructure in the future city: Theoretical perspective", *Procedia Soc. Behav. Sci.,* vol. 156, pp. 247-251, 2014. [http://dx.doi.org/10.1016/j.sbspro.2014.11.183]

[16]   L. Mora, and M. Deakin, *Untangling smart cities: From utopian dreams to innovation systems for a technology-enabled urban sustainability.* Elsevier, 2019.

[17]   T. Singh, A. Solanki, and S. Sharma, "Role of smart buildings in smart city-components.technology, indicators, challenges, future research opportunities", In: *Digital Cities Roadmap: IoT-Based Architecture and Sustainable Buildings* Wiley Online Library, 2021. [http://dx.doi.org/10.1002/9781119792079.ch14]

[18]   A. Solanki, and A. Kumar, "A system to transform natural language queries into SQL queries", *Int. J. Inf. Technol.,* vol. 14, no. 12, pp. 437-446, 2018. [http://dx.doi.org/10.1007/s41870-018-0095-2]

[19]   G. Singh, and A. Solanki, "An algorithm to transform natural language into SQL queries for relational databases", *Selforganizology,* vol. 3, no. 3, pp. 100-116, 2016.

[20]   J. Qiu, Y. Chai, Y. Liu, Z. Gu, S. Li, and Z. Tian, "Automatic non-taxonomic relation extraction from big data in smart city", *IEEE Access,* vol. 6, pp. 74854-74864, 2018. [http://dx.doi.org/10.1109/ACCESS.2018.2881422]

[21]   D. He, and S. Zeadally, "An Analysis of RFID authentication schemes for internet of things in healthcare environment using elliptic curve cryptography", *IEEE Internet Things J.,* vol. 2, no. 1, pp. 72-83, 2015. [http://dx.doi.org/10.1109/JIOT.2014.2360121]

[22]   R. Rajput, and A. Solanki, "Real time sentiment analysis of tweets using machine learning and semantic analysis", *In Commun Comput Syst-Proc Int Conf Commun Comput Syst ICCCS,* vol. 2016, pp. 687-692, 2017. [http://dx.doi.org/10.1201/9781315364094-123]

[23]   N. Kaur, and A. Solanki, "Sentiment Knowledge Discovery in Twitter Using CoreNLP Library", *2018*

8th International Conference on Cloud Computing, Data Science & Engineering (Confluence), pp. 574-580, 2018.
[http://dx.doi.org/10.1109/CONFLUENCE.2018.8442439]

[24]   A. Sharma, and A. Solanki, "A hybrid page rank algorithm for web pages", *Int. J. Sci. Res. Dev.,* vol. 3, no. 3, pp. 3702-3708, 2015.

[25]   V. Singh, and B. Saini, "An effective tokenization algorithm for information retrieval systems", *Computer Science,* vol. 4, 2014.
[http://dx.doi.org/10.5121/csit.2014.4910]

[26]   A.M. Saeed, T.A. Rashid, A.M. Mustafa, P. Fattah, and B. Ismael, "Improving kurdish web mining through tree data structure and porter's stemmer algorithms", *UKH J. Sci. Eng.,* vol. 2, no. 1, pp. 48-54, 2018.
[http://dx.doi.org/10.25079/ukhjse.v2n1y2018.pp48-54]

[27]   D. Wei, B. Wang, G. Lin, D. Liu, Z. Dong, H. Liu, and Y. Liu, "Research on unstructured text data mining and fault classification based on RNN-LSTM with malfunction inspection report", *Energies,* vol. 10, no. 3, p. 406, 2017.
[http://dx.doi.org/10.3390/en10030406]

[28]   S. Li, W. Li, C. Cook, C. Zhu, and Y. Gao, "Independently recurrent neural network (IndRNN): Building A Longer and Deeper RNN", *ArXiv,* 180304831 Cs.
[http://dx.doi.org/10.1109/CVPR.2018.00572]

[29]   Available from: https://www.pluralsight.com/guides/introduction-to-lstm-units-in-rnn (accessed Mar. 03, 2022)

[30]   M. Patil, P. Rekha, A. Solanki, A. Nayyar, and B. Qureshi, "Big data analytics using swarm-based long short-term memory for temperature forecasting", *Computers, Materials & Continua.,* 2021.

[31]   Available from: https://towardsdatascience.com/understanding-encoder-decoder-sequence-to-sequence -model-679e04af4346 (accessed Mar. 03, 2022)

[32]   I. Sutskever, O. Vinyals, and Q.V. Le, "Sequence to sequence learning with neural networks", *ArXiv,* p. 14093215 Cs, 2014. Available from: http://arxiv.org/abs/1409.3215

[33]   K. Cho, "Learning phrase representations using RNN encoder-decoder for statistical machine translation", *ArXiv,* p. 14061078 Cs Stat, 2014.

[34]   D. Bahdanau, K. Cho, and Y. Bengio, "Neural machine translation by jointly learning to align and translate", *ArXiv,* p. 14090473 Cs Stat, 2016. Available from: http://arxiv.org/abs/1409.0473

[35]   Available from: https://github.com/google/seq2seq (Mar. 03, 2022)

[36]   Z. Ullah, F. Al-Turjman, L. Mostarda, and R. Gagliardi, "Applications of artificial intelligence and machine learning in smart cities", *Comput. Commun.,* vol. 154, pp. 313-323, 2020.
[http://dx.doi.org/10.1016/j.comcom.2020.02.069]

[37]   Available from: https://www.taylorfrancis.com/chapters/edit/10.1201/9781003156123-13/predictio- -breast-lung-cancer-comparative-review-analysis-using-machine-learning-techniques-- run-solanki-sandeep-kumar-rohan-simar-preet-singh-akash-tayal (accessed Oct. 20, 2022)

[38]   D.J. Clement, and P.N. Crutzen, "How local policy priorities set the smart city agenda", *Technol. Forecast. Soc. Change,* vol. 171, p. 120985, 2021.
[http://dx.doi.org/10.1016/j.techfore.2021.120985]

[39]   A. Solanki, A. Goel, and A. Singh, "Evaluation of fuzzy logic mechanism in fuzzy expert systems to improve the decision making process", *presented at the International Conference on Emerging Trends and Developments in Science, Management and Technology, RKGIT, GZB,* 2013.

[40]   T. Singh, A. Nayyar, and A. Solanki, "Multilingual opinion mining movie recommendation system using RNN", *Proceedings of First International Conference on Computing, Communications, and Cyber-Security (IC4S 2019).,* vol. 121, Springer: Singapore, no. Apr, pp. 589-605, 2020. [http://dx.doi.org/10.1007/978-981-15-3369-3_44]

CHAPTER 6

Machine Learning-based Intrusion Detection for Position Falsification Attack in the Internet of Vehicles

Olfa Masmoudi[1], **Hanen Idoudi**[1,*] and **Mohamed Mosbah**[2]

[1]*National School of Computer Science, University of Manouba, Manouba, Tunisia*
[2]*LaBRI (UMR5800), CNRS, University of Bordeaux, Talence, France*

Abstract: Intelligent transportation system (ITS) is a promising technology to enhance driving safety and efficiency within smart cities. It involves public transportation management, infrastructure control and road safety. Its main purpose is to avoid risks and accidents, reduce traffic congestion and ensure safety for road users. Vehicular ad hoc networks (VANET) are core components of ITS where wireless communications between vehicles, as well as between vehicles and infrastructure, are possible to allow exchanging road, traffic or infotainment information. VANET is vulnerable to several security attacks that may compromise the driver's safety.

Using misbehavior detection approaches and information analysis demonstrated promising results in securing VANET. In this context, Machine Learning techniques proved their efficiency in detecting attacks and misbehavior, especially zero-day attacks.

The goal of this chapter is twofold. First, we intend to analyze the security issue in VANET by reviewing the most important vulnerabilities and proposed countermeasures. In the second part, we introduce a comprehensive Machine Learning framework to design a VANET IDS. We used the framework to evaluate the performances of several Machine Learning techniques to detect position attacks using the VeReMi security dataset. Experimental results prove that KNN, Decision Tree and Random Forest outperform Logistic Regression, SVM and Gaussian Naïve Bayes in terms of Accuracy, F-measure, Precision and Recall.

Keywords: Internet of vehicles, Intrusion detection, Machine learning, Position attack, Vanet security.

* **Corresponding author Hanen Idoudi:** National School of Computer Science, University of Manouba, Tunisia;
E-mail: hanen.idoudi@ensi-uma.tn

Arun Solanki and Anuj Kumar Singh (Eds.)

INTRODUCTION

Vehicular Ad hoc NETworks (VANET) are core components of intelligent Transportation Systems (ITS). In VANET, vehicles are able to construct a self-organizing network to communicate with each other or with some road infrastructure [1]. VANET relies on two main components: Road Side Unit (RSU) and On Board Unit (OBU). Road Side Unit (RSU) is the roadside communication equipment. It provides internet access to vehicles and ensures exchanging application information between vehicles. On Board Unit (OBU) is the mobile terminal placed on the vehicle. It allows communication with other vehicles or with infrastructure equipment.

VANET enables different communication architectures, such as Vehicle-to-Vehicle (V2V), Vehicle-to-Infrastructure (V2I), Infrastructure-to-vehicle (I2V), Infrastructure-to-Infrastructure (I2I) and Hybrid communications [1].

In the vehicular plane, each vehicle is equipped with OBU. The latter allows V2V communications. The RSU plane facilitates V2I, I2V and I2I communications. VANET is intended for different applications such as infotainment, payment, Internet and cloud-based services. The service plane also involves the certificate authority (CA) or trusted authority (TA) of the PKI-based authentication system [2].

VANET has a highly dynamic topology due to vehicle movement. Target vehicles are reached depending on their geographical location, and signal propagation is affected by the environment, such as buildings, trees, wall panels, forests, *etc*. Moreover, energy, storage failure and computing capacity are not critical problems for VANET. In spite of that, the main challenge for VANET is processing huge amount of data in a real-time manner [1].

The main purpose of VANET communications is to improve transportation safety. In order to achieve this goal, security requirements such as authentication, integrity, confidentiality, non-repudiation and availability have to be ensured. Furthermore, safety and emergency messages are broadcasted and exchanged *via* wireless channels. As a result, VANET is subject to various security attacks.

Several existing works studied VANET security issues and introduced novel countermeasures that can tackle VANET vulnerabilities. Intrusion detection systems (IDS) are a commonly used approach to detect misbehavior and malicious activities Since few years, the adoption of Machine Learning (ML) techniques is attracting a growing interest because of their ability to detect unknown and zero-day attacks [3, 4].

This chapter has the following objectives:

- We review the most important communication standard protocols and architecture for VANET.
- We analyze the security issues in VANET by reviewing the most important attacks and countermeasures while focusing on IDS.
- We introduce a novel and comprehensive framework for ML-based IDS targeting position falsification attacks in VANET.
- We evaluate the performances of ML classifiers using the VeReMi security dataset.

The chapter is organized as follows. Section II is devoted to the background and related works on VANET communications and security issues. Section III depicts the proposed ML framework for IDS. Finally, section IV is dedicated to experimental results.

The following table depicts the main used acronyms throughout the chapter.

Table 1. List of abbreviations.

CA	Certificate authority
DCC	Decentralized Congestion Control
DOS	Denial of Service
ECDSA	Elliptic Curve Digital Signature Algorithm
EDCA	Enhanced Distributed Channel Access
I2V	Infrastructure-to-Infrastructure
IDS	Intrusion detection systems
ITS	Intelligent transportation system
OBU	On Board Unit
OFDM	Orthogonal Frequency Division Multiplexing
PKI	Public Key Infrastructure
RSU	Road Side Unit
SVM	Support Vector Machines
TA	Trusted authority
V2I	Vehicle-to-Infrastructure
V2V	Vehicle-to-Vehicle
VANET	Vehicular ad hoc networks
VeReMi	Vehicular Reference Misbehavior Dataset

WAVE	Wireless Access in Vehicular Environments
WSM	WAVE Short Messages

VANET COMMUNICATION AND SECURITY

In this section, we review the most important standard communication protocols and architectures for VANET, and then we discuss the security issue and some prominent security attacks; afterwards, the existing security counter measures and their limitations have been described.

VANET Communication Standards

VANET has specific requirements that need the development of dedicated communications technologies such as DSRC, ITS-G5 and LTE-V [2, 5, 6].

DSRC is based on IEEE 802.11 technology. IEEE WAVE (Wireless Access in Vehicular Environments) and ETSI ITS-G5 are also based on IEEE 802.11p. DSRC is more suitable for highly mobile environments. Therefore, it is commonly used in vehicular communication systems [7].

IEEE 802.11p

IEEE added 802.11p to his IEEE 802.11 protocols family in order to standardize the DSRC band specific to vehicular networks [6]. The standard IEEE 802.11p specifies the physical and MAC layers for VANET. In fact, the definition of the physical layer and the QoS are based respectively on IEEE 802.11a and IEEE 802.11e [6].

• **The physical layer**:

The physical layer of IEEE 802.11p is based on the OFDM (Orthogonal Frequency Division Multiplexing) [6].

• **The MAC layer**:

The IEEE 802.11p MAC layer is based on EDCA (Enhanced Distributed Channel Access) as an enhancement of DCF (Distributed Coordination Function). To improve messages safety and to ensure their timely transmission, the EDCA uses 4 Access category (AC) to manage QoS: Background traffic (AC0), Best Effort traffic (AC1), Video traffic (AC2) and Voice traffic (AC3), Access category AC3 has the highest priority.

IEEE WAVE

WAVE IEEE 1609 (Standard for Wireless Access in Vehicular Environments) was intended to achieve interoperability in a VANET environment and to establish different communications schemes, such as V2I and V2V. This architecture is based on the following layers [6].

• The MAC Layer:

IEEE 1609.4 is an improvement to 802.11 MAC. It defines wireless multi-channel radio operations, and it specifies priority access parameters, interval timers, service channel operations and control channels. In addition, it defines switching parameters, management services and channel routing.

• The Network and Transport Layer:

IEEE 1609.3 defines services for the transport and network layers, mainly addressing and routing for secure data exchange. In addition, it introduced WAVE Short Messages (WSM) protocol.

• The Facilities Layer:

The facilities Layer, defined by IEEE 1609.6 standard, is an intermediate layer between the transport and application layers. It ensures the management of interoperable services. It defines an identification service and remote management for WAVE devices (RSU and OBU), using WAVE management services defined by IEEE Std 1609.3. This standard also includes identification services based on WSM protocol.

ETSI ITS-G5

ITS-G5 enables the information exchange in V2V and V2I schemes. ITS-G5 defines a new scheme to minimize the probability of radio channel congestion [5]. Its architecture is based on:

• Mac Layer:

This layer is built upon IEEE 802.11p and the Decentralized Congestion Control (DCC). DCC ensures load balancing, flow and forward data packets. It controls the network load by tuning channel access parameters such as the transmitting power, the transfer rate and the radio sensitivity.

- **Network and Transport Layer**:

The Geo-networking protocol is implemented at the network layer to support location information. During data forwarding, the selection of the next-hop node is based on its geolocation information.

In the transport layer, the Basic Transport protocol offers a point-to-point connectionless transport service. Its main objective is to multiplex and demultiplex messages at the Facilities level to be forwarded using the Geo-networking protocol.

- **Facilities Layer**:

In the facilities layer, new messages are defined. These messages are both cooperative awareness message, which is a periodic message, and decentralized environmental, which is an event message. These messages cause supplementary channel load because of their retransmission. For that reason, facilities layer uses some special techniques, allowing an effective radio channel loading as well as specific protocols to transmit packets efficiently.

VANET Security Attacks

VANET is subject to various security attacks that target all security requirements: integrity, authentication, confidentiality, non-repudiation and availability. VANET is vulnerable to all general security attacks that target wireless environments in general as well as specific attacks that exploit inherent characteristics of VANET [8]. Some of the most exploited and most studied vulnerabilities are given here-after:

- **Denial of Service (DOS):** In a DOS attack, malicious nodes generate a huge number of useless requests on the network. These requests overload the network for the sake of blocking the transmission channel and interrupting services. Consequently, vehicles are prevented to receive critical messages and information from both security applications and other legitimate users [6, 9].

- **Man in the Middle:** Man in the middle attacks have serious consequences on VANET. Indeed, a malicious node can eavesdrop on and modify messages and packets exchanged in the network. The exchanged information may be delay-intolerant and sensitive. There are two types of this attack: passive and active.

- **Sybil:** In a Sybil attack, a malicious node takes illegitimately multiple identities. This attack is quite harmful to VANET. It creates an illusion of traffic congestion. For example, a malicious vehicle gives the impression that there are many extra vehicles in the network traveling nearby. This illusion influences other vehicles' path choices [10].
- **Impersonation:** In an impersonation attack, the attacker stoles the identity of a legitimate vehicle and acts as an authorized node. During the communication between two legitimate nodes, the attacker modifies the message from the sender and then transmits it to the receiver. Therefore, the malicious node is represented as legitimate, and it passes false information. This type of attack takes place mainly during the time of an accident [11, 12].
- **Wormhole:** A wormhole attack is a severe attack that targets routing protocols in VANET. In this attack, malicious nodes affect routing request packets and decrease the hop counts number. Consequently, the malicious nodes build a private tunnel with a reduced hop count. As a result, this tunnel attracts packets, and all exchanged packets between legitimate vehicles are transmitted through the private tunnel of the malicious nodes. Hence, an attacker can control packets or delete them [13].
- **Blackhole:** In a blackhole attack, the attacker node sends Route Reply messages indicating optimal path details. So, the other nodes are attracted by the optimal path and transmit their packets through it. The malicious node collects all packets without retransmitting them. Consequently, routing tables are disrupted, and messages cannot reach their destinations. As a result, the malicious node drops the messages silently and creates the blackhole effect [6, 14].
- **Replay:** In the replay attack, in order to misguide legitimate nodes, the messages are preserved and then reused. Firstly, the intruder stores some of the network-transmitted messages. After the expiry of these messages, the attacker re-sends them [15]. The injection back of packets received into the network causes the replay of beacons. Consequently, the attacker is able to manipulate the location and the nodes routing tables [6, 8].
- **Timing:** The main objective of VANET safety applications is to deliver the right information to vehicles at the right time in order to avoid accidents and ensure driver's and vehicle's safety. To ruin this requirement, the malicious nodes carry on this attack by creating a delay slot to block the message. Consequently, the destination node cannot receive the messages at the appropriate time [16, 17].

- **Position Falsification:** In VANET, the location information is critically important. It is about providing other vehicles a false position information rather than the right position information that can simply be retrieved from GPS [6,

15]. Circulating erroneous position information has an effect on the node authentication in the network, the reliability of packet forwarding, and the network performance. In the vehicular context and especially with safety traffic, insecure information transmission leads to hazardous dangers. In fact, a successful attack may lead to serious accidents, economic loss and even human losses. As a consequence, putting up security countermeasures is of utmost importance.

VANET Countermeasures

ETSI defined a specification for ITS security requirements. This specification defined a general framework for a secure ITS architecture [25]. Moreover, to secure VANET communications, several security countermeasures have to be adopted.

Public Key Infrastructure

Public Key Infrastructure (PKI) ensures exchanging data in a secure way. In addition, it enables identity verification of involved entities. PKI is composed of policies, standards, software and hardware. All these components work together in order to create, administrate, distribute and revoke keys and digital certificates. PKI incorporates the following key elements [18]:

• Root Certificate Authority (Root CA): The Root CA presents the center of trust. It provides services in order to authenticate entities' identities.
• Registration Authority (RA): It is also called a subordinate CA. It is certified by, and protects the Root CA. It also provides VANET users with their authorized certificates. In fact, the communication between users and Root CA passes through the RA. Hence, the attack may be detected in the RA before reaching the Root CA.
• Certificate database: The certificate database stores certificate requests as well as issued certificates and revoked certificates. Both Root CA and RA have access to the certificate database.
• Certificate store: The certificate store exists in each vehicle in order to store private keys and issued certificates.

Cryptographic Mechanisms

Their aim is to ensure the confidentiality of data while being transmitted from a source to a destination. Moreover, they involve encryption algorithms, hash functions, and signature algorithms and can provide solutions for diverse types of threats at different levels in VANET. New lightweight solutions for data encryption are also considered to tackle the limited computation capacities of different VANET equipment. For instance, Elliptic Curve Digital Signature Algorithm (ECDSA) is intended to implement a digital signature system for IoT in general and for securing VANET communication [19].

Key Management Systems

They are responsible for credentials and key management in a network. Public-key infrastructure (PKI) is used to verify node's authenticity when they communicate. They can be implemented as centralized, decentralized, or distributed systems [20].

PKI are widely used since they prove their efficiency against attacks from unauthorized and outside attackers. Nevertheless, PKI verifications are not sufficient to ensure the reliability of messages. Dealing with compromised entities and inside attackers, as well as misbehaviors detection in the communication process, are serious challenges of PKI-based security architectures [3].

Anonymity, Unlinkability and Traceability Techniques

These techniques aim at preventing unauthorized access and ensuring data privacy. They offer a countermeasure against several attacks, such as eavesdropping, trajectory tracking, or location disclosure. For instance, anonymity techniques are based on the use of pseudonyms by Group Signature and Pseudonymous Authentication schemes. In group signature mechanisms, a vehicle uses a private group key, while in pseudonymous authentication schemes, each vehicle holds a set of identities [21, 22]. Traceability is difficult to achieve while keeping data privacy. Subsequently, some solutions were proposed to trace and revoke malicious vehicles [23].

Security Protocols

Several security protocols are proposed or adapted to the context of IoT communications in general, such as TLS, DTLS, and IPSec [24]. These protocols are also considered to secure VANET communication at the transport layer.

Intrusion Detection Systems

IDS are used to detect insider attacks and misbehaviors. Decentralized IDS, Centralized IDS and Hybrid IDS are several ways of IDS deployment. IDS can be classified into 4 categories based on the technique used to detect threats: Signature-based, Watchdog-based, Anomaly-based and Hybrid IDS.

Machine Learning(ML)-based IDS are Anomaly IDS. This approach assumes that intrusive activities are a subclass of abnormal activities. In ML-based IDS, different ML techniques are used to recognize the unobserved misbehavior pattern. In fact, it extracts relations between different attributes and builds attack models [28]. This mechanism allows the RSU or OBU to detect any misbehavior in the network by analyzing received messages and network information. Unlike other types of IDS, ML-based IDS are able to detect zero-days and unknown anomalies.

Some existing works have already defined ML-based IDS for security breach detection in VANET. In [26], Random forest, Bagging, and AdaBoosting methods are trained and tested on the Can-hacking dataset, and the DT-based model results in yield performance. A tree-based Intelligent IDS for the internet of vehicles (IoV) that detects DoS and Fuzzy attacks is proposed by Li Yang *et al.* [27]. The authors evaluated the performance of the Decision tree, Random Forest, Extra trees, and XGradient Boost Methods using the Car-Hacking Dataset.

Fuad A. Ghaleb [28]. proposed a Misbehavior detection model based on Machine Learning techniques. The authors used a real-world traffic dataset, namely Next Generation Simulation (NGSIM), to train and evaluate the model. They used Artificial Neural Network. To evaluate the work, the authors used the F-measure and the false positive rate. Pranav Kumar Singh and al [3]. used ML-based IDS to detect wormhole attacks in VANET. Firstly, the authors generated a simulated dataset. In fact, they used both a traffic simulator, namely, Simulation of Urban Mobility Model (SUMO), and NS3 as a network simulator. Secondly, two different ML algorithms were applied to the generated dataset to train the model. These ML algorithms are k-nearest neighbors (k-NN) and Support Vector Machines (SVM). Finally, to evaluate the different models, the authors used the accuracy rate and four different alarms, which are True Positive, False Positive, True Negative and False Negative. As a result, both the SVM and k-NN performed well. Pranav Kumar Singh and al [3]. proposed an ML-based IDS to detect Position falsification attacks in VANET. The authors used Logistic Regression and SVM models. To evaluate the work, they used F-measure. As a result, they proved that SVM performed better than logistic regression.

Based on the study works, we noticed that a position attack is one of the specific and critical security attacks that a VANET may encounter. This attack can lead to direct alteration within the safety information and decisions, which are mainly based upon position information. Yet, few works have already focused on studying this attack and defining efficient IDS towards it.

Therefore, in the following section, we aim to define a comprehensive Machine Learning framework to detect position falsification attacks.

PROPOSED MACHINE LEARNING FRAMEWORK FOR POSITION ATTACK DETECTION

Our aim is to develop a decentralized ML-based IDS for VANET. Each vehicle has its own IDS, which uses ML techniques to detect nodes sending false position information.

This system uses three phases, as depicted in Fig. (**1**):

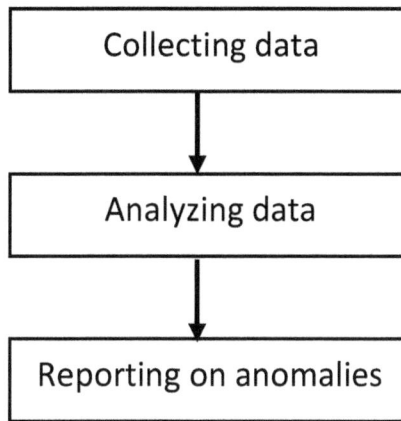

Fig. (1). Steps of the proposed ML framework.

- **Collecting Data:** Each vehicle instantly receives many safety messages. In addition, it collects a lot of data from its numerous different sensors.
- **Analyzing Data:** The Machine learning software deployed in each vehicle is responsible for analyzing collected data and for making the decision.
- **Reporting Engine:** In case of malicious node detection, the vehicle sends an alarm message to the RSU. If the RSU receives several alerts in a defined time interval from different vehicles, it has to inform the Certification Authority in order to revoke the authentication certification of the malicious node.

On the one hand, this architecture has to satisfy the VANET requirements. On the other hand, it could take advantage of the VANET network characteristics.

A decision based on exchanged information has to be taken and broadcasted instantly because the VANET system is very dynamic, critical and time-sensitive. Real-time decisions could benefit from the VANET characteristics as the availability of energy storage, and computation capacity is not critical [28]. In fact, this decentralized ML-based IDS takes the characteristics of both decentralized deployment and ML-based IDS. In addition, it benefits from the important computation and storage resources in each vehicle.

As a result, it is characterized by its high performance in detecting position falsification attacks with different signatures owing to the ML techniques. We expose the following the different phases of applying our ML framework.

Dataset Description

The vehicular Reference Misbehavior Dataset (VeReMi) is a simulated public dataset. Its main objective is to provide researchers with a high-quality simulation dataset to be used in misbehavior detection studies [29].

VeReMi dataset was generated based on the Luxembourg traffic scenario (LuST). It consists of 225 simulation executions, taking into account the following:

- 5 different attacker types:
  - The constant attacker which uses a constant and pre-configured position.
  - The constant offset attacker which adds a constant offset to the real position.
  - The random attacker: It transmits a random position for each new message.
  - The random offset attacker: It transmits a random position depending on the preconfigured area around the vehicle. For each message, it takes a new random value.
  - The eventual stop attacker: It behaves normally for a period of time. After this period, it acts as if it has stopped. If fact, it sends the current position repeatedly.
- 3 different attacker densities;
- 3 different traffic densities:
  - the low density: In this case, there are between 35 and 39 vehicles,
  - the medium density: In this case, there are between 97 and 108 vehicles,
  - the high density: In this case, there are between 491 and 519 vehicles.

For each simulation, a ground truth file is generated. It specifies the behavior of each node. In fact, it contains information about each vehicle, such as attacker type (if it is an attacker or not), as well as the real position of the vehicle and its speed.

In addition, for every vehicle belonging to the simulation, a message log file is generated. This file contains two types of messages:

- Safety messages sent by other nodes containing basic information such as: the message ID, the sender position and speed as well as the send and receive time.
- Position data sent by the GPS device of the local vehicle and containing the actual location of the node.

Data Preprocessing

In this section, we expose the different steps required to prepare the dataset in order to be used by the ML classifiers. In fact, we explain the extraction of suitable data from VeReMi. Then, we clarify the reduction of the dataset dimensions. Finally, we standardize the data.

Dataset Preparation

In order to use VeReMi as a training dataset in our study, its files were preprocessed. These are the preprocessing steps:

- First, several treatments were applied to all the log files of each simulation. We used only the safety messages received from other vehicles. In addition, we decomposed features such as position and speed. As a result, each log file has the features presented in Table **2**.

Table 2. Features and their descriptions.

Feature	Description
send-time	The time of sending the message
rcvTime	The time of receiving the message
sender	The ID of the sender vehicle
messageID	The ID of the message
pos_z	The value of the position on the x-axis
pos_z	The value of the position on the y-axis
pos_z	The value of the position on the z-axis
spd_x	The value of the speed on the x-axis
spd_y	The value of the speed on the y-axis
spd_z	The value of the speed on the z-axis
RSSI	The received signal strength indicator

- Second, we concatenated these files in order to generate a file that contains all the safety messages broadcasted during the simulation.

- Third, in order to train the models, we added the target to the dataset. In fact, the Ground Truth file contains all information about each vehicle. Thus, we extracted the information about each broadcasted safety message from this. As a result, we considered the following features: sendTime, rcvTime, sender, messageID, pos_x, pos_y, pos_z, spd_x, spd_y, spd_z and attack, which is a boolean value that indicates if the received message is issued from an attacker or not.
- Fourth, after analyzing the resulting dataset, we noted that it is full of similar lines. Actually, this duplication is caused by the broadcasted criteria of the safety messages. Thus, it causes overfitting problem for ML algorithms. Consequently, we had to treat this dataset and delete similar lines.
- Fifth, we repeated this process for different scenarios, and we concatenated the final files in order to increase the dataset size as well as to have the different implemented attacks because every scenario has one specific attack.

As a result, we get a dataset with 15509 samples classified into two classes:

- Falsified messages: This class contains 2178 samples distributed equally between all the different attacks defined in the previous section.
- Non-falsified messages: This class contains 13331 samples.

Hence, our resulting dataset is highly skewed.

Dimensionality Reduction

High-dimensional data leads to high computational cost and memory usage [30]. Therefore, preprocessing these data is necessary. There are two dimensionality reduction techniques known as feature selection and feature extraction.

- **Feature Selection:** High dimensional dataset consists of an important number of features that can be redundant, irrelevant and misleading. This huge number of features leads to an increase in search space size as well as more difficulties in data processing. Despite the fact that some of these features do not contribute to the learning process. Hence, feature selection is the process of sorting out the most useful features able to discriminate classes.
- **Feature Extraction:** This technique uses initial features in order to generate other features which are more significant. In fact, it applies linear combinations of original features. Hence, the size of the feature space decreases without losing consistent information.

In conclusion, the dimensionality reduction techniques have the following advantages:

- They increase the accuracy of the ML models. In fact, these techniques improve the data quality by removing irrelevant and noisy data.
- They prevent overfitting by removing redundant data and highly correlated features.
- They provide computational efficiency. In fact, the dimensionality reduction of the feature space limits the storage requirements and obviously increases the learning algorithm's speed. In order to apply these techniques to our dataset, we used correlation analysis. The correlation analysis aims at exploring the relationship between features.

We used the correlation coefficients for the aim of analyzing the relationship between features. We used the Pearson correlation coefficient. The results are shown in Fig. (**2**).

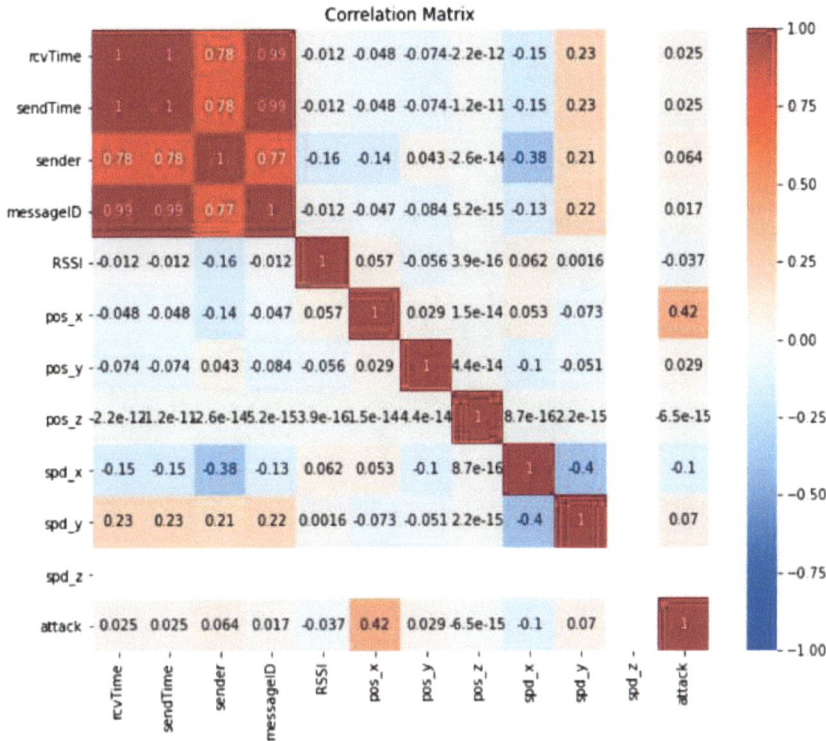

Fig. (2). Correlation matrix.

The correlation matrix depicts the correlation between all features. It especially points out the relation between the target and the other features. Firstly, we notice that the spd_z feature does not correlate with any other feature. This result was already expected because spd_z value equals zero during the simulation. In addition, the correlation coefficient between attack and pos_z is very low. Thus, we eliminate pos_z and spd_z features. Secondly, we noticed that rcvTime, sendTime, messageID and sender features are highly correlated with each other.

Taking into account this correlation and to eliminate the redundancy of values, we eliminated the messageID and sender features, as well as extracted a linear combination between rcvTime and sendTime. Instead, we defined a new feature which is transmissionTime depicted in equation 1. It defines the duration needed for a message to be transmitted from the sender to the receiver.

To sum up, after several treatments, we used the following features: transmissionTime, RSSI, pos_x, pos_y, spd_x and spd_y, as well as the target attack. In Fig. (**3**), we present the obtained correlation matrix.

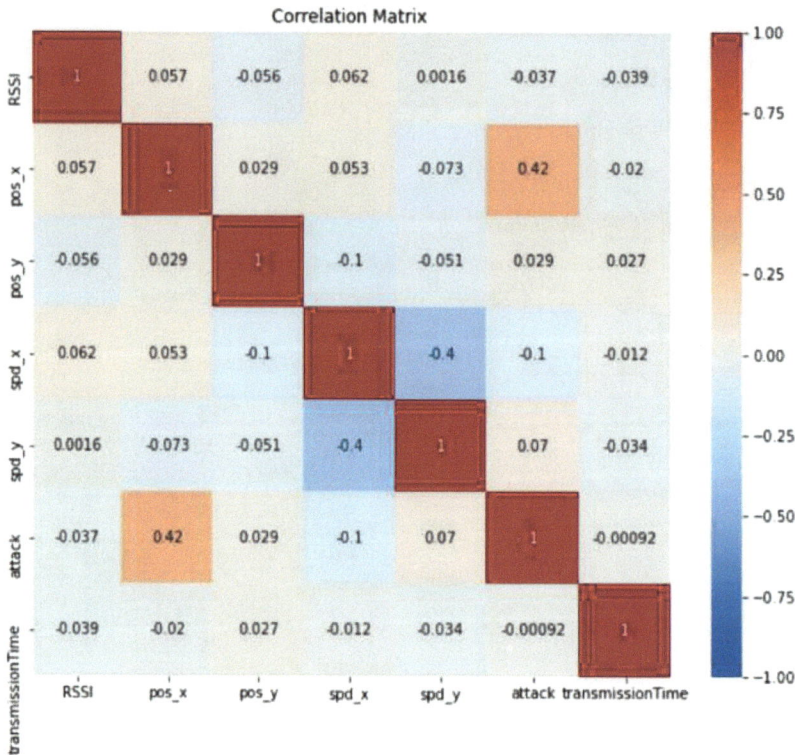

Fig. (3). Correlation Matrix after dimensionality reduction.

$$transmissionTime = rcvTime - sendTime \qquad (1)$$

Data Standardization

Standardization of a dataset is required for many machine learning algorithms. It removes the sample mean. Then, it scales all the values to unit variance. However, outliers influence negatively the sample mean or variance. For that reason, the median and the interquartile range often give better results. Therefore, in this work, we will use the RobustScaler. In fact, it removes the median and scales the data according to the quantile range.

PERFORMANCE EVALUATION

This section exposes the main results of conducted experiments to evaluate the proposed ML-based framework.

Metrics

In order to measure the performance of ML classifiers, we used different metrics such as *Accuracy*, *Precision*, *Recall* and *F-measure*. These metrics were calculated according to true positives (*TP*), false positives (*FP*), true negatives (*TN*) and false negatives (*FN*).

- **Accuracy:** Accuracy is the ratio between the number of correct predictions to the total number of predictions made. It is defined as:

$$Accuracy = \frac{TP+TN}{TP+TN+FP+FN} \qquad (2)$$

- **Precision:** Precision is the ratio between correctly predicted positive and total predicted positive samples. It is calculated according to the equation below. Hence, high precision indicates low *FP*.

$$Precision = \frac{TP}{TP+FP} \qquad (3)$$

- **Recall:** Recall is the ratio between correctly predicted positive samples and all samples that belong actually to the positive class. It is calculated according to the equation below. Hence, high recall indicates low *FN*. Consequently, this metric is important for the evaluation of an ML model in the security field.

$$Recall = \frac{TP}{TP+FN} \tag{4}$$

- **F-measure:** F-measure is a combined metric as the harmonic average of both *Recall* and *Precision*. It is calculated according to the equation below:

$$F - measure = \frac{2 \times Precision \times Recall}{Precision + Recall} \tag{5}$$

$$F - measure = \frac{2 \times TP}{2 \times TP + FP + FN} \tag{6}$$

Hyperparameters Optimization

Hyperparameter optimization is an essential step in our work. However, finding the best hyperparameter settings manually takes too much time. For that reason, there are many techniques used for hyper-parameter optimization, such as Grid search [31]. Grid search is an approach that builds and evaluates a model for every combination of the algorithm hyperparameters indicated in the grid. In this part, we will compare the best results of the grid search functions for the different used ML classifiers. This comparison allows the selection of the most efficient hyperparameters.

- **Logistic Regression (LR):** We applied the grid search on the solver hyperparameter. Table **3** presents the most efficient solvers and their results. According to the results presented, the two solvers have the same performance. However, the liblinear solver has a lower execution time than the lbfgs solver. Therefore, the liblinear solver will be selected as the most efficient solver.

Table 3. Logistic regression results.

Hyper Parameters	Accuracy	F-measure	Precision	Recall	Execution Time (Sec)
Solver: liblinear	0.9049	0.5193	0.9075	0.3644	0.02570
Solver: lbfgs	0.9049	0.5193	0.9075	0.3644	0.21115

- **Support Vector Machine (SVM):** For this classifier, we apply the grid search method on the different kernels in order to find the most suitable kernel for our problem. Table **4** depicts the most efficient kernels and their results. According to the results, the rbf kernel has higher performances and lower execution time than the polynomial kernel. Therefore, the rbf kernel will be selected as the most efficient kernel.

Table 4. SVM Results.

Hyper Parameters	Accuracy	F-measure	Precision	Recall	Execution Time (Sec)
Kernel: poly	0.9047	0.5055	0.9463	0.3455	35.66028
Kernel: rbf	0.9101	0.5461	0.9531	0.3833	1.93050

- **K-Nearest Neighbors (KNN):** We applied the grid search on different KNN hyperparameters. In fact, the number of neighbors, the weight and the metric were taken into consideration. The most efficient combinations are:
  - (1): n neighbors= 3, weights= distance and metric= manhattan
  - (2): n neighbors= 15, weights= uniform and metric= manhattan

Table **5** presents these combinations and their results. According to the previous results, combination (1) presents the most efficient hyperparameters. In fact, it gives the highest metrics values, especially the *F-measure, Recall* and execution time.

Table 5. KNN Results.

Hyper Parameters	Accuracy	F-measure	Precision	Recall	Execution Time (Sec)
(1)	0.9901	0.9640	0.9944	0.9354	0.10221
(2)	0.9809	0.9276	0.9977	0.8669	0.15711

- **Decision Tree:** In this classifier, we tested two hyperparameters which are the criterion and the maximal depth. The combinations that give the best metrics are:
  - (1): criterion= entropy and max depth= 12
  - (2): criterion= gini and max depth= 8

Performances of these combinations are presented in Table **6**.

Table 6. Decision Tree Results.

Hyper Parameters	Accuracy	F-measure	Precision	Recall	Execution Time (Sec)
(1)	0.9975	0.9914	0.9941	0.9882	0.11419
(2)	0.9935	0.9776	0.9979	0.9582	0.08539

The combination (2) gives the best execution time. The execution time of the combination (1) is higher than the execution time of the combination (2).

However, the combination (1) has the best *Accuracy*, *F-measure* and *Recall* metrics. Therefore, it will be selected as the most efficient combination.

- **Random Forest:** In this classifier, we tested three hyperparameters which are the criterion, the maximal depth and the number of estimators. The combinations that give the best metrics are:
  - (1): criterion= entropy, max depth= 12 and n estimators= 100
  - (2): criterion= entropy, max depth= 12 and n estimators= 50
  - (3): criterion= entropy, max depth= 6 and n estimators= 100

These combinations are presented in Table **7**. The combination (1) has a long execution time, which is not suitable for VANET real-time requirement. The combination (3) has the shortest execution time. However, the combination (2) gives the best *Accuracy*, *F-measure* and *Recall* metrics. For that reason, it will be selected as the most efficient combination.

Table 7. Random Forest Results.

Hyper Parameters	Accuracy	F-measure	Precision	Recall	Execution Time (Sec)
(1)	0.9980	0.9927	0.9980	0.9889	3.52673
(2)	0.9981	0.9931	0.9960	0.9889	1.73117
(3)	0.9811	0.9389	0.9977	0.8331	1.07872

Comparison between ML Models

After optimizing the hyperparameters of each model, we will compare the performance of these algorithms for our IDS. In Fig. (**4**), the performances of different ML models are presented.

These results prove that Logistic Regression, SVM and Gaussian Naïve Bayes are not efficient for our problem. KNN, Decision Tree and Random Forest are obviously more powerful. Comparing these models, we notice that the Random Forest gives the highest *Accuracy*, *F-measure*, Precision and *Recall*. Besides, it evidently needs a longer execution time than KNN and Decision tree models. This long execution time could affect the efficiency of our proposed solution.

KNN and decision trees have significantly shorter execution times with acceptable metrics. Decision Tree shows the highest *F-measure* and *Recall* metrics. Therefore, it is considered the most efficient model.

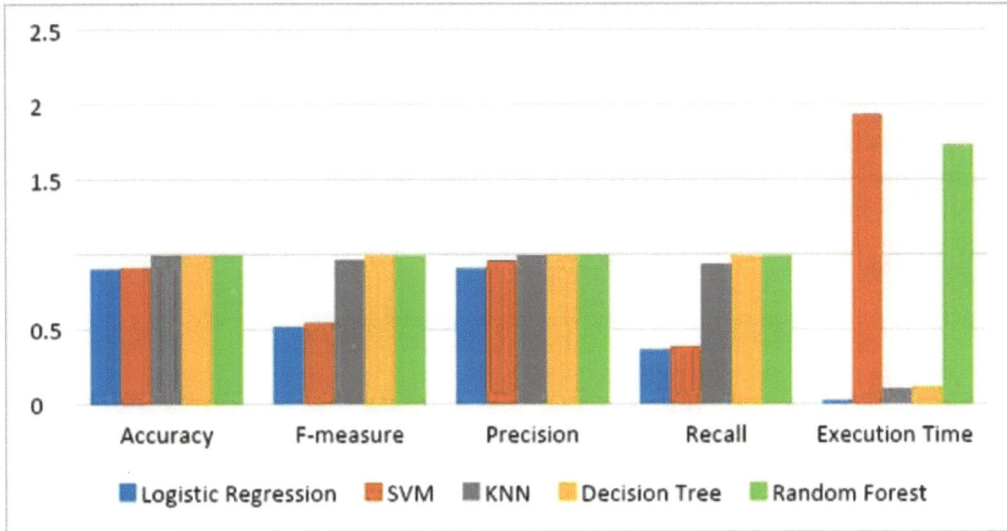

Fig. (4). Comparison between ML models.

CONCLUSION

Security is a main concern in VANET as they are subject to many threats and they inherit from all wireless network vulnerabilities. VANET is mainly used for transmitting safety information to users. As these data are related to human safety, therefore any alteration or suppression can be a serious threat. To secure sensitive safety date, security countermeasures should be set up within VANET communications.

This chapter reviews the security issue of VANET communication, which is exposed; then, a comprehensive framework to design ML-based IDS for VANET is introduced. Furthermore, we used a recent dataset, namely VeReMi, to evaluate the performances of several Machine learning techniques to detect position falsification attacks.

For the data preprocessing phase, and after data cleaning, we used Grid to search for hyper-parameter optimization for each used ML model. Experimental results prove that KNN, Decision Tree and Random Forest outperform Logistic Regression, SVM and Gaussian Naïve Bayes in terms of *Accuracy, F-measure, Precision* and *Recall*.

Incorporating ML techniques when designing IDS is undoubtedly a promising way to detect all sorts of security threats. Position falsification attack is one of the harmful ones that may endanger safety applications. Further work should be done to combine the use of IDS with other efficient security countermeasures that are able to block access to malicious nodes and eliminates erroneous generated data at as the right moment. At this end, future work will consider the integration of a ML-based framework within a complete communication architecture, combining not only prevention but also curative techniques to tackle zero-day attacks. Such architecture should benefit from the current integration of Edge technology with VANET infrastructure.

REFERENCES

[1]   J. Wang, J. Liu, and N. Kato, "Networking and communications in autonomous driving: A survey", *IEEE Commun. Surv. Tutor.,* vol. 21, no. 2, pp. 1243-1274, 2019.
[http://dx.doi.org/10.1109/COMST.2018.2888904]

[2]   F. Cunha, L. Villas, A. Boukerche, G. Maia, A. Viana, R.A.F. Mini, and A.A.F. Loureiro, "Data communication in VANETs: Protocols, applications and challenges", *Ad Hoc Netw.,* vol. 44, pp. 90-103, 2016.
[http://dx.doi.org/10.1016/j.adhoc.2016.02.017]

[3]   P.K. Singh, R.R. Gupta, S.K. Nandi, and S. Nandi, "Machine learning based approach to detect wormhole attack in VANETs", In: *Workshops of the International Conference on Advanced Information Networking and Applications,* Matsue, Japan, 2019.
[http://dx.doi.org/10.1007/978-3-030-15035-8_63]

[4]   A. Ghosal, and M. Conti, "Security issues and challenges in V2X: A Survey", *Comput. Netw.,* vol. 169, no. 107093, 2020.
[http://dx.doi.org/10.1016/j.comnet.2019.107093]

[5]   A. Abunei, C. Comşa, and I. Bogdan, "Implementation of ETSI ITS-G5 based inter-vehicle communication embedded system", In: *2017 International Symposium on Signals, Circuits and Systems (ISSCS),* Romania, 2017.
[http://dx.doi.org/10.1109/ISSCS.2017.8034921]

[6]   M.N. Mejri, "Securing vehicular networks against denial of service attacks", PhD thesis. Sorbonne University, France, 2016.

[7]   G. Naik, B. Choudhury, and J.M. Park, "IEEE 802.11bd & 5G NR V2X: Evolution of Radio Access Technologies for V2X Communications", *IEEE Access,* vol. 7, pp. 70169-70184, 2019.
[http://dx.doi.org/10.1109/ACCESS.2019.2919489]

[8]   M.A.H. Al Junaid, A.A. Syed, M.N.M. Warip, K.N.F.K. Azir, and N.H. Romli, "Classification of Security Attacks in VANET: A review of requirements and perspectives", *Information & Communication Technology (ICT), Science (SCI) & Mathematics (SM),* 2018.
[http://dx.doi.org/10.1051/matecconf/201815006038]

[9]   Y. Lahrouni, C. Pereira, B.A. Bensaber, and I. Biskri, "Using mathematical methods against denial of service (dos) attacks in VANET", *15th ACM International Symposium on Mobility Management and Wireless Access, USA,* 2017.
[http://dx.doi.org/10.1145/3132062.3132065]

[10]   B. Yu, C.Z. Xu, and B. Xiao, "Detecting sybil attacks in VANETs", *J. Parallel Distrib. Comput.,* vol. 73, no. 6, pp. 746-756, 2013.
[http://dx.doi.org/10.1016/j.jpdc.2013.02.001]

[11]   R. Mishra, A. Singh, and R. Kumar, "VANET security: Issues, challenges and solutions", *International Conference on Electrical, Electronics, and Optimization Techniques (ICEEOT),* 2016.
[http://dx.doi.org/10.1109/ICEEOT.2016.7754846]

[12]   R. Raghav, R. Danu, A. Ramalingam, and G.K. Kumar, "Detection of node impersonation for emergency vehicles in VANET", *Int. J. Eng. Res. Technol.,* vol. 2, no. 12, pp. 3383-3389, 2013.

[13]   S.M. Safi, A. Movaghar, and M. Mohammadizadeh, "A novel approach for avoiding wormhole attacks in VANET", In: *Second International Workshop on Computer Science and Engineering,* China, 2009.

[14]   A. Upadhyaya, and J.S. Shah, "Blackhole Attack and its effect on VANET", *Int. J. Comput. Sci. Eng.,* vol. 5, pp. 25-32, 2017.

[15]   M. Arif, G. Wang, M. Zakirul Alam Bhuiyan, T. Wang, and J. Chen, "A survey on security attacks in VANETs: Communication, applications and challenges", *Vehicular Communications,* vol. 19, p. 100179, 2019.
[http://dx.doi.org/10.1016/j.vehcom.2019.100179]

[16]   A. Quyoom, A.A. Mir, and D.A. Sarwar, "Security attacks and challenges of VANETs : A literature survey", *J. Multim. Inform. Sys.,* vol. 7, no. 1, pp. 45-54, 2020.
[http://dx.doi.org/10.33851/JMIS.2020.7.1.45]

[17]   I.A. Sumra, J-L. Ab Manan, and H. Hasbullah, "Timing attack in vehicular network", *15ᵗʰ WSEAS International Conference on Computers, World Scientific and Engineering Academy and Society (WSEAS),* 2011.

[18]   H. Hasrouny, "Trust management and security solutions for vehicular networks", PhD thesis, Telecommunications National Institute, France, 2018.

[19]   D. Koo, Y. Shin, J. Yun, and J. Hur, "An online data-oriented authentication based on merkle tree with improved reliability", *IEEE International Conference on Web Services (ICWS), Honolulu, USA,* 2017.
[http://dx.doi.org/10.1109/ICWS.2017.102]

[20]   R. Barskar, M. Ahirwar, and R. Vishwakarma, "Secure key management in vehicular ad-hoc network: A review", *International Conference on Signal Processing, Communication, Power and Embedded System (SCOPES), India,* 2016.
[http://dx.doi.org/10.1109/SCOPES.2016.7955730]

[21]   D. Manivannan, S.S. Moni, and S. Zeadally, "Secure authentication and privacy-preserving techniques in Vehicular Ad-hoc NETworks (VANETs)", *Vehicular Communications.* vol. 25, pp. 100247, 2020.

[22]   N. Parikh, and M.L. Das, "Privacy-preserving services in VANET with misbehavior detection", *IEEE International Conference on Advanced Networks and Telecommunications Systems (ANTS), India,* 2017.
[http://dx.doi.org/10.1109/ANTS.2017.8384146]

[23]   L. Chen, S.L. Ng, and G. Wang, "Threshold anonymous announcement in VANETs", *IEEE J. Sel. Areas Comm.,* vol. 29, no. 3, pp. 605-615, 2011.
[http://dx.doi.org/10.1109/JSAC.2011.110310]

[24]   A. Perez, "TLS and DTLS protocols, network security", Network Security, 1ˢᵗ ed. John Wiley & Sons Inc., pp. 109-132, 2014.

[25]   "Intelligent Transport Systems (ITS); Security; ITS communications security architecture and security management", *ETSI TS 102 940 V1.3.1 (2018-04),* 2018.

[26]   S.C. Kalkan, and O.K. Sahingoz, "In-vehicle intrusion detection system on controller area network with machine learning models", *11th International Conference on Computing, Communication and Networking Technologies (ICCCNT), India,* 2020.
[http://dx.doi.org/10.1109/ICCCNT49239.2020.9225442]

[27]   L. Yang, A. Moubayed, I. Hamieh, and A. Shami, "Tree-based intelligent intrusion detection system in internet of vehicles", *IEEE Global Communications Conference (GLOBECOM), Waikoloa, HI, USA,* 2019.
[http://dx.doi.org/10.1109/GLOBECOM38437.2019.9013892]

[28]   F.A. Ghaleb, A. Zainal, M.A. Rassam, and F. Mohammed, "An effective misbehavior detection model

using artificial neural network for vehicular ad hoc network applications", *IEEE Conference on Application, Information and Network Security (AINS), Malaysia,* 2017.
[http://dx.doi.org/10.1109/AINS.2017.8270417]

[29] J. Kamel, M. Wolf, R.W. van der Hei, A. Kaiser, P. Urien, and F. Kargl, "VeReMi Extension: A dataset for comparable evaluation of misbehavior detection in VANETs", *IEEE International Conference on Communications (ICC), Dublin, Ireland,* 2020.
[http://dx.doi.org/10.1109/ICC40277.2020.9149132]

[30] S. Khalid, T. Khalil, and S. Nasreen, "A survey of feature selection and feature extraction techniques in machine learning", In: Science and Information Conference, London, UK, 2014.
[http://dx.doi.org/10.1109/SAI.2014.6918213]

[31] M. Feurer, J. Springenberg, and F. Hutter, "Initializing bayesian hyperparameter optimization via meta-learning", *AAAI Conference on Artificial Intelligence, Austin, Texas, USA,* 2015.

CHAPTER 7

Implementation of Smartphone-based Indoor Positioning Application Using Trilateration

Saptarshi Paul[1,*]

[1] *Department of Computer Science, Assam University, Silchar, India*

Abstract: Positioning applications using GPS, A-GPS, and other technologies are now commonly found in most held hand smart devices. The advents in applications/tools such as Google Maps have made outdoor positioning and guidance much easier. Compared to outdoor positioning, Indoor positioning has always been more challenging. Indoor positioning faces an uphill task of proper Position fixing due to an array of issues that are otherwise absent in the outdoor environment. In this chapter, through trilateration, we have devised an application that takes the help of Wi-Fi signals and does Position fixing in an indoor environment. Indoor localization and positioning is still a challenging topic in Wireless Sensor Networks, and also it is vital because of its effects on monitoring, power consumption, *etc.*, for our work distance calculation of an object using the proposed path loss model, and Trilateration method is implemented to calculate the unknown Position of a device under the environment. It collects all the Wi-Fi signals and finds the exact matches with the database to calculate the user's actual Position on the map. It reduces the complexity of computing the distance of different access points from the user and reduces error. The tool was found to be quite promising in detecting the Position of the host device. Future work that can be extended from this work can include work with a path loss model, Multi-Sensor Fusion, to the inclusion of pattern recognition.

Keywords: A-GPS, Indoor positioning, Position-fixing, Trilateration, Wi-Fi.

INTRODUCTION

Smartphones have become a 'part and parcel' of life. Rapid growth in Smartphone technology made our work comfortable and easy. For ease to use and uncountable features, the uses of Smartphone users are increasing exponentially. The growth is observed both in software technology (Operating system based/third party applications) as well as in hardware variety and companies. The gradual increase in technological accuracy and decrease in the cost of handheld wireless devices

[*] **Corresponding author Saptarshi Paul:** Department of Computer Science, Assam University, Silchar, India; E-mail: paulsaptarshi@yahoo.co.in

Arun Solanki and Anuj Kumar Singh (Eds.)

propelled the functionality and availability of mobile stations. These factors, coupled with low price, has led many to switch to handheld mobile stations. It naturally created competition with desktops in use. Fig. (**1**) shows the international mobile *versus* desktop user base [1].

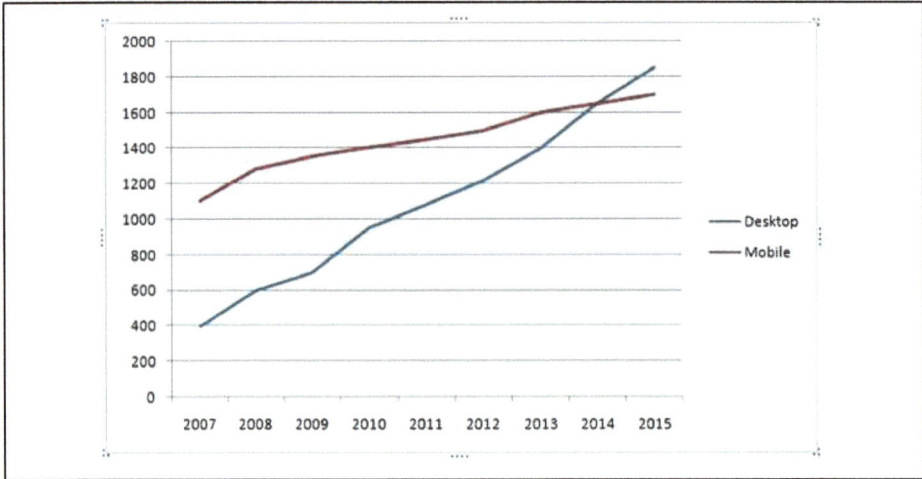

Fig. (1). Mobile *versus* desktop users in million-world wide.

The World Wide Web has been fueling growth in the fields of IOT, Information technology, and technology-enabled business areas. Statistics show that almost 95% of mobile station users prefer having internet connectivity. Fig. (**2**) shows the comparison of Internet users among Desktop, Mobile, and other connected devices.

Internet-enabled smartphones have become a commonly held hand mobile station that enables us to locate our position in the outdoor environment through a host of application programs using technologies such as GPS and AGPS, among others. Indoor positioning through the same device can be achieved by a host of other technologies. Though accurate indoor positioning is much tougher to achieve due to an array of problems, it can still be achieved. This work describes how the positioning was achieved in an indoor environment using the trilateration method. The chapter has been organized into the following sections: Section 2 lists the problem statement and technical challenges. Section 3 lists similar work done for indoor positioning in recent times. Section 4 discussed the methodology undertaken. Section 5 discusses the positioning technologies in brief Section 6 takes up, in detail, the development of the application, including the algorithm and the flowchart. Section 7 is used to show the snapshots of the client and server sides. Section 8 describes the Comparison Study (Existing Trilateration *versus* Implemented Trilateration). Section 9 deals with the conclusion. Section 10 takes up the future practical extensions of the work.

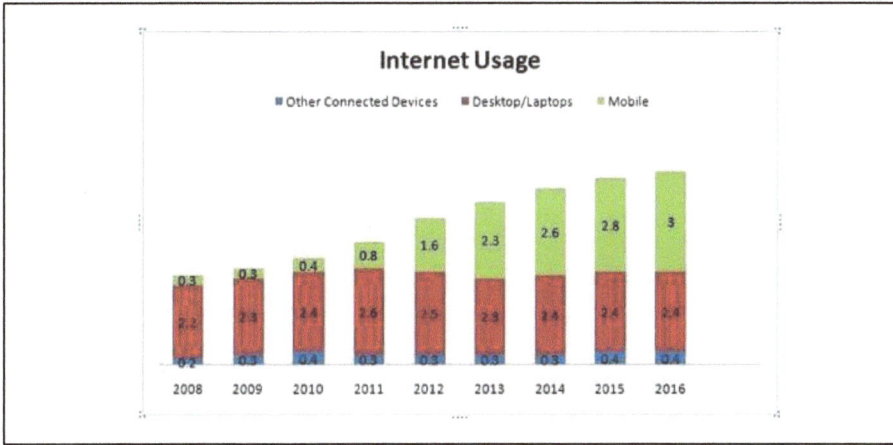

Fig. (2). Internet user.

Problem Statement and Technical Challenges

Opposed to outdoor navigation, the problem of Indoor navigation and positioning is quite challenging. Both of them aim to determine the actual position of an object or device accurately. The past few decades have seen positioning systems (GPS, GLONASS, *etc.*) widely used to track devices. Finding the best possible route to travel is one of the multitudes of applications that exist for positioning systems. In-door positioning and localization techniques are highly motivated by outdoor Positioning Systems but are a different challenge altogether. Outdoor positioning systems do not work properly in Indoor environments because of multiple factors such as high-story buildings, obstruction because of the roof, walls, and other obstacles that ultimately attenuate the signal coming from the satellites. After attenuation, the receiver receives fluctuating and faded signals, leading to a miscalculation of coordinates by GPS devices. To address the problem, an array of alternate techniques has been proposed for indoor positioning, navigation, and tracking. These include methods such as Assisted Global-Positioning-System, Wireless-Fidelity, Bluetooth, Zigbee, Beacon, and Radio-Frequency-Identifier (RFID). For our research purpose, we take up Indoor positioning and navigation using a received signal strength indicator (RSSI) based on IEEE 802.11. For position fixing, trilateration with the received signal strength indicator (RSSI) method will be implemented in a smartphone. The mobile platform can be a smart device with a low-quality WLAN antenna and low memory. Low battery consumption is also considered for the platform. Many technical challenges were faced during the design and implementation of the RSSI-based indoor navigation mobile platform. The instability of the received signal strength was the major challenge, as trilateration was to be based on the WLAN positioning system. Successful Indoor positioning and navigation system can be designed depending on the existing infrastructure inside any building structure. Such positioning systems can be based on Wi-Fi technology. Wi-Fi is a wireless technology used mainly as Pico-cell. With the advent of multiple Fiber optic-based service providers, it is a very commonly found technology in most apartment households [2]. A network of Wi-Fi access points, often known as Wi-Fi hotspots, makes up this system. Our indoor positioning and navigation are based on the Wi-Fi access point (modem/router) signal that a smartphone picks up. Many methods, including the JTC path loss model and the free Space path loss model, can determine the distance. Any trilateration algorithm was also applied to find the current user position based on the distance calculated by the path loss model. Therefore the user position fully depends on the Received Signal Strength (RSS). The occurrence of any disturbance, such as the wall, magnetic field, or other nearby objects, may attenuate the signal strength, which causes an error in Position fixing. Therefore, it is evident that accurate Position fixing depends on the Indoor environment and the density of Wi-Fi access points. Since accuracy increases depending on the number of access positions in the area.

Similar Work

Work in an indoor environment has been carried out earlier, and various methods have been adopted. Table **1** summarizes some important work done in this field:

Table 1. Table showing similar work in the domain.

The Approach Explored/Undertaken	Author /Book /Reference
Wi-Fi-Based Indoor Positioning System Using handheld devices [2]	Bin Hu, Engineering and Health Royal Melbourne Institute of Technology (RMIT)
RSS-based technique for indoor positioning [3]	Ubiquitous Positioning and Mobile Location-Based Services in Smart Phones
A-GPS-based system for accurate indoor positioning [4]	ChittorSundaramurthy, The University of Texas at San Antonio [3]
High-sensitivity GPS-enabled system for indoor positioning [5]	A.BARBEAU, G. Nidhan
Trilateration Based Localization Algorithm for Wireless Sensor Networks [6]	Oguejiofor O.S, Aniedu A.N, Ejiofor H.C, Okolibe A.U
Indoor localization and navigation for the Android platform [7]	JurajBenicek, MaSaryk University

(Table 1) cont.....

The Approach Explored/Undertaken	Author /Book /Reference
Improved Wi-Fi Indoor Positioning [8]	Rui Ma, QiangGuo, Changzhen Hu, and JingfengXue.
AGPS and Infrared based guidance system for Android and I-phone [9].	Denis Huber School of Electrical and Computer Engineering Technical University
Indoor Navigation System for Handheld Devices [10]	Manh Hung V. Le, Dimitris Saragas, Nathan Webb

Table **1** shows that various methods, such as A-GPS, RSS, Infrared, and Wi-Fi-based methods, have been explored for indoor positioning with varying degrees of accuracy. Our study of the above works gave us the advantages and disadvantages of the explored method and encouraged us to come up with the implemented work.

POSITIONING TECHNOLOGIES

Technologies for positioning include Global Positioning Systems, Assisted-GPS, Wireless-Fidelity, Radio Frequency Identification (RFID), and infrared-based systems. All the mentioned technologies have more or less been explored as potential use and capability in positioning. Indoor positioning technologies such as finger-printing [11], Offline acquisition process, and online positioning methods are available for use [12, 13].

Positioning Technologies in Common Use

Positioning technologies nowadays are numerous to find the exact location of people or mobile devices depending on the environment and situation; positioning methodologies are used. Different type of techniques gives different levels of accuracy and complexity to user needs. Commonly used positioning technology is Global Positioning System (GPS), which can offer accuracy in two different levels one high accuracy (centimeter), and another low accuracy (meter) depending on positioning methods used to determine the Position and type of the system (receiver) used to determine the Position. In the outdoor environment, the output is satisfactory; whenever it comes into an indoor environment, the accuracy level decreases. For this reason, Global Positioning System is used in the outdoor environment, and alternatively, indoor navigation and positioning system uses assisted GPS, Wi-Fi, Bluetooth beacon, and other devices having small coverage area are used for certain features. *e.g.*, Wireless Fidelity based location technology found more use despite its challenges. In this chapter, we oversee some of the location technologies with their basic system requirements, performance, and their accuracy in the practical field. Popular Positioning techniques to navigate and locate different kinds of smart devices many of the positioning techniques are used in outdoor and indoor environments. For outdoors commonly used Global Positioning System is used for high accuracy, is easily available, and is user-friendly. But the drawback of the global positing system is it does not work perfectly for the indoor environment due to the attenuation of the signal by different obstacles. Therefore, many other solutions have to explore to achieve positioning capabilities. Some of the common methods have been introduced below.

Global Positioning System

Global Positioning System is the first of many LEO satellites' radio navigation grids. Put into orbit by the Government of the United States, it is operated by a special branch of the USAF. It is a navigation system that spans the whole globe. This LEO satellite system can provide locations and time information to the GPS receiver, provided the user has an unobstructed line of sight to the satellites. Four LEO satellites are required for the greatest reception. 24 satellite constellations make up the Global Positioning System, which is used to travel the whole globe simultaneously. Three or more satellites at once can be used to find a single smart device or GPS receiver.It was originally developed for the United States army to make military navigation applications, after 1980, the Positioning system was made available to all civilians.

Assisted Global Positioning System

Assisted Global Positioning System is capable of enhancing the standard of operations of LEO-based Global Positioning. It uses a standard GSM network to provide a backup location and time information. This method helps in determining the location with improved accuracy of the Mobile Station. The improved accuracy is generally achieved in two different patterns. The first method is to increase the accuracy of the time to first fix. In doing so, Assisted Global Positioning Systems makes Mobile stations get Location Area information from the GSM or other cellular networks. As such, the LA information need not be downloaded from the LEO satellites. Secondly, it can be used to assist a Mobile station to gather location information in cases where and when LEO signals fluctuate or in rare cases when not available at all. LEO signals, in cases where they are impacted by concrete structures or natural ones, can make use of nearby GSM BTS to determine the exact location and time data.

Systems Based on Wireless Fidelity

One of the most widely approved and utilized technology for determining to position is Wireless Fidelity. Indoor environments where determining positions can be hard to determine been known to achieve a good degree of accuracy using an available Wireless Fidelity facility. Systems using Wireless Fidelity to achieve location accuracy are the same as GSM MS location updating systems. Latest Wireless Fidelity location systems are known to use Signal strength finger-printing technology. This method is known to use Wireless Fidelity signal strengths emitted from access points in the concerned location. The Signal data from various AP is stored in a central repository which the MS uses for implementing real-time location determination using sensors in the MS.RSS values in the data repository are used in determining the exact MS location by matching the current MS Wireless Fidelity signal data.

Other Systems

Apart from Wireless Fidelity, other technologies using various radio frequencies (Bluetooth, infrared, *etc.*) have been tried as a base for location identification and positioning. These methods have been thoroughly experimented upon. Bluetooth is known to be a common technology being used for the communication of packet data over short ranges. For transmitting the identity of an entity, RFID is used. For a technology with long wavelengths, used for short-range communication, Infrared is used. Though found useful for indoor environments, an IR device does not possess the capability to penetrate walls creating serious constraints for communicating between rooms. Modern mobile stations using GSM and other technologies have been found useful for all the technologies mentioned above. Ultrasonic is a term used to describe a technique that uses oscillating sound pressure waves to locate things and gauge distances. It typically employs a frequency that is higher than the human hearing range's upper limit. These methods can be employed individually or collectively to locate indoor placement with a given level of accuracy.

AIM OF THE WORK

The aim of this research is the development of an android application for navigating a smartphone in an indoor environment with an increase in accuracy. The objectives of this project are:

- To study different types of commercial applications that have been used in different fields and Indoor navigation and positioning (Google Indoor navigation).
- To identify problems faced by different approaches.
- Identification of the best possible method for identification of location and positions to the best possible extent.
- Calculate the actual distance from the nearby Wi-Fi access point to the device.
- Development of an android platform-based application for the client that can be used for collecting signals from various Wi-Fi access points and measuring the

distance from them, calculating the user position, and navigating a user in an indoor area.

- Developing a server-side application with a Database that can store and provide maps of different Indoor areas.

The proposed navigation and positioning system is a preliminary application software coded in Java and XML (extensive-markup-language) that runs on the Android platform (Android, Kit-Kat), MySQL database is used to support the back end of the server application. A database can store the basic information of the Wi-Fi access points that are situated in different positions in the indoor environment [14].

TECHNIQUES FOR INDOOR NAVIGATION

The main aim of Indoor navigation is to locate and navigate any person or device in an indoor environment where a global positioning system (GPS) does not work properly. For this reason, Wi-Fi, Bluetooth, and Beacon can be used to track person or advice depending on their received signal-strength indicator, Time-of Arrival-of signal, or Angle-of arrival-of the signal. Positioning using Wi-Fi has a big challenge signal fluctuation of Wi-Fi access terminals is very high due to various kinds of objects and magnetic fields in the nearby area. Much research has been done on designing and developing a model for a different environment to get the correct result. The commonly used methodologies used for the calculation of MS positions can be summarized:

Fingerprinting

Fingerprinting is a traditional technique to track any device or person based on the RSSI. This technology generally makes use of the various signal strengths that are emitted from multiple access points that the MS can access in the concerned indoor environment. The signal strength of several access points is stored in the database along with user coordinates. During the tracking of any device or a person in the specified indoor environment, the unknown user location and the signal strength are compared with the fingerprint that is stored in the online database to get the actual Position of the user. Such a positioning system gives an accuracy of 0.6 m on average and 1.3 on maximum. The traditional fingerprinting algorithms are mainly composed of two phases: Online and offline positioning methods.

Off-Line Acquisition Method

The off-line acquisition method is composed of 3 stages:

First Stage-Collection of Wi-Fi signal in an indoor environment: This stage is concerned with the collection of Wi-Fi signals. These signals are based on a map that depicts the Access Points. The Access Points map is engineered by forming a grid of access points that are equidistant from each other. The physical movement of the MS collects the Wi-Fi signals by moving to every Access Point location as depicted in the map. Opposed to 3-D modeling, this particular approach makes use of indoor 2-D modeling structures. Here different floors are not considered. Once 2-D modeling of the locations is determined in the indoor environment, division of the indoor architecture takes place into a grid of points, that are equidistant from each other. This turns the location of each Access Point to be denoted as (AP, X, Y). Where AP means id-point for each collecting Access Point. Coordinated for each collecting point is represented by (X, Y). Ultimately, the original Wi-Fi point information is collected by using an MS. These data are collected as original Wi-Fi signals, and their respective location information is then uploaded into a central repository (in a server).

Second stage - Indoor Wi-Fi signal Error handling: Processing of the initial Wi-Fi signals gathered from various Access Points takes place at this step. When the gathering process is ongoing, various mistakes are classified and handled accordingly. Systematic, gross, and random errors are the three main categories under which errors are commonly classed. This step is really crucial.

Third stage - Construction of Database containing Location-Fingerprints: Various location fingerprints are generally used in the whole process. Location finger-print is generally expressed as (ID, X, Y, MAC_k, AVG_k, $PAVG_k$, DEV_k) where the value of k is (k = 1, 2, . . ., n). A single location fingerprint means it is the concerned information collected from an Access Point. If we consider that a particular collecting point can receive an "n" number of different Wi-Fi signals, then by default, that particular location finger-print will, in turn, contain an "n" number of WiFi signal strengths. (ID, X, Y) is used to represent one particular location of one collecting point. The physical address of the "k" th Wi-Fi access point is denoted by MAC_k. The average value of the "k"th original Wi-Fi signal strength is given as AVG_k. Now the average value of the "k"th processed Wi-Fi signal strength will be given as $PAVG_k$. If we consider the standard deviation of the "k"th original Wi-Fi signal. Then the strength is denoted by DEV_k.

On-Line Positioning Method

The online acquisition method is composed of 4 stages:

Stage one: location fingerprints going through Pre-matching. To shorten the time for positioning, we need to reduce the number of possible fingerprints. This stage is responsible for this reduction. This phase is also used for pre-matching the various location fingerprints collected throughout. We apply the algorithm proposed in the online positioning method, then we obtain the Wi-Fi signal information of the desired target. The information gathered from the various Wi-Fi signals can be expressed as (MAC_k, AVG_k, $PAVG_k$, DEV_k) where the value of k stands for (k = 1, 2, . . ., m). The meaning of the symbols is the same as described in Section 3.2.3. In this case, the signal data are received at the target place. In the next step, the gathered contents will use the information gathered from Wi-Fi signals to estimate the location of the target place. This methodology, also known as pre-match, is used to reduce the count of location fingerprints. The method can be divided into two steps:

I: The calculation of MAC addresses will be done from the information gathered from the Wi-Fi signal (on the target place). It can be put as follows

If PAVG > FLAG, (FLAG value is used to distinguish the stronger Wi-Fi Access Point) and FLAG = average value of the total "k" PAVGs.

II: Those possible fingerprints will be chosen as the location fingerprints that contain the above MAC IDs.

Stage two: This stage is used to calculate the improved-Euclidean-distance-positioning after pre-match. The intermediate positioning result (X1, Y1) is obtained from Improved-Euclidean-distance. To consider the traditional Improved-Euclidean-distance-positioning, we choose possible K_d fingerprints and then make use of the locations for estimating the result (X1, Y1). It is observed that The improved-Euclidean-distance points obtained from the fingerprints are found to be the smallest among all possible fingerprints.

Stage three: Calculating the Improved-joint-probability-positioning. After stage three, to get an intermediate positioning result (X2, Y2), the improved joint probability is utilized. For calculating the improved-joint-probability-positioning, we decide to pick the possible Kp fingerprints Wi-Fi-AP. Original Wireless Fidelity signal strength Sensor is used to their location for estimating the result (X2, Y2). The largest possible fingerprints are the improved-joint-probability points of these fingerprints.

Stage four: Calculating Weighted-fusion-positioning. In this stage, we use the values of X1, Y1, X2, and Y2 for the calculation of the final result (X, Y). Here we use the weighted fusion method. But there lies a great drawback. It was found that any changes made to the surrounding (addition or removal of furniture or structures) lead to changes in the fingerprint. Each fingerprint corresponds to each location. As a result, there is a requirement of updating to the records containing the fingerprints [15, 16]. However, this problem of changing surroundings and environment can be dealt with by integrating with other more real-time sensors (photo-camera).

METHODOLOGY USED

In this chapter, we have discussed the design and development of an android application for navigating in an indoor environment with increased accuracy with a Smartphone. To do so, multiple objectives came up, which can be listed as follows:

1. To study different types of commercial applications that have been used in both outdoor and indoor navigation and positioning.
2. To identify the basic problems faced by the currently existing methods.
3. To fix the optimal approach for enhancing position estimate accuracy for the indoor environment.
4. To calculate the actual distance from the nearby Wi-Fi access point to the device.
5. To develop a server-side application with a Database that can store and provide maps of different Indoor areas.
6. Develop an application that can address the client side. It is to be based on the android platform for a collection of signals from the Wi-Fi access point and measuring the distance from them, calculating the user position, and navigating a user in an indoor area.

DEVELOPMENT OF THE APPLICATION

Software used for the Application

The proposed navigation and positioning system is a preliminary application software coded in Java and XML (extensive markup language) that runs on the Android platform (Android, Kitkat), MySQL database is used to support the back end of the server application. A database can store the basic information of the Wi-Fi access points that are situated in different positions in the Indoor environment.

Development Kit, Tools, and Platform

For our Indoor navigation and positioning system, we used android as the software platform, Java Programming language, and MySql server as Database (Database Back End). The idea is to have a smartphone application/tool that can collect Wi-Fi signal data from multiple access points to match the details of an access point with the online database. Based on this decision, the environment is fixed and the Floor map is loaded accordingly [17, 18]. Signal strength is then processed using the model of path loss and an algorithm designed to calculate the distance depending on the path loss, which sends back the result in the form of KK (Kilometer) or meter [19, 20]. Again trilateration algorithm is then executed based on the distance given by the path loss model to give the actual Position of the user.

Platform used (Android)

Android is a commonly used operating system used in MS around the world. It was developed by Google. It is based on the Linux kernel designed for screen touch devices as used in Smartphones and tablets. The graphical-user-interface (GUI) of Android is completely based on systems such as manipulation, using touch, shake, and gesture; they loosely correspond to the actions of the real world, such as pinching, poking, and swiping to be able to modify objects in screen with a virtual keyboard for the text input. In addition to screen-touch devices, Google then developed GoogleTV for Television, smart-wrist-watches android based on O/S, and Android Auto for a car. Each of them is a specialized graphical user interface and variants of Android are also used in Digital cameras, Notebooks, *etc.* Initially, Android was developed by Android Inc. to make users comfortable with touchscreen phones. Android Inc. chooses Java because of Platform Independence. In 2005 Google bought it. In 2007, Android was launched. In the same year, the Open-Handset-Alliance was founded. It brought together enterprises of hardware, software, and telecommunication. It was devoted to the idea of open standards for various mobile stations. The first Android device launched for commercial use was made in September 2008. The O/S has made it through many major releases. The current release is Android 12. It is supposed to be the 12th major release and the 19th version of Android.

MySQL Database

MySQL is open-source relational database management (RDBMS) software owned by oracle, which named combines the name of co-founder Michael Widenius' daughter and SQL, which stands for structured Query Language. MySQL has made the software open source under the GNU General Public License, as well as under a variety of proprietary agreements. MySQL was owned and sponsored by a single for-profit firm, the Swedish company MySQL AB, now owned by Oracle Corporation. For proprietary use, several paid editions are available and over additional functionality.

Server-side Development

In this project, has been used PHP as server sides back-end language to run the application on the server. CSS, HTML, JQuery, and Bootstrap for designing user interfaces and JSON to retrieve data from the Server.

Algorithm used

The localization algorithm used is the RSSI-based trilateration localization technique. This is based on the lacerations method. If we consider the basic formula for the general equation of a circle, then it is as follows:

$$x^2 + y^2 = r^2 \tag{1}$$

For a circle center at x_0; y_0

The equation of the circle will be:

$$(x - x_0)^2 + (y - y_0)^2 = d^2 \tag{2}$$

Considering all the nodes are in the same plane A, B, and C, respectively, we have the following diagram, as shown in Fig. (**3**):

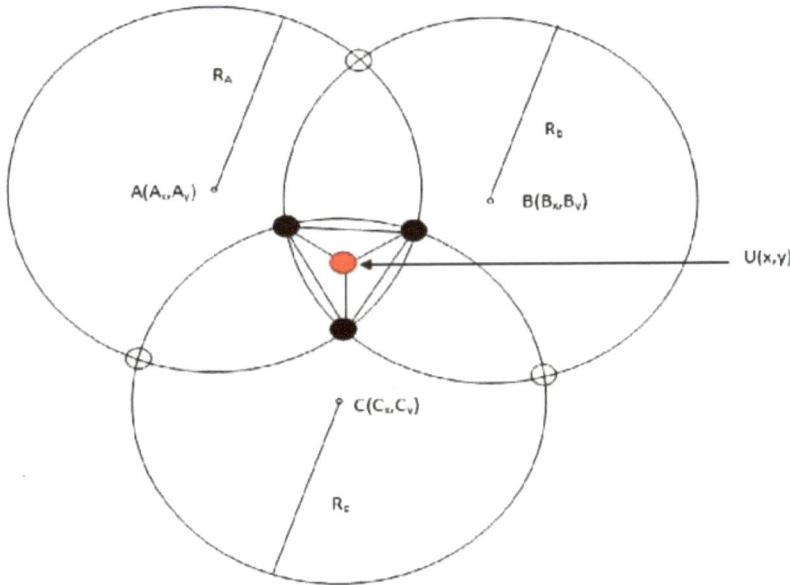

Fig. (3). Localization using trilateration.

$$d_a^2 = (x - x_b)^2 + (y - y_c)^2 \tag{3}$$

$$d_b^2 = (x - x_b)^2 + (y - y_c)^2 \tag{4}$$

$$d_b^2 = (x - x_c)^2 + (y - y_c)^2 \tag{5}$$

To calculate the intersection points of two circles of different radii, let us take an example to illustrate the process of finding intersection points of the circle:

$$(x - 2)^2 + (y - 3)^2 = 9 \tag{6}$$

$$(x - 1)^2 + (y + 1)^2 = 16 \tag{7}$$

We first expand the two equations as follows:

$x^2 - 4x + 4 + y^2 - 6y + 9 = 9 \ x^2 - 2x + 1 + y^2 + 2y + 1 = 16$

Multiply all terms in the first equation by -1 to obtain an equivalent equation and keep the second equation unchanged:

$-x^2 + 4x - 4 - y^2 + 6y - 9 = -9 \ x^2 - 2x + 1 + y^2 + 2y + 1 = 16$

We now add the same sides of the two equations to obtain a linear equation:

$2x - 3 + 8y - 8 = 7$

Which may be written as:

$x + 4y = 9$ or $x = 9 - 4y$

We now substitute x by 9 - 4y in the first equation to obtain:

$(9 - 4y)^2 - 4(9 - 4y) + 4 + y2 - 6y + 9 = 9$

This may be written as $17y2 - 62y + 49 = 0$

Solving the quadratic equation for y we obtain two solutions:

$$y = \frac{31 + 8\sqrt{2}}{17} \approx 2.49, \text{ and} \tag{8}$$

$$y = \frac{31 + 8\sqrt{2}}{17} \approx 1.16 \tag{9}$$

We now substitute the values of y already obtained into the equation x = 9 - 4y to obtain the values for x as follows:

$$x = \frac{29+32\sqrt{2}}{17} \approx -0.96 \text{ and} \tag{10}$$

$$x = \frac{29+32\sqrt{2}}{17} \approx 4.37 \tag{11}$$

The two points of intersection of the two circles are given by (-0.96, 2.49) and (4.37, 1.16).

Similarly, this process can be used to calculate the intersection points of each circle with others. Now if the distance between the node and the intersection point is less than the threshold, then it belongs to that circle. By this method, the respective intersection points are considered. These points represent an intersection area and result in a triangle, whose mid-point can be calculated by the formula given below:

$$ox = \frac{Ax+Bx+Cx}{3} \text{ and } oy = \frac{Ay+By+Cy}{3} \tag{12}$$

Where "Ax" and "Ay" are the x and y coordinates of point A *etc.* This mid-point represents the Position of the device which is the key attention of the work. Plotting this point into the map shows the Position of the smart device on the indoor map.

To have a better idea of how our system works, we have depicted it through an algorithm that is described next and through a flowchart as given in Fig. (4).

Implementation Algorithm

Step1: Scan Wi-Fi Access Points and store them in an array.

Step 2: Check the Internet connection.

Step 3: Match the access points with the database in the server store in the array.

Step 4: If several matches are more than or equal to three, then go through step5 to step 12.

Step 5: Get RSSI of the APs.

Step 6: Store the top three from the matches depending on signal strength.

Step 7: Get Location information(floor id, floor name) from the database against the APs.

Step 8: Get a map from the database against floor id;

Step 9: Set Map in the application.

Step 10: Calculate the distance of three APs using the Path loss model and store it in d1, d2, and d3.

Step 11: Calculate the Position using the trilateration algorithm.

Step 12: Return the Position and depict it in the Floor Map.

The stepwise explanation of how the accurate location in an indoor environment is deduced is shown in our flowchart as Fig. (**4**).

Algorithm:

1. Scan Wi-Fi Access Points and store them in an array.
2. Check the Internet connection.
3. Match the access points with the database in the server store in the array.
4. If the number of matches three more than three, then do.
5. Get RSSI of the APs.
6. Store the top three from the matches depending on signal strength.
7. Get location information (floor id, floor name) from the database against the APs.
8. Get a map from the database against the floor id.
9. Set Map in the application.
10. Calculate the distance of three APs using the path loss model and store it in d1, d2, and d3.
11. Calculate Position using the trilateration algorithm.
12. Return the Position and put in the Floor image.

Screenshots of Server Side and Client Side Interface

Client Side applications

While Fig. (**5**) and Fig. (**6**) show the screenshots of the server side, for testing the application, Maps were created for the building. Existing laboratories on different floors and classrooms were uploaded. The figures shown below are examples of laboratories on various floors. The maps are as being displayed in Fig. (**7**), while (Fig. **8**) depicts the exact location of the device in the Building. (Laboratory 3 and Laboratory 4, Ground floor). So we see that the application can accurately locate the position of the smartphone not only with the accuracy of floors but also concerning rooms wise as uploaded in the maps.

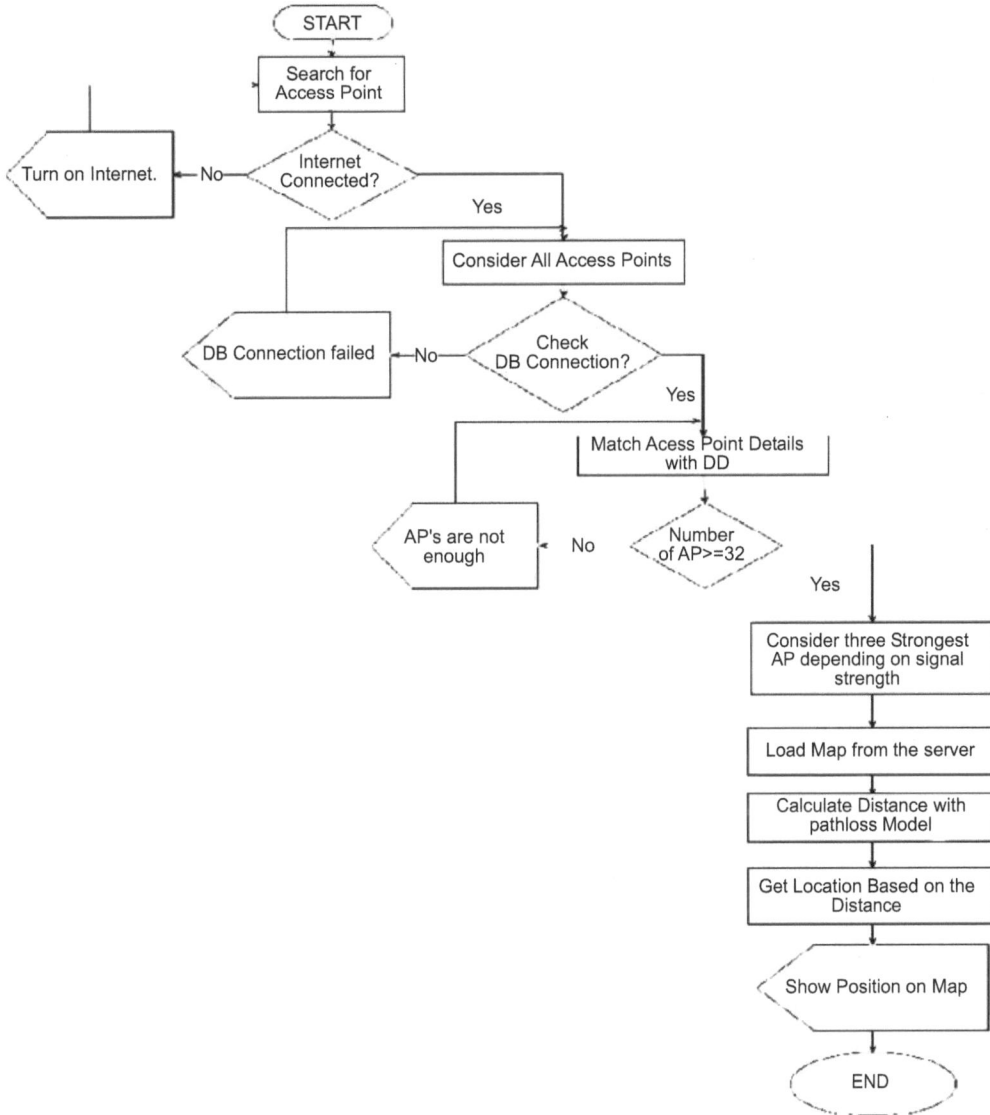

Fig. (4). Flowchart of the indoor positioning application.

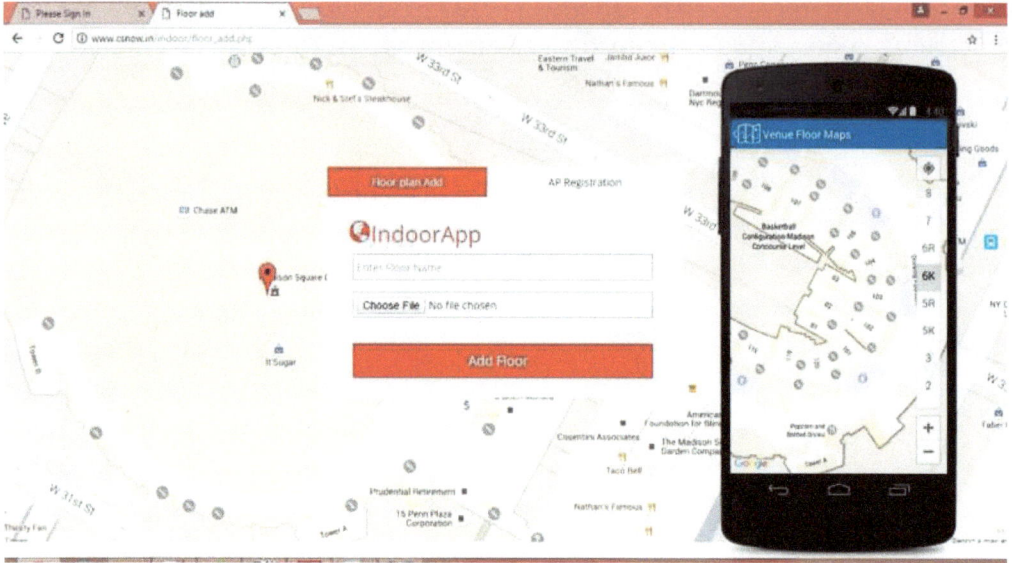

Fig. (5). Screenshot of Server Side application.

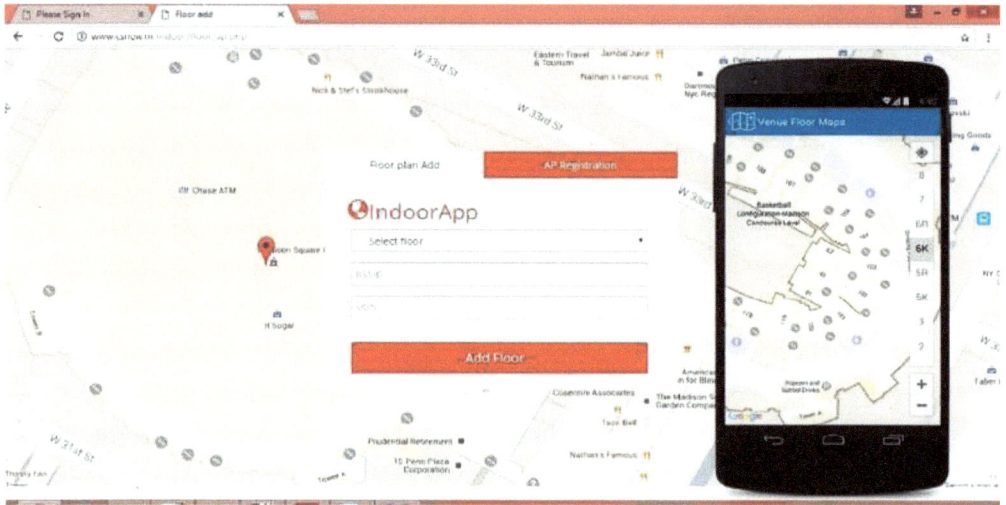

Fig. (6). Screenshot of Access Point on Server Side.

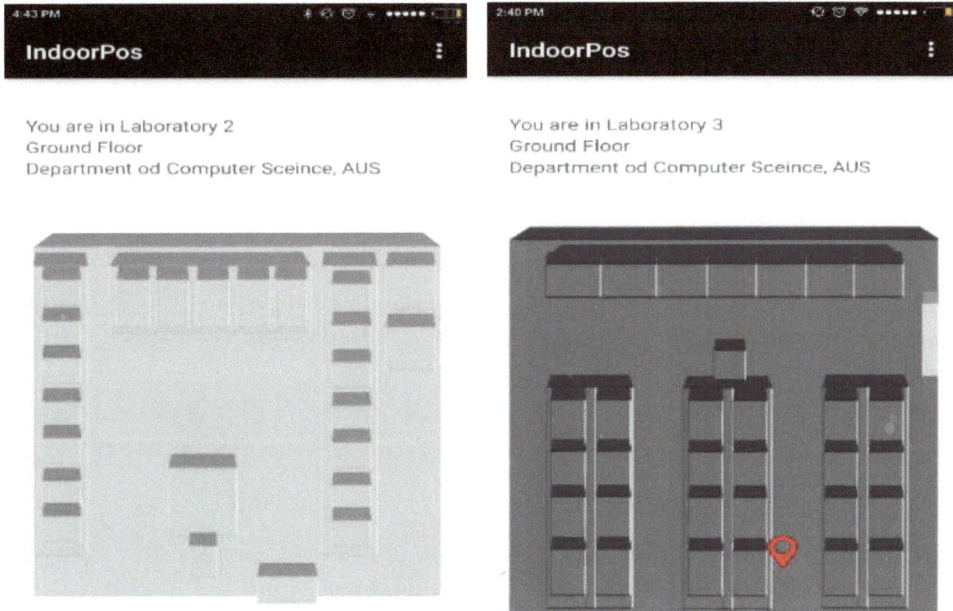

Fig. (7). Loaded maps for the laboratories.

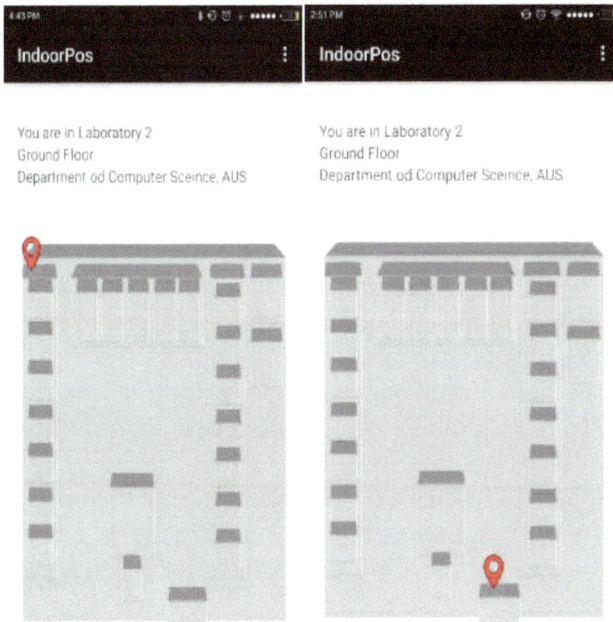

Fig. (8). Position as shown by the application on the client side for different indoor locations.

DISCUSSION OF RESULTS

In Fig. (**8**), we see that the details of the GUI are shown. It also shows the exact location of the Mobile Station/smart device using our algorithm. In the 1st picture, the location of the user is on the extreme left of laboratory 2, while in the second picture, we see that the location has changed to near the exit. Let us now discuss the results by comparing them with the existing methods.

1. Existing trilateration algorithm needs intersection points to calculate the user position; on the other hand, our implemented algorithm/ work needs an area of intersection to calculate the user position.
2. In the existing trilateration algorithm, the intersection point is the user position, and in our implemented algorithm, from the intersection area, it finds the midpoint, which is the user position.
3. In existing trilateration, intersection points are rarely found because of the fluctuation of RSSI. Whereas the implemented algorithm needs an intersection area that is easily available even if RSSI fluctuates.

CONCLUSION AND FUTURE SCOPE

The IEEE W/L protocols were released about fifteen years back, therefore, Wireless Fidelity technical standards are well developed. Meanwhile, it is widely used because of its high speed and extensive coverage. Almost every phone and smart devices have a Wi-Fi facility. For outdoor environments, the Global Positioning System can achieve high accuracy up to three meters in the result. But in the Indoor environment, due to the attenuation of signal for various obstacles like roofs, walls, and magnetic fields, GPS technology does not work perfectly. So, it becomes hard for the user to determine location information in an Indoor environment. This work represents the localization and positioning of a person/ a device in an Indoor environment using the concept of trilateration. Indoor localization and positioning is still a challenging topic in Wireless Sensor Networks and also it is vital because of effecting on monitoring, power consumption, *etc.* To determine an object's distance, the proposed path loss model and trilateration approach are used. This allows us to determine an object's location inside the environment. To determine the user's precise location on the map, it gathers all Wi-Fi signals and searches the database for exact matches. It reduces the complexity of computing the distance of different access points from the user and reduces error.

In this work, the attempt was to calculate the distance of different Wi-Fi access points from the user, based on the signal strength using the path loss model. After calculating the distance in the meter, the trilateration method was applied to calculate the user position. Several domains can be explored further to increase the performance of the positioning and navigation system:

Working with path loss model: Since the path loss models fluctuate when some other object comes nearby, therefore the system can apply different path loss models dynamically depending on the indoor environment.

Multi-Sensor Fusion: Combining different sensors like Gyroscope and proximity makes the application a bit more intelligent, such that the device can understand how far a user can go within a fraction of a second. It can be very much applicable for the reduction of high fluctuations.

Direction of the user: Using inbuilt sensors of mobile devices like proximity and Gyroscope, a path can be created to detect the direction of the user and calculate the distance of a nearby object to navigate the user perfectly.

Hybrid method: A combination of a Global Positing System and an Indoor positioning system can be created to navigate in both environments. Users may navigate outdoors accurately using GPS, and whenever it comes under an indoor environment, it will hand over to the Indoor System is that installed on the server.

Pattern recognition: An advanced system can be developed which can predict the user destination by consulting its history log. Therefore a pattern-matching algorithm can be applied to predict the user destination based on the previous data that is stored in the database.

ACKNOWLEDGEMENTS

The work was implemented by Mr. Biswajit Das of the Department of Computer Science, Assam University, with the help of the resources locally available. The work was carried out under supervision.

REFERENCES

[1]   Available from: http://www.smartinsights.com /mobile-marketing/mobile-marketing-analytics/mob-le-marUniversity of Illinois, Urbana-Champaign, Fundamentals of wireless communication

[2]   B. Hu, "Wi-Fi based indoor positioning system using smartphones", In: *School of Mathematical and Geospatial Sciences College of Science* Engineering and Health Royal Melbourne Institute of Technology (RMIT) University, Master thesis, 2013.

[3]   R. Chen, "Ubiquitous positioning and mobile location-based services in smart phones", IGI Global, 2012.

[http://dx.doi.org/10.4018/978-1-4666-1827-5]

[4]   C.M. Sundaramurthy, *Wi-Fi assistance to a SUPL-based A-GPS simulator for indoor positioning* M.S. 1475836, The University of Texas at San Antonio, 2010.

[5]   P.A. Barbeau, "Positional Accuracy of Assisted GPS Data from High Sensitivity GPS-enabled Mobile Phones", *J. Navig,* pp. 381-399, 2011.

[6]   O.S. Oguejiofor, A. NAniedu, H.C Ejiofor, and A. UOkolibe, "Trilateration based localization algorithm for wireless sensor network", *Int. J. Sci. Mod. Eng.,* vol. 1, no. 10, 2013.

[7]   J. Benicek, "In-door localization and navigation for Android platform", Masaryk University, Faculty of Informatics, 2015.

[8]   M. Rui, and Q. Guo, "An improved wifi indoor positioning algorithm by weighted fusion", In: *School of Software* Beijing Institute of Technology: Haidian District, Beijing, China, 2017.

[9]   Denis Huber School of Electrical and Computer Engineering Technical University, Berlin Background Positioning for Mobile Devices -Android *vs.* iPhone, 2015.

[10]   M.H.V. Le, and D. Saragas, *N.Webb, "Indoor Navigation System for Handheld Devices".* Worcester Polytechnic Institute Worcester: Massachusetts, USA, 2016.

[11]   L. Lovisolo, and R. Campos, "Two-Stage Indoor Positioning using Deep Learning and RF Fingerprinting in WiFi Networks", *Conference on Brazilian Symposium of Telecommunications and Processing of SINAIS,* 2020.

[12]   R. Bill, C. Cap, M. Kofhal, and T. Mundt, "Indoor and outdoor positioning in mobile environments : A review and some investigations on WLAN positioning", *Geograp. Inform.Sci.,* vol. 10, no. 2, 2004.

[13]   H. Liu, H. Darabi, P. Banerjee, and J. Liu, "Survey of wireless indoor positioning techniques and systems", *IEEE Trans. Syst. Man Cybern. C,* vol. 37, no. 6, pp. 1067-1080, 2007.
[http://dx.doi.org/10.1109/TSMCC.2007.905750]

[14]   C. Laoudias, and P. Hui, "The Airplace indoor positioning platform for Android smartphones", *IEEE 13th International Conference on Mobile Data Management (MDM),* pp. 312-315, 2012.
[http://dx.doi.org/10.1109/MDM.2012.68]

[15]   R.S. Campos, A. Chawdhry, and U. Pravir, "Search space reduction in DCM positioning using unsupervised clustering", *Proceedings of IEEE 10th Workshop on Positioning Navigation and Communication (WPNC).* pp. 1–6, Dresden, Germany, 2013.
[http://dx.doi.org/10.1109/WPNC.2013.6533271]

[16]   R.S. Campos, L. Lovisolo, and M.L.R. de Campos, "Wi-Fi multi-floor indoor positioning considering architectural aspects and controlled computational complexity", *Expert Syst. Appl.,* vol. 41, no. 14, pp. 6211-6223, 2014.
[http://dx.doi.org/10.1016/j.eswa.2014.04.011]

[17]   A. Varshavsky, "The SkyLoc Floor Localization System", *Proceedings of the Fifth Annual IEEE International Conference on Pervasive Computing and Communications (PerCom'07), White Plains, USA,* pp. 125-134, 2007.
[http://dx.doi.org/10.1109/PERCOM.2007.37]

[18]   N. Moayeri, J. Mapar, S. Tompkins, and K. Pahlavan, "Emerging opportunities for localization and tracking Guest Editorial", *IEEE Wirel. Commun.,* vol. 18, no. 2, pp. 8-9, 2011.
[http://dx.doi.org/10.1109/MWC.2011.5751290]

[19]   S. Kullback, and R.A. Leibler, "On information and sufficiency", *Ann. Math. Stat.,* vol. 22, no. 1, pp. 79-86, 1951.
[http://dx.doi.org/10.1214/aoms/1177729694]

[20]   Y. Bai, W. Jia, H. Zang, and M. Sun, "Helping the blind to find the floor of destination in multistory buildings using a barometer", *35th Annual International Conference of the IEEE Engineering in Medicine and Biology Society (EMBC).* pp. 4738–4741, 2013.

CHAPTER 8

How the 'Things' Speak: The Usage and Applications of Sensors in IoT

Amartya Chakraborty[1,*]

[1] *University of Engineering and Management, Kolkata, India*

Abstract: The Internet of Things (IoT) has been massively revolutionizing human lives for the last few decades. The powerful and steady advancements in the field of science and technology have aided this process immensely. As a result, almost all aspects of our lives have grown smarter. Nowadays, life is almost unthinkable in the absence of IoT-enabled smart devices, such as smart televisions, smart computers, smart-phones, smart fitness trackers, *etc.* Needless to say, all these devices enjoy ever-growing popularity in this era of smart technology. This development is propelled by the existing digital communication backbone – the Internet. The very Internet, over which human communication started just a few decades back, is now being used by each and everything in our surroundings, be it natural or man-made. The advent and inclusion of IoT in recent times have highlighted how trees, crops, fruits, chairs and tables, electrical appliances, and all other objects around us can interact with each other. They are capable of communicating as freely as humans, and based on such communications, these things' can even behave smartly, individually, and in unison, by making informed decisions in real-time! Given that these things do not possess the gift of life naturally, their ability to express themselves comes from the use of numerous types of sensing devices, also called sensors. The intelligent manufacturing and easy availability of these miniature, cost-effective sensing devices have given a new shape to almost all aspects of our lives. The data regarding the behavior of things, as captured by sensors, is essentially what the things express, and it carries meaning in the particular setting. This data may then be processed and analyzed at the source, transmitted over the internet and processed in a cloud or remote machine. While in some day-to-day applications, the data is used directly for decision-making (for example, in smart electric appliances), in more critical problems, the data needs ample processing and analysis (healthcare, activity recognition, *etc.*). In the latter case, different mathematical model-based machine learning algorithms are utilized to learn hidden patterns or features in acquired data and extracted features. With the use of a trained learning algorithm called a classifier, the new data is then used for decision-making purposes. The choice of such algorithms is often dependent on the type of sensor data being used and the corresponding application area. Thus, it is seen that IoT-based systems find application in various domains, starting with research and development up to industry, agriculture, defense, *etc.* In reality, the progress of researchers in different domains leads to smart products that, in turn, make human lives easier. Research in several pop-

---

[*] **Corresponding author Amartya Chakraborty:** University of Engineering and Management, Kolkata, India; E-mail: amartya3@gmail.com

Arun Solanki and Anuj Kumar Singh (Eds.)

ular verticals, such as Human Activity Recognition, Remote Healthcare, Remote Monitoring, Smart Automation, Smart Agriculture, *etc.*, have yielded many such products. This chapter focuses on the deep-seated relationship between IoT and sensors from the perspective of state-of-the-art research. It offers discussions on the usage of various types of sensing devices, associated data, and their contribution towards solving specific research problems in the respective IoT-based applications. This includes the Video Camera, Inertial Measurement Unit (IMU) Sensors, Ultrasonic Sensors, Electrocardiogram (ECG) Sensors, Passive Infra-Red (PIR) Sensors, Electromyogram (EMG) Sensors, and some commonly used sensing devices for Environmental and Agricultural Smart system development. A pertinent case study is also included to demonstrate the role of sensors in the development of IoT-based systems. This study also highlights how little effort it takes to implement an IoT-based data acquisition system. The different popular application areas are discussed thereafter in terms of some broad categories. This is followed by the description of some of the standard metrics used for evaluation and benchmarking the performance of smart sensing systems. The future of sensing devices has been discussed, followed by the pertinent challenges faced by IoT-enabled smart systems in implementation. Finally, the concluding remarks are offered. The chapter aims to serve as a wholesome source of knowledge, and relevant information to researchers and practitioners who wish to indulge in the development of smart IoT enables sensing systems.

Keywords: Internet of things, Sensors, Smart applications, Sensor applications, IoT.

INTRODUCTION

The extensive usage of the internet framework has been making human lives more connected for a few decades, highlighting how instant communication can be achieved and utilized in social, business, education, and healthcare scenarios with ease. The Internet of Things (IoT) thrives on this same framework by replacing the human factor with things – both natural and man-made. However, a logical restriction in this process is that things, whether natural or man-made, cannot communicate; they lack the gift of life. Similarly, they cannot sense, think or speak. This is where the sensors pray a pivotal role in IoT. This is also noted from the conventional 3-layer architecture of IoT systems, which starts with the sensing layer as illustrated in Fig. (**1**). The data that is sensed in the first layer is then sent with proper network policies and frameworks to the application layer. In this final layer, the data is analyzed for making decisions and executing different applications based on the extracted information.

A sensor is an electronically controlled device that is capable of detecting particular events or measuring the changes in its immediate environment. For instance, the measurement of change in temperature or the detection of infra-red radiation-emitting object presence is a simple function performed by the temperature sensor and Passive Infra-Red (PIR) sensor, respectively. In application, the sensors need to be controlled with proper triggers and power provision so that they work as per requirement. For this purpose, micro-controllers or micro-processors are utilized, where the latter has the added advantage of immediate data processing and decision-making. In other cases, the microcontroller uses Bluetooth modules [1], Wi-Fi modules [2], or GSM [3] modules to communicate the gathered data to a server where the processing or analysis is undertaken. The sensors can also be grouped into two classes based on their usage, while some are deployed in the target environment for detecting any changes in the same, other sensors need to be fit onto specific objects or locations for proper sensing to take place. This also varies according to the particular application field in question. So to properly develop any IoT-based system, it is crucial to determine all the computational and logistic requirements involved in the particular problem. Accordingly, sensors and controllers or processors are to be selected and deployed. A widely used family of micro-controller circuits is the family of Arduino boards [4], whereas, for microprocessors, a popular choice is the Raspberry Pi family [5]

In this chapter, a detailed discussion has been conducted on the usage of various sensing devices in the different popular IoT-based research domains, such as Human Activity Recognition, Smart Healthcare, Smart Environment Monitoring, Smart Agriculture, *etc.* All mentioned electronic components and research work are duly cited for the benefit of the readers, students, and researchers so that they can utilize this work as a ready reference. Some sensor discussions include drawn images for a better understanding of the sensor working principle; readers may refer to the cited web pages for actual product images.

SENSOR PLACEMENT IN IOT-BASED SYSTEMS

Almost all IoT-based systems rely on the effective deployment of sensors, and this deployment can be categorized into two types. This section aims to highlight these deployment scenarios in brief.

Wearable/On-body sensor placement: In this sensor deployment scheme, the main concept is that the IoT-enabled system works outdoors. This essentially means that there is no fixed set of points or locations from where sensors can gather the necessary data. For instance, let us consider the example of a person walking outdoors. This is a general problem in the domain of Human Activity Recognition, where it is critical to obtain data regarding human movement and activity from sensors. However, since the premise is outdoors, it cannot be pre-determined where the person will move towards. In such situations, it becomes necessary to obtain the necessary data from sensors which are placed at fixed positions on the volunteer/person's body. This type of sensing setup is called wearable setup or on-body setup. Miniature sensors can be embedded in clothing or straps/belts to be worn by the monitored person, such that all physiological changes during the volunteer's movement can be successfully captured. With reference to the previous example, we find different systems that utilize foot-worn, leg-worn, wrist-worn, waist-worn, glove-embedded, *etc.*, types of sensing units. It is to be noted that in all such cases, there is no change in the sensor requirement. The effective embedding or placement and robustness of the overall embedded system determine the successful data acquisition in an outdoor environment.

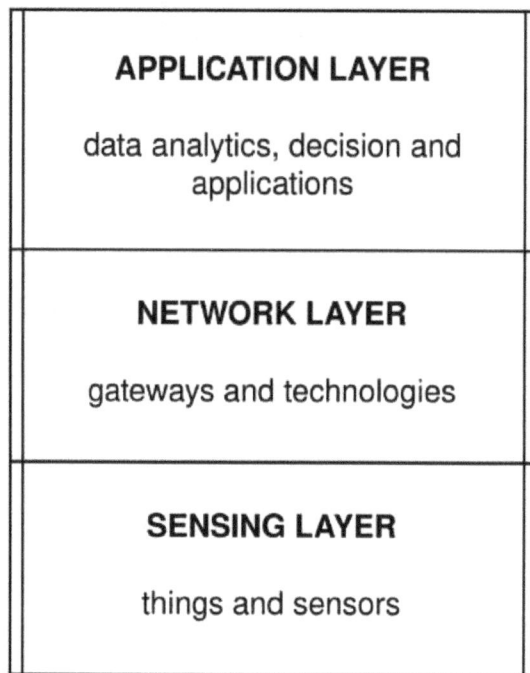

APPLICATION LAYER

data analytics, decision and applications

NETWORK LAYER

gateways and technologies

SENSING LAYER

things and sensors

Fig. (1). 3-layer IoT architecture.

Environment-deployed systems: In contrast to the previous sensor-deployment scenario, in this scheme, the sensors are placed at different fixed positions in the natural environment where the volunteer will perform the activities. This essentially implies that the activities or events to be sensed will be performed at a pre-determined location or place. For example, we can consider the situation where an elderly person is being monitored in a hospital room. In this case, the different sets of sensors can be attached to fixed points, such as the bed stand, the roof, the walls, the floors, *etc.* In any such scenario, when the sensed subject is confined indoors, it is a preferred approach to place the sensors in the environment itself. In comparison to the wearable scheme, this system of sensor deployment has some inherent issues. It may so happen that the arrangement of objects like furniture *etc.* changes in the monitored hospital room. Therefore it becomes necessary to re-align and re-position the sensors fixed in different places of the room in order to sense effectively. Such sensing approaches are thus prone to constant maintenance and supervision. However, there is another advantage of using such device-free setups for data acquisition. For wearable systems, there is an implicit factor of invasiveness – the setups have to be worn constantly for proper data acquisition. This can often lead to discomfort and abnormal activity patterns by the subjects, who are constantly reminded of the fact that each and every movement is being recorded. The acquisition of natural activity data can be hindered in such cases. This is an advantage in the case of device-free systems where the subject need not be concerned about any of the sensors or their working. Natural, normal activities will be performed, and the environment-fitted sensors will keep doing their job properly. This scheme is thus much less invasive and does not invoke any discomfort in the sensed subjects.

Hybrid model: In a few specialized applications, it may so happen that multi-modal data is being gathered using heterogeneous sensors. This means that sensors acquiring different types of data need to be used together to serve a common purpose. As an example, we may consider the problem of group-activity recognition using environment-deployed ultrasonic sensors and smart-phone microphones. The former provided location information of the subjects, whereas the latter helped to provide context to the different group activities that are being performed by the subjects.

SOME POPULAR SENSORS IN IOT-BASED APPLICATIONS

In this section, we have listed a set of commonly used sensors that are utilized in the different types of IoT-based applications. For each sensor, the various domains of application have been discussed with reference to state-of-the-art research works. For each sensor type, there are different products manufactured by various companies. The commonly used and popular sensor models are also cited in the text in this section. This will benefit the readers who wish to start working on any of the research problems.

Video Camera

The video camera works much the same way as any normal camera, with the only difference being that it is capable of recording a temporal sequence of images.

Each image in this sequence pictorially illustrates the condition of the objects in the environment at that particular instant. This approach is widely used for the detection, monitoring, and tracking of human activities and in human healthcare. Any change in the posture, position, or motion of human objects in the zone of coverage of a video camera can be identified and utilized for automated recognition of their activities. As it is difficult to process video signals directly, frame-by-frame analysis is undertaken and advanced principles of image processing and machine learning are utilized. A more enhanced camera imaging system called Kinect is also used for enhanced applications. This system is also called a depth camera, capable of detecting skeleton images of living objects and motion, thus enhancing its applicability.

The maximum usage of video camera-based sensing is seen in Human Activity Recognition Systems (HARS). The recognition of hand gestures has been undertaken in works such as by Sharma *et al.* [6]. The estimation of hand pose has been performed by Czuszynski *et al.* [7]. Ullah *et al.* [8] demonstrated how player actions during sports events can be analyzed from video frames. Other activities like dancing [9], actions in movies [10], and sports events [11] can also be detected accurately from video data. With data of the same modality, works like the identification of abnormal activities in a crowded [12] have also been performed. In healthcare, the detection of Parkinson's disease from video data has been done by Arifoglu *et al.* [13]. Fall detection and monitoring have been performed by Panahi *et al.* [14] and Nizam *et al.* [15] using video frames. In other applications, such as IoT-based video surveillance systems, the video data is analyzed for intruder detection and alarm system [16].

Inertial Measurement Unit (IMU) Sensor

The IMU sensor is a Micro-Electro-Mechanical System (MEMS) based electronic chip that generally consists of the Accelerometer, Gyroscope, and Magnetometer sensors. Each of these sensors is capable of acquiring respective data in the context of a 3-axis coordinate system. The accelerometer measures the linear acceleration of an object in m/s2, the Gyroscope reads the angular velocity of an object in degrees/second and the magnetometer senses the intensity of the magnetic field for an object in terms of μT (micro Tesla) or Gauss. In simpler terms, the Accelerometer expresses the amount of force (and resultant acceleration) that an object is experiencing in the X, Y, and Z axes. At rest, an object experiences only acceleration due to gravity. Depending on the sensor's orientation, a different amount of force will be experienced in the axes. In contrast to the former, a Gyroscope is capable of measuring the rotational motion and lateral orientation of an object. Lastly, the magnetometer is similar to a compass and returns the object's orientation with reference to the Earth's magnetic field. The accelerometer is used for determining the pitch and roll of an object, while the magnetometer provides the yaw value. The gyroscope is generally used in fusion with the data from the Accelerometer data due to its unreliability as a real-time feature in different problems. The concepts of pitch, roll and yaw are illustrated in Fig. (2). Pitch is the rotation of the body in the axis through the side of an object, Roll is the rotation in the axis that goes through the object from front to back, and yaw is the rotation of an object around the vertical axis. These are treated as the different dimensions of movement for any object in motion. One popularly used IMU sensor is the MPU-6050 sensor module [17].

The IMU sensors find application in various practical fields but are mostly used for Human Activity Recognition related problems. The Activities of Daily Living (ADL) were identified using IMU data in the works of [18, 19, 20]. The sports activities like cycling, rowing, *etc.*, can also be determined from IMU data along with ADLs [21]. Similarly, bad habits like smoking and drinking are also identifiable from data gathered using IMU sensors in combination with other sensors [22]. In healthcare, fall detection and monitoring using IMU sensors have been researched successfully in the works of [23, 24, 25], *etc.*

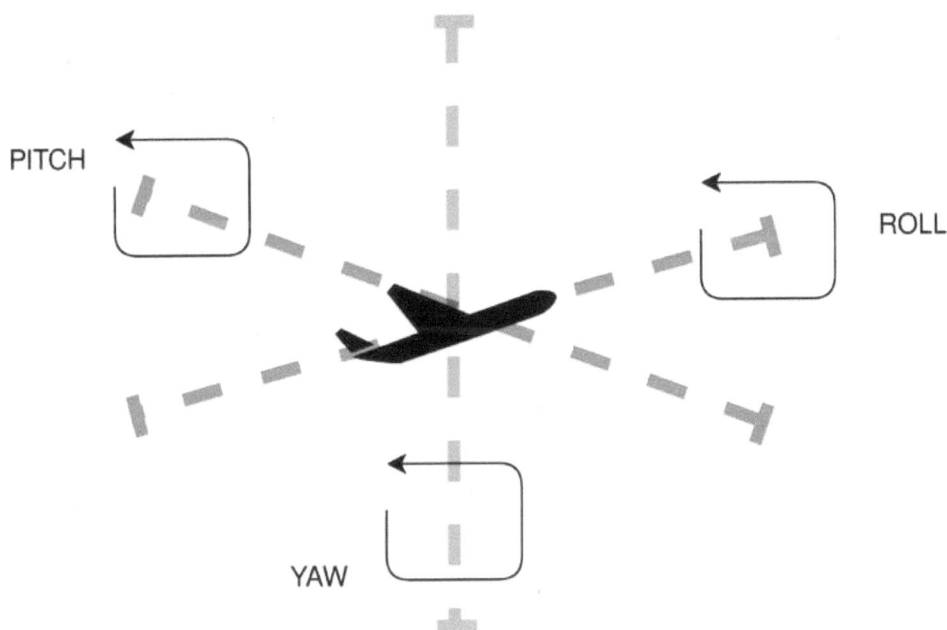

Fig. (2). Pitch, roll, and yaw.

Ultrasonic Sensor

The ultrasonic sensors are based on the same principle that is utilized in SONAR (Sound Navigation and Ranging) in ships and by bats for communication, *i.e.*, the ultrasonic waves. These sensors essentially consist of a transmitter and a receiver, the former emits an array of ultrasonic pulses, and the latter receives the reflected pulse. The time taken by the first reflected pulse is used to determine the distance between an obstacle and the sensor itself, given the speed of sound in the medium. This has been illustrated in Fig. (**3**). The working principle has also been utilized by IoT-based applications and research works. One commonly used Ultrasonic Sensor module is the HC-SR04 module [26].

This type of sensor has been used mainly for obstacle detection and avoidance in Smart Automation systems [27]. In the domain of HARS, these sensors have been used for detecting single-person activities [28] and postural changes [29], group [30] and collective activities [31], as well as for tracking [32], towards indoor localization. Other domains of usage include healthcare, where works like [33] aim to monitor elderly patients prone to falling. A very different field also utilizes this family of sensors for monitoring the health of structures and their degradation over time [34].

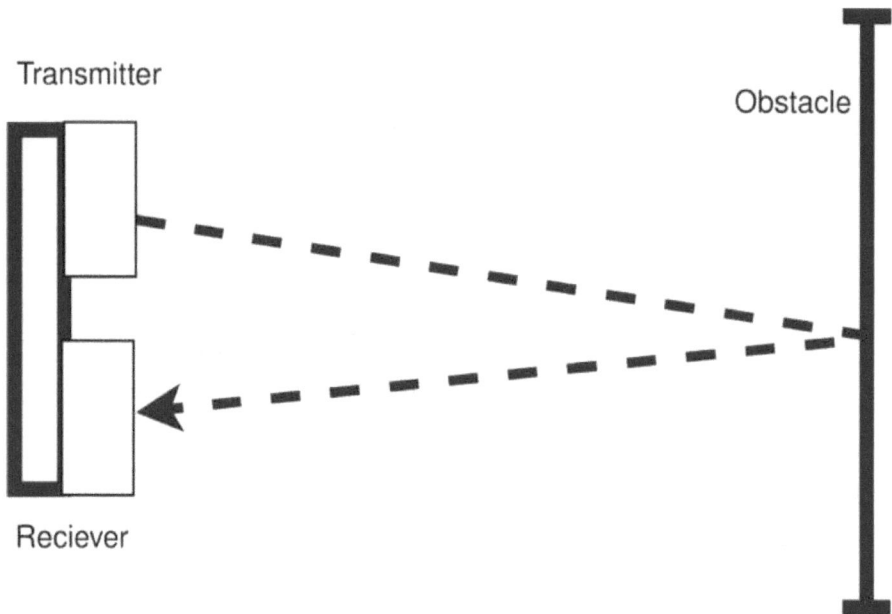

Fig. (3). Working of ultrasonic sensor.

Electrocardiogram (ECG) Sensor

These sensors measure the electrical activity of the human heart during each cardiac cycle. This activity is detected with the help of electrodes fit on different sections of a volunteer's body. In medical-grade conventional 12-lead ECGs, 10 are placed on limbs and the remaining 2 on the chest of the subject. The electric potential of the heart muscles is measured over time, and this is representative of the depolarization and repolarization of heart muscles; visually, these phenomena during a cardiac cycle can be represented as a P-wave, QRS complex, and a T-wave. This has been illustrated in Fig. (4). A popular single-lead ECG monitor sensor is the AD8232 module [35].

The ECG sensor signals are used for applications in IoT-based healthcare. In general, the diseases and defects associated with heartbeat patterns and rhythms are identified by researchers with the help of ECG sensor data [36]. The work by Bsoul *et al.* [37] detects sleep apnoea in patients from ECG signals. Different types of heart arrhythmia and the detection of normal versus defective heartbeat patterns have been performed by Wang *et al.* [38], Krishevsky *et al.* [39], and Rajpurkar *et al.* [40]. The detection of situations of stress versus those of non-stress is also possible from ECG signals, as demonstrated in the work of Jacqueline *et al.* [41].

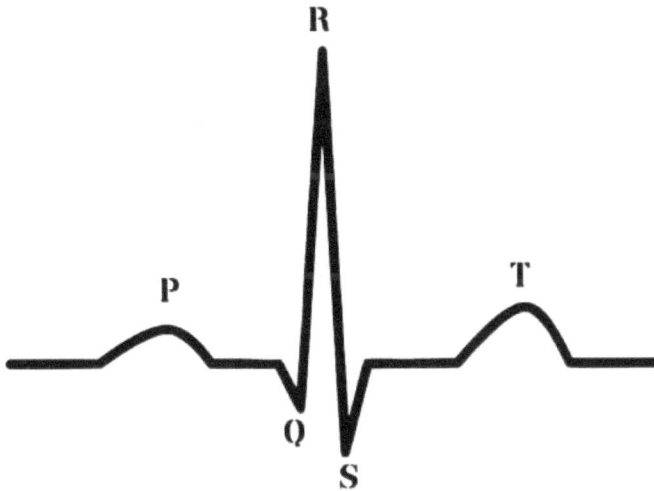

Fig. (4). ECG signals of a heart in normal rhythm.

Passive Infra-Red (PIR) Sensor

The Passive Infrared Sensor is based on the principle of detecting the heat emitted by objects as electromagnetic radiations of Infrared (IR) wavelength. These radiations are not visible to humans but can be picked up by IR-sensitive material. The PIR sensor attempts to detect the change from ambient heat when a warm body, such as a person, passes through its sensing zone. This change occurs in two phases, first when the body's heat is pickup up and next when the warm body leaves the sensing zone. Usually, a lens is used to increase the detection area or sensing zone of PIR sensors, called the Fresnel lens. This lens is not required to be made of glass; cheaper plastic variants also serve the purpose of the sensor despite the possibility of some distortion in lens shape. A popularly used PIR sensor is the HC-SR501 PIR Motion Sensor [42].

The PIR sensors are mainly used in IoT-based HARS and Healthcare solutions. The works by Luo *et al.* [43], Kashimoto *et al.* [44, 45], Luo *et al.* [46], Yang *et al.* [47], *etc.*, are instances of the state-of-the-art research in this domain spanning across both the domains.

Electromyogram (EMG) Sensor

This sensor is purely based on the measurement of the electrical potential in muscle cells. This electric potential is measured in terms of the voltage difference between electrodes. This technique is referred to popularly as Electromyography and is a two-step procedure. Initially, a baseline reading is defined depending on the voltage difference for the human subject when he/she is in a calm or relaxed state. It has been noted that this base level is variable and unique for all human beings. Next, the subject is exposed to some external stimulus and the consequent voltage difference is now measured. The impact or effect of the stimulus is identified as the ratio of the base value and the stimulus-induced value. The electrodes that are used in EMG can be of two types – surface/skin electrodes and inserted electrodes.

The EMG-based applications mainly focus on healthcare-based research, specifically in the detection of neuro-muscular defects or abnormalities and in recognition of human emotions. Some state-of-the-art research works are those by Girardi *et al.* [48], Martinez-Rodrigo *et al.* [49], Nakasone *et al.* [50], Wagner *et al.* [51], *etc.*

Sensors used for Environment Monitoring

The past few decades have witnessed a rise in industrial pollution and pollution as a whole. Consequently, IoT-based environment monitoring systems aim to gather data about this problem, analyze the data, and make decisions based on the results. As these sensors are mostly used only for solving problems concerning environment monitoring, these have been grouped together. The following sensors are most common in this group:

i. CO_2 sensor: Used for measuring the concentration of Carbon Dioxide gas in the air. MG-811 is a commonly used sensor for measuring CO2 [52].

ii. CO sensor: Used for measuring the concentration of Carbon Monoxide gas in the air. MQ7 is one such popular CO sensor [53].

iii. Temperature sensor: Measures the temperature of the air.

iv. Humidity sensor: Measures the relative humidity in the air. DHT11 and DHT22 are two popular sensors used for the detection of air temperature and relative humidity.

v. Gas sensor: This sensor family detects a number of different gases such as hydrogen, propane, alcohol, Liquefied Petroleum Gas (LPG), Carbon Monoxide (CO), *etc.* MQ2 is one such popular gas sensor [54].

vi. Air Quality sensor: Similar to the previous case, this sensor detects a variety of air components, such as NOx, Benzene, Ammonia, CO2, Smoke, *etc.* MQ135 is one such popular sensor [55].

Other than these sensors, there are several other sensors used in specific cases depending on the requirement of the research problem. State-of-the-art research works have used this category of sensors for environmental monitoring, such as in the works of Shah *et al.* [56], Jaladi *et al.* [57], Mamun *et al.* [58], *etc.*

Sensors used in Smart Agriculture

Similar to the previous case, there are only a handful of sensors that are used in combination, commonly for the development and usage of smart agricultural monitoring systems. A few of the popular sensors are given here:

i. Temperature sensor - measures the temperature of the air at that location.

ii. Humidity sensor - measures the relative humidity of the air.

iii. Soil Moisture sensor – senses the water content in the soil in terms of volume. A commonly used sensor of this type is Sensor 13322 [59].

There are other sensors used for the deployment of smart IoT-based agricultural systems. Some state-of-the-art works that have worked towards this research problem are [60 - 64], *etc.*

Smart-phones

Nowadays, one inseparable part of our daily life is the Smart-phone. The usage of mobile devices has come a long way and nowadays encompasses multiple utilities that we are largely dependent on – such as instant messaging, photography, *etc*. Consequently, a standard smartphone is equipped with a number of sensors that make it suitable as an IoT device. These sensing modules include but are not limited to – video camera, sound sensor, proximity sensor, IMU sensor, fingerprint sensor, *etc*.

The use of smartphones as sensor devices minimizes the extra effort and cost involved in system setup for data acquisition. Thus, there are many researchers who have utilized the smart-phone based sensors for the development of IoT-based applications. This is evident from the recent studies of state-of-the-art research work, undertaken by [65 - 67], *etc*. Various IoT-based applications are also noted, such as IoT-enabled road condition monitoring [68], fall detection towards healthcare monitoring [69], agriculture monitoring [70], *etc*.

CASE STUDY: USE OF SMART-PHONE AS SENSING DEVICE IN IOT APPLICATION

In this part of the discussion, the IMU sensor data for two different activities have been acquired using a standard smart-phone. For data acquisition with smart-phone sensors, several free-to-use android applications are available, such as *Sensor Record* [71]. The data gathered from the 3-axis Accelerometer sensor of the smart-phone is saved in Comma Separated Values (CSV) format in the smart-phone storage first. Next, this data is transmitted over the Internet to a computation-capable device where further visualization, processing, and decision-making may be applied. Often, the smart-phone itself is used for computation and processing. On the processing device, the CSV files are processed using programming software such as Python or R.

Table **1** and **2** illustrate the raw data as acquired by the smart-phone's 3-axis accelerometer sensor using a free-to-use application [71]. The data correspond to two different activities, namely, *smart-phone at rest* and *walking with smart-phone in hand,* respectively.

Table 1. Raw data for smart-phone at rest.

Timestamp	Milliseconds	X	Y	Z
2021-06-26 09:52:36	1	-0.591368	0.272939	9.986216
2021-06-26 09:52:36	11	-0.572214	0.284910	9.876082

(Table 1) cont.....

Timestamp	Milliseconds	X	Y	Z
2021-06-26 09:52:36	21	-0.533907	0.270545	9.849746
2021-06-26 09:52:36	31	-0.545878	0.287304	9.842564
2021-06-26 09:52:36	41	-0.545878	0.294487	9.837775

Table 2. Raw data for walking with smart-phone in hand.

Timestamp	Milliseconds	X	Y	Z
2021-06-26 09:54:00	0	-1.503559	1.738190	9.744401
2021-06-26 09:54:00	10	-1.711854	2.375048	9.361329
2021-06-26 09:54:00	20	-1.333570	2.580950	8.918402
2021-06-26 09:54:00	30	-1.156399	2.676718	8.726865
2021-06-26 09:54:00	40	-1.747767	2.741361	7.824251

The acquired accelerometer data is better observed by plotting the temporal sequence of 3-axis data in the form of a line plot. This is usually the first step before data processing and is important for visual understanding of the data. Figs. (**5**) and (**6**) illustrate the line plots corresponding to the activities described above.

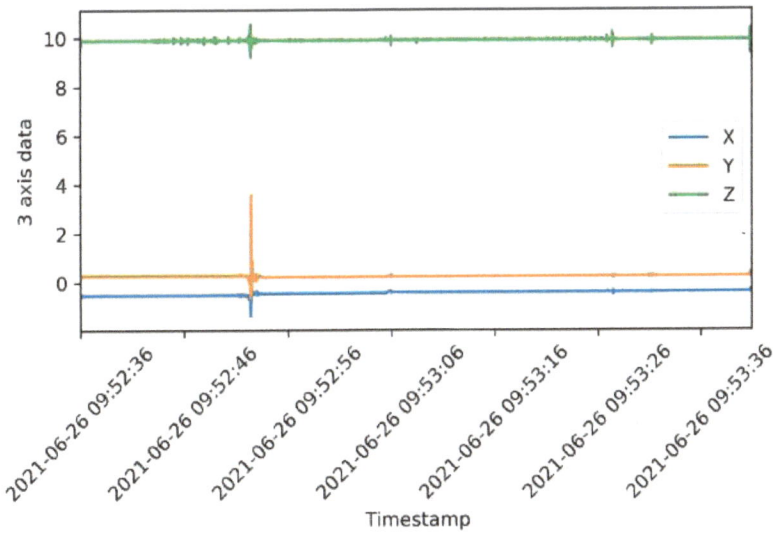

Fig. (5). Illustration of 3-axis Accelerometer data for smart-phone at rest.

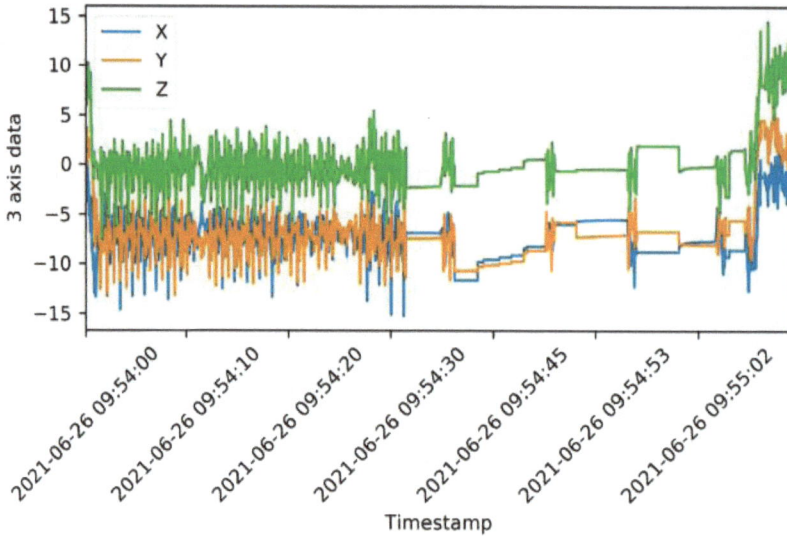

Fig. (6). Illustration of 3-axis Accelerometer data for walking with smart-phone in hand.

It is evident from the two figures that there is a clear distinction between the patterns of temporal data for the two activities. These patterns may be extracted meaningfully with statistical, frequency-domain, or other feature-extraction methods for effective learning and classification purposes towards developing an IoT-based smart activity recognition system. Thus, this case study highlights how sensor data, gathered even from smartphones, capture the essence of different events occurring in the surroundings of any object.

IOT ENABLED APPLICATION AREAS

Since its induction in the technological domain, IoT has touched upon almost all arenas of human existence. IoT-influenced domains range from manufacturing to healthcare, and most of the state-of-the-art research problems are also being conducted in these domains. In this section, we have attempted to focus on some of the common IoT-enabled application areas that have revolutionized our standard of living.

   i. Transportation – The availability of smart sensor-based systems and the advantage of leveraging the internet framework has brought in a new age in transportation systems. Automated, driverless cars are one of the many wonders that have resulted from this innovation. Popular brands, such as Tesla, have developed cars capable of sensing traffic, weather, *etc.*, conditions and driving around without any human intervention. Apart from this, the advent of IoT-enabled transportation systems has resulted in increased road safety, ease of driving, efficient fuel usage, minimized exhaust release, *etc*.

ii. Manufacturing – The production and manufacturing processes in industry involve a lot of manpower as well as human decision-making. IoT-enabled solutions are being successfully adopted in manufacturing for efficient working of the complete process. Augmented Reality (AR) enabled shops, remote monitoring of machine wear and tear, automated quality checking and maintenance, *etc*., are applications that have increased the efficiency of the manufacturing industry as a whole. These applications not only influence performance but also reduce resource wastage and minimize risk in production lines.

iii. Smart Cities – automated solutions have become part and parcel of many households across the globe. IoT-enabled smart solutions are becoming more and more convenient and dependable for adapting in our very households. Consequently, many cities around the world have inculcated IoT-enabled smart solutions in each and every aspect of the functioning of the city, ranging from governance to healthcare and transportation services. A notable example is the city of Singapore which uses the Smart Nation Sensor Platform repository for obtaining sensor data for the betterment of city planning and quality of life.

iv. Agriculture – With the ever-increasing population on earth, there is going to be a dire need for more and more food in the near future. Conventional or traditional agricultural practices may not be able to supplement this amount of demand. IoT-enabled agricultural solutions are thus being adapted to provide round-the-clock optimized solutions without the constant intervention of farmers. The utilization of smart sensing systems helps in better crop produce quality, higher amount of yield, and also in reduction of resource wastage such as wastage of fertilizers and insecticides. Apart from these, IoT-enabled systems have been effectively adopted in dairy farming, greenhouses, *etc*.

v. Healthcare – Affordable and convenient healthcare solutions have always been rarely available, and in high demand. With the inclusion of IoT, such solutions are becoming more and more practical and effective. Remote monitoring of patients, telehealth-based consultations, and even robotic assistance in surgeries are some of the many solutions provided by IoT-based smart healthcare systems. This is projected to improve the overall quality of life for patients and the elderly who are in need of healthcare but there is no availability of medical personnel. The development of smart healthcare solutions goes hand in hand with the growth of an IoT-enabled smart city.

BASIC METRICS FOR SENSOR-DATA-BASED SYSTEM PERFORMANCE EVALUATION

Most sensor-based applications and systems rely on smart decision-making in almost real-time situations. The effectiveness of such systems is to be pre-determined before deploying them in a real-life scenario. This efficiency can be measured in terms of many different evaluation techniques. However, the most commonly used evaluation technique in any of the sensor-data-based supervised learning problems is the determination of Precision, Recall, F1 score, and Accuracy. In this section, a discussion is offered on the relevance of the basic metrics that result in the aforementioned results and their relevance in any sensor-data-based smart system performance evaluation.

During the experimentation in the research phase, the sensor data is labeled, that is the sequence of events and their significance, both are already known from data acquisition. It is this information that the machine learning algorithms utilize in order to gather insights into the data. The label information is also referred to as the Ground Truth, whereas the decision made by a system that has gained knowledge from sensor data, is known as its prediction. The relation between this ground truth information and the system prediction leads to the identification of True Positive (TP), True Negative (TN), False Positive (FP), and False Negative (FN) values.

Let us consider a system for a two-class problem, where different features and parameters are captured using environmental sensors, and which predict either rainy or dry weather. Now, depending on the ground truth and system prediction, there are four possibilities that arise when these values are tallied.

True Positive is the situation where the ground truth is of a rainy day, and the prediction by the system is of a rainy day. So, the prediction by the system is True, hence the name True Positive.

Next, it may happen that the system has predicted dry (not rainy) weather, and that is verified by the ground truth information. So, the negative prediction by the system is true, hence True Negative.

In some cases, it may so happen that the system predicts a rainy day, whereas the ground truth is dry weather. In this situation, the rainy (positive) decision by the classifier is false, thus False Positive.

The last possibility is that the classifier predicts that the weather is not rainy, but in reality, the ground truth indicates that the weather is rainy. So, the system decision is negative, which in turn is false, hence called False Negative.

Based on these 4 values, the metrics Precision, Recall, and F1 score are calculated. Though these metrics are not discussed in this chapter in detail, this section attempts to highlight the significance of TP, TN, FP, and FN as elementary metrics of any sensor-based systems performance evaluation.

SENSORS AND THE FUTURE OF IOT

Given the rapid technological advancements that are fuelling the design and development of affordable sensing units, the sensors can be identified as the actual working unit of any IoT-enabled smart system. In the near future, sensors and actuators are destined to grow smarter – in terms of intelligent actions and decision-making capability. The augmentation of analytical decision-making along with the usual purpose of a sensing device at the sensor level will enhance the real-time performance of the system as a whole while reducing network latency and system-level dependencies. At the same time, the shelf life of sensing units is expected to be increased manifold, or they need to be upgradable via firmware upgrades in order to develop sustainable systems. Scalability and miniaturization are both critical for the rapid adaption of sensing units, and must also be treated as important features of future sensors. Lastly, bio-compatible, bio-communicable sensing units will lead the way to better means of human-machine interaction and inter-operation.

CHALLENGES IN SENSOR-BASED IOT-ENABLED SYSTEMS

This chapter has illustrated how the sensors are an integral part of IoT-enabled smart and automated systems. However, there exist different challenges in the adoption of such systems as reliable products of daily use. In this section, some challenges pertinent to IoT-enabled smart systems are discussed.

i. Management of data: The data generated by the various types of sensors and actuators, differ in many ways. The overall sensor data being aggregated by IoT-enabled systems gives rise to the issue of handling Big Data. The data differ in terms of the sensor sampling rate, data format, data type, captured noise, *etc*. Consequently, different database and data handling requirements need to be taken care of. The inclusion of parallel-processing capability, efficient database access, and management are quintessential for the success of sensor-enabled products.

ii. Lack of ease-of-use: Often, it is noted that there exists a technological barrier to the usage of IoT-enabled systems. The requirements for the proper working of any such system require knowledge about the internal working principle and a level of sophistication exists, though unwanted. This becomes a hindrance in the adoption of such products for daily use. There needs to be easy interfacing such that patients, for instance, can use the setup to capture necessary data for perusal by remotely located doctors, without the intervention of any third party. The development of such systems as products should consider the feedback of common users in the initial phases of testing.

iii. Privacy Protection: As the big data contains sensor-captured data regarding different critical parameters of the subjects, it is only normal that data privacy is expected to be maintained by such systems. However, any unfortunate instance where the subject's data is leaked or misused can lead to a massive loss of faith in such systems. The mistrust and negative perception that arises from such experiences act as a massive hindrance in their adoption. Irrespective of whether the acquired data is stored locally or in the cloud, security assurance over the network is a big challenge for IoT-enabled systems. Country-specific regulatory norms should be put in place to ensure that there is no data misuse and no unwarranted access.

iv. Supervision and Maintenance: Usually the sensing systems are designed using low-cost and miniature sensing units. However this has a drawback – often, these sensors have low precision and reduced lifespan or service-life. Also, their sensing coverage, range, and sensitivity may get affected over time. So, any practically deployed system needs to be regularly monitored for the replacement of faulty units. It is essential to detect when a necessary replacement needs to be made, such that performance is not affected in real-time applications. This is particularly critical in applications where timely and optimum performance is quintessential, such as in some healthcare problems, manufacturing, *etc.*

CONCLUSION

In this chapter, some of the major IoT-based applications have been discussed with respect to the different types of sensing devices and sensing modalities used in each of them; widely used sensors such as IMU, Ultrasonic, PIR, Air Quality, ECG, *etc.*, have been included. The working principle of some sensors has been discussed, along with their usage in the development of IoT-based smart applications and related research. It is seen for some sensors how they find widespread utility across multiple research domains, such as the Ultrasonic Sensor, which is used for IoT-based smart healthcare monitoring as well as structural fitness monitoring of buildings. In contrast, for some domains of application, there are a limited number of sensors whose use is restricted to that particular domain; IoT-based environment monitoring is such an example. All the sensor-based research work has been duly cited, along with links to the commonly used model of each sensor type. The case study included in the latter part of the chapter demonstrates how easily IoT-based applications are developed with the use of sensors embedded in everyday electronic devices, such as smart-phones. A brief discussion has been added on the challenges and future of IoT-based sensing systems in the rapidly advancing era of smart systems. In the future, the discussions may be extended by including the and-to-end details of the development of an automated, smart IoT-enabled system fuelled by intelligent learning algorithms. This chapter highlights the important role that sensors play in IoT applications by acquiring data on behalf of things in their current environment, and it has been written in order to serve as an easy reference manual for all students and researchers who endeavor to start working in sensing for IoT-based problems.

REFERENCES

[1]　Available from: https://www.electronicshub.org/hc-05-bluetooth-module/ (accessed: Oct. 21, 2022)

[2]　Available from: https://www.electronicwings.com/arduino/esp8266-wifi-module-interfacing--ith-arduino-uno (accessed: Oct. 21, 2022)

[3]　Available from: https://www.electronicscomp.com/sim900a-gsm-gprs-module-india (accessed: Oct. 21, 2022)

[4]　Available from: https://www.arduino.cc/ (accessed: Oct. 21, 2022)

[5]　Available from: https://www.raspberrypi.org/ (accessed: Oct. 21, 2022)

[6]　R.P. Sharma, and G.K. Verma, "Human computer interaction using hand gesture", *Procedia Comput. Sci.,* vol. 54, pp. 721-727, 2015.
[http://dx.doi.org/10.1016/j.procs.2015.06.085]

[7]　K. Czuszynski, J. Ruminski, and J. Wtorek, "Pose classification in the gesture recognition using the linear optical sensor", *10th International Conference on Human System Interactions (HSI),* pp. 18-24, 2017.
[http://dx.doi.org/10.1109/HSI.2017.8004989]

[8]　A. Ullah, K. Muhammad, I.U. Haq, and S.W. Baik, "Action recognition using optimized deep autoencoder and CNN for surveillance data streams of non-stationary environments", *Future Gener. Comput. Syst.,* vol. 96, pp. 386-397, 2019.
[http://dx.doi.org/10.1016/j.future.2019.01.029]

[9]　K.V. Kumar, P.V. Kishore, D.A. Kumar, and E.K. Kumar, "Indian classical dance action identification using adaboost multiclass classifier on multifeature fusion", In: *2018 Conference on Signal Processing and Communication Engineering Systems (SPACES),* 2018, pp. 167-170.
[http://dx.doi.org/10.1109/SPACES.2018.8316338]

[10]　P. Wang, Y. Cao, C. Shen, L. Liu, and H.T. Shen, "Temporal pyramid pooling-based convolutional neural network for action recognition", *IEEE Trans. Circ. Syst. Video Tech.,* vol. 27, no. 12, pp. 2613-2622, 2017.
[http://dx.doi.org/10.1109/TCSVT.2016.2576761]

[11]　M. Qi, Y. Wang, J. Qin, A. Li, J. Luo, and L. Van Gool, "Stagnet: An attentive semantic RNN for group activity and individual action recognition", *IEEE Trans. Circ. Syst. Video Tech.,* vol. 30, no. 2, pp. 549-565, 2020.
[http://dx.doi.org/10.1109/TCSVT.2019.2894161]

[12]　Y. Feng, Y. Yuan, and X. Lu, "Learning deep event models for crowd anomaly detection",

Neurocomputing, vol. 219, pp. 548-556, 2017.
[http://dx.doi.org/10.1016/j.neucom.2016.09.063]

[13]   D. Arifoglu, and A. Bouchachia, "Activity recognition and abnormal behaviour detection with recurrent neural networks", *Procedia Comput. Sci.,* vol. 110, pp. 86-93, 2017.
[http://dx.doi.org/10.1016/j.procs.2017.06.121]

[14]   L. Panahi, and V. Ghods, "Human fall detection using machine vision techniques on RGB–D images", *Biomed. Signal Process. Control,* vol. 44, pp. 146-153, 2018.
[http://dx.doi.org/10.1016/j.bspc.2018.04.014]

[15]   Y. Nizam, M.N.H. Mohd, and M.M.A. Jamil, "Human fall detection from depth images using position and velocity of subject", *Procedia Comput. Sci.,* vol. 105, pp. 131-137, 2017.
[http://dx.doi.org/10.1016/j.procs.2017.01.191]

[16]   S.P. Gulve, S.A. Khoje, and P. Pardeshi, Implementation of IoT-Based Smart Video Surveillance System.*Computational Intelligence in Data Mining.,* H. Behera, D. Mohapatra, Eds., vol. 556. Springer: Singapore, 2017, pp. 771-780.
[http://dx.doi.org/10.1007/978-981-10-3874-7_73]

[17]   Available from: https://www.sparkfun.com/products/11028 (accessed: Oct. 21, 2022)

[18]   L.C. Jatoba, U. Grossmann, C. Kunze, J. Ottenbacher, and W. Stork, "Context-aware mobile health monitoring: Evaluation of different pattern recognition methods for classification of physical activity", *2008 30th Annual International Conference of the IEEE Engineering in Medicine and Biology Society,* 2008.
[http://dx.doi.org/10.1109/IEMBS.2008.4650398]

[19]   L. Fan, Z. Wang, and H. Wang, "Human activity recognition model based on decision tree", *2013 International Conference on Advanced Cloud and Big Data,* 2013.
[http://dx.doi.org/10.1109/CBD.2013.19]

[20]   D. Anguita, A. Ghio, L. Oneto, X. Parra, and J.L. Reyes-Ortiz, "Human activity recognition on smartphones using a multiclass hardware-friendly support vector machine", *Lect. Notes Comput. Sci.,* vol. 7657, pp. 216-223, 2012.
[http://dx.doi.org/10.1007/978-3-642-35395-6_30]

[21]   K. Altun, and B. Barshan, "Human activity recognition using inertial/magnetic sensor units", *Human Behavior Understanding,* pp. 38-51, 2010.
[http://dx.doi.org/10.1007/978-3-642-14715-9_5]

[22]   M. Shoaib, S. Bosch, H. Scholten, P.J.M. Havinga, and O.D. Incel, "Towards detection of bad habits by fusing smartphone and smartwatch sensors", *IEEE International Conference on Pervasive Computing and Communication Workshops (PerCom Workshops),* 2015.
[http://dx.doi.org/10.1109/PERCOMW.2015.7134104]

[23]   D. Yacchirema, J.S. de Puga, C. Palau, and M. Esteve, "Fall detection system for elderly people using IoT and Big Data", *Procedia Comput. Sci.,* vol. 130, pp. 603-610, 2018.
[http://dx.doi.org/10.1016/j.procs.2018.04.110]

[24]   V.S. Kumar, K.G. Acharya, B. Sandeep, T. Jayavignesh, and A. Chaturvedi, Wearable sensor-based human fall detection wireless system. *Wireless Communication Networks and Internet of Things,* pp. 217-234, 2018.
[http://dx.doi.org/10.1007/978-981-10-8663-2_23]

[25]   I. Chandra, N. Sivakumar, C.B. Gokulnath, and P. Parthasarathy, "IoT based fall detection and ambient assisted system for the elderly", *Cluster Comput.,* vol. 22, no. S1, pp. 2517-2525, 2019.
[http://dx.doi.org/10.1007/s10586-018-2329-2]

[26]   Available from: https://www.sparkfun.com/products/15569 (accessed: Oct. 21, 2022)

[27]   A. Ali, H. Akbar, and Z. Sartaj, "Obstacle detection for blind people using ultrasonic sensors and ardino processor", *ScienceOpen,* 2022.

[http://dx.doi.org/10.14293/S2199-1006.1.SOR-.PPVQFLG.v1]

[28]   A. Ghosh, "On automatizing recognition of multiple human activities using ultrasonic sensor grid", *2017 9th International Conference on Communication Systems and Networks (COMSNETS)*, 2018.
       [http://dx.doi.org/10.1109/COMSNETS.2017.7945440]

[29]   A. Ghosh, D. Chakraborty, D. Prasad, M. Saha, and S. Saha, "Can we recognize multiple human group activities using ultrasonic sensors?", *2018 10th International Conference on Communication Systems & Networks (COMSNETS)*, 2018.
       [http://dx.doi.org/10.1109/COMSNETS.2018.8328272]

[30]   A. Ghosh, A. Chakraborty, D. Chakraborty, M. Saha, and S. Saha, "UltraSense: A non-intrusive approach for human activity identification using heterogeneous ultrasonic sensor grid for smart home environment", *J. Ambient Intell. Humaniz. Comput.*, 2019.
       [http://dx.doi.org/10.1007/s12652-019-01260-y]

[31]   A. Ghosh, A. Chakraborty, J. Kumbhakar, M. Saha, and S. Saha, "HumanSense: A framework for collective human activity identification using heterogeneous sensor grid in multi-inhabitant smart environments", *Pers. Ubiquitous Comput.*, vol. 26, no. 3, pp. 521-540, 2022.
       [http://dx.doi.org/10.1007/s00779-020-01402-6]

[32]   V.T. Pham, Q. Qiu, A.A.P. Wai, and J. Biswas, "Application of ultrasonic sensors in a smart environment", *Pervasive Mobile Comput.*, vol. 3, no. 2, pp. 180-207, 2007.
       [http://dx.doi.org/10.1016/j.pmcj.2006.07.002]

[33]   Y. Huang, and K. Newman, "Improve quality of care with remote activity and fall detection using ultrasonic sensors", *Annual International Conference of the IEEE Engineering in Medicine and Biology Society*, 2012.
       [http://dx.doi.org/10.1109/EMBC.2012.6347325]

[34]   Yinghui Lu, and J.E. Michaels, "Feature extraction and sensor fusion for ultrasonic structural health monitoring under changing environmental conditions", *IEEE Sens. J.*, vol. 9, no. 11, pp. 1462-1471, 2009.
       [http://dx.doi.org/10.1109/JSEN.2009.2019339]

[35]   Available from: https://www.sparkfun.com/products/12650 (accessed: Oct. 21, 2022)

[36]   H. Yüksel, "IoT-based smart healthcare monitoring system", *Healthcare Monitoring and Data Analysis using IoT: Technologies and applications*, pp. 71-98, 2022.
       [http://dx.doi.org/10.1049/PBHE038E_ch5]

[37]   M. Bsoul, H. Minn, and L. Tamil, "Apnea MedAssist: Real-time sleep apnea monitor using single-lead ECG", *IEEE Trans. Inf. Technol. Biomed.*, vol. 15, no. 3, pp. 416-427, 2011.
       [http://dx.doi.org/10.1109/TITB.2010.2087386] [PMID: 20952340]

[38]   J.S. Wang, W.C. Chiang, Y.L. Hsu, and Y.T.C. Yang, "ECG arrhythmia classification using a probabilistic neural network with a feature reduction method", *Neurocomputing*, vol. 116, pp. 38-45, 2013.
       [http://dx.doi.org/10.1016/j.neucom.2011.10.045]

[39]   A. Krizhevsky, I. Sutskever, and G.E. Hinton, "ImageNet classification with deep convolutional neural networks", *Commun. ACM*, vol. 60, no. 6, pp. 84-90, 2017.
       [http://dx.doi.org/10.1145/3065386]

[40]   N. Katsaouni, F. Aul, L. Krischker, S. Schmalhofer, L. Hedrich, and M.H. Schulz, "Energy efficient convolutional neural networks for arrhythmia detection", *bioRxiv*, vol. 13, no. 100127, 2022.
       [http://dx.doi.org/10.1101/2021.09.23.461522]

[41]   J. Wijsman, B. Grundlehner, H. Liu, H. Hermens, and J. Penders, "Towards mental stress detection using wearable physiological sensors", *2011 Annual International Conference of the IEEE Engineering in Medicine and Biology Society*, 2011.
       [http://dx.doi.org/10.1109/IEMBS.2011.6090512]

[42] Available from: https://robu.in/product/pir-motion-sensor-detector-module-hc-sr501/ (accessed: Oct. 21, 2022).

[43] X. Luo, T. Liu, B. Shen, J. Hong, Q. Chen, and H. Chen, "Human Daily Activity Recognition Using Ceiling Mounted PIR Sensors", *Proceedings of the 2nd International Conference on Advances in Mechanical Engineering and Industrial Informatics (AMEII 2016),*, 2016
[http://dx.doi.org/10.2991/ameii-16.2016.169]

[44] Y. Kashimoto, M. Fujiwara, M. Fujimoto, H. Suwa, Y. Arakawa, and K. Yasumoto, "ALPAS: Analog-PIR-sensor-based activity recognition system in smarthome", *2017 IEEE 31ˢᵗ International Conference on Advanced Information Networking and Applications (AINA),* 2017.
[http://dx.doi.org/10.1109/AINA.2017.33]

[45] Y. Kashimoto, "Low-cost and device-free activity recognition system with energy harvesting PIR and Door Sensors", *Adjunct Proceedings of the 13ᵗʰ International Conference on Mobile and Ubiquitous Systems: Computing Networking and Services,* 2016.
[http://dx.doi.org/10.1145/3004010.3006378]

[46] X. Luo, Q. Guan, H. Tan, L. Gao, Z. Wang, and X. Luo, "Simultaneous indoor tracking and activity recognition using pyroelectric infrared sensors", *Sensors,* vol. 17, no. 8, p. 1738, 2017.
[http://dx.doi.org/10.3390/s17081738] [PMID: 28758934]

[47] D. Yang, B. Xu, K. Rao, and W. Sheng, "Passive Infrared (PIR)-based indoor position tracking for smart homes using accessibility maps and a-star algorithm", *Sensors,* vol. 18, no. 2, p. 332, 2018.
[http://dx.doi.org/10.3390/s18020332] [PMID: 29364188]

[48] D. Girardi, F. Lanubile, and N. Novielli, "Emotion detection using noninvasive low cost sensors", *2017 Seventh International Conference on Affective Computing and Intelligent Interaction (ACII),* 2017.
[http://dx.doi.org/10.1109/ACII.2017.8273589]

[49] A. Martínez-Rodrigo, R. Zangróniz, J.M. Pastor, J.M. Latorre, and A. Fernández-Caballero, "Emotion detection in ageing adults from physiological sensors", *Ambient Intelligence - Software Applications,* pp. 253-261, 2015.
[http://dx.doi.org/10.1007/978-3-319-19695-4_26]

[50] "Emotion recognition based on heart rate and skin conductance", *In Proceedings of the 2ⁿᵈ International Conference on Physiological Computing Systems,* 2015.
[http://dx.doi.org/10.5220/0005241100260032]

[51] J. Wagner, "From physiological signals to emotions: Implementing and comparing selected methods for feature extraction and classification", *IEEE International Conference on Multimedia and Expo,* 2005.
[http://dx.doi.org/10.1109/ICME.2005.1521579]

[52] Available from: https://robu.in/product/mg811-module-air-carbon-dioxide-co2-sensor/ (accessed: Oct. 21, 2022)

[53] Available from: https://www.dfrobot.com/product-686.html (accessed: Oct. 21, 2022)

[54] Available from: https://robu.in/product/mq-2-mq2-smoke-gas-lpg-butane-hydrogen-gas-sensor-detector-module/ (accessed: Oct. 21, 2022)

[55] Available from: https://www.rhydolabz.com/sensors-gas-sensors-c-137_140/air-quality-sensor-mq135-p-1115.html (accessed: Oct. 21, 2022)

[56] J. Shah, and B. Mishra, "IoT enabled environmental monitoring system for smart cities", *2016 International Conference on Internet of Things and Applications (IOTA),* 2016.
[http://dx.doi.org/10.1109/IOTA.2016.7562757]

[57] J. Agajo, and A. Theophilus, "Using wireless sensor networks for industrial monitoring", *IET International Conference on Wireless Sensor Network 2010 (IET-WSN 2010),* 2010.

[http://dx.doi.org/10.1049/cp.2010.1039]

[58] M.A.A. Mamun, and M.R. Yuce, "Sensors and systems for wearable environmental monitoring toward IoT-enabled applications: A review", *IEEE Sens. J.,* vol. 19, no. 18, pp. 7771-7788, 2019.
[http://dx.doi.org/10.1109/JSEN.2019.2919352]

[59] Available from: https://www.sparkfun.com/products/13322 (accessed: Oct. 21, 2022).

[60] S.V. Mukherji, R. Sinha, S. Basak, and S.P. Kar, "Smart agriculture using internet of things and MQTT protocol", *2019 International Conference on Machine Learning, Big Data, Cloud and Parallel Computing (COMITCon),* 2019.
[http://dx.doi.org/10.1109/COMITCon.2019.8862233]

[61] Suma N, Samson SR, Saranya S, Shanmugapriya G, Subhashri R, "IOT based smart agriculture monitoring system", *Int J Recent Innovation Trends Comp Comm,* vol. 5, no. 2, pp. 177-181, .
[http://dx.doi.org/10.31838/jcr.07.13.210]

[62] P. Kuruba, and V. Madhusudhan, "Smart growth monitoring system in agriculture using IoT", *J. Adv. Res. Dynam.Cont. Sys.,* vol. 11, no. 12-SPECIAL ISSUE, pp. 620-630, 2019.
[http://dx.doi.org/10.5373/JARDCS/V11SP12/20193258]

[63] T.A. Khoa, M.M. Man, T.Y. Nguyen, V. Nguyen, and N.H. Nam, "Smart agriculture using IoT multi-sensors: A novel watering management system", *J. Sens. Actu.Netw.,* vol. 8, no. 3, p. 45, 2019.
[http://dx.doi.org/10.3390/jsan8030045]

[64] M. Ayaz, M. Ammad-Uddin, Z. Sharif, A. Mansour, and E.H.M. Aggoune, "Internet-of-things (IoT)-based smart agriculture: Toward making the fields talk", *IEEE Access,* vol. 7, pp. 129551-129583, 2019.
[http://dx.doi.org/10.1109/ACCESS.2019.2932609]

[65] M. A. E. Khaddar, and M. Boulmalf, *Smartphone: The ultimate iot and ioe device.* intechopen, 2017, pp. 1-422.
[http://dx.doi.org/10.5772/intechopen.69734]

[66] B.D. Marah, Z. Jing, T. Ma, R. Alsabri, R. Anaadumba, A. Al-Dhelaan, and M. Al-Dhelaan, "Smartphone architecture for edge-centric iot analytics", *Sensors,* vol. 20, no. 3, p. 892, 2020.
[http://dx.doi.org/10.3390/s20030892] [PMID: 32046133]

[67] S.M. Elatawy, "IoT-based smart lab system in schools using arduino and bluetooth based android smartphone", *Int. J. Comput. Appl.,* vol. 175, no. 19, pp. 52-59, 2020.
[http://dx.doi.org/10.5120/ijca2020920724]

[68] A. Ghose, P. Biswas, C. Bhaumik, M. Sharma, A. Pal, and A. Jha, "Road condition monitoring and alert application: Using in-vehicle smartphone as internet-connected sensor", *2012 IEEE International Conference on Pervasive Computing and Communications Workshops,* 2012.
[http://dx.doi.org/10.1109/PerComW.2012.6197543]

[69] H.A. Tran, Q.T. Ngo, and V. Tong, "A new fall detection system on Android smartphone: Application to a SDN-based IoT system", *2017 9th International Conference on Knowledge and Systems Engineering (KSE),* 2017.
[http://dx.doi.org/10.1109/KSE.2017.8119425]

[70] M.A. Patil, A.C. Adamuthe, and A.J. Umbarkar, "Smartphone and IoT based system for integrated farm monitoring", *Techno-Societal,* vol. 2018, pp. 471-478, 2020.
[http://dx.doi.org/10.1007/978-3-030-16848-3_43]

[71] Available from: https://play.google.com/store/apps/details?id=de.martingolpashin.sensor_record&hl=en_IN&gl=US (accessed May 2nd, 2021).

CHAPTER 9

IoT and Cloud-based Data Analytics for Real Life Applications and Challenges

Sartaj Ahmad[1,*]

¹ KIET Group of Institutions Delhi-NCR, Affiliated to AKTU, Lucknow, UP, India

Abstract: Due to the massive development in the field of Internet technology, data communication and its processing make it easy for people to access and interact with various physical devices around the world. It has led to many buzzwords, such as the Internet of Things, cloud computing, data analysis, *etc.* It is important to understand the relationship between them. Every day, many devices connect to the internet and share a large amount of data that needs to be processed for future reference. Therefore, the cloud concept plays a big role in storing such a large and fast operation. The use of this type of data depends on the personal needs of the end user. Some users' devices are the sources of their communication. For some, user data is important to understand customer behavior. For some users, how to manage massive data and devices are important. Similarly, few users pay attention to data to improve their goods and services. In this chapter, we focus on the Internet of Things, cloud computing, and data mining, and try to find the connection between them in terms of users, services, and applications. Furthermore, to get an insight into the data, this chapter consists of an introduction, research methodology, and conclusion.

Keywords: Big data, Big data analytics, Cloud computing, Data mining, Internet of things, Utility computing.

INTRODUCTION

The Internet of things produces a lot of data that may be used for further analysis and decision-making for the business. So, it is important to know the relationship between the Internet of things, the Cloud and Data Analytics. With the advancement of Internet speed and bandwidth, many devices are connecting daily, and this leads to a problem in terms of the huge amount of data produced by each device. The main challenge is how to deal with this data for the benefit of the business. Therefore, it becomes important to find different patterns from this data to get an insight into the business. It means there is a need to understand the relat-

---

* **Corresponding author Sartaj Ahmad:** KIET Group of Institutions Delhi-NCR, Affiliated to AKTU, Lucknow, UP, India; E-mail: sartaj.ahmad@kiet.edu

Arun Solanki and Anuj Kumar Singh (Eds.)

ionship between IoT, Cloud, and Big data. It is essential to know about these three concepts before going into detail.

IoT (Internet of Things)

It can be said collection of devices or appliances which are connected through the Internet. These devices may send and receive data and can be controlled from the other devices through the Internet [1]. Such generated data can be used further for decisions. Different patterns can be found and interpreted from such huge data using different data mining techniques. Generated data may be historical or real-time, but it depends on the individual how to use it. Machine learning, deep learning, data science, and statistical techniques can play a great role to handle such types of data.

Challenges in IoT: IoT is used in different areas like agriculture, transportation, traffic control, smart cities, healthcare, and many more. Besides its vast scope, it faces many challenges few of which are as follows.

Scalability: Billions of devices are connected through the internet and generate lots of data per unit of time. Therefore, storing and analysis of such real-time data is one of the challenges.

Security Issues: People are not aware of how to use such devices and how to secure the devices and data produced by these devices. This may lead to some problems in the future.

Health Care Issues: Sometimes wearable devices are used to take care of the patient; time mishandling, technical error, or lack of knowledge may be life-threatening to the patient.

Lack of Government Regulation: There is rapid advancement in this area, but still, government regulation is not so strong to keep our data and device security.

Insufficient Bandwidth: Devices are connecting exponentially and producing huge data, and the transfer of such data from one place to another place requires high bandwidth. This time of demand for bandwidth will increase over time which is also a challenge.

Electricity: IoT requires a 24x7 power supply, but in some countries, irregularity in electricity supply is also a major issue. Therefore, searching for and producing a new source of power is also a major challenge in this area.

Big Data

Data which is having features called 4Vs. like volume, variety, velocity, and veracity [2]. Volume means data is coming from different data sources, variety means data is in different formats, velocity means data is produced very fast and veracity means trustworthy quality data. There may be so many challenges in the case of Big Data related to data cleaning, transformation loading finally, processing for further interpretation. As the size of the data is increasing very fast, there is a need for some technology to store, process, and analyze. This technology is called Cloud computing and will be explained in the next paragraph.

Challenges in Big Data: IoT devices generate large amounts of real data that are difficult to store and manage. There are many tools available to manage such a large amount of data, but there are still a few challenges.

Lack of Knowledgeable Big Data Professionals: Big Data is very demanding nowadays, but there is a lack of professionals. There are several tools available, but people don't know how to use them. The company began to spend a lot of money on employee training. It produces many types of jobs, such as data scientists, data analysts, machine learning professionals, *etc.*

Data Size Increasing: The size of data is increasing day by day, and it becomes difficult to store and manage. For this, skilled professionals are needed.

Confusion in the Selection of Tools: With so many tools available on the market, it is sometimes difficult to choose the right tool according to the requirements.

Data Integration Issues: Collecting data from different sources and integrating it for analysis is also a daunting task. Data may have many forms, text form, image, audio, and video form. Therefore, the integration of various data is also an arduous task.

Security Issues: For a company or organization, protecting data is very important because it can cause huge financial losses. Insecure data may be stolen, or knowledge leakage may occur.

Cloud

It is an on-demand IT service of resources for storing huge data and powerful computation. It has multiple locations called data centers where different functions are distributed to handle huge data and process data [3, 4]. It reduces the cost required for software and hardware. We can sell up or scale down the IT services as per our requirements and anywhere as far as location is concerned.

It provides a secure, reliable, and speed-up environment for storing, computing, and transferring data.

Challenges in Cloud Computing: It provides users with hardware, software, and computing facilities according to their requirements. Therefore, it must be flexible enough in terms of users and resources. However, it still faces many of the following challenges.

Scalability in terms of Users and Hardware: As the number of users grows exponentially, hardware scalability is required to meet their needs. But the performance of the cloud should not decrease with the increase in users.

Efficient and Flexible Access Mechanism: Users should have enough ability to easily access and store data. Users should be flexible enough to run queries and get quick responses. The system should also be flexible enough to support parallel queries.

Elasticity: The system should have enough capacity to grow and shrink according to the current state of the cloud. According to the needs of users, resources should always be available [5].

Sharing: Sometimes, different applications may share the same resources and data. Therefore, effective methods are needed to support this type of sharing between different users and applications [6].

Diverse Environment: It should support the heterogeneity of hardware and software, such as disk speed, network, storage, and different computing capabilities [7, 8].

Free from Location and Placement: The cloud should be unaffected by location and data placement. Data and resources should be available on demand and not restricted by location. For this reason, it may have the concept of data replication, the concept of load balancing, and high bandwidth [9, 10].

Effective Handling and Storing of Large Datasets: There should be an effective and efficient mechanism to process and store large data sets because, with the connection of new devices, the data sets grow very fast. It should also support the concept of distributed systems because different applications may use the same data set in parallel.

Privacy in Cloud Computing: Data privacy is very important because data in the cloud is stored and outsourced according to user requirements. Encryption and decryption can be used to achieve privacy, but it will add additional costs.

Billing for Service: Customers can be charged for storing data, computing, and accessing data. So, the charge in the bill may vary as per these three components by the service provider.

Network Issue: As multi-user access to data requires a high-bandwidth and non-congested network. Therefore, the network should be efficient, and there should not be any packet loss.

Relationship between IoT, Big Data, and Cloud: After some understanding of IoT, Big Data, and Cloud [11], it is important to understand the relationship among them, as shown in Fig. (**1**).

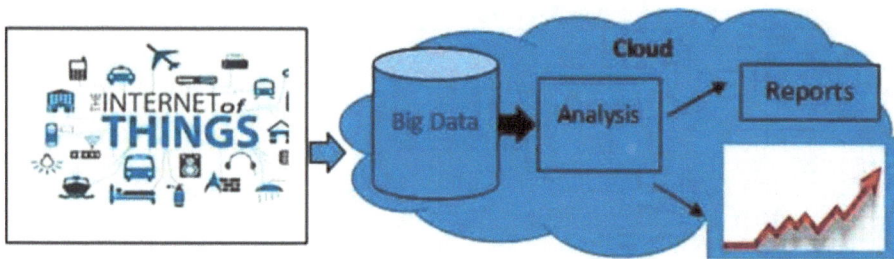

Fig. (1). IoT, Big Data, and Cloud.

It shows that the data generated by any device from the Internet of Things is huge and is stored in the form of big data for further processing. For storing purposes, cloud service can be considered to reduce software and hardware cost. Now we can apply analytical tools to gain insight into these data. The result can be further interpreted as a decision. Similarly, summaries and reports can be generated to prepare business action plans.

DATA ANALYTICS AND ITS TECHNIQUES

In this, we try to discover knowledge from the data. Based on this information, businessmen can make some decisions. This process includes data collection, cleaning, transformation, loading, and modeling using some statistical and analytical tools. It may have different steps, as discussed and shown [12] shown in Fig. (**2**).

Data Collection

Data is collected from different sources like excel sheets, survey data, flat files (JSON, XML), relational database management systems, *etc.*, after the collection cleaning process takes place.

Transformation

The main objective of this step is to clean and convert data into the general format. For example, the transformation from the different date format to the required date format. Similarly, identifying and removing the outlier (not fit data). This process also smooths noisy data by the binning method. This step can also be used for normalization, where the data can be converted from one scale to another scale.

Loading

Once data is properly transformed, it can be loaded in the target data warehouse for the data mining process to get an insight into the data.

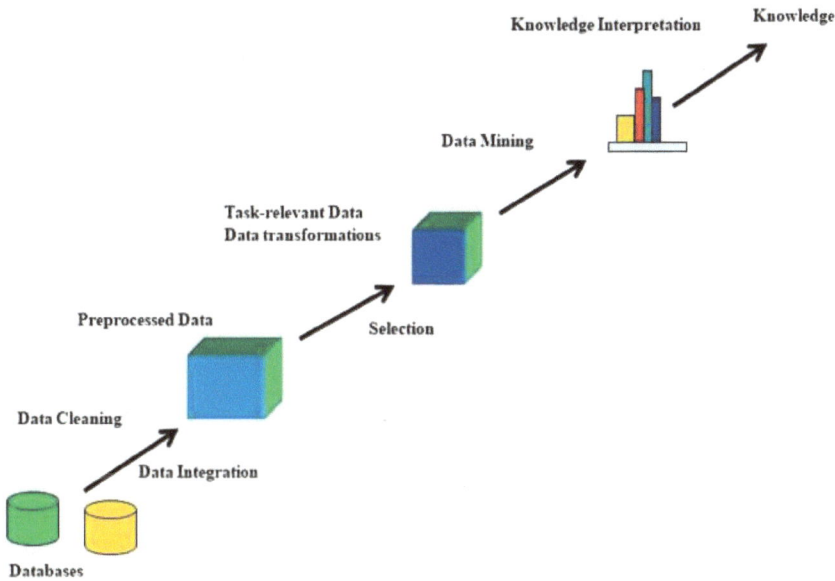

Fig. (2). Steps carried out in data analytics.

Modeling Techniques

It may have different statistical or analytical tools. In this, we try to use some mathematical models to find some hidden patterns in the data. A few of them are as follows.

1. Correlation
2. Chi^2 Test
3. Regression

4. Association
5. Classification
6. Decision Tree
7. Neural Network
8. Clustering *etc.*

Correlation

It is used to find the type of relationship between two variables. The relation may be positive, negative, or equal. It can be calculated in terms of Karl Pearson's coefficient (r) [13], whose value lies between -1 to 1 and can be calculated as follows:

$$r = \frac{\sum (x - \bar{x})(y - \bar{y})}{\sqrt{\sum (x - \bar{x})^2 \sum (y - \bar{y})^2}} \tag{1}$$

if r = 0 It means no relationship

r = 1 It means +ve relationship

For example:

Price of commodity and its demand

r = -1 It means -ve relationship

For example:

Sales of woolen clothes and temperature increasing.

Therefore, it describes the degree of relationship between two variables.

Chi² Test

It is also used to check the association between two or more variables. It means whether two or more variables are independent of each other or whether there is any relationship [14]. Initially, we set the null hypothesis that variables are independent of each other. Next, we find the Chi² value, and if the chi-square statistic > the calculated chi-square value, then there is no need to reject the null hypothesis. It means variables are independent of each other.

For example: Is there any relationship between gender and English Newspaper reading?

Regression

Correlation describes the degree of the relationship, not the exact relationship. Regression is used to find the relationship or nature of the relationship between attributes or variables. Once we find the exact relationship, it will be useful for prediction purpose [15]. Such a relationship may be between two variables called linear regression, where one is dependent, and another is an independent variable. Similarly, it can be between more than two variables, called multivariate regression, where one is dependent, and others are independent variables. Therefore, such a technique has great importance for forecasting and regression purposes.

$$y = a + bx \qquad\qquad (2)$$

This equation describes the relationship between y and x, where y (dependent variable) can be predicted in terms of x (independent variable).

For example, there may be a relationship between blood pressure and the age of different persons. Further same relation can be used to predict the blood pressure of individual age.

Association Technique

As the size of data grows, it becomes difficult to analyse it. In such cases, we try to find hidden patterns [16]. Association mining is also helpful for finding frequent patterns in the data. It also helps in finding the subsequence of the items. There are two measures called support and confidence; in terms of these, we can find frequent item sets and subsequences (in some order).

Support describes the popularity of the pattern in the transactions, while confidence describes the popularity of one item over another item.

Such association can be represented as:

$$d > X \to Y \qquad\qquad (3)$$

It means if a customer by X item, then Y will be the next item to be bought. For this purpose, the minimum threshold of support and confidence is set. If any rule satisfies such a threshold, then the same rule can be said to be a strict rule. Therefore, a strict rule helps in finding some association between the items.

For example:

In a general store Milk, Bread, Butter can be the frequent pattern in the different transactions. It means most of the customers buy such a set of items. It also describes that if the customer buys milk, bread then the next item in sequence will be butter. Such type of technique is mainly used in Market Basket Analysis. The Apriori algorithm is used in this technique.

According to this algorithm, support and confidence will be as follows:

Support = No. of the transaction having X and Y items both/Total no. of transaction

Confidence = No. of the transaction having X and Y items both/No. of the transaction having X item

Classification

This is also called supervised learning, where we have training data, and this data works as a supervisor. Training is also called labeled data. Using this data, a model is prepared called a classifier [17]. Such a classifier can be used further to classify new records as per the training provided. There are the following measures to check the performance of the classification model.

Precision

It describes what portion of the output positive is identified correctly.

Recall

It means what portion of the existing positive is identified correctly.

Accuracy

It means how often the classifier classifies the records correctly. The misclassification rate can be calculated by subtracting the accuracy value from 1. For example, patients can be classified as shown in the following Table **1**, where 'YES' means the patient has a particular disease, and 'NO' means the patient not having the disease.

Precision = TP/ (TP+FP)

= 100/ (100+10)

$= 0.91$

Recall = TP/(TP+FN)

$= 100/ (100+5)$

$= 0.95$

Accuracy = (TP + TN) / (TP + TN + FP + FN)

$= (100+50) / (100 + 50 + 10 + 5)$

$= 0.91$

Misclassification rate or error rate $= 1 - 0.91$

$= 0.09$

Table 1. Confusion matrix.

n=165	Predicted: NO	Predicted: YES	
Actual: NO	TN = 50	FP = 10	60
Actual: YES	FN = 5	TP = 100	105
	55	110	

Decision Tree

It is a tree structure as shown in Fig. (**3**), where each internal node (non-leaf node) denotes a test on an attribute, each branch represents an outcome of the test, and the leaf node (terminal node) holds a class label. In this, a given tuple X which has no class label initially is tested for its attributes, and a proper path is found from the root to the leaf [18]. This path predicts the class of that tuple. It is very important for high-dimensional data. The learning and classification steps of the decision tree are simple and fast. It has good accuracy. If a person's age is senior and their credit rating is fair, then he can be offered a credit card.

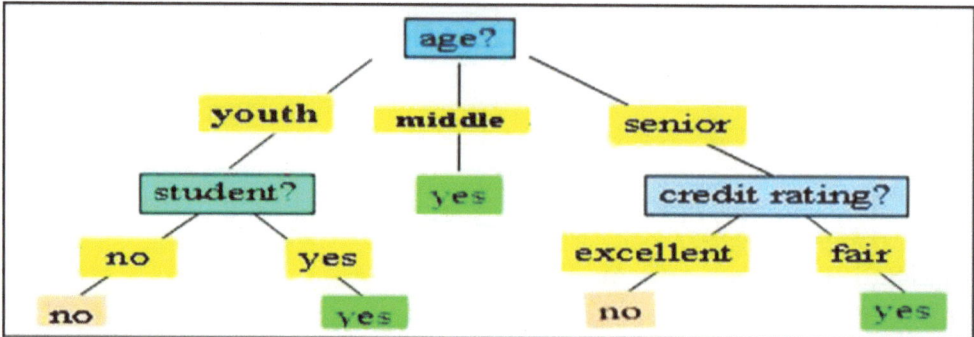

Fig. (3). Example of a decision tree.

Neural Network

It is a computational analogous of neurons [19]. It is a set of connected input/output units in which each connection has a weight associated with it. During the learning phase, the network learns by adjusting the weights to be able to predict the correct class label of input tuples. Schematic diagram of multi-layer feedforward neural network as shown in Fig. (4).

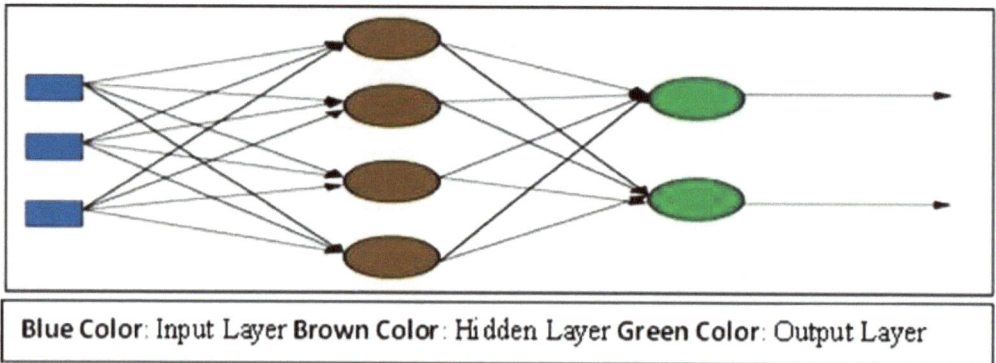

Blue Color: Input Layer **Brown Color**: Hidden Layer **Green Color**: Output Layer

Fig. (4). Multi-layer feedforward neural network.

Such a type of neural network has an input layer, one more hidden layer, and an output layer. Each layer is made of units. The input to the network corresponds to the attributes measured for each training tuple. A neural network can be used when we have little knowledge of the relationships between attributes and classes. It is also well suited for continuous values.

Clustering

In this technique, we try to extract information from unlabeled data. That is why it is also called unsupervised learning. In this technique, similar objects are put in a group, and dissimilar objects are put in a different group [20]. Similarity and dissimilarity are found in terms of the characteristics or features of the objects. It can also be defined as the process of grouping the data into classes or clusters so that objects within a cluster have high similarity but high dissimilarity from the objects of other clusters. It can be used in different applications, like categorizing customers as per their buying behavior. In medicine, to find the groups of patients as per symptoms, *etc*. There are many algorithms that support this concept. For example, Partition Based Algorithms, Hierarchical Based and Density-based algorithms, *etc*. It is difficult here to explain each algorithm however, just for awareness, I am introducing the K Means algorithm. It consists of the following steps:

Step 1: Arbitrary choose K (number of clusters) objects from data D as the initial centers of the clusters.

Step 2: Compute the mean (center) or centroid of each cluster of the current partition. Assign each object to the cluster with the most similar (closest) center.

Step 3: Go back to step 2.

Step 4: Until no change in the mean values of centroids.

Similarity can be checked in terms of the Euclidean distance formula or Manhattan distance formula. Further, this chapter describes an application based on the case study to understand the relationship between IoT, Cloud, and data analytics.

CASE STUDY

In this case study, we consider data [21] which is about the weather. It is collected by Chicago Park District through sensors at the beaches of Chicago Lake. These sensors capture the data hourly during the summer, as shown Table **2**.

No of Instances collected: 59144

Attributes considered: 6

Table 2. Filtered attributes and their data type.

Attribute name	Data Type
Wet Bulb Temperature (In Celsius)	Number
Humidity (In %)	Number
Total Rain (In mm/hour)	Number
Wind Direction (In Degrees)	Number
Maximum Wind Speed (In Meters per second)	Number
Solar Radiation (Solar radiation in watts per square meter)	Number

There are many data mining techniques like classification, association, clustering, neural network, *etc.*, to find insight into the data. It depends on the data and the individual how to use such techniques to get hidden patterns. Here it is found that clustering is a more suitable technique because data is unlabeled. This is an unsupervised approach called the clustering approach, where the KMeans algorithm is used to analyze this data. Following is the information related to the different parameters.

Number of iterations: 12

Sum of within-cluster distances: 31189.14376858875

Initial starting points (random):

Cluster 0: 10.643001,79,185.445529,326,4.7,0

Cluster 1: 2.5,50,12.2,322,2.8,0

Cluster 2: 10.643001,84,185.445529,261,4.4,0

In this model, missing values are replaced with mean/mode. The cluster centroids have been illustrated as presented in Table **3**.

Table 3. Final cluster centroids.

Attribute	Full Data (59144)	Cluster#1 17004(29%)	Cluster#2 16454(28%)	Cluster#3 25686(43%)
Wet Bulb Temperature	10.643	10.643	10.643	10.643
Humidity	71	77	53	77
Total Rain	185.4455	185.4455	185.4455	185.4455
Wind Direction	196	269	258	72
Maximum Wind Speed	3.8	4	4.3	3.4
Solar Radiation	3	2	2	4

In the chart as given in Fig. (**5**), it can be observed that there is a major shift in the wind direction which is from 196 to 72 units. Similarly, maximum wind speed and solar radiation are changing from 3.8 to 3.4 units and 3 to 4 units, respectively. This shows Cluster#3 size is bigger than Cluster#1 and Cluster#2. It means there is some part of summer that is not suitable for tourism purposes on such types of beaches.

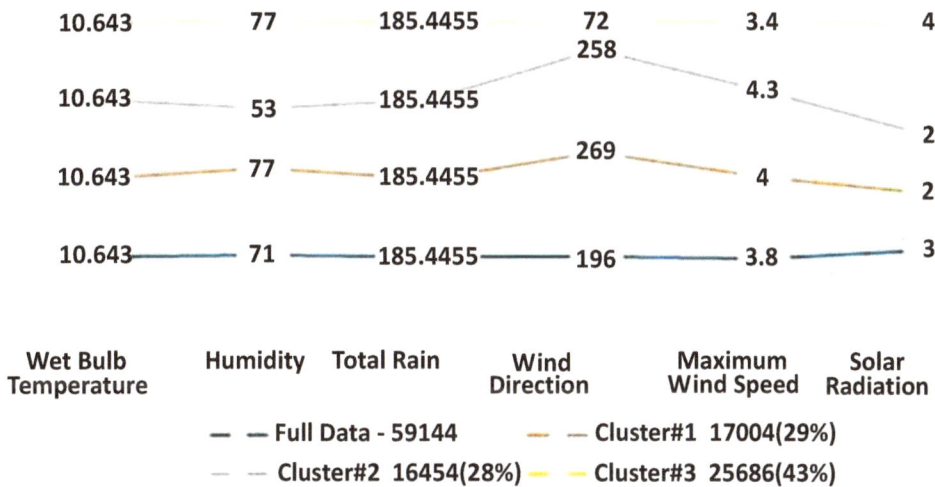

Fig. (5). Attributes wise centroid in the different clusters.

APPLICATIONS OF IOT, CLOUD, AND DATA ANALYTICS

There are several areas where a combination of IoT, cloud, and data analytics can be used. A few of them are listed below.

Healthcare

Compared with manual processes, medical devices based on the Internet of Things can more effectively monitor the health of patients [22]. This type of equipment reduces human error in collecting data and monitoring the health of patients, which supports the timely saving of lives.

Smart City

The data generated by the Internet of Things can be used to build smart cities by reducing pollution, controlling traffic, waste management, and making citizens' lives more comfortable and safer [23].

Education

The Internet of Things also plays an important role in the education field, like Smartboard and digital attendance registration. IoT sensors also help to detect natural disasters so that timely action can be taken [24]. Similarly, the Internet of Things can be used to transfer text from books, documents, and papers to computers or mobile phones.

Agriculture

The Internet of Things can remotely monitor farm conditions, and infrastructure can free up time, labor, and capital for investment, allowing farmers to focus on other things. For example, agricultural drones are relatively inexpensive drones equipped with advanced sensors that provide farmers with new ways to increase yields and reduce crop damage [25]. Another area where IoT technology is applied is vertical agriculture, which allows the control of soil moisture through computers or mobile devices.

Transportation and Logistics

Information can be gathered with the help of sensors and devices embedded in the vehicle, about the level of fuel, driver's behavior, and about the condition of the vehicle, *etc*. IoT helps companies and customers to get real-time information about the product from order to delivery [26]. IoT is also useful in logistics, where the location of goods can be kept under watch. This can be used to determine whether there is theft or delay in goods. It also helps in a secure supply chain by tracking vehicles, cargo, parcels, trolleys, and deliveries in progress.

Social Networking

It is known that IoT connects people, devices, and sensors. It leads to social networks which manage to connect and maintain the communication of billions of people using social relationships. Therefore, social IoT (IoT) [27] is an emerging field that uses social relations to connect and maintain devices in IoT networks. It is a new paradigm based on social relationships among objects in IoT networks. Social relationships, such as parents (devices with the same brand and batch), hosting (devices in the same location), co-working (devices used for collaboration), ownership (devices owned by the same user), and social objects (with data) based on irregular connected devices users used to connect smart objects. The goal of IoT is to "maintain the two levels of people and things; allow objects to have their social networks; allow humans to impose rules to protect their privacy, and only access the results of autonomous object interactions that occur on the social network of objects".

CONCLUSION

This chapter focuses on the Internet of Things as a source of data, the cloud for storing large amounts of data, and data analytics for discovering data insights. It also describes how to use the data obtained from the sensors for analysis. In this chapter, clustering techniques are used for analytical purposes and require interpretation to make certain decisions. Such decisions are very important in business processes. In the future, data streams and other techniques can be used to find more insights into the data. Likewise, advances in machine learning and artificial intelligence can also play an important role in automating processes and systems. Device security and privacy also matter of concern. Mutual authentication of devices and networks is also an issue for secure communications.

REFERENCES

[1]   M. Vögler, J.M. Schleicher, C. Inzinger, and S. Dustdar, "Ahab: A cloud-based distributed big data analytics framework for the internet of things", *Softw. Pract. Exper.,* vol. 47, no. 3, pp. 443-454, 2017. [http://dx.doi.org/10.1002/spe.2424]

[2]   A. Sungheetha, and R. Sharma, "Real-time monitoring and fire detection using internet of things and cloud-based drones", *J. Soft. Comp. Parad.,* vol. 3, no. 2, pp. 168-174, 2020.

[3]   H.N. Dai, H. Wang, Guangquan Xu, and J. Wan, "Big data analytics for manufacturing internet of things: Opportunities, challenges and enabling technologies", *Enterp. Inform. Sys.,* vol. 9-10, no. 9-10, pp. 1279-1303, 2020.

[4]   S. Says, and J.S. Raj, "Internet of things and big data analytics for health care with cloud computing", *J. Inform. Technol.,* vol. 1, no. 1, pp. 9-18, 2019.

[5]   B. Cooper, A. Silberstein, E. Tam, R. Ramakrishnan, and R. Sears, "Benchmarking Cloud Serving Systems YCSB", *SOCC,* 2010.

[6]　B. Hindman, A. Konwinski, M. Zaharia, A. AliGhodsi, A. Joseph, R. Katz, and S. Scott Shenker, "A platform for fine-grained resource sharing in the data center", In: *Usenix NSDI*, 2011.

[7]　E. Krevat, J. Joseph Tucek, and G. Gregory, "Disks are like snowflakes: no two are alike", In: *HotOS*, 2011.

[8]　M. Zaharia, A. Konwinski, A. Joseph, R. Katz, and I. Stoica, "Improving map reduce performance in heterogeneous environments", In: *Usnix OSDI*, 2008.

[9]　Y. He, R. Lee, Y. Huai, Z. Shao, N. Jain, X. Zhang, and Z. Xu, "RC File: a fast and space-efficient data placement structure in MapReduce-based warehouse systems", In: *IEEE ICDE*, 2011.

[10]　L. Qiao, "Integration of server, storage and database stack: moving processing towards data", *2008 IEEE 24ʰ International Conference on Data Engineering,* p. 1200, 2008.
[http://dx.doi.org/10.1109/ICDE.2008.4497529]

[11]　Available from: https://www.evelta.com/blog/iot-sensors/ (Accessed: 5th March 2022)

[12]　U. Fayyad, G. Piatetsky-Shapiro, and P. Smyth, "From data mining to knowledge discovery in databases", *AI Mag.,* vol. 17, no. 3, pp. 37-37, 1996.

[13]　N.J. Gogtay, and U.M. Thatte, "Principles of correlation analysis", *J. Assoc. Physicians India,* vol. 65, no. 3, pp. 78-81, 2017.
[PMID: 28462548]

[14]　B.M. Padhy, R.R. Mohanty, S. Das, and B.R. Meher, "Therapeutic potential of ivermectin as add on treatment in COVID 19: A systematic review and meta-analysis", *J. Pharm. Pharm. Sci.,* vol. 23, pp. 462-469, 2020.
[http://dx.doi.org/10.18433/jpps31457] [PMID: 33227231]

[15]　S. Chatterjee, and A.S. Hadi, *Regression analysis by example.* John Wiley & Sons, 2015.

[16]　B. Varija, and N.P. Hegde, *An Association Mining Rules Implemented in Data Mining. In Smart Computing Techniques and Applications* Springer: Singapore, 2021, pp. 297-303.

[17]　M.L.R. AbdElNabi, M.J. Wajeeh, M EL-Bakry, H.N. Taha, and N.E. M. Khalifa, "Breast and colon cancer classification from gene expression profiles using data mining techniques", *Symmetry,* vol. 12, no. 3, p. 408, 2020.
[http://dx.doi.org/10.3390/sym12030408]

[18]　B. Charbuty, and A. Abdulazeez, "Classification based on decision tree algorithm for machine learning", *J. Appl. Sci. Technol.Tren.,* vol. 2, no. 1, pp. 20-28, 2021.
[http://dx.doi.org/10.38094/jastt20165]

[19]　D. Bau, J.Y. Zhu, H. Strobelt, A. Lapedriza, B. Zhou, and A. Torralba, "Understanding the role of individual units in a deep neural network", *Proc. Nat. Acad. Sci.,* vol. 117, pp. 30071-30078, 2020.
[http://dx.doi.org/10.1073/pnas.1907375117]

[20]　V. Zarikas, S.G. Poulopoulos, Z. Gareiou, and E. Zervas, "Clustering analysis of countries using the COVID-19 cases dataset", *Data Brief,* vol. 31, p. 105787, 2020.
[http://dx.doi.org/10.1016/j.dib.2020.105787] [PMID: 32523977]

[21]　Available from: https://data.cityofchicago.org/d/k7hf-8y75 (Accessed: 1st Jan 2022).

[22]　A. Kulkarni, and A.S. Sathe, "Healthcare applications of the internet of things: A review", *Int. J. Comput. Sci. Inf. Technol.,* vol. 5, no. 5, pp. 6229-6232, 2014.

[23]　Y. Mehmood, F. Ahmad, I. Yaqoob, A. Adnane, M. Imran, and S. Guizani, "Internet-of-things-based smart cities: Recent advances and challenges", *IEEE Commun. Mag.,* vol. 55, no. 9, pp. 16-24, 2017.
[http://dx.doi.org/10.1109/MCOM.2017.1600514]

[24]　J. Marquez, J. Villanueva, Z. Solarte, and A. Garcia, IoT in education: Integration of objects with virtual academic communities. *New Advances in Information Systems and Technologies.* Springer, 2016, pp. 201-212.

[http://dx.doi.org/10.1007/978-3-319-31232-3_19]

[25]   R. Gómez-Chabla, K. Real-Avilés, C. Morán, P. Grijalva, R. Gómez-Chabla, K. Real-Avilés, C. Morán, P. Grijalva, and T. Recalde, "IoT applications in agriculture: A systematic literature review", In: *2ⁿᵈ International Conference on ICTs in Agronomy and Environment* Springer, 2019, pp. 68-76.

[26]   N. Manoj Kumar, and A. Dash, "Internet of things: An opportunity for transportation and logistics", *Proceedings of the International Conference on Inventive Computing and Informatics (ICICI 2017),* pp. 194-197, 2017.

[27]   A.M. Ortiz, D. Hussein, S. Park, S.N. Han, and N. Crespi, "The cluster between internet of things and social networks: Review and research challenges", *IEEE Internet Things J.,* vol. 1, no. 3, pp. 206-215, 2014.
[http://dx.doi.org/10.1109/JIOT.2014.2318835]

CHAPTER 10

Cloud-Based Secure Framework for Service Authentication and Access Control in Smart Cities Architecture Employing IOE

Amit Wadhwa[1,*], **Neerja Arora**[2] and **Ankit Garg**[3]

[1] GL Bajaj Institute of Technology and Management, Greater Noida, India

[2] Ajay Kumar Garg Engineering College, Ghaziabad, Uttar Pradesh, India

[3] Apex Institute of Technology, Computer Science and Engineering, University Center for Research and Development, Chandigarh University, Mohali, Punjab, India

Abstract: Cloud Computing has evolved as a next-generation technology and used as an integrated technology solution or feature in many evolving computing areas. One of the areas is in the field of Smart Cities, employing the internet of things or everything. A smart city is similar to a next-generation city, where services are being provided to users just like in the cloud computing domain. The focus of using such a system is to provide smart services to users or people living around. In previous works, presented by authors around the world, many solutions in different domains related to smart cities are provided, catering to different needs of users but still, there is scope for better access control and authentication mechanisms for accessing various services provided to users over a cloud-based environment. Smart cities are based on the usage of online computing services provided by various ICT/IOT technologies. It also faces many challenges and security threats, just like services in a cloud computing environment. The work presented here will discuss the concepts of the convergence of IOE and cloud computing in smart cities and the challenges faced in future-generation cities employing IOE. Along with this catering to security requirements in smart cities, this work proposes a security framework focussed on providing secure access control and authentication services delivered over the cloud-based system used in smart cities.

Keywords: Access control, Authentication, Cloud computing, Internet of things, Internet of everything, Smart cities, Security.

INTRODUCTION

"Smart city" is a term known since 1994 when Cisco invests a large amount of around $25m for a period of 5 years to research different perspectives of smart cities. In 2008, IBM started its "Smarter Planet" initiative to identify the usage

---

* **Corresponding author Amit Wadhwa:** GL Bajaj Institute of Technology and Management, Greater Noida, India; E-mail: am1012it@gmail.com

Arun Solanki and Anuj Kumar Singh (Eds.)

and suitability of applying sensors with analytics and networks for issues in urban areas. Since then, over the years, the ability of technology to provide a holistic or comprehensive view of all facets of city functionality/operations and improved quality of life has become a reality today.

The primary goal behind the concept of smart cities is to automatize and optimize their functions. Using smart data analysis and technology support amplifies economic growth, thereby improving citizens' quality of life. The salient factor in this would be using technology appropriately rather than how much technical support is available.

The primary goal behind the concept of smart cities is to automatize and optimize their functions. Using smart data analysis and technical support helps improves economic growth, thereby improving citizen's quality of life. An important factor in this would be, using technology appropriately rather than how much technical support is available.

A smart city, moreover, uses ICT (Information and Communication Technology) technology [1, 2] to provide the benefits of improved operational efficiency, thereby providing a better quality of service for the welfare of citizens of the city. There exist many formal definitions for a Smart City, like IBM, defines a smart city as "one that makes optimal use of all the interconnected information available today to better understand and control its operations and optimize the use of limited resources".

The main idea behind the concept is to identify and provide technology-based solutions to problems faced by people in urban areas. The smart city uses different types of software, UI's (user interfaces) and networks for communication mechanisms [1] alongside IoT (Internet of Things) to provide technology-oriented solutions to issues faced by citizens in their day-to-day life. The important term or technology concept used in smart cities is IoT. IoT is referred to as the network of physical objects like sensors or actuators for collecting useful information about various activities performed in cities which would help in driving decisions for the well-being of the citizens.

The main goals for the development of a smart city are:

- Improving transportation services,
- Reducing industrial or generic waste and preventing inconvenience to citizens living around,
- Improving social and economic standards and
- Maximizing social inclusion

Further, cloud computing also plays a vital role alongside IoT [1] as its features are, used as the backbone for effectively utilizing the power of IoT. An IoT system involves devices like sensors *etc.*, with limited storage, computation power and connectivity options, to provide enhanced support in terms of the above said features, the power of cloud computing can be utilized. Cloud computing is a system for on-demand network access to a shared pool of resources with expandable storage, high computational capability, and multiple supported connectivity options. So, an amalgamation of IoT with cloud computing would enhance the power of IoT for Machine to Machine inter-communication [3], providing a viable technology solution for issues of people. IoT is a major technology component in the development of Smart Cities, so using it alongside the cloud would solve inherent problem faced in Smart Cities functionality compared to when IoT is used alone.

IoT has remarkable effects in work and home scenarios, where it can play a leading role in the next future with features like assisted living, robotics, e-health, smart transportation, *etc.* Following it, in 2008, IoT was reported by the US National Intelligence Council as one of the six technologies with a potential impact on US interests towards 2025 [2]. The IoT ecosystem works by providing a system where internet-connected devices can sense/fetch data from the environment/equipment and further share it with other devices without the involvement of people/human intervention. It is also referred to as (M2M) Machine to Machine communication technology.

Number of devices that interconnected with each other in 2011 crossed the population of people in the world [3]. While the Internet of Things is still looking for its own form, its effects have already begun to make incredible advances as a universal solution for the connected scenario [4]. Due to the importance of IoT technology, various IoT-based applications have been developed, like Smart City, Smart Home, Smart Grid, Smart Health, *etc.* [5 - 8]. With massive urbanization in the world recently, using ICT to perform urban city operations has become quite an effective solution. The Smart City concept is selected based on other previously coined urban development models like digital city and telicity *etc.*, as it provides a better abstraction among others [9].

In smart cities, the services are provided to users over the internet just like we do in the cloud computing domain. So, likewise cloud computing systems, smart cities also possess or encounter the challenge of security vulnerabilities in the services provided by the system. Here in this work, initially, we have focused our attention on the identification of various vulnerable or susceptible entities involved in the smart city environment. As the services in the system are susceptible to security breaches or issues, a cloud-based solution for secure authentication and access control has been proposed with enhanced or multilevel access control protection.

In this work, the initially unification of IoE (Internet of Everything) and the Cloud is discussed with a comparison of features provided by the Cloud, and a comparison of it with IoT and IOE is elaborated. Next, challenges faced by smart cities employing IOE are discussed. Further, issues faced in the Smart City environment and the interrelation with cloud architecture are provided in this work. The work discussed here focuses on unifying cloud computing, IoT and IOE [6, 9]. Mainly, the focus is on features, challenges, and security issues faced in the Smart Cities employing IOE. In the end, a cloud-based framework for secure access control and authentication is proposed for usage in future smart cities, followed by future directions in the field of work.

UNIFICATION OF CLOUD COMPUTING AND IOE

Cloud computing has emerged as a booming domain area, as many of the day-to-day applications used by internet users employ the power of cloud computing. Further, mobile devices are also commonly used by a large set of the world population, mainly smart mobile devices requiring the internet. It leads to the requirement for a technology that could cope with ever increasing demand for computing power, storage, and an expandable network [10]. Cloud computing technology over the years has proved to be a viable solution for satisfying the said requirements of flexible storage, network, and computation power. In this section of work, initially, cloud services supporting IoT and IOE are presented, followed by a differentiation between IoT and IOE.

Cloud Services - Supporting IOT and IOE

Cloud computing provides a set of services or features which form the basis for its development. The services provided to cloud users are designed keeping in mind the features and functionality the cloud system provides. Like a cloud, users don't have to think about the ever-growing computational power requirements of the application being designed [10]. The cloud also supports broad network access and provides appropriate storage to meet all the data requirements of applications that might require to be scaled up or down. Following it, one could say that services provided over a cloud environment will justify usability and role in the field of IOT and IOE, as both these fields lack features that are the backbone of a cloud-based system [11]. Services or features provided by a cloud computing environment are depicted as shown in Fig. (**1**).

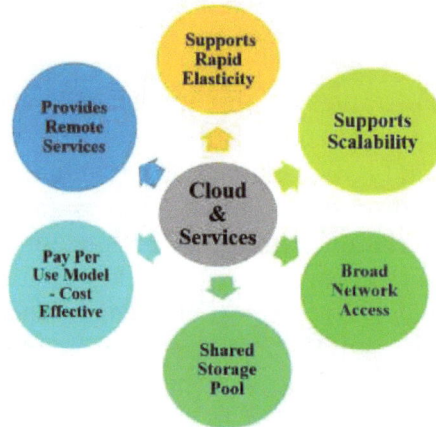

Fig. (1). Cloud computing services.

Rapid Elasticity

It specifies that the services provided over the cloud platform are elastic in nature and can be provisioned in an elastic way by users in any number at any time and size [11].

Scalability

It is the property by which any service provisioned by the user over the cloud, like storage, computation power [11], *etc.*, can be easily scaled up or down as per the user's requirements.

Broad Network Access

With this feature, the services of cloud-based systems are accessed and supported by a variety of devices over the internet, like mobile phones, laptops, Smart TV's and tabs [11].

Pay Per Use Model – Cost Effective

Due to this feature, one could make out that the services are accessible on a payment basis, like Netflix, amazon prime and Hotstar. As much as one wants to use a service, one needs to only pay for that duration, making the solution cost-effective compared to the traditional system.

Shared Storage Pool and Remote Services

Storage provided in a cloud-based system is unlimited in size; as per requirement, storage can be increased in size, which enhances flexibility in the system [11].

Also, services can be deployed on or accessed from remote locations or servers, which makes the architecture location independent.

Differentiating IOT and IOE

The term Internet of Things was coined in 1999, although what we see today is its transformed version. Earlier, people connected by connecting devices like landline phones, TV and radio, but interacting with them was an impossible task [12 - 14]. Now people connect through internet-based smart devices like smartphones or TV, *etc.* IoT opens a possibility for all smart devices to communicate or exchange information with others, laying down the basis for machine-to-machine communication.

Defining IoT

IoT can be defined as the collection of unlimited or un-countable internet-connected physical devices that sense and share data without any human intervention [5, 7, 10]. The sensing devices can be configured to communicate with other devices in the system and share data for achieving specific tasks.

Working of IOT System

IoT system works by the use of embedded sensors in devices or objects connected through the internet, which further integrates data collected from different sources like IOT-enabled devices and analyzes the information for processing, thereby drawing useful conclusions and helping in decision making [11, 13]. After processing the information, some useful patterns can be detected from the analysis drawn, or recommendations can be made using the analysis to draw conclusions about any real-time situation.

For example, Sensors deployed in a shopping mall [13] can be used to make many observations or draw useful conclusions like:

- Which sections of the shopping area are visited by the customers most?
- Where can overcrowding happen on certain days (like during sales or public holidays [15])?
- Track no. of people of different genders visit per day.
- Which items are selling fast, and useful in making advance orders for the same?

Fig. (2) sums up the working flow of the process followed in IOT based ecosystem for making useful decisions for real-life scenarios.

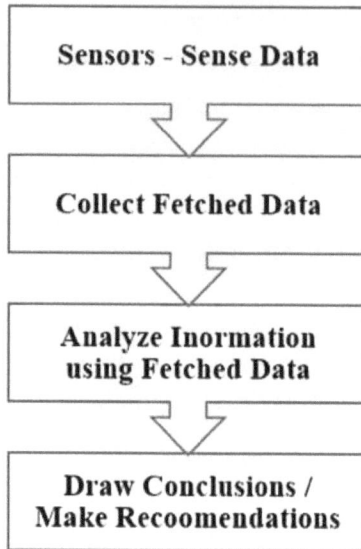

Fig. (2). IOT Process Flow.

Components Enabling IOT

There are different components that enable or support the working of the IOT-enabled system [13], which are as follows:

RFIDs

Uses radio waves to track the tags attached to the physical devices used in the IOT network.

Sensors

These are the components that are used to detect changes in the environment or surroundings.

Smart Networks

These are composed of different topologies which can be supported by the IOT-enabled system to interconnect devices.

Gateways

Sensors in the system provide data collected to Gateways, and a particular sort of pre-processing is incorporated at this level.

IOT technology majorly involves "Things" and "Networks".

Defining IOE and differentiating from IOT

IOE is the term most often confused with IOT, but the two differ in many ways. IOE can be said to be the superset of IOT, where the focus of IOT lies mainly on interconnecting things or objects, but IOE is concerned with things, people, data, and processes [14, 16, 17]. It works as a complete system where everything is interconnected. IOE supports not only machine-to-machine communication, but also supports Machine to People, and People to People by using underlying technology.

The foundation of the IOE is laid down on 4 pillars, *i.e.*, people, things, data, and process [18, 19], whereas IOT works with only Things or objects. This is the major difference between the concepts of IOT and IOE. The essential components of IOE [18, 20] are described below:

Things

Things are referred to as the components or objects which collect information using sensors embedded into them. They use the network to share information with each other. An example of such a device is a smartwatch used for monitoring the health parameters of a person like BP, calories burned [18], oxygen levels, *etc.*

People

People refer to humans without which any connection can't be said as Intelligent [10, 20]. This type of communication is like doctors using sensors embedded or attached to patient's body for analyzing and monitoring their health.

Data

Data refer to humans without which any connection can't be said as Intelligent. This type of communication is like doctors using sensors embedded or attached to patient's body for analyzing and monitoring their health.

Process

The process specifies or determines how each of the above-mentioned components works together to achieve the required goal. The basic idea is to deliver accurate information to the correct user (person or machine) at the right time [14].

Apart from these four pillars, another thing or component that is required is Network, without which nothing works, neither IOT nor IOE [21, 22]. So, one could conclude that IOE is all about its 4 Pillars and Network. IOE can be defined as a network of networks where billions of connections create unprecedented opportunities and new risks [23].

Unification of Cloud and IOE

From the above-discussed concepts, one clear thing is that IOT is a subset of IOE or IOE, which can be said as a superset of IOT. So, limitations or issues encountered during the integration of IOT with the Cloud are also applicable for Cloud and IOE unification with a set of additional inclusions. As per the literature presented by the researcher over the years, certain areas in a Cloud-based system can benefit from IOE. On the other hand, there are certain advantages IOE can reap by integrating with a Cloud computing environment that justifies the unification of the Cloud with IOE. There are certain drivers driving the Integration of the Cloud with IOE. There are certain features of the Cloud that are aligned with respect to IOE, as shown in Fig. (**4**).

As shown in Fig. (**3**), these features can be said as the differentiating points between the cloud and IOE environment.

Justification for Unification of Cloud with IOE

Cloud has features like centralized architecture, unlimited computation power, works with virtual resources, supports big data management and services are delivered over cloud using the internet.

Whereas IOE, as its extension of IOT, works in a distributed architecture, has limited computation power and storage and works with real objects or things [21, 24], generating an enormous amount of data which acts as the source of big data. Based on these features, although they contrast each other, in another sense, one can see that the shortfalls of one could be countered by the other technology, which will justify the reason for their unification. There are certain drivers or major features based on which these technologies work and support each other, which are described here as Drivers supported by IOE, benefitting the Cloud environment are listed as follows:

- Communication Oriented
- Storage Oriented and
- Computation Power Oriented [11]

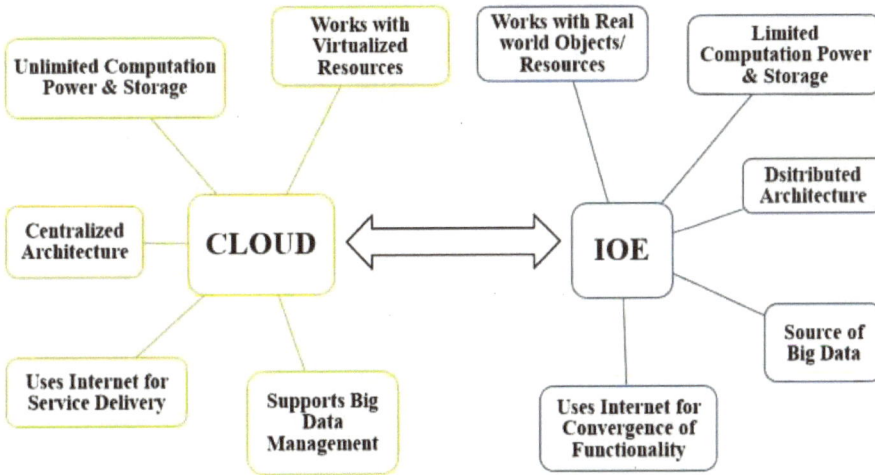

Fig. (3). Features of Cloud Aligned in Accordance with IOE.

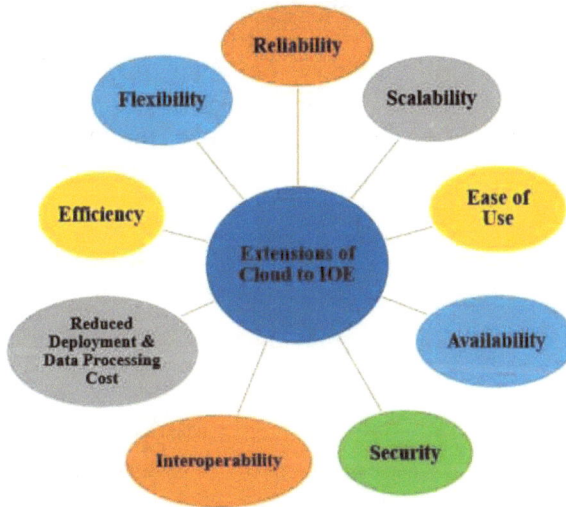

Fig. (4). Cloud-Based Extensions or Features to IOE.

Communication Oriented

- Cloud offers an effective and low-cost solution to connect, track, and manage anything from anywhere at any time by using customized portals and built-in apps [11].
- Utilizing high-speed networks provides support for remote things to be controlled, monitored, and communicated with in an effective manner [13]. Apart from this real-time access to generated data is also made effectively and efficiently [11].

Storage Oriented

- IOE-based things produce large amounts of structured and semi-structured data, which could be easily managed by Cloud [25].
- Security is required for data collected or generated out of IOT devices.

Computation Power Oriented

Requirements of IOE for extensive processing power and energy resources can be handled by Cloud based system with capabilities for effectively and efficiently analyzing and processing the real-time data.

The above amalgamation of Cloud with IOE will harness the power of both technologies and would make way for a new set of paradigms like "Things as a Service", or "Sensors as a Service"/"Sensing as a Service" [11].

Benefits to Cloud by its Convergence with IOE

- Cloud can benefit from IOE and can work with related Objects in a well-organized manner.
- Cloud can act as an intermediary between IOE-based objects and their applications, with complexities and functionalities of applications hidden.
- It can support IOE by extending it with its features of unlimited storage and processing power.

Also, there are certain drivers which are missing in IOE and will be available to it during its integration with the Cloud environment, which is shown in Fig. (**5**).

As shown in Fig. (**4**), it represents the features of the Cloud that could be extended to IOE to support its shortfalls.

Further, Cloud can provide reliability, scalability, efficiency, and flexibility to IOE applications. Also, applications built in IOE would become interoperable if integrated over a cloud environment. Availability of data and applications is ensured as the cloud advocates for on-demand service access supporting backup and replication by providing continued services even in adverse situations emerging due to SPOF's [26] (Single point of failures). Apart from the Cloud, if integrated with IOE, it would benefit IOE with its support for multiple security measures [26 - 28]. Further, this integration or unification will also be cost-effective as data processing and deployment costs are reduced in cloud environments. All these discussed features are like additional internal drivers used for integration and usage of the Cloud and IOE.

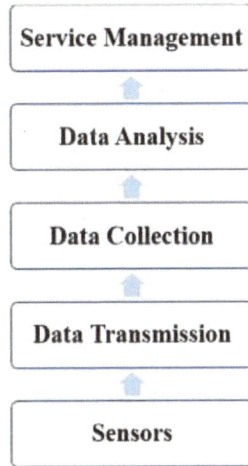

Fig. (5). Process flow in a smart city system.

CHALLENGES FOR SMART CITIES EMPLOYING IOE

This section of work covers the basic concept of Smart cities employing IOE, where IOE can be further integrated with the Cloud to reap the benefits as discussed in the previous section. Further to this, the focus will be towards identifying challenges from literature, faced while thinking of building futuristic Smart Cities [29], required to be built considering the ever-growing urban population in the world. It will be considered as the possible choice catering to the challenges faced by countries whose major population is shifting towards Urban areas and adopting urban living standards.

Defining Smart Cities

The technology of Smart City is based on the concept of IOT and, in a broader sense IOE. With the swift increase in the population and urbanization around the world has impacted the way of managing the massive expansion of urbanization, resulting in an impact on the environment and lifestyle of the people [10]. The idea of building Smart Cities is still in the evolving stage, as not many countries across the world are fully accustomed to Smart City architecture [10] due to financial and technological factors [18].

As the concept of Smart Cities is built on the foundations of IOE, so technological innovations or advancement in IOE is required to make the culture of Smart City fully realizable. The main idea behind building Smart Cities is to provide its occupants with services to meet their needs, automatically identified by their behavior [10]. A smart city uses different ICT-based digital tools for the betterment of the life of citizens living in it. The term digital city is used interchangeably to refer to a smart city. It seems obvious that the smart city often stems from the digital city for better urban management [24].

Although Smart City seems to be a generic concept, the notion of Smart City can vary from city to city. Since problems in many cities are different, they have to be dealt with differently. The generic realization of the smart city concept could not apply to every scenario. New technologies and ideas can be useful in enhancing the lives of citizens with a vision for creating a brighter future for them.

Building smart cities using technological innovations would help in improving efficiency, sustainability and competitiveness with a better economy and high quality of life for citizens [30]. The process flow for the working of a smart City is shown in Fig. (**5**).

There are certain parameters cities can use to work around and try to improve to achieve their goals of a better economy and high-quality life for citizens [22]. Those parameters can be like:

- Economy
- Standard of Living
- Education
- Environment
- Security &
- Mobility/Transportation

Economy

Requirements from a financial perspective can be dynamic and healthy and done by using technology to make following city-wide regulations more feasible and responsive for citizens.

Standard of Living

It means improving the daily life of citizens by focusing on their health of citizens, both mental and physical, thereby allowing them to make better choices in their lives.

Education

Virtual learning platforms could be developed for better reach within remote users. Augmented and virtual reality-oriented technologies could also help transform the way one understands and learn.

Environment

Working with the digital world in a city can have an environmental impact also. The use of sensor-based technology solutions can help improve decisions about physical infrastructure.

Security

As the city works on digital technology, it also requires measures to secure every checkpoint in the city to enhance public safety. Access to service should be properly authenticated using multi-factor type authentication mechanisms.

Mobility/Transportation

Digital technology-based Transportation is another important factor in keeping a city smarter. Sensor-driven location searching, dynamic pricing and ride/vehicle sharing could help improve the traffic situation across the city.

Characteristics of Smart Cities

As the transition of a city to a smarter one takes time, making the right step-forward towards the desired goal should be monitored across four major pillars that must be thoroughly practiced. The pillars of importance are:

• Engaging Stakeholders [22]
• Policy Changes
• Funds and finances &
• Experimentation

Stakeholders

The right idea is to engage all stakeholders in preparing the plan and vision for a futuristic Smart City. It will include Governments, Industry, Academia, and citizens to build upon this plan and decide on the perception after thoroughly understanding the architecture.

Policy Changes

Living standards and the way citizens want things to work might collide with the law and enforcement agencies' thought processes. So that should be considered before making any advancements.

Funds and Finances

Some of the projects under smart city development might require funding from not only government bodies but also from private partners or external agencies. For example, investment can be raised from public-private partnerships, crowdfunding, charging users for keeping up with operational costs and development funds from private or public players. So, all that should be aligned with the requirements.

Experimentation

There should be physical or virtual testing grounds for checking the implementable ideas or innovations, enhancing the benefits of holistic development. Application or characteristics of smart cities [30] are as follows:

- Smart Economy [30] (Involves Competitiveness and Flexibility)
- Smart People [30] (Involves Social and Human Capital)
- Smart Governance [30] (Active Participation among related Entities)
- Smart Transportation [30] (Involves Sustainable, Innovative and Safe Transport System)
- Smart Infrastructure (Supports Smart Accessible Infrastructure)
- Smart Industries (Automated control and working)
- Smart Energy and Environment [30] (Using Smart meters - environment friendly in nature)
- Smart Living [30] (Talks about Quality of Life, like health conditions, social cohesion, *etc.*)

Smart City – Challenges

Challenges faced by Smart Cites are elaborated here as follows:

- One challenge would be ensuring data generated out of different employed sensors is not compromised [30, 31, 32] – *i.e.*, Who will ensure that data is not altered or mishandled or not forged, and not shared with unauthorized users, and only accessible by legitimate users?
- Another challenge would be to identify the faulty or erroneous sensed data – *i.e.*, How to ensure that the data fetched using available sensors is correct or not? As decision making or drawing conclusions for applicable systems are totally dependent on the sensed data. If it includes irregularities or inaccuracies to some greater extent, then it will affect the functioning of the whole system or service.
- Trusting other SP's(Service Providers) providing similar sorts of services – The idea here is that it will be difficult for people to trust other SP's providing

similar sorts of services. It will make the users aligned to only limited service providers of any given domain.

- Another challenge would be sharing and storing data as per regulatory body guidelines – A lot of data is collected and which could be of varying types like structured, semi-structured or unstructured [27], so storing and sharing a different variety of data would be a difficult task considering the regulatory body guidelines.

- Another challenge would be to provide a trust framework, which would ensure trustworthy services for legitimate users.

- Services that are derived or employed in the functioning of Smart cities are not possessing malicious intent, *i.e.*, if an application is designed to gather useful data and sell it to some unreliable or wrong persons, then it might result in hampering the trust of users on services or the quality of Smart city environment.

- Another challenge would be restricting access to user data and service access in a smart city environment - It will be susceptible to attacks as data with services are provided over the network using the internet. A multi-factor authentication system and a secure Access control protection mechanism are needed to suppress the attacks if encountered over the network during service access.

SECURITY ATTACKS AND IMPLICATIONS IN SMART CITIES ARCHITECTURE

The concept of smart cities has its usability in many application-specific roles, which are elaborated as shown in Fig. (**6**).

• Security and Surveillance

Smart security measures must be adopted for sensor data and services provided to citizens. Surveillance involves monitoring access to live feeds for a video stream [30, 33] to a restricted set of users, like for crime detection and prevention.

• Patient Health Monitoring

The patient health monitoring system is susceptible to attacks as information collected from sensors embedded with the patient's body is available to unauthorized users [33, 34]. The information can contain data like heart rate, blood pressure, the status of kidneys, liver and other vital or private organs *etc.*, for which an integrated security solution to maintain privacy is needed [29].

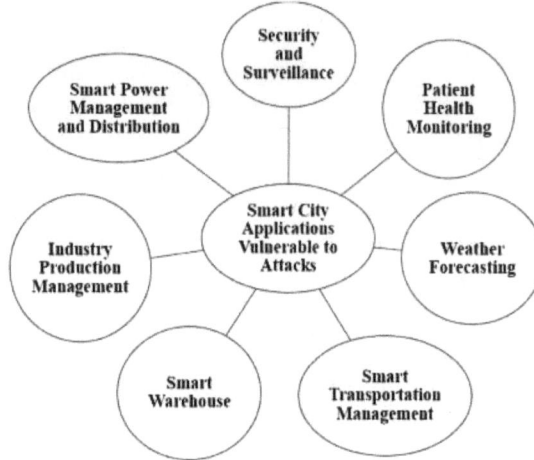

Fig. (6). Smart city applications vulnerable to attacks.

• Weather Forecasting

It includes information regarding temperature, pressure, wind speed, *etc.* or any chances of natural disasters happening in the near future, information if altered after the attack then, it will lead to some unpredictable situations like no or wrong information about disasters being circulated among authorities [29].

• Smart Transportation Management

It involves issues like parking and congestion on roads, for which following smart parking and traffic management is required. It acts as a viable application for smart city architecture. Solutions to trafficmanagement are like car or bike pooling [10] systems handled by smart applications, which are also susceptible to network-level attacks. To prevent them, there is a need for encryption of information while communicating; identifying legitimate car or bike poolers is a challenge to be handled by smart technology.

• Industry/Factory Production Management

It includes the use of robotic equipment-based operation management of industry, thereby keeping a check on the production capacity of items manufactured in the company. The smart assembly line employed for production and manufacturing involves using sensors to indicate completion or issues with a specific operation in desired time for immediate action by the concerned personnel or team. If sensors are not correct in identifying the root cause of the problem in time, happens due to any reason like a faulty sensor or sensor vulnerability to attacks [34, 35], it will hamper the generic operation of the industry.

• Smart Power Management and Distribution

It involves operations like power monitoring, power plan controlling, underground cable system monitoring, smart meter reading management, solar panels management [30], *etc.* All these are the application of IOE for providing smart power-related services to citizens in smart cities.

• Smart Warehouse

Involves operations like auto identification of stock availability in the warehouse. Moreover, inventory management and supporting stock management would be helpful in circumstances where a few items in the warehouseare wiped out fast than others so as to maintain availability. The sensors can be deployed for easy identification of shortfalls in stocks. It can be susceptible to MIM attacks.

Security Perspective

Smart cities system provides support for various application areas, as discussed above, which are susceptible to many security issues or attacks.

Various examples of attacks or security issues can be like:

- Cyber Security Issues (Can occur with smart grid development)
- Attack on IOT based Objects (susceptible to common wireless network attacks)
- Attacks or threats like DDOS (Distributed denial of service), MIM(Man in the middle attack), *etc.*
- Device Hijacking
- Access control issues
- Authentication and Authorization issues

To prevent attacks or threats and counter any such issues, prevention methods are required to be adopted as given in Table **1**.

Table 1. Attack types with attack surface and their prevention methods.

Attack Types	Attack surface/Prevention Mechanisms
Device Hijacking	Maintain Unique Identification and Strong Access Control Mechanism

Attack Types	Attack surface/Prevention Mechanisms
DOS/DDOS	Incorporating Two-factor Authentication, Encryption, and Access Control [30].
MIM attack	Prevention by Effective Authentication and Encryption
Data Privacy and Identity theft	Countered by Strong Authentication, Encryption and Access Control [30]
Masquerading	Strong Authentication
Eavesdropping	Strong Encryption of Data in Transit, Network Segmentation [32]
Steganography	Configure Anti-Malware for detecting binders/ use software from trusted sites [33]

Other means of protection are like:

- Building Security Policy to prevent them, but the cost should be low.
- Lightweight cryptographic methods could be identified and applied to maintain CIA (Confidentiality, Integrity and Availability [18, 30, 34]) of transmitted data over the network.
- Hijacking can be countered by Device's unique identification and adoption of strong access control mechanism.
- DDOS can be countered by Strong 2 factor Authentication [34, 36] Encryption, and access control.
- MIM can be countered by effective authentication and encryption.
- Privacy data and identity theft can be countered by Authentication, Encryption and Access Control [10, 18, 30].

Security Challenges and Solutions in Smart City Environment

Apart from above-discussed attacks and their countermeasures, these security challenges are categorized into different types:

- Operational and Transition Challenges [18] – These challenges involve issues encountered during the transition from a traditional architecture to a smart city-based system. It's being specified that there is a crucial role of case study-based research in the rapid development of smart cities throughout the world [6, 18].
- Technological Challenges – From a technology perspective, the development of smart cities poses the biggest challenge, for incorporating all requirements, different technologies are required to be integrated, like WSN's, IOT, Big Data [16], ML(Machine Learning), AI(Artificial intelligence), *etc.* And with these technologies, their related security issues will also merge.
- Sustainability Challenges [18] – These challenges specify that a thorough

understanding of human behavior and the feeling of safety and security of the citizens are to be considered before actually implementing the smart city ecosystem in place.

- Trust Challenges [18] – Trust factor is important while designing Smart City as it relies upon a lot of data and its movement across the network, and the data belongs to the citizens of Smart city. Without the consent and willingness of citizens, to move to a smart city, architecture would be catastrophic. So, trust should be enbibed in the citizen's mind about new architecture.

Security Risks and Implications in Smart Cities

Apart from the above-discussed security issues and attack points, there are risks in the system with their implications which are given in Table **2**:

Table 2. Security risks and their implications.

Security Risks	Implications
Hardware In-secured	Resulting in IOT/IOE-based vulnerability and Botnet attacks [30]
Irregulated Smart Devices	Vendors might be evading regulations to develop low-cost smart devices
Insufficient Bandwidth	Results in Infrastructure failure or breakdown [30]
Vulnerable Applications	Every smart device is at potential Risk
Large Attack area	Entire system is exposed to attacks
No Data Privacy and Protection	Privacy or data breach, unauthorized data access
Lack of Centralized Security [30]	Compromising DC (Data center's) and Infrastructure

Smart Cities Architecture

Smart city architecture involves a few layers based on which the entire system works. There is a vital role of IOE and IOT in the functioning and development of smart cities as many of the components involved with IOE are useful in smart city-wide applications, like RFID, Sensors, actuators [20, 34], *etc.* The components or layers involved in smart city architecture are as follows:

• Smart Devices

Includes things like wireless sensors, CCTV surveillance cameras, weather sensors, smart meters, traffic management digital components, RFID's, *etc.*

• Communication Network

Includes various communication-related protocols and methods for connecting all digital or electronic devices. Also supports communication network types like 2G, 3G, 4G, LTE, Bluetooth, WIFI and Zigbee protocols.

• Transport Layer

It works to support security system alerts, IOT-based data movements and data transmission tracking features or devices.

• Security Systems or Devices

Includes components like firewalls, gateways, routers, and switches, and supports authentication and access control methods [37] for interacting with customer applications. Above all these layers, there exists a layer of customer or consumer-based applications [38] through which users perform all interactions. The whole architecture of a smart city can be seen as shown in Fig. (7).

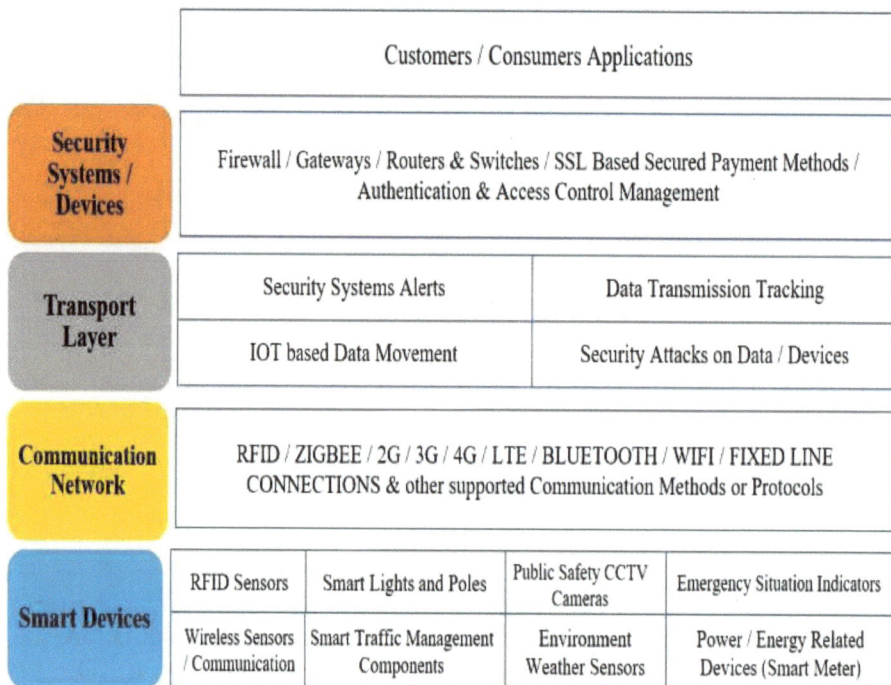

	Customers / Consumers Applications			
Security Systems / Devices	Firewall / Gateways / Routers & Switches / SSL Based Secured Payment Methods / Authentication & Access Control Management			
Transport Layer	Security Systems Alerts		Data Transmission Tracking	
	IOT based Data Movement		Security Attacks on Data / Devices	
Communication Network	RFID / ZIGBEE / 2G / 3G / 4G / LTE / BLUETOOTH / WIFI / FIXED LINE CONNECTIONS & other supported Communication Methods or Protocols			
Smart Devices	RFID Sensors	Smart Lights and Poles	Public Safety CCTV Cameras	Emergency Situation Indicators
	Wireless Sensors / Communication	Smart Traffic Management Components	Environment Weather Sensors	Power / Energy Related Devices (Smart Meter)

Fig. (7). Smart City Architecture.

As illustrated in Fig. (**7**), in smart city architecture, there are various layers based on it, and the whole system works.

As smart devices are concerned, they work on some communication protocol, through which communication happens, and further data or information travels through the transport layer [38, 39] and may become vulnerable to attacks there and might be at the next layer of security, governed by Gateways, firewalls and other security mechanisms [40].

As per the types of attacks discussed in Table **1**, along with the information gathered from the literature, it's found that many types of attacks and security breaches can be countered using strong Authentication and Access Control mechanisms [37]. Based on this extracted information, the next section of the work presents a proposed framework for the security of services in IOE based Smart City system [41], which would be effective in preventing or handling different types of security breaches, either affecting the data or information in transit at the transport layer or available at the application level.

FRAMEWORK FOR SECURE ACCESS CONTROL AND SERVICE AUTHENTICATION IN SMART CITIES

Security in cloud-based systems can be implemented at various levels. In IOE-based security is sought at various levels:

1. As different nodes are there in the sensor-based network, so security is required for authenticating nodes and ensuring access control to services within a network.
2. Then security is also sought for nodes in different sensor-based networks, as nodes in IOE-based systems require to communicate, so they need to share some common shared key to authenticate themselves for the network. Also, controlling access to services can be managed and authenticated using it.
3. Security is also needed for data travelling between different nodes in the same network or other networks through gateways.

As per the above discussion, it's required to have multi-level security scenarios in a sensor-based IOE system. So as per the discussion, the following security measures or attributes are required to be maintained in a Smart City system employing IOE: Confidentiality, Integrity and Authentication [37] (CIA).

Toa achieve these attributes following Security Framework is proposed to work:

Step 1: Device-to-Device Security is sought to prevent external devices which are not part of the network to not enter the communication network. It is prevented by sharing a common key between nodes.

The requirement of the system is that key sharing should be securely done so that key can not be accessible to external nodes in the network. This is done by using the approach from MLBAAC [42] model of security as implemented for a Cloud-based system providing services to users. Service access key distribution happens using Double braker mechanism as done in a cloud-based system [42], ensuring Authenticity.

In the double braker mechanism [42] for key sharing, the encrypted key can be shared using multiple platforms, partly on email and partly on the mobile system. Which makes it more protected against attacks compromising one location like email or mobile device for key sharing [42]. Encrypted keys shared on the mobile device can be decrypted using a suitable application to be installed for service access by users of the Smart City environment [43].

Step 2: Device to Gateway or Cloud level security can be achieved using every sensor node in the network is having their own private key generated using Random key generator algorithm, which is again shared using a previous algorithm, and along with it keys are encrypted using suitable AES + SHA3 based digital signature algorithm for ensuring confidentiality and integrity [42] in the communication.

Step 3: Another shared key is used to ensure the information sent across the network is encrypted with AES 256 algorithm and the key to be shared can be encrypted using it and shared using the same double braker algorithm for extended security.

So, the above steps, if employed, can prevent attacks on different sensor network nodes using double braker [42] based key sharing mechanism providing strong access control and authentication features and further using the keys to encrypt data or information as well as communicating among nodes of the network ensures confidentiality and integrity in the system. Overall, this will ensure achieving essential attributes of CIA in the system.

CONCLUSION AND FUTURE DIMENSIONS

In the end, one could say that the IOE-based system with integration of the cloud for access control and authentication can be ensured using a shared key system where key sharing can be achieved confidentially by a double braker system. Also, for protecting the key for direct use, it can be encrypted with a strong AES256 method for extended protection, which can be decrypted using an application designed for the same, which is to be installed by Smart city service user on his or her mobile or smart device. The system can achieve CIA features using it and enable secure access control and authentication to services over IOE-based Smart city environment using MLBAAC [42] model as deployed for the cloud-based system to access services available over the cloud.

Further, in future testing, the above-discussed steps and the model using real-time sensors data for analyzing the time required in operation for implementing the system for services in a Smart City environment can be done, which would further provide the results to identify the impact of implementing such kind of system with extended security features, in terms of time required for service access and total execution time of the system and further comparing it with the previous less secure system.

REFERENCES

[1]   A. Botta, W. de Donato, V. Persico, and A. Pescapé, "Integration of cloud computing and internet of things: A survey", *Future Gener. Comput. Syst.,* vol. 56, pp. 684-700, 2016.
[http://dx.doi.org/10.1016/j.future.2015.09.021]

[2]   S.R.I. Consulting, ""Disruptive Civil Technologies: Six Technologies With Potential Impacts on US Interests Out To 2025", In: *Tech. Report CR 2008-07.* SRI Consulting Business Intelligence, North America, 2008.

[3]   J. Gubbi, R. Buyya, S. Marusic, and M. Palaniswami, "Internet of Things (IoT): A vision, architectural elements, and future directions", *Future Gener. Comput. Syst.,* vol. 29, no. 7, pp. 1645-1660, 2013.
[http://dx.doi.org/10.1016/j.future.2013.01.010]

[4]   P. P. Ray, "A survey on Internet of Things architectures", *J King Saud University Comp Info Sci,* vol. 30, no. 3, pp. 291-319, 2018.
[http://dx.doi.org/10.1109/IEMCON.2018.8614931]

[5]   A. Das, M.S.C. Sharma, and K.B. Ratha, "The new era of smart cities, from the perspective of the internet of things", *Smart Cities Cybersecurity and Privacy,* pp. 1-9, 2019.
[http://dx.doi.org/10.1016/B978-0-12-815032-0.00001-9]

[6]   B.R. Stojkoska, and K.V. Trivodaliev, "A review of internet of things for smart home: Challenges and solutions", *J. Clean. Prod.,* vol. 140, no. 3, pp. 1454-1464, 2016.

[7]   Q. Yang, "Internet of things application in smart grid: A brief overview of challenges, opportunities, and future trends", *Smart Power Distribution Systems,* pp. 267-283, 2019.
[http://dx.doi.org/10.1016/B978-0-12-812154-2.00013-4]

[8]   H. Hamidi, "An approach to develop the smart health using internet of things and authentication based on biometric technology", *Future Gener. Comput. Syst.,* vol. 91, pp. 434-449, 2019.
[http://dx.doi.org/10.1016/j.future.2018.09.024]

[9]   S.P. Mohanty, U. Choppali, and E. Kougianos, "Everything you wanted to know about smart cities: The Internet of things is the backbone", *IEEE Consum. Electron. Mag.,* vol. 5, no. 3, pp. 60-70, 2016.
[http://dx.doi.org/10.1109/MCE.2016.2556879]

[10]   D. Saba, Y. Sahli, B. Berbaoui, and R. Maouedj, Towards smart cities: Challenges, components, and architectures.*Toward Social Internet of Things (SIoT): Enabling Technologies, Architectures and Applications.* Springer: Cham, 2019, pp. 249-286.

[11]   B.B.P. Rao, P. Saluia, N. Sharma, A. Mittal, and S.V. Sharma, "Cloud computing for Internet of Things & sensing based applications", *Sixth International Conference on Sensing Technology (ICST),* 2012, Kolkata: India.

[http://dx.doi.org/10.1109/ICSensT.2012.6461705]

[12]   A. Garg, and A. Negi, "Structure preservation in content-aware image retargeting using multi-operator", *IET Image Process.,* vol. 14, no. 13, pp. 2965-2975, 2020.
[http://dx.doi.org/10.1049/iet-ipr.2019.1032]

[13]   G.C. Fox, S. Kamburugamuve, and R.D. Hartman, "Architecture and measured characteristics of a cloud based internet of things", *International Conference on Collaboration Technologies and Systems (CTS),* pp. 6-12, 2012.
[http://dx.doi.org/10.1109/CTS.2012.6261020]

[14]   Available from: https://www.geeksforgeeks.org/difference-between-IoE-and-iot/ (Accessed: 17th Feb. 2023)

[15]   T. Alam, "Cloud-Based IoT Applications and their roles in smart cities", *Smart Cities,* vol. 4, no. 3, pp. 1196-1219, 2021.
[http://dx.doi.org/10.3390/smartcities4030064]

[16]   A. Garg, and A.K. Singh, Applications of Internet of Things (IoT).*Intelligence of Things: AI-IoT Based Critical-Applications and Innovations.,* G. Computing, Ed., Springer: Cham, 2021, pp. 1-34.
[http://dx.doi.org/10.1007/978-3-030-82800-4_1]

[17]   A. Siriweera, and K. Naruse, "Internet of Cross-chains: Model-driven cross-chain as a service platform for the internet of everything in smart city", *IEEE Consum. Electron. Mag.,* no. Nov, pp. 1-1, 2021.
[http://dx.doi.org/10.1109/MCE.2021.3127429]

[18]   E. Ismagilova, L. Hughes, N.P. Rana, and Y.K. Dwivedi, "Security, privacy and risks within smart cities: Literature review and development of a smart city interaction framework", *Inf. Syst. Front.,* no. July, pp. 1-22, 2020.
[PMID: 32837262]

[19]   A.K. Singh, and B.D.K. Patro, "Elliptic curve signcryption based security protocol for RFID", *KSII Transac. Intern. Inform.Sys.,* vol. 14, no. 1, pp. 344-365, 2020.

[20]   C. Badii, P. Bellini, A. Difino, and P. Nesi, "Sii-Mobility: An IoT/IoE architecture to enhance smart city mobility and transportation services", *Sensors,* vol. 19, no. 1, p. 1, 2018.
[http://dx.doi.org/10.3390/s19010001]

[21]   N. Gavrilović, and A. Mishra, "Software architecture of the internet of things (IoT) for smart city, healthcare and agriculture: Analysis and improvement directions", *J. Ambient Intell. Humaniz. Comput.,* vol. 12, no. 1, pp. 1315-1336, 2021.
[http://dx.doi.org/10.1007/s12652-020-02197-3]

[22]   S. Anand, and M.V. Ramesh, "Multi-layer architecture and routing for internet of everything (IoE) in smart cities", *Sixth International Conference on Wireless Communications, Signal Processing and Networking (WiSPNET),* pp. 411-416, 2021.
[http://dx.doi.org/10.1109/WiSPNET51692.2021.9419428]

[23]   D. Evans, "The Internet of Everything: How More Relevant and Valuable Connections Will Change the World", In: *Cisco Internet Business Solutions Group (IBSG).* Cisco Systems, Inc.: San Jose, 2012, pp. 1-9.

[24]   R. Kitchin, "The real-time city? Big data and smart urbanism", *Geo J.,* vol. 79, no. 1, pp. 1-14, 2014.
[http://dx.doi.org/10.1007/s10708-013-9516-8]

[25]   R. Kitchin, "Making sense of smart cities: Addressing present shortcomings", *Camb. J. Regions Econ. Soc.,* vol. 8, no. 1, pp. 131-136, 2015.
[http://dx.doi.org/10.1093/cjres/rsu027]

[26]   U.S. Soni, and R.H. Talwekar, "Internet of things in smart grid: An overview", *J. Commun. Eng. Sys.,* vol. 8, no. 2, pp. 28-36, 2019.

[27]   S. Aguzzi, D. Bradshaw, M. Canning, M. Cansfield, P. Carter, G. Cattaneo, S. Gusmeroli, G.

Micheletti, D. Rotondi, and R. Stevens, "Definition of a research and innovation policy leveraging Cloud Computing and IoT combination", *Tech. Report, European Commission, Directorate-General for Communications Networks, Content and Technology Eur. Union,* 2016.

[28]   A. Kumar Singh, and B.D.K. Patro, "A novel security protocol for wireless sensor networks based on elliptic curve signcryption", *Int. J. Comp. Netw. Commun.,* vol. 11, no. 5, pp. 93-112, 2019.
[http://dx.doi.org/10.5121/ijcnc.2019.11506]

[29]   J. Maria de Fuentes, L. Gonzalez-Manzano, A. Solanas, and F. Veseli, "Attribute-based credentials for privacy-aware smart health services in iot-based smart cities", *Computer,* vol. 51, no. 7, pp. 44-53, 2018.
[http://dx.doi.org/10.1109/MC.2018.3011042]

[30]   O. Saber, and T. Mazri, "Smart city security issues: The main attacks and countermeasures, ISPRS", *Int. Arch. Photogramm. Remote Sens. Spat. Inf. Sci,* pp. 465-472, 2021.
[http://dx.doi.org/10.5194/isprs-archives-XLVI-4-W5-2021-465-2021]

[31]   A.K. Singh, and B.D.K. Patro, "Security requirements and attacks in wireless sensor networks", *Int. J. Appl. Eng. Res.,* vol. 14, no. 2, pp. 158-161, 2019.

[32]   Available from: https://www.fortinet.com/resources/cyberglossary/eavesdropping (Accessed: 21st Oct. 2022)

[33]   Available from: https://www.mcafee.com/enterprise/en-us/assets/solution-briefs/sb-quarterly-thr-ats-jun-2017-2.pdf (Accessed: 21st Oct. 2022)

[34]   Available from: https://www.libelium.com/libeliumworld/iot-security-infographic-privacy-authenticity-confidentiality-and-integrity-of-the-sensor-data-the-invisible-asset/ (Accessed: 21st Oct. 2022)

[35]   A. Garg, A. Negi, and P. Jindal, "Structure preservation of image using an efficient content-aware image retargeting technique", *Signal Image Video Process.,* vol. 15, no. 1, pp. 185-193, 2021.
[http://dx.doi.org/10.1007/s11760-020-01736-x]

[36]   Available from: https://www.tatacommunications.com/wp-content/ uploads/2019/02/Tata-Commun-ications-Smart-City-Security-Brochure.pdf (Accessed: 21st Oct. 2022)

[37]   A. Wadhwa, and V.K. Gupta, "Proposed framework with comparative analysis of access control & authentication based security models employed over cloud", *Int. J. Appl. Eng. Res.,* vol. 12, no. 24, pp. 15715-15722, 2017.

[38]   I. Romdhani, "Existing Security Scheme for IoT", In: *Securing the Internet of Things,* Syngress, Science Direct, 2017, pp. 119-130.
[http://dx.doi.org/10.1016/B978-0-12-804458-2.00007-X]

[39]   A.K. Singh, and B.D.K. Patro, Security attacks on RFID and their countermeasures. *Computer Communication, Networking and IoT.* Springer: Singapore, 2021, pp. 509-518.
[http://dx.doi.org/10.1007/978-981-16-0980-0_49]

[40]   B.N. Silva, M. Khan, and K. Han, "Towards sustainable smart cities: A review of trends, architectures, components, and open challenges in smart cities", *Sustain Cities Soc.,* vol. 38, pp. 697-713, 2018.
[http://dx.doi.org/10.1016/j.scs.2018.01.053]

[41]   N. Kalbo, Y. Mirsky, A. Shabtai, and Y. Elovici, "The security of IP-based video surveillance systems", *Sensors,* vol. 20, no. 17, p. 4806, 2020.
[http://dx.doi.org/10.3390/s20174806] [PMID: 32858840]

[42]   A. Wadhwa, and V.K. Gupta, "Practical implementation and analysis of mlbaac model for cloud", *Int. J. Comp. Eng. Technol.,* vol. 9, no. 3, pp. 14-22, 2018.

[43]   M. Kalinin, V. Krundyshev, and P. Zegzhda, "Cybersecurity risk assessment in smart city infrastructures", *Machines,* vol. 9, no. 4, p. 78, 2021.
[http://dx.doi.org/10.3390/machines9040078]

CHAPTER 11

Blockchain Technologies and Smart Contracts in Smart Cities

Aditya Gupta[1,*], **Parth Malkani**[1], **Chitra Krishnan**[2], **Neelesh Thallam**[1] and **Aman Verma**[1]

[1] *Amity University, Noida, Uttar Pradesh, India*

[2] *Symbiosis Center for Management Studies, Symbiosis International Deemed University, Noida, India*

Abstract: Smart Cities are gaining attention due to the ever-increasing population. The increasing population and expanding urbanization resulted in increased congestion and numerous environmental problems. Due to COVID-19, more efficient urbanization increased the need for smart cities. To address the societal and efficient urban management challenges of these Smart Cities, advanced technologies like Blockchains can play vital roles. Smart Contracts are blockchain-based applications. Smart contracts are used to automate agreements without the involvement of a middleman. Smart contracts are executed by a network of computers once predefined conditions are met. The execution action can be in the form of the release of funds to parties, vehicle registration, sending notifications, and issuing a ticket. The information on the transactions completed is updated on the blockchain. This chapter provides insight into how blockchain technology works for smart contracts, which deliver numerous services in Smart cities ecosystems' in more reliable, data secured, and beneficial for the population in Smart cities. The chapter will contribute to the planning of Smart cities planners, developers, architects, and thinkers for using smart contracts to deliver various services in the smart city's governance.

Keywords: Blockchain technologies, Smart contracts, Smart cities.

INTRODUCTION

Blockchain is a technological invention that has disrupted the recent computer paradigm. With the help of blockchain and smart contracts, many applications that are notoriously difficult and complex, have been able to improve their service [1]. With tamper-proof smart contracts and algorithmic executions, blockchain technology allows decentralized consensus and potentially expands the contractual field. Meanwhile, achieving decentralized consensus necessitates the dissemination of knowledge, which changes the informational environment.

---

[*] **Corresponding author Aditya Gupta:** Amity University, Noida, Uttar Pradesh, India; E-mail: akgupta@amity.edu

Everyone today must adapt to digital platforms for information sharing, data services, buying, selling, and transactions, among other things, because of the advancement of contemporary technology [22]. These digital marketplaces facilitate the exchange of specialized data from producer to consumer and vice versa (activity of receiver). Digital material, on the other hand, needs proof of delivery (PoD) to show that the desired content number was provided to the consumer. The PoD also assures that digital content is provided to both parties without manipulation and exactly as requested. This safeguards both parties' rights while also building confidence in the event of a future occurrence.

There are currently a lot of digital markets where customers and digital artists may engage. Despite their prominence, these platforms still account for a sizable portion of income. As a result, the author only earns a small profit [23]. Other digital services with more brand and revenue share flexibility are also available, but the main issue with all existing solutions is that they are all centralized.

The centralized system has a single point of failure. In addition, there is a lack of transparency, and authority is not distributed fairly. As a result, they are more likely to be bribed. These solutions also rely on payments made through a Trusted Third Party (TTP). As a result, they are untrustworthy and unreliable. Blockchain technology, on the other hand, has enabled a decentralized proof of the delivery system. This distribution system is known for its tamper-proof and unchangeable qualities because of its decentralized distributed ledger. Due to its security properties, it is feasible to have transparency, traceability, and auditability.

Smart Contracts

As a result of their application on blockchain-based distributed ledger infrastructures, smart contracts have achieved widespread acceptance since they do away with the need for trusted third parties to carry out and be liable for automated transactions [2]. The contractual parties must have faith in and trade with the middlemen when smart contracts are implemented on a centralized system governed by intermediate agents. In the case of smart contracts that are implemented on a distributed ledger, the execution and recording of transactions are handled by a decentralized infrastructure that is protected by cryptography. The blockchain system, which is a sort of distributed ledger technology, is the subject of this chapter. This would enable us to have a better understanding of how bitcoin, blockchain, and smart contracts operate, which is critical in today's fast-paced environment.

Blockchain

There are two sorts of blockchain: public and private. The primary difference between a public and private blockchain is that the former functions in a decentralized open environment with no limits on the number of people who can join the network, whilst the latter operates within the boundaries set by a governing institution. Blockchain is a distributed ledger technology that is managed in a decentralized (usually autonomous) way. It was originally widely known as the technology behind the cryptocurrency Bitcoin [3]. It comes in several other forms, usually with the ability to store and run computer programs. This has resulted in applications such as smart contracts, which are characterized by tamper-proof contingent consensus-triggered payments and funding through the initial issuance of tokens. A block is a grouping of records, which are referred to as transactions or events. The decentralized ledger of the blockchain network is shared by all participants. During the verification and agreement process between the parties to the blockchain, these transactions are recorded in the ledger and added to the blockchain. The characteristics of the blockchain, such as decentralization, immutability, and encrypted (cryptographic) linkages, are all critical.

The decentralization of the blockchain distributes power across network contributors. It is a blockchain distinction that allows redundancy, unlike centralized systems controlled by a trusted third party [4]. Decentralization improves service availability, reduces the likelihood of failure, and improves service dependability by assuring uptime. The transaction entries in the public ledger, which are still spread throughout the nodes, are permanent and unchangeable.

Immutability (inalterability) is a key property of blockchain-based centralized database systems, which elevates data integrity on the public ledger to new heights. From a computer viewpoint, records are tamper-proof due to the presence of cryptographic links.

Each record's cryptographic connection is structured chronologically to ensure the chain's integrity across the blockchain. A digital signature verifies the integrity of each record using asymmetric key cryptography and hashing techniques. The integrity of a transaction block or record is jeopardized when it is modified, rendering the block and record invalid. The technology that underpins cryptocurrency appears to be promising. A global ledger, which is based on blockchain and maintains an account of all transactions, is one of the most fundamental components of cryptocurrencies. To comprehend blockchain, we must first comprehend a few fundamental concepts: The words "hash", "linked list", and "hash pointers" all refer to the same object.

Hash is a basic function that returns a fixed-length string from any input, such as:

- We are unable to acquire input from hash.
- We can't find two messages with the same hash as the computation we have (no in a practical time).

The hash will be drastically different if we modify a single bit in the input message. As no two inputs will have the same hash, we can use the hash to uniquely identify extremely big files (at least theoretically). Instead of storing and comparing the whole file the next time we come across it, we may just compare its hash to the hash we remember [5].

Not only does a hash pointer maintain track of the variable's location, but it also keeps track of the hash of the data stored there. A hash reference can not only be used to retrieve data but can also be used to check if it has changed.

A linked list is a collection of nodes that each have a pointer to the node before, after, or both. As each node holds a pointer to the preceding node, you only need to preserve the position/reference of the top node. To explore the whole list, just move each node over the location recorded in each node of its neighboring node.

We may now point the main pointer to a new node whenever we require one, with the new node referencing the previous top-level node. Ethereum is a Blockchain that was developed by Vitalik Butarin, Martin Wood, and others in 2013 and debuted in 2015. They wanted to overcome Bitcoin's various limitations and, most all, make it possible to run modest Blockchain apps. While Bitcoin focuses on decentralized payments, Vitalik and the rest of the team are developing a decentralized financial system based on Blockchain applications. They came up with an initial notion that would allow users or programs to upload arbitrary code to the Blockchain *via* transactions. For the first time, the concept of a Smart Contract (or contract for short) was mentioned.

SMART CONTRACTS AND BLOCKCHAIN

Simple computer programmes that are executed when specific criteria are satisfied and recorded on a blockchain are what smart contracts are all about. In many cases, they are used to automate contract execution so that all parties may be confident in conclusion right away, without the need for any intermediaries or wasted time. They can also automate operations that trigger when conditions are met. Smart contracts are written to the blockchain's code and consist of a sequence of "if/when... then..." phrases. The computer network performs the task when the predetermined condition is completed and confirmed. These actions can release funds in this part and save the vehicle, send notifications, or include ticket problems. When the transaction is complete, the block string is updated. This cannot change the transaction, and only the result of the authorized parts can be seen.

Business laws may be translated into computer programming using smart contracts. To meet the demands of diverse sectors, numerous smart contract platforms have been developed. Each smart contract platform comes with its own set of capabilities that are geared to certain applications. Ethereum, for example, is primarily intended for cryptographic applications. Immutable computer code, a decentralized ledger, and a consensus layer are all necessary components of a smart contract system, and almost all platforms contain them [6].

When a condition is met, the contract is instantly executed. As smart contracts are digital and automated, there is no paperwork to deal with and no time to correct mistakes that may occur when manually filling out paperwork. This means that speed, efficiency, and precision will improve. As no third parties are involved and encrypted transaction logs are distributed among participants, there is no doubt that the information has been manipulated for personal advantage. This ensures openness and confidence. Blockchain transaction records are difficult to compromise since they are encrypted. Furthermore, since each item on a distributed ledger is linked to the entries that came before and after it, hackers would have to alter the whole chain in order to modify a single record. It is no longer necessary to use a middleman to coordinate transactions, which eliminates the delays and expenses that arise with using a middleman.

SMART CITY CONCEPT

For a long time, the concept has been referred to as "digital city", "knowledge city", "intelligent city", and "ubiquitous city". The idea of a city with autonomous operations that manage several aspects of urban life through the widespread use of information and communication technology is like all of these conceptual models. At its heart, the Internet of Things is where we deconstruct the components of a smartphone and implant them in our homes, streets, and autos — in short, everything with network connectivity that may have economic value. These ubiquitous sensors, which may be found on our bodies as well as in our infrastructure, are crucial components of the city of the future.

SHARING ECONOMY IN SMART CITIES

In the sharing economy, huge groups of people collaborate to better use underutilized assets, with supply and demand intertwined to enable the supply side to directly provide products and services to those who are in need. The fundamental purpose of a sharing corporation, whether for profit or not, is to optimize asset usage while simultaneously minimizing transaction costs [7]. On the supply side, individuals may offer short-term leases of their unused autos or spare rooms in their apartments or houses to others who are looking for temporary housing. The demand side may profit from consumers renting items at a lower cost or with lower transactional overhead than they would benefit from buying or renting from a traditional source on the supply side.

As Uber and Airbnb have demonstrated, long-established sectors like transportation and housing may be disrupted by the introduction of networked alternatives built from the bottom up. Due to ubiquitous internet access and location services accessible *via* mobile devices, digital networks can better handle the supply and demand of current marketplaces. However, legislatures all over the globe are pushing back against these internet corporations because they refuse to recognize service providers (drivers, renters) as workers (which consequently allows them to maintain lower prices). In a relatively short amount of time, two technologies that make it easier to allocate scarce resources (space, time, and vehicles) through linked mobile devices have produced a fundamental shift in commerce: individuals may now provide and access on-demand resources to one another.

How is it Driven?

The sharing economy is fueled by digital connectivity technologies, which serve as the foundation for these improvements by offering immediacy. Individuals' real-time data and skills are critical for improving asset utilization and transitioning a city into a "smart" city [8]. Citizens, objects, and utilities in smart cities may use ubiquitous technology to connect effortlessly, dramatically increasing information exchange on the state and the trading of idle assets. Due to digital connection, people may rent out spare houses and basements, keep parking lots full, ride an idle bicycle along the street, and even share a taxi with a stranger heading in the same direction.

As described in Fig. (1), an emphasis is placed on the interaction that exists between the sharing economy and smart cities. Smart cities are propelled forward by a combination of social, economic, and technological enablers. The purpose of a smart city, as seen in the figure's outer ring, is to accomplish smart government, living, people, mobility, the environment, and the economy, among other things.

Greater efficiency in the use of urban resources, such as land and water, as well as public transportation, services, food, goods, and money, contributes to the growth of smart cities in the middle ring [9]. As the sharing economy is concerned with how urban resources are shared, seeing smart cities through this perspective may help us better understand how it grows from the viewpoint of resource allocation and how it will affect the future of the sharing economy.

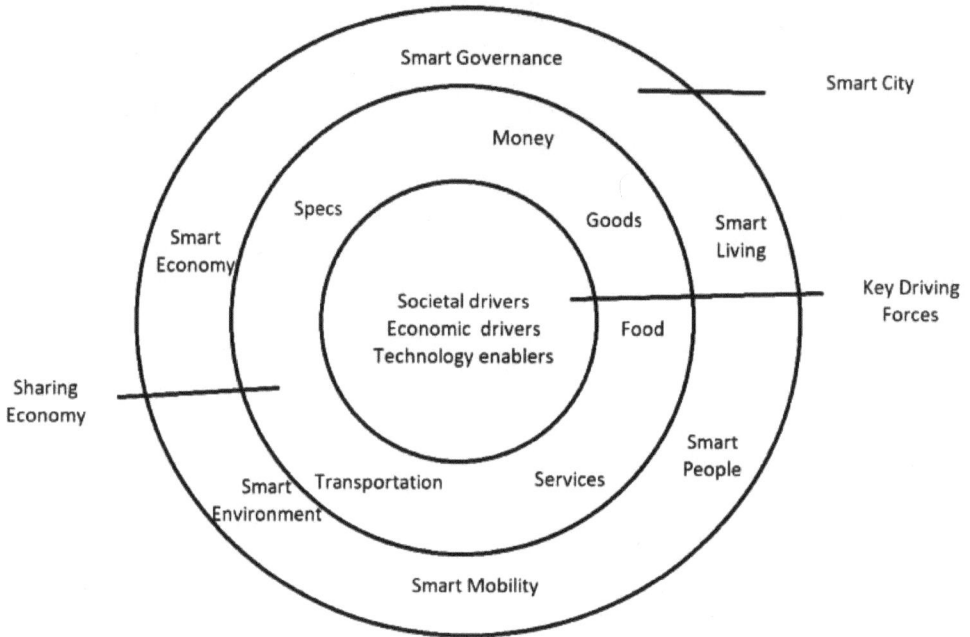

Fig. (1). Smart cities and sharing economy.

Arithmetic Proof of Data

A linked list in which hash points substitute ordinary pointers is referred to as a "blockchain". This enables each blockchain node to determine not just the next node's location, but also if the data on that node has changed. We'll use the same nomenclature since nodes in a blockchain are referred to as blocks. The Head hash pointer will also point to the most recent block on the network. Any new blocks will be placed next to B3, with a link to B3 in this blockchain and data that must be maintained up to date (in the case of bitcoin multiple transactions).

Advanced Signature

Multi-signatures are a feature of Bitcoin that allows a transaction to be redeemed if at least t out of n valid signatures are present. By distributing decryption or singing powers among several users, multi-signatures are resistant to unscrupulous persons. The Lightning Network, a Bitcoin extension with near-instant payment confirmation, uses multi-signatures to deposit mutual funds on the blockchain first. Payments from the funds can be made outside of the blockchain with quick confirmation after they've been confirmed. Finally, the funds can be closed by signing transactions with all the needed signatures. ECDSA may be used to build extensions to the Bitcoin multi-signature method.

How is the Blockchain Tamper-proof?

The blockchain's hash function contributes to the impossibility of data tampering. When transactions are turned to blocks, each block is tagged with the hash of the previous block, producing a chain. A hash is an algorithm that converts unencrypted input material into an encrypted code that mirrors it. Any amount of data may be transformed into a string of a certain length using a hash function. For example, the hash length for "7" is the same as for "Blockchain is about to revolutionize the way the industry does business".

Decrypting the hash is exceedingly difficult since the hacker has no way of knowing whether the input is long or short based on the length of the output. In addition, even modest changes to the entry generate a new and unexpected hash, which must be re-verified by the blockchain network, or the hash will become invalid. Because these blocks and their associated hash functions are stored on several machines, changes to a hash function on a single system are quickly observed by the rest of the network. Attempts to change data in the blockchain are quickly detected and reversed in this way.

SMART CONTRACT PROGRAMMING LANGUAGES

Pact, Vyper, and Liquidity are the names of three popular programming languages used in smart contracts. The execution of smart contracts in the actual world is discussed in detail below, with reference to each sample contract [9].

Vyper

Vyper, like Solidity, is an essential programming language that works with EVM bytecode. It is frequently utilized because it aids in the identification and interpretation of smart contracts for more transparency when two or more parties are involved. Ethereum platform is specifically used to create a smart contract. Ethereum is a decentralized, open-source platform that helps developers to make smart contracts with the language [10]. It allows for the construction and execution of complex programs, as well as the execution of large-scale computing instructions on a distributed platform. The Ethereum Virtual Machine (EVM) is at the heart of Ethereum, and it runs code of varying algorithmic complexity.

Ethereum has a P2P network protocol, communicating with every participating network through nodes. Nodes linked to the Ethereum network provide transparency by applying rules throughout the blockchain database. EVM is facilitated to run on each node in the network and can be accessed anywhere in the world through the nodes.

The Ethereum platform is featureless or value-neutral. Organizations and developers must determine what it will be utilized for. However, the features of Ethereum favor some application types more than others. Ethereum is best suited for applications that automate direct P2P contact or allow network-wide coordinated group action. Apps for organizing P2P markets, for example, like a connecting pool of investors and borrowers [11]. There are a few crucial elements to remember from the Ethereum Design Rationale document when it comes to developing on Ethereum.

As shown in Fig. (**2**), we demonstrate a smart contract for a hypothetical cryptocurrency called 'NEOCrypto'. Only the developer of NEOCrypto may issue it, and it can only be sent to a recipient with his or her address.

```
1  pragma solidity ^0.4.0;
2  /*Sample contract for NEOCrypto */
3  contract NEOCrypto{
4       address public developer;
5       mapping (address => uint) public balance;
6
7       //Notifies when a transaction is complete
8       event transaction(address from, address to, uint amount);
9
10 function NEOCrypto()
11 {
12 developer = msg.sender;
13 }
14 function create(address receiver, uint amount)
15 {
16      if(msg. sender! developer)
17          throw;
18      balance[receiver] += amount;
19 }
20
21 function receiver(address receiver, uint amount)
22 {
23      if(balance[msg.sender] < amount)
24          throw;
25      balance[msg. sender]
26      amount;
27      balance[receiver] +- amount;
28      transaction(msg.sender, receiver, amount);
29 }
```

Fig. (2). Solidity (Author's creation).

Pact

Pact is a programming language used to develop smart contracts that run on the Kadena blockchain in a simple and secure manner. Pact enables developers to create transactional logic that is both durable and performant, allowing mission-critical business transactions to be completed swiftly and safely. It is immutable and supported by Turing-incomplete, which fixes the overall safety of transactions. This makes it more difficult to write bugs and simpler to identify them. Complex, speculative application logic has no place at this key layer. A pact was developed for overcoming formal verification of data and can be upgraded in a matter of time for high computational.

As shown in Fig. (3), we demonstrate how to utilize Pact to create a simple "account balance" smart contract, replete with account creation and money transfer functionality. A detailed explanation of the contract can be found here, which includes instructions on how to install the module, define keysets, define modules, create tables, and finally invoke the 'accounts' module.

```
(define-keyset 'accounts-admin
  (read-keyset "accounts-admin-keyset"))

(module accounts 'accounts-admin
 "Simple account functionality."

 (defschema account
  "Schema for accounts table."
  balance:decimal
  amount:decimal
  keyset:keyset
  note)

 (deftable accounts:{account})

 (defun create-account (address keyset)
  (insert accounts address
        { "balance": 0.0, "amount": 0.0, "keyset": keyset,
          "note": "Created account" }))

 (defun transfer (src dest amount)
  "transfer AMOUNT from SRC to DEST"
  (with-read accounts src
        { "balance":= src-balance
        , "keyset" := src-ks }
   (enforce-keyset src-ks)
   (check-balance src-balance amount)
   (with-read accounts dest { "balance":= dest-balance }
    (write accounts src
        { "balance": (- src-balance amount)
        , "amount": (- amount)
        , "note": { "transfer-to": dest } })
     (write 'accounts dest
        { "balance": (+ dest-balance amount)
        , "amount": amount
        , "note": { "transfer-from": src } })))))

 (defun check-balance (balance amount)
  (enforce (<= amount balance) "Insufficient funds"))
)

(create-table accounts)
```

Fig. (3). Account Balance by Pact (Author's creation).

LIQUIDITY

Tezos' Liquidity is a powerful smart-contract language. It's a highly structured functional language that utilizes the OCaml syntax and follows the Michelson security policy [12]. Furthermore, the Michelson programming language, which provides formal verification, ensures the security of smart contracts.

Three main aspects of the Liquidity language are:

1. Complete coverage of the Michelson language: Liquidity can write everything that can be written in Michelson.
2. Instead of stack operations, local variables can be used to store values. Local variables do not survive Contract, which is the sole constraint. Call, following Michelson's idea of forcing explicit value storage to prevent reentrancy problems.
3. High-level types: Liquidity programs may define and utilize kinds like sum-types and record-types. The contract format for Liquidity may be found in.

DISCUSSION

Solidity failed because it was regarded as the most vulnerable to security problems. Although being helpful is a huge benefit, being vulnerable to security flaws is a significant disadvantage, as recent assaults on the Ethereum network have revealed, because these flaws may be used by unscrupulous users to cause financial loss. Meanwhile, Liquidity and Pact are still relatively unknown languages, but they appear to be more secure than Solidity for the time being. Finally, each language has its unique set of advantages and disadvantages. The interesting thing to note here is that as time and research pass, all three languages change and evolve. As a result, we expect that our effort will help to build a body of knowledge that will benefit the domain's future growth and success.

As shown in Fig. (**4**), the contract is a simple bidding system that requires a user to have at least 2 tz in order to participate. The contract will display the error message "Insufficient money, at least 2 tz to bid" if a user attempts to bid with a balance of less than 2 tz.

THE FUTURE GROWTH POTENTIAL OF BLOCKCHAIN-BASED SMART CONTRACTS

Stakeholders are interested in smart contracts because of their efficacy and efficiency in sharing and gaining access to them. Smart contracts may automate, compute, and organize payments before automatically carrying out their terms and conditions [13]. Contracts may be executed promptly when all promises have been fulfilled, improving transparency, removing middlemen, and allowing multi-party consensus-based verification, saving money, time, and increasing reliability. As shown in Fig. (5), smart contracts have the potential to change several industries, including banking, real estate, healthcare, insurance, and even elections. While smart contracts and their use in the banking and insurance industries offer a lot of advantages and benefits, blockchain technology is still in its early stages and will take some time to establish itself as the preferred method.

```
1   let%init storage (myname : string) =
2       Map.add myname 0 (Map ["ocaml", 0; "pro", 0]

4   let%entry main
5       (parameter : string)
6       (storage : (string, int) map)
7       : unit * (string, int) map =

9   let amount = Current.amount() in

11  if amount < 5.00tz then
12      Current.failwith "Not enough money, at least 5tz to vote"
13  else
14      match Map.find parameter storage with
15      None -> Current,failwith "Bad vote"
16      Some x - >
17          let storage = Map.add parameter (x+1) storage in
18              ( () , storage )
```

Fig. (4). Smart contract with liquidity, (Author's creation).

Smart Contract in Financial Services

Smart contracts will allow the financial services industry to make significant infrastructural and operational improvements. A distributed ledger could be a viable choice for managing large numbers of transactions. These savings are estimated to amount to $15 to $20 billion per year by 2022.

Smart Contracts in Real Estate

Smart contracts are used in this industry to record the ownership of any real estate. By removing the need for a lawyer or broker, they enhance transaction speed and efficiency. The vendor could take over the procedure. Smart contracts make title administration less expensive and more transparent [14]. The transaction might be blocked by title flaws, costing you money in legal fees. Smart contracts, on the other hand, keep track of the property's history, asset location, and other relevant data. They help to avoid fraud by using secure and tamper-proof encrypted codes.

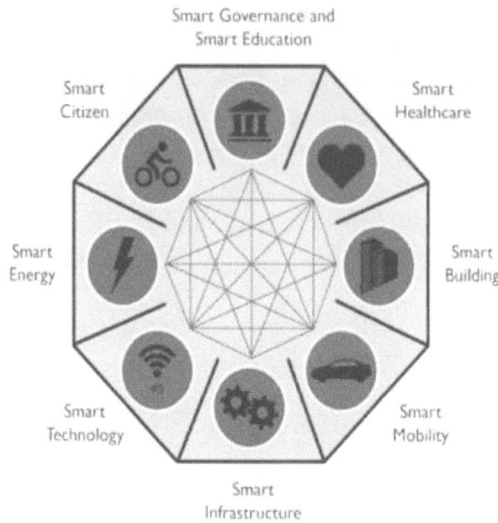

Fig. (5). Smart city Conceptual Framework (Author's Creation).

Smart Contract in Healthcare

In this scenario, maintaining care standards entails guaranteeing safe patient data interchange across healthcare providers. Patients' data can be safely kept and securely accessed on a blockchain using smart contracts, which can only be accessed with the patient's private key. Patients can also rest assured that their healthcare providers will always have access to the information they require, and that their personal information will be kept private and secure [15].

Smart Contract in Voting

Elections may be held in the future using a blockchain-based voting system. By making voting secure and simple with digital technology, blockchain voting solutions can expand accessibility, promote greater voter turnout, and speed up the process of counting and publishing results. Smart contracts will be able to validate voters' identities, preventing election hackers from casting multiple ballots, which is a common goal of theirs.

Smart Contract in Insurance Industry

Each year, the insurance industry spends millions of dollars on claims processing. Worse, money is wasted on fraudulent claims. By allowing for frequent error checks and claims processing, smart contracts make it easier for consumers and companies to handle insurance plans [16]. Consumers will benefit from speedier processing times since their prices, especially premium plans, will be lower.

Smart contracts may be used for peer-to-peer transactions, supply chain management, product creation, and inventory control, to name a few. Smart contracts are swiftly being utilized to demonstrate the transparency, accountability, and efficiency that they were supposed to deliver, even while there is always room for improvement and innovation [17]. Smart contracts are swiftly being utilized to demonstrate the transparency, accountability, and efficiency that they were supposed to deliver, even while there is always room for improvement and innovation. The initiatives taken by the Government of India for smart cities have been listed in Table **1**.

Table 1. Indian government initiatives for smart cities.

Smart Governance	Smart Energy	Smart Environment	Smart Transport	Smart Information and Communication	Smart Buildings
83 million USD for Digital India Initiative	Establish smart grid test bed and knowledge center.	Add 30,000 MW in five-year plan.	Ministry to invest more than 20 billion USD on metro rail.	Broadband connection to 175 million users.	3rd largest construction market, by adding 11.5 million homes every year.
PPP model to upgrade infrastructure	8 smart grid pilot projects with 10 million USD.	Invest 50 billion in the water sector.	Monorail project at Mumbai at 500 million USD.	Safe City project, Union ministry to invest 333 million USD.	Intelligent building management system market is 1,891 million USD.
Develop at least 2 smart cities in each state.	88,000 MW power generation in a five-year plan.	Yamuna action plan at 276 million USD.	-	-	Smart buildings will save up to 30% of water usage and 40% of energy usage.
DMICDC plans to develop 7 cities with 100 billion USD investment.	Install 130 million smart meters.	GOI and World Bank signed a 500 million USD credit for rural water supply and sanitation.	-	-	-

THREATS AND LIMITATIONS OF BLOCKCHAIN-POWERED SMART CONTRACTS

As a novel technology, smart contracts have a variety of challenges, including legal constraints, dependency on "off-chain" resources, immutability, scalability, and other concerns [17].

A mechanism for achieving a compromise.

To begin, there are legal issues:

i. Because each country has its own set of rules and regulations, ensuring that all requirements are met is tough.
ii. Even though legal terms or conditions are not measurable, modelling them in a smart contract is difficult, making them acceptable and quantifiable for a computer that performs them; and
iii. Governments are interested in using blockchain technology in a regulated and controlled manner in a variety of applications, but one challenge is that it is reliant on "off-chain" suppliers. Some smart contracts claim to be able to obtain data or parameters from off-chain, or non-blockchain, resources.
iv. Oracles are dependable third parties who collect data off-chain and then upload it to the blockchain at regular intervals, serving as the blockchain's data collecting point. Although the current spells have been thoroughly tested, they may result in a "point of failure" if employed. An oracle, for example, may be unable to deliver critical information, supply incorrect data, or just cease to function. As a result, these scenarios must be considered before smart contracts may be widely used.

There's also the matter of immutability to consider. The code of a smart contract cannot be modified once it has been launched. The disadvantage of immutability in smart contracts is that if there is a bug in the code, the smart contract's immutability function prevents it from being fixed [18]. Similarly, if the circumstances change, there is no easy way to proceed (for example, the parties have agreed to modify the parameters of their commercial transaction, or if the legislation changes, *etc.*). To address the immutability issue, in-depth and potentially costly professional audits of smart contracts are required prior to blockchain deployment.

Fourth, scalability is always a problem since, in today's digital world, when everything is automated, the only limit is the number of transactions that can be confirmed in a second on any digital platform. The blockchain is affected by the same problem [19]. Due to scalability constraints, network congestion, higher transaction commission rates, and longer confirmation times are required. The consensus technique used by smart contract platforms, on the other hand, is required for transaction verification [20].

Scalability is thus dependent on the consensus process, which is another issue with smart contracts. Other blockchain networks (such as Cardano), which will revolutionize blockchain technology by the end of this year and improve transaction rates by a million times, are working on a test network region to address it [21].

CONCLUSION AND FUTURE SCOPE

This chapter examines blockchain technology and smart contracts in the context of smart cities, a notion that is still developing. The smart city concept is seen by the Indian government as a way to increase the productivity of a number of activities for Indian inhabitants, including real estate, health care, infrastructure, mobility, education, and energy. Implementing blockchain technology through smart contracts has solved the problem of putting multiple activities into practice. Smart contracts and blockchains are building the foundation for future urban infrastructure and communication technologies [22]. The most recent achievements in overcoming these problems were examined, culminating in a comparison of some of the most popular smart contract applications in smart cities. Smart contract applications across a variety of sectors, as well as popular use cases for each, have been rigorously validated [23]. As a result, smart contract challenges are emphasized in certain areas of smart contract design, deployment, execution, and conclusion. Smart contracts have a lot of potentials when combined with the smart city concept. One of the issues about the smart city programme is the potential for fragmentation as businesses want to express their opinions on the city, while officials approve or prohibit developments. The smart city shared economy framework has added new dimensions to the management of a variety of smart city verticals. Finally, we hope that this chapter will help developers create secure and scalable smart contract applications while also advancing blockchain technology [24]. Despite a slew of roadblocks, the use of smart contracts, which are constructed on top of blockchains, is rapidly growing. Smart contracts, like other computer software tools, include a range of flaws that can be caused by human error.

Smart contracts provide a number of advantages and benefits, and they are currently being employed in a number of smart city activities. Smart contracts will be widely used in the future in high-potential areas such as governance, energy, the environment, transportation, information and communication, and buildings in smart city processes [25]. The application of smart contracts reduces fraud, lowers costs, and increases immutability in all of these aspects of smart city operations.

Smart contracts are currently self-executing, business automation apps that run on a decentralized network such as blockchain, but we may expect this network to be switched to a contract management solution, which will give traceability or demonstrate authenticity. For example, one of the most recent contract management solutions on the market is Fabasoft Contracts, a cloud-based contract management solution that is ready-to-use and designed to support users throughout the entire contract life cycle, from cross-company contract preparation to efficient review and approval processes to revision-secure contract archiving. It allows for the creation of contract rights and duties that may be validated and enforced automatically in a variety of ways.

REFERENCES

[1]   H.R. Hasan, and K. Salah, "Proof of delivery of digital assets using blockchain and smart contracts", *IEEE Access,* vol. 6, pp. 65439-65448, 2018.
        [http://dx.doi.org/10.1109/ACCESS.2018.2876971]

[2]   L.W. Cong, and Z. He, "Blockchain disruption and smart contracts", *Rev. Financ. Stud.,* vol. 32, no. 5, pp. 1754-1797, 2019.
        [http://dx.doi.org/10.1093/rfs/hhz007]

[3]   T.M. Hewa, Y. Hu, M. Liyanage, S.S. Kanhare, and M. Ylianttila, "Survey on blockchain-based smart contracts: Technical aspects and future research", *IEEE Access,* vol. 9, pp. 87643-87662, 2021.
        [http://dx.doi.org/10.1109/ACCESS.2021.3068178]

[4]   Available from: https://corporatefinanceinstitute.com/resources/knowledge/deals/smart-contracts/

[5]   S.N. Khan, F. Loukil, C. Ghedira-Guegan, E. Benkhelifa, and A. Bani-Hani, "Blockchain smart contracts: Applications, challenges, and future trends", *Peer. Peer. Netw. Appl.,* vol. 14, no. 5, pp. 2901-2925, 2021.

[6]   Available from: https://academy.shrimpy.io/post/the-best-smart-contract-platforms

[7]   T. Nugent, D. Upton, and M. Cimpoesu, "Improving data transparency in clinical trials using blockchain smart contracts", *F1000Res,* vol. 5, p. 2541, 2016.
        [http://dx.doi.org/10.12688/f1000research.9756.1]

[8]   Available from: https://ethereum.org/en/developers/docs/smart-contracts/#further-reading (August 6, 2021.)

[9]   Available from: https://www.kaleido.io/blockchain-blog/5-examples-of-blockchain-smart-contracts (February 13, 2020)

[10]   H. Watanabe, S. Fujimura, A. Nakadaira, Y. Miyazaki, A. Akutsu, and J. Kishigami, "Blockchain contract: Securing a blockchain applied to smart contracts", In: *2016 IEEE international conference on consumer electronics (ICCE), IEEE,* 2016.
        [http://dx.doi.org/10.1109/ICCE.2016.7430693]

[11]   S. Wang, L. Ouyang, Y. Yuan, X. Ni, X. Han, and F.Y. Wang, "Blockchain-enabled smart contracts: Architecture, applications, and future trends", *Trans. Sys. Man. Cybern.Sys.,* vol. 49, no. 11, pp. 2266-2277, 2019.

[12]   Available from: https://techjury.net/blog/blockchain-statistics/ (August 5, 2021)

[13]   A. Kosba, A. Miller, E. Shi, Z. Wen, and C. Papamanthou, "Hawk: The blockchain model of cryptography and privacy-preserving smart contracts", *In 2016 IEEE symposium on security and privacy,* pp. 839-858, 2016.

[14]   Available from: https://execed.economist.com/blog/industry-trends/5-applications-blockchain--our-business (February 13, 2018)

[15]   T.M. Hewa, Y. Hu, M. Liyanage, S.S. Kanhare, and M. Ylianttila, "Survey on blockchain-based smart contracts: Technical aspects and future research", *IEEE Access,* vol. 9, pp. 87643-87662, 2021.
        [http://dx.doi.org/10.1109/ACCESS.2021.3068178]

[16]   G. Governatori, F. Idelberger, Z. Milosevic, R. Riveret, G. Sartor, and X. Xu, "On legal contracts,

imperative and declarative smart contracts, and blockchain systems", *Artif. Intell. Law,* vol. 26, pp. 377-409, 2018.

[17] G. Destefanis, M. Marchesi, M. Ortu, R. Tonelli, A. Bracciali, and R. Hierons, "Smart contracts vulnerabilities: A call for blockchain software engineering?", *2018 International Workshop on Blockchain Oriented Software Engineering (IWBOSE),* p. 19-25, 2018.
[http://dx.doi.org/10.1109/IWBOSE.2018.8327567]

[18] Available from: https://blockgeeks.com/guides/different-smart-contract-platforms/ (April 24, 2020)

[19] Available from: https://www.fabasoft.com/en/products/fabasoft-contracts (Accessed: 10th Nov. 2021)

[20] Available from: https://medium.com/inspiredbrilliance/is-blockchain-really-tamper-proof-88d1bc5ee338 (June 25, 2018)

[21] Available from: https://levelup.gitconnected.com/what-is-blockchain-and-how-it-is-tamper-proof-f86744cb77 (May 25, 2020.)

[22] P.K. Kapur, A. Gupta, and N. Sachdeva, "Measuring brand health", *2015 4th International Conference on Reliability, Infocom Technologies and Optimization (ICRITO) (Trends and Future Directions),* p. 1-6 02-04, 2015.
[http://dx.doi.org/10.1109/ICRITO.2015.7359353]

[23] V. Aggarwal, S. Dash, P.D. Yadav, and A.K. Gupta, "Role of ICT enabled Cloud Learning Management System tools in Fostering Entrepreneurship Amongst Youth", *2022 2nd International Conference on Innovative Practices in Technology and Management (ICIPTM),* pp. 508-515, 2022.
[http://dx.doi.org/10.1109/ICIPTM54933.2022.9754158]

[24] C. Krishnan, A. Gupta, A. Gupta, and G. Singh, Impact of artificial intelligence-based chatbots on customer engagement and business growth. *Deep Learning for Social Media Data Analytics. Studies in Big Data.,* T.P. Hong, L. Serrano-Estrada, A. Saxena, A. Biswas, Eds., vol. 113. Springer: Cham, 2022.
[http://dx.doi.org/10.1007/978-3-031-10869-3_11]

[25] A.K. Gupta, V. Aggarwal, P.D. Yadav, M. Naved, S. Dash, and T. Chandwani, "Effectiveness of technological based classroom engagement", *2022 3rd International Conference on Intelligent Engineering and Management (ICIEM),* pp. 887-893, 2022.
[http://dx.doi.org/10.1109/ICIEM54221.2022.9853199]

SUBJECT INDEX

A

AdaBoosting methods 153
Ad hoc networks 144, 146
AGI systems 44
Agricultural smart system development 191
AI-based 41, 92, 94, 96, 103
   applications 94, 103
   data 94
   sensors 96
   technologies 41
   traffic management system 92
AI-natural language processing 140
Air pollution 73, 82
Air quality 74, 98, 123, 125, 200, 207
   and pollution sensors 125
   indoor 74
ANI computing systems 44
ANN for smart computing 53
Anomalies 48, 70
   magnetic 70
Anomaly detection process 71
Apps, business automation 272
Artificial 40, 43, 46, 51, 52, 58, 130, 153
   neural networks (ANN) 40, 46, 51, 52, 58, 130, 153
   super Intelligence (ASI) 43
Artificial intelligence 7, 14, 40, 41, 43, 53, 54, 55, 57, 75, 87, 88, 89, 91, 96, 98, 103, 112
   systems 43, 75
   techniques 41
   technology 14, 96
Automating processes 228
Automation 4, 7, 20, 46, 48, 55, 65, 76, 87, 94, 97, 100
   control mechanisms 55
   smart constructing 76
Automobile(s) 19, 29, 76, 125
   electrical 76
   vehicle identification 29

B

Big data 6, 14, 40, 45, 46, 47, 58, 98, 109, 110, 134, 213
   analytics 6, 40, 45, 46, 47, 58, 109, 110, 134, 213
   and artificial intelligence technology 14
   tools 98
Bitcoin 103, 258, 259, 260, 263
   cryptocurrency 259
Blockchain 89, 91, 103, 104, 113, 257, 258, 259, 260, 264, 265, 268, 271, 272
   applications 260
   database 265
   network 104, 259, 264, 271
   system 104, 258
   technology 89, 91, 103, 104, 113, 257, 258, 268, 271, 272
Blockchain-based 259, 267, 269
   centralized database systems 259
   smart contracts 267
   voting system 269

C

Cameras 7, 11, 52
   sensor-enabled 52
Carbon emissions 113
CCTV surveillance cameras 250
Chemical substances, toxic 94
Cloud 55, 98, 213
   analytics 55
   and data analytics 213
   networks 98
   processing techniques 98
Cloud computing 17, 55, 56, 81, 87, 95, 96, 104, 213, 215, 216, 231, 233, 234
   systems 233
   technologies 104, 234
Cognitive techniques 17

www.ingramcontent.com/pod-product-compliance
Lightning Source LLC
Chambersburg PA
CBHW050814220326
41598CB00006B/206